This book examines the influence of angelology on the christology of the Apocalypse of John. In the Apocalypse, Jesus appears in glorious form reminiscent of angels in Jewish and Christian literature in the period between 200 BCE and 200 CE. Dr Carrell asks what significance this has for the christology of the Apocalypse. He concludes that by portraying Jesus in such a way that he has the form and function of an angel, and yet is also divine, the Apocalypse upholds monotheism while at the same time providing a means for Jesus to be presented in visible, glorious form to his church.

SOCIETY FOR NEW TESTAMENT STUDIES

MONOGRAPH SERIES

General editor: Richard Bauckham

95

JESUS AND THE ANGELS

Jesus and the angels

Angelology and the christology of the Apocalypse of John

PETER R. CARRELL

CAMBRIDGE
UNIVERSITY PRESS

PUBLISHED BY THE PRESS SYNDICATE OF THE UNIVERSITY OF CAMBRIDGE
The Pitt Building, Trumpington Street, Cambridge CB2 1RP, United
Kingdom

CAMBRIDGE UNIVERSITY PRESS
The Edinburgh Building, Cambridge CB2 2RU, United Kingdom
40 West 20th Street, New York, NY 10011–4211, USA
10 Stamford Road, Oakleigh, Melbourne 3166, Australia

First published 1997

Printed in the United Kingdom at the University Press, Cambridge

Typeset in Times 10/12pt

A catalogue record for this book is available from the British Library

Library of Congress cataloguing in publication data
Carrell, Peter R.
Jesus and the angels : angelology and the christology of the Apocalypse
of John / Peter R. Carrell.
    p.   cm. – (Society for New Testament Studies. Monograph series : 95)
Includes bibliographical references and index.
ISBN 0 521 59011 6 (hardback)
1. Jesus Christ – History of doctrines – Early church, c. 30–600.
2. Angels – History of doctrines – Early church, c. 30–600.
3. Bible. N.T. Revelation – Criticism, interpretation, etc.   I. Title.
II. Series: Monograph series (Society for New Testament Studies) : 95.
BT198.C32   1997
232′.09′015–dc21   96–47526   CIP

ISBN 0 521 59011 6 hardback

CE

CONTENTS

vii

Contents

PREFACE

My interest in the christology of the Apocalypse began during my BD studies at Knox Theological Hall, Dunedin, New Zealand, and resulted in a small dissertation on Lamb christology. The observation that comparatively little work has been done on the christology of the Apocalypse led me to maintain an interest in this subject as I embarked on postgraduate studies at the University of Durham, England, under the supervision of Professor James Dunn. The resulting PhD dissertation is the basis for this book. I remain grateful for all the assistance I received from Professor Dunn and other teachers in the Department of Theology at Durham, fellow students, family, and friends in the completion of that project. I also gratefully acknowledge the helpfulness of my examiners, Professor Richard Bauckham and Dr Robert Hayward. I remain thankful for a Post-Ordination Scholarship from the St John's College Trust Board, Auckland, NZ, which contributed the greatest part of my financial support while studying in Durham. In the process of turning the dissertation into a monograph it is my pleasant task to thank Professor Dunn for his continuing encouragement and Dr Margaret Thrall for her patient encouragement and helpful direction. To fellow Kiwi scholars also go my thanks for their interest and support: Dr Paul Trebilco, Dr Derek Tovey, Revd Ren Kempthorne, Dr Peter Lineham, and Dr Tim Meadowcroft. I am also thankful that twelve thousand miles from the Libraries of the University of Durham and Tyndale House, Cambridge I have been able to find help in time of need from the Kinder Library, the College of St John the Evangelist, Auckland, the Bishopdale College Library, Nelson, and the Hewitson Library, Knox College, Dunedin. My extended family have been supportive in various ways for which I gladly thank them. Teresa Kundycki-Carrell, my wife, and our children, Leah, Bridget, Andrew, and Alice, have patiently borne with me through the period of revision.

I gratefully dedicate this book to them and to four Bible teachers (among others) who haved fired my passion for biblical study: Dick Carson, Derek Eaton, Milton Hayward, and my father, Brian Carrell.

ACKNOWLEDGEMENTS

A number of biblical quotations are taken from the New Revised Standard Version of the Bible, copyright 1989 by the Division of Christian Education of the National Council Churches of Christ in the USA. All rights reserved. Used by permission. A number of other biblical quotations are from the New Revised Standard Version Apocryphal/Deuterocanonical Books, copyright 1989 by the Division of Christian Education of the National Council of Churches of Christ in the USA. Used by permission. All rights reserved.

Quotations of various ancient Jewish, Christian, and patristic writings are acknowledged where they occur. Permission has been secured from the publishers to quote from A. F. J. Klijn and G. J. Reinink (eds.), *Patristic Evidence for Jewish–Christian Sects* (Novum Testamentum Supplements 36), Leiden: E. J. Brill, 1973, and R. E. Heine (ed.), *Origen: Commentary on the Gospel of John, Books 1–10* (The Fathers of the Church 80), Washington, DC: Catholic University of America, 1989. Translations from James H. Charlesworth (ed.), *The Old Testament Pseudepigrapha*, 2 vols., London: Darton, Longman & Todd; New York: Doubleday, 1983, 1985, are by permission of the publishers. Translations from H. F. D. Sparks, *The Apocryphal Old Testament*, Oxford: Clarendon Press, 1984 are by permission of Oxford University Press. Translations from E. Hennecke, W. Schneelmelcher (eds.), *New Testament Apocrypha*, 2 vols., 1959, 1964 (ET: R. McL. Wilson, Philadelphia: Westminster Press, 1963, 1964) are by permission of the publishers, Westminster, John Knox Press, and James Clarke & Co.

Translations of classical and Hellenistic texts are usually taken from the Loeb Classical Library, published by William Heinemann Ltd. (London) and Harvard University Press (Cambridge, MA), with acknowledgement where they occur. Permission to cite Chr.

Burchard's reconstructed Greek text of *Joseph and Aseneth* in A.-
M. Denis, *Concordance Grecque des Pseudépigraphes d'Ancien
Testament: concordance, Corpus des Textes, Indices*, Louvain: Uni-
versité Catholique de Louvain, 1987, is gratefully acknowledged.

ABBREVIATIONS

ABD	D. N. Friedman (ed.), *Anchor Bible Dictionary* (6 vols.)
Adam & Eve	*Books of Adam and Eve*
Adv. haer.	*Adversus haereses* (Irenaeus)
AGJU	Arbeiten zur Geschichte des antiken Judentums und des Urchristentums
AJBI	*Annual of the Japanese Biblical Institute*
ANCL	Ante Nicene Christian Library
ANRW	H. Temporini and W. Haase (eds.), *Aufstieg und Niedergang der römischen Welt*
ANTJ	Arbeiten zum Neuen Testament und Judentum
AOS	American Oriental Series
AOT	H. E. D. Sparks (ed.), *The Apocryphal Old Testament*
Apc.	Apocalypse of John = Revelation of John
Apoc. Abr.	*Apocalypse of Abraham*
2–3 Apoc. Bar.	Syriac, Greek *Apocalypse of Baruch*
Apoc. Esdras	*Apocalypse of Esdras*
Apoc. Mos.	*Apocalypse of Moses*
Apoc. Paul	*Apocalypse of Paul*
Apoc. Pet.	*Apocalypse of Peter*
Apoc. Zeph.	*Apocalypse of Zephaniah*
Apol.	*Apology* (Justin)
APOT	R. H. Charles (ed.), *The Apocrypha and Pseudepigrapha of the Old Testament in English* (2 vols.)
As. Mos.	*Assumption of Moses*
Asc. Isa.	*Ascension of Isaiah*
ATANT	Abhandlungen zur Theologie des Alten und Neuen Testaments

Aug.	*Augustianum*
b.	Babylonian Talmud
BA	*Biblical Archaeologist*
BAG	W. Bauer, W. F. Arndt, and F. W. Gingrich (eds.), *A Greek–English Lexicon of the New Testament and Other Early Christian Literature*
Barn.	*Epistle of Barnabas*
BASOR	*Bulletin of the American Schools of Oriental Research*
BCE	Before Common Era
BETL	Bibliotheca ephemeridum theologicarum lovaniensium
BHS	*Biblia hebraica stuttgartensia*
BHT	Beiträge zur historischen Theologie
Bib.	*Biblica*
Bib. Ant.	*Biblical Antiquities* (Pseudo-Philo)
BibLeb	*Bibel und Leben*
BiKi	*Bibel und Kirche*
BJRL	*Bulletin of the John Rylands University Library of Manchester*
BR	*Biblical Research*
BTB	*Biblical Theology Bulletin*
BWANT	Beiträge zur Wissenschaft vom Alten und Neuen Testament
BZ	*Biblische Zeitschrift*
BZAW	Beihefte zur *ZAW*
BZNW	Behefte zur *ZNW*
BZRGG	Beihefte der *Zeitschrift für Religions- und Geistesgeschichte*
CBQ	*Catholic Biblical Quarterly*
CBQMS	Catholic Biblical Quarterly Monograph Series
CE	Common Era
CNT	Commentaire du Nouveau Testament
CSCO	Corpus scriptorum christianorum orientalium
CSEL	Corpus scriptorum ecclesiasticorum latinorum
CTM	*Concordia Theological Monthly*
DBAT	*Dielhammer Blätter zum Alten Testament*
De Benef.	De Beneficiis (Seneca)
Dial.	*Dialogue with Trypho* (Justin)
Did.	*Didache*

DJD	Discoveries in the Judean Desert
DSSE	G. Vermes, *The Dead Sea Scrolls in English*
1, 2, or 3 *Enoch*	Ethiopic, Slavonic, or Hebrew *Book of Enoch*
Ep. Apost.	*Epistula Apostolorum*
ESTNT	Exegetische Studien zur Theologie des Neuen Testaments
ET	English Translation
Eth.	Ethiopic
ETL	*Ephemerides theologicae lovanienses*
ETR	*Etudes théologiques et religieuses*
EUS	European University Studies
EvQ	*Evangelical Quarterly*
ExpTim	*Expository Times*
fr.	fragment
FRLANT	Forschungen zur Religion und Literatur des Alten und Neuen Testaments
FS	*Festschriften*
GCS	Die Griechischen Christlichen Schriftsteller der Ersten Drei Jahrhunderte
GNS	Good News Studies
HDR	Harvard Dissertations in Religion
HKAT	Handkommentar zum Alten Testament
HKNT	Handkommentar zum Neuen Testament
HNT	Handbuch zum Neuen Testament
HSM	Harvard Semitic Monographs
HSS	Harvard Semitic Studies
HTR	*Harvard Theological Review*
IB	*Interpreter's Bible*
ICC	International Critical Commentary
ICS	*Illinois Classical Studies*
Int.	*Interpretation*
JBL	*Journal of Biblical Literature*
JJS	*Journal of Jewish Studies*
Jos. and Asen.	*Joseph and Aseneth*
Josephus	
Ant.	*Jewish Antiquities*
JW	*Jewish Wars*
JQR	*Jewish Quarterly Review*
JSHRZ	Jüdische Schriften aus hellenistisch-römischer Zeit

JSJ	*Journal for the Study of Judaism in the Persian, Hellenistic, and Roman Period*
JSNT	*Journal for the Study of the New Testament*
JSNTSup	Journal for the Study of the New Testament Supplement Series
JSP	*Journal for the Study of the Pseudepigrapha*
JSPSup	Journal for the Study of the Pseudepigrapha Supplement Series
JSS	*Journal of Semitic Studies*
JTC	*Journal for Theology and the Church*
JTS	*Journal of Theological Studies*
Jub.	*Book of Jubilees*
Ladd. Jac.	*Ladder of Jacob*
Lat.	Latin
LXX	The Septuagint
m.	Mishnah
Mor. Def. Orac.	*Moralia: De Defectu Oraculorum* (Plutarch)
MS	Manuscript
MSS	Manuscripts
MT	Masoretic Text
NA^{26}	E. Nestle, K. Aland, and B. Aland (eds.), *Novum Testamentum Graece*, 26th edn, 1979
NCB	New Century Bible
NEB	New English Bible
Neot.	*Neotestimentica*
NIV	New International Version
NLC	New London Commentary
NovT	*Novum Testamentum*
NovTSup	Novum Testamentum Supplements
NRSV	New Revised Standard Version
NT	New Testament
NTA	E. Hennecke and W. Schneelmelcher (eds.), *New Testament Apocrypha* (2 vols.)
NTAbh	Neutestamentliche Abhandlungen
NTD	Das Neue Testament Deutsch
NTS	*New Testament Studies*
OCD	*The Oxford Classical Dictionary*, 2nd edn, 1970
Odes Sol.	*Odes of Solomon*
Origen	
Comm. Joh.	*Commentarii in Johannis*
Comm. Matt.	*Commentarii in Matthaei*

OT	Old Testament
OTP	James H. Charlesworth (ed.), *Old Testament Pseudepigrapha* (2 vols.)
OTS	*Oudtestamentische Studiën*
Pan.	*Panarion seu adversus lxxx haereses* (Epiphanius)
Pap.	Papyrus
Pesiq.	*R. Pesiqta Rabbati*
PG	J. Migne (ed.), *Patrologia graeca*
Philo	
Agr.	*De Agricultura*
Cher.	*De Cherubim*
Conf.	*De Confusione Linguarum*
Det.	*Quod Deteris Potiori insidiari solet*
Fug.	*De Fuga et Inventione*
Leg.	*De Legatione ad Gaium*
Leg.All.	*Legum Allegoriae*
Mig. Abr.	*De Migratione Abrahami*
Mos.	*De Vita Mosis*
Mut.	*De Mutatione Nominum*
Quaest. in Ex.	*Quaestiones et Solutiones in Exodum*
Quaest. in Gn.	*Quaestiones et Solutiones in Genesin*
Quis Her.	*Quis Rerum Divinarum Heres*
Quod Deus	*Quod Deus Immutabilis sit*
Sac.	*De Sacrificiis Abelis et Caini*
Som.	*De Somniis*
Pirqe R. El.	*Pirqe Rabbi Eliezer*
PL	J. Migne (ed.), *Patrologia latina*
Pr. Jos.	*Prayer of Joseph*
Pr Man	Prayer of Manasseh
Praep. ev.	*Praeparatio evangelica* (Eusebius)
PS	Pseudepigrapha Series
Ps. Clem.	*Pseudo Clement*
Pss. Sol.	*Psalms of Solomon*
PTA	Papyrologische Texte und Abhandlungen
PVTG	Pseudepigrapha Veteris Testamenti Graece
Qumran literature	
1Q, 2Q, 3Q, etc.	Numbered caves of Qumran
1Q19 fr. 3	(means) text 19 from Qumran Cave 1, fragment 3
1QapGen.	*Genesis Apocryphon* of Qumran Cave 1

1QH	*Thanksgiving Hymns* from Qumran Cave 1
1QM	*War Scroll* from Qumran Cave 1
1QS	*Rule of the Community* from Qumran Cave 1
1QSa	Appendix A (*Rule of the Congregation*) to 1QS
1QSb	Appendix B (*Blessings*) to 1QS
4Q 'Amram[b]	*Testament of Amram* from Qumran Cave 4
4QM[a]	*War Scroll* fragment from Qumran Cave 4
4Q400–5	Shirot 'Olat Ha- Shabbat, liturgical texts 400–405 from Qumran Cave 4
11QMelch	Melchizedek text from Qumran Cave 11
RAC	*Reallexikon für Antike und Christentum*
RB	*Revue Biblique*
Rec.	Recension
Ref. omn. haer.	*Refutation omnium haeresium* (Hippolytus)
RevQ	*Revue de Qumran*
RHPR	*Revue d'histoire et de philosophie religieuses*
RTP	*Revue de théologie et de philosophie*
SBL	Society of Biblical Literature
SBLDS	SBL Dissertation Series
SBLMS	SBL Monograph Series
SBLSCS	SBL Septuagint and Cognate Studies
SBLSP	SBL Seminar Papers
SBLTT	SBL Texts and Translations
SBT	Studies in Biblical Theology
ScripAeth	Scriptores Aethiopice
Shepherd of Hermas	
Herm. Mand.	*Hermas, Mandates*
Herm. Sim.	*Hermas, Similitudes*
Herm. Vis.	*Hermas, Visions*
Sib. Or.	*Sibylline Oracles*
SJ	Studia judaica
SJLA	Studies in Judaism in Late Antiquity
SJT	*Scottish Journal of Theology*
Slav.	Slavonic
SNT	Studien zum Neuen Testament
SNTSMS	Society for New Testament Studies Monograph Series
SPB	*Studia postbiblica*
SSS	Semitic Study Series
ST	*Studia theologica*
STDJ	Studies on the Texts of the Desert of Judea

StudNeot	Studia Neotestamentica
SVTP	Studia in Veteris Testamenti pseudepigrapha
Syh.	*Syro-Hexapla*
TA	Theologisches Arbeiten
TAQ	E. Lohse (ed.), *Die Texte aus Qumran: Hebräisch und Deutsch*
TDNT	G. Kittel and G. Friedrich (eds.), *Theological Dictionary of the New Testament* (10 vols.)
T. Ben.	*Testament of Benjamin*
T. Dan	*Testament of Dan*
T. Levi	*Testament of Levi*
T. Jos.	*Testament of Joseph*
Test. Abr.	*Testament of Abraham*
Test. Sol.	*Testament of Solomon*
Tg.	*Targum*
Tg. Onq.	*Targum Onquelos*
Tg. Neof.	*Targum Neofiti I*
Tg. Ps.-J.	*Targum Pseudo-Jonathan*
Tg. Yer. I	*Targum Yerusalmi I*
Tg. Yer. II	*Targum Yerusalmi II*
Th.	Theodotion
TLZ	Theologische Literaturzeitung
TQ	*Theologische Quartalschrift*
TRu	*Theologische Rundschau*
TS	*Theological Studies*
TSAJ	Texte und Studien zum antiken Judentum
TU	Texte und Untersuchungen
TynBul	*Tyndale Bulletin*
TZ	*Theologische Zeitschrift*
UBSGNT³	United Bible Societies, *The Greek New Testament*, 3rd edn, 1983
VC	*Vigiliae christianae*
VE	*Vox Evangelica*
VT	*Vetus Testamentum*
VTSup	Vetus Testamentum Supplements
WBC	Word Bible Commentary
WMANT	Wissenschaftliche Monographien zum Alten und Neuen Testament
WTJ	*Westminster Theological Journal*
WUNT	Wissenschaftliche Untersuchungen zum Neuen Testament

ZAW	*Zeitschrift für die alttestamentliche Wissenschaft*
ZBKNT	Zürcher Bibel Kommentare Neue Testament
ZNW	*Zeitschrift für die neutestamentliche Wissenschaft*

1

INTRODUCTION

Previous study of the christology of the Apocalypse

In general the study of the christology of the Apocalypse in this century has trodden well-worn paths along thematic valleys and over titled mountains largely similar to the study of christology elsewhere in the New Testament. A good deal of this study is presented in the introductory sections to commentaries,[1] or in chapters of general books about the Apocalypse,[2] or in the course of studies of NT christology.[3] The list of articles,[4] dissertations,[5] and monographs[6] specifically devoted to the christology of the Apocalypse is not overly long. For our present purposes most of the arguments and counter-arguments advanced in these studies do not concern us except in two respects. First, we are interested in what has been said in studies such as these about the divinity of Jesus Christ in the Apocalypse. Secondly, we have noted in such studies the virtual absence of reference to the question which is the

---

[1] E.g. Charles, i, cxi–cxiv; Beckwith, 312–7; Swete, clv–clix; Ford, 12–19. (Commentaries on the Apocalypse itself are referred to by the author's name only.)

[2] E.g. Scott, *Revelation*; Guthrie, *Relevance*; Bauckham, *Theology*.

[3] E.g. Cullmann, *Christology*; Hahn, *Hoheitstitel*; Müller, *Messias*; Schillebeeckx, *Christ*; De Jonge, *Christology*; Dunn, *Christology*; Hare, *Son*.

[4] E.g. Ellwanger, 'Christology'; Beck, 'Christology'; Scott, 'Behold'; Harlé, 'L'Agneau'; Schmitt, 'Interpretation'; Silberman, 'Farewell'; Rissi, 'Erscheinung'; Hillyer, 'Lamb'; Roberts, 'Lamb'; Mounce, 'Christology'; Van Unnik, 'Worthy'; Bovon, 'Le Christ'; Sabugal, 'El titulo'; Gerhardsson, 'Aussagen'; De Jonge, 'Use'; Guthrie, 'Lamb'; Carnegie, 'Worthy'; Edwards, 'Christological'; Jankowski, 'Chrystus'; Lohse, 'Menschensohn'; Moore, 'Jesus'; Läpple, 'Geheimnis'; Reddish, 'Martyr'; Satake, 'Christologie'; Boring, 'Narrative', 'Voice'; Slater, 'King'.

[5] E.g. Cook, *Christology*; Carrell, 'Lamb'; Jones, 'Study'. The present author has not been able to obtain a dissertation by Engelbrecht, Johannes Jacobus, 'The christology of the Book of Revelation' (DTh. Diss., University of Pretoria, 1980 (Afrikaans text)).

[6] Büchsel, *Christologie*; Comblin, *Christ*; D'Sousa, *Lamb*; Holtz, *Christologie*; Hohnjec, *Lamm*.

1

chief concern of this monograph, namely, the possibility of angelological influence on the christology of the Apocalypse.

With respect to the question of the divinity of Christ we may
note on the one side the views of scholars such as E. F. Scott who
argued that it is doubtful if John regarded Christ as being 'in any
full sense divine',[7] and Maurice Casey who has argued that 'the
lamb is carefully distinguished from God, and he is not said to be
divine'.[8] But on the other side the majority of scholars have had no
difficulty in affirming a 'high christology' for the Apocalypse.
Caird, for example, has argued that John believes that 'the glory of
God has been seen in the face of Jesus Christ' (cf. 2 Cor. 4.6).
Consequently, Christ bears 'all the attributes of deity' in his initial
portrayal (Apc. 1.12–16), is marked by the titles of God (e.g.
22.13), and, as the Lamb, has his name coupled together with the
name of God (e.g. 22.1,3). In short, 'God, once hidden from human
sight, [is] now revealed in the known person of his Son'.[9] A similar
conclusion is reached by Schillebeeckx who argues that the secret
name in Apocalypse 19.12 signifies that 'Revelation explicitly
maintains the mystery of the eschatological identity of the person
of Jesus . . . The author evidently means to suggest that the nature
of Christ is intrinsically bound up with that of God himself'.[10]
Most recently Bauckham has argued that the pattern of 'I am' self-
declarations by God (1.8, 21.6) and Christ (1.17, 22.13) reveals 'the
remarkable extent to which Revelation identifies Jesus Christ with
God'.[11] In particular, Apocalypse 22.13 (where Christ is 'the Alpha
and the Omega, the first and the last, the beginning and the end')
reveals 'unambiguously that Jesus Christ belongs to the fullness of
the eternal being of God'. Accordingly the Apocalypse implies
neither an adoptionist christology, nor that Christ is understood as
a second god. Thus the worship of Jesus in the Apocalypse (e.g.
Apc. 5.9–13, 22.1–3), a work which is distinctly monotheistic in
outlook, 'must be understood as indicating the inclusion of Jesus in
the being of the one God defined in monotheistic worship'.[12]

On the question of angelological influence we note an article by
Fischer which typifies the inattention of scholars to this influence.[13]

[7] Scott, *Revelation*, 116. Cf. Swete, clv–clix; Charles, i, cxii.
[8] Casey, *Jewish*, 142.   [9] Caird, 289–301; cf. Boring, 102–3.
[10] Schillebeeckx, *Christ*, 432–62; citation from p. 443.
[11] Bauckham, *Theology*, 54–5.
[12] Ibid., 56–60; citations from pp. 56–7 and 60, respectively.
[13] Fischer, 'Christlichkeit' (1981).

Writing on the Christian character of the Apocalypse, Fischer
devotes a small but profound section to the christology of the
Apocalypse. He perceives John to be expressing the form of Christ
in four ways: (i) co-regent of God; (ii) supreme archangel; (iii) son
of man-judge and (iv) the 'one sacrificing himself for us'. Yet
Fischer does not develop the idea that Christ is the supreme
archangel (which arises out of Apc. 12.10–12 where Christ is
honoured as victor after Michael's struggle with the dragon).[14]

If any aspect of christological study appears to provide a starting
point for our task it would be 'angel christology'. Yet, as we shall
see, our starting point is better found elsewhere. Angel christology
certainly existed after the first century CE (and we examine this in
more detail in chapter 5 below) but the question of whether it
existed in the first century CE has for the most part received a
negative answer. In 1941 Werner argued that the oldest christology
was in fact an angel christology.[15] For example, behind the conception of Christ as 'messiah–son of man' was 'a high angelic being'
(cf. 1 *Enoch* 46.3) and the son of man was represented as 'the Prince
of Angels' (e.g. Mark 8.38; Matt. 13.41–2; Luke 22.43).[16] Critical
response to this thesis was swift[17] and decisive,[18] although some
recent assessments have not been totally dismissive.[19] In any case,
Werner himself had very little to say about the christology of the
Apocalypse and offers no discussion at all of key christological
texts such as Apocalypse 1.13–16, 14.14, and 19.11–16.[20] Some
speculation about angel christology in the NT has continued in
recent years, mostly in connection with books such as the Fourth
Gospel and Jude.[21] Karrer, however, devotes a short but important

[14] Ibid., 170.
[15] Werner, *Die Entstehung des Christlichen Dogmas* (Bern: Paul Haupt, 1941, 1954).
We have used the ET, Werner, *Formation*.
[16] Ibid., 120–4.
[17] Michaelis, *Engelchristologie*; with vigorous response in Werner, *Formation*, 130,
n. 1.
[18] E.g. Barbel, *Christos*, 348: 'in the NT there is no consciousness of an angel
christology'; cf. Balz, *Methodische*, 208; Kretschmar, *Studien*, 220–2, and, more
recently, Dunn, *Christology*, 154–8, 322, n. 106.
[19] E.g. Hengel, *Son*, 84; 'A real *angel christology* could only become significant right
on the fringe of the Jewish–Christian sphere . . . Werner much exaggerated the
role of "angel christology" in early Christianity' (italics in original). Cf. Knight,
Disciples, 73.
[20] Discussion of the Apocalypse does not feature in Bakker's important article,
'Christ', on angel christology.
[21] E.g. Fossum, 'Kyrios', with reply by Bauckham, *Jude*, 310–2. Knight (*Disciples*,
91), sees an angel christology in John 8.58 and 12.41; contrast with Dunn,

4 _Introduction_

Excursus to the question of angel christology in the Apocalypse and argues that Apocalypse 1.5 and 14.14 particularly show signs of the influence of angel christology.[22] We may also note a dissertation by Brighton,[23] and an article by Gundry,[24] both of which will be referred to in chapter 7.

Werner's thesis and the debate it generated did not foreclose the possibility that an alternative approach to the relationship between angelology and christology might prove more acceptable. Daniélou and Longenecker avoided replicating Werner's 'extreme thesis' by arguing for 'angelomorphic christology' as a feature of Jewish Christianity. In this view the development of christology was influenced by the angelology of the OT but not to the point that Christ was designated an angel; rather, this influence led to 'angelomorphic categories' being attributed to Christ.[25] As we shall see, the term 'angelomorphic christology' is particularly useful for describing important aspects of the christology of the Apocalypse.[26]

A starting point

In relation to the Apocalypse the discussion of 'angelomorphic christology' has been principally led in recent times by Christopher Rowland. In our view the best starting point for research into the influence of angelology on the christology of the Apocalypse is an observation made by Rowland in the course of his work on Jewish and Christian apocalypticism, especially in relation to angel and _merkabah_ speculations within this phenomenon.[27] For Rowland some visions of glorious angels in Jewish apocalyptic writings seem

---

Christology, 154–8. Bühner (_Gesandte_, 316–433), discerns angelological influence in the background to the christology of the Fourth Gospel; note also Segal, 'Ruler', 258–9. Sanders ('Dissenting') argues for an angelic background to Phil. 2.5–11.

[22] Karrer, _Johannesoffenbarung_, 147–9.   [23] Brighton, _Angel_.

[24] Gundry, 'Angelomorphic'.

[25] Longenecker, _Christology_, 26–32; Daniélou, _Theology_, 117–46; cf. Carr, _Angels_, 143ff.; Fossum, 'Jewish–Christian'.

[26] Note most recently Stuckenbruck, 'Refusal'. In this article Stuckenbruck indicates that more extensive treatment of angelomorphic christology in the Apocalypse is given in his forthcoming volume, now published, but not yet sighted by the present author: _Angel Veneration and Christology. A Study in Early Judaism and in the Christology of the Apocalypse of John_ (WUNT 2.70), Tübingen: Mohr (Paul Siebeck), 1995.

[27] Rowland, 'Vision', _Heaven_, 'Man'.

to imply 'some kind of bifurcation in the conception of God', so that, even if the earliest Christians did not think of Christ as an angel, aspects of Jewish angelology may have provided a means for grasping how Christ could be a divine being alongside God.[28] Rowland's work is particularly valuable because he develops his thesis with the christophany in Apocalypse 1.13–16 as one focus.

In essence Rowland argues that Ezekiel 1.26–8, 8.2–4, and Daniel 10.5–6 disclose a trend whereby the human form of God (Ezek. 1.26–8) is separated from the divine throne-chariot and functions as 'a quasi-angelic mediator' (Ezek. 8.2–4) similar to the angel in Daniel 10.5–6. On the one hand, the form of the angel in Daniel 10.5–6 appears to have been influenced by Ezekiel, especially the theophany in chapter 1.[29] On the other hand, the figure in Ezekiel 8.2–4 may be compared with 'one like a son of man' in Daniel 7.13: both are heavenly figures who are spoken of in 'quasi-divine terms'.[30] The divine status of the Danielic son of man figure, according to Rowland, is even more apparent in Daniel 7.13 LXX which speaks of the figure coming 'as the Ancient of Days' rather than 'unto the Ancient of Days'.[31] The LXX variant was probably responsible for the identification of the risen Jesus with the Ancient of Days in Apocalypse 1.14.[32]

A similar explanation may be given for the background to the glorious angel Yahoel in *Apocalypse of Abraham* 10–11 (an apocalypse dating from a similar period to the Apocalypse). This suggests that the developments Rowland adduces were part of a broad tendency in Jewish angelology in which the conception of God is bifurcated: alongside God is another divine figure who acts in God's place with the form and character of God.[33] Thus Rowland has advanced the very important thesis that the appearances of the risen Jesus in Apocalypse 1, and of certain other glorious angels in apocalyptic literature, may be explained in terms of developments in Jewish theology and angelology, in which a glorious angel 'embodied the attributes of the glorious God whom the prophet Ezekiel had seen by the river Chebar'.[34]

---

[28] As recognized by, e.g., Dunn, *Christology*, xxiv (whence the citation) and Hurtado, *God*, 74.

[29] Rowland, 'Vision', 1–5, *Heaven*, 94–101.   [30] Rowland, *Heaven*, 97.

[31] This matter will be examined more closely in chapter 2.

[32] Rowland, *Heaven*, 97–8.

[33] 'Bifurcating' is used by Rowland, 'Vision', 2; our explanation in the second part of the sentence draws on Rowland, *Heaven*, 97–8.

[34] Rowland, *Heaven*, 103.

We shall have more to say about Rowland's proposal in subsequent chapters. But at this point it is appropriate to mention briefly several related contributions in the study of angelology and christology. Segal, for example, has examined rabbinic traditions about the (so-called) 'two powers' heresy, in which, contrary to the strict monotheism of rabbinic Judaism, scripture was interpreted 'to say that a principal angelic or hypostatic manifestation in heaven was equivalent to God'.[35] The opposition of the rabbis to this heresy is dated by Segal to the second century CE, but with the observation that 'the rabbis' second-century opponents had first-century forebears', such as Philo's talk of a 'second god' and Paul's polemic against angelology in Galatians 3.19–20.[36] As far as Segal could discern, an interest in the principal angel or in hypostases which was *heretical* had not developed in the first century CE.[37] The interest in the glorious angel Yahoel in the *Apocalypse of Abraham*, for example, is 'not clearly heretical'.[38]

With particular reference to Samaritan religious traditions, Fossum has investigated the origins of the Gnostic demiurge. He attempts to show that the demiurge, as conceived in Gnosticism, was preceded by 'Jewish ideas about the creative agency of the hypostasized divine Name and the Angel of the Lord'.[39] An example of such agency is the angel Yahoel.[40] A named angel represents a shift from the stage when the Angel of the LORD was more or less indistinguishable from God: the Angel of the LORD now has personality and personal existence.[41] According to Fossum this development which envisaged, or at least tended to envisage, another power alongside God predates the Christian era.[42]

We cannot here develop a detailed criticism of Fossum's work. Nevertheless its importance, which in the present context principally lies in its claim that a 'two powers' belief may have predated the Christian era, requires that we outline a response to his approach. First, Fossum does not substantiate his claim that angels such as Yahoel 'shared God's own . . . nature or mode of being'.[43] Secondly, Fossum does not demonstrate that a second power alongside God such as the Angel of the LORD was worshipped in the

[35] Segal, *Powers*, 18.   [36] Ibid., 260–2.   [37] Ibid., 192, 196, 200.
[38] Ibid., 196; cf. summary remark in Hurtado, *God*, 32: 'an interest in angelic beings is one thing and the worship of them another'.
[39] Fossum, *Name*, v.   [40] Ibid., 319–21, 333.   [41] Ibid., 337.
[42] Ibid., 307, 318, 332.   [43] Ibid., 333.

pre-Christian era.[44] Thirdly, Fossum supports his argument with evidence drawn from periods later than the first century CE. It is always problematic when developments attested in later periods are read back into earlier stages of religious history.[45]

Rowland, Segal, and Fossum, therefore, have explored evidence concerning the shift from strict monotheism to a kind of dualistic or binitarian position in some Jewish circles. Taking the interpretation of the status of the angel Yahoel as something of a yardstick, Segal is least inclined to see heretical developments in the first century CE, Fossum is most inclined, while Rowland sees the potential for heretical development in, perhaps even before, the first century CE.

Not unexpectedly the challenges posed by Rowland and Fossum have drawn a response. Chief among the respondents has been Hurtado who argues that principal angel figures, in common with exalted patriarchs (such as Moses and Enoch), and divine hypostases (such as *Sophia* and the *Logos*), reflect an underlying interest in the concept of 'divine agency'. Hurtado argues that divine agency 'operated within the traditional Jewish concern for the uniqueness of God'.[46] In other words, Hurtado argues, against Rowland and Fossum, that traditions concerning the chief divine agent involved no 'mutation' in the monotheistic belief and devotional practice of post-exilic Judaism. In particular, Hurtado challenges Rowland's and Fossum's understandings of the significance of Yahoel in *Apocalypse of Abraham* 10–11. The glorious appearance of this angel is not an expression of the belief that the divine Glory had become a personalized divine agent.[47] Rather, the portrayal of Yahoel is a creative attempt to show 'the visual majesty accorded to the angel chosen by God as his chief agent'.[48] The majesty of Yahoel is not evidence for 'a bifurcation of the deity'; rather it is a reflection of 'the pattern of ancient imperial regimes [which] required that the figure holding the position of God's vizier should be described in majestic terms'.[49] Positively, Hurtado advances the hypothesis that the divine agency tradition

[44] Hurtado, *God*, 38.
[45] Ibid. An extreme example of this tendency is Fossum's citing in *Name* (329–32) of the Magharian sect's teaching about the Angel of the LORD, which is attested to in tenth- and twelfth-century writings!
[46] Hurtado, *God*, 38.
[47] Fossum, *Name*, 319–20; Rowland, *Heaven*, 102–3. Rowland is more hesitant on this matter than Fossum.
[48] Hurtado, *God*, 88.   [49] Ibid., 89.

contributed to the development of the earliest christology. Briefly, the exalted Jesus was understood to be the chief divine agent,[50] but a 'mutation' in belief took place whereby Jesus Christ was included in the devotional thought and practice of the early Christians as 'a second object of devotion alongside God'.[51]

Hurtado is not the only critic of Rowland and Fossum,[52] but he is the one who has responded most fully to their work. At the heart of Hurtado's criticism of Rowland and Fossum, and of his hypothesis concerning the development of christology, lies the importance of worship as a test of doctrine. It is the absence of evidence for the worship of a second 'divine' being (whether hypostasis, angel, or patriarch) which cautions Hurtado against claims such as Fossum's that there were substantial modifications of monotheism in post-exilic Judaism.[53] Conversely, it is the worship of Jesus which sets the Christian concept of divine agency on its head compared with its Jewish counterpart.[54]

Hurtado's work has been subjected to a critical review by Rainbow.[55] The details of this cannot be elucidated here, save to note that Rainbow identifies a class of intermediaries not considered as a separate category by Hurtado, namely, 'eschatological figures in the Bible' (e.g. Enoch). The importance of this category is that a figure manifestly distinct from God (i.e. not a personification), yet conceived of having 'an aureola of deity' (i.e. not a patriarch or angel), could have been considered worthy of worship. Rainbow argues that a separate category is appropriate because 'Hurtado's test of cultic veneration is not applicable to eschatological beings. No one would offer worship to a person who was still awaited in the future.'[56] Worship might be offered, however, to a person whose followers were convinced he was a now-present eschatological figure. Such conviction could have arisen if Jesus convinced his followers that he would share in the status of the one God as Messiah in the terms set forth in Psalm 110.1 and Daniel 7.13. This would explain the worship of Jesus by the first Christians. But to maintain this hypothesis it would have to be demonstrated that texts such as Matthew 26.64 *par.*, where Psalm 110.1

---

[50] Ibid., 93–9.   [51] Ibid., 100, cf. 99–124.

[52] Cf. Dunn, *Christology*, xxiv–xxvi; Karrer, *Johannesoffenbarung*, 143–7; Kim, *Origin*, 244–6.

[53] Hurtado, *God*, 38; cf. Dunn, *Partings*, 219.   [54] Hurtado, *God*, 100.

[55] Rainbow, 'Monotheism'.   [56] Ibid., 88, n. 22.

and Daniel 7.13 are combined in the words of Jesus at his trial, are historically reliable. A tall order – as Rainbow admits![57]

When Hurtado emphasizes the importance of worship as a test for developments within or away from monotheism he acknowledges his debt to Bauckham who has examined the worship of Jesus in apocalyptic Christianity, principally in connection with the Apocalypse and the *Ascension of Isaiah*.[58] Since the worship of Jesus has less significance in an environment with a lax attitude to monotheism, Bauckham first establishes that, at least in the circles represented by the two apocalypses in question, there was a strict adherence to monotheism.[59] The evidence for this lies principally in the refusal of angels to be worshipped (Apc. 19.10, 22.8; *Asc. Isa.* 7.21, 8.5). With this evidence may be contrasted those passages which explicitly acknowledge Jesus' worthiness to be worshipped (e.g. Apc. 5.8–12; *Asc. Isa.* 9.28–32). In the present context Bauckham's discussion is particularly noteworthy because it involves the interface between angelology and christology, at least with respect to the Apocalypse (and to the *Ascension of Isaiah*). Bauckham argues that there is 'a sharp theological distinction between Christ and angels'.[60] This distinction is demonstrated in three ways.

First, Christ is worshipped and not the angels. But, secondly, this worship arises from the fact that only Christ is *worthy* to open the scroll. The angels also have a role in the implementation of the divine purposes, but no special worthiness is demanded for this role and no praise results from its fulfilment.[61] Thirdly, this distinction parallels that made in respect of the giving of the revelation. Jesus 'belongs with God as giver, while the angel belongs with John as instrument' in the transmission of the revelation.[62] Bauckham's work in this area is of great importance for the discussion of the influence of angelology on the christology of the Apocalypse as it unfolds in succeeding chapters.[63]

All the scholars discussed so far in this section have something to say about monotheism. The work of Rowland and Fossum, for

---

[57] Ibid., 88–90. For a different, but in our opinion unconvincing, set of criticisms of Hurtado see Knight, *Disciples*, 57–109, esp. p. 97.

[58] Bauckham, 'Worship'; cf. Hurtado, *God*, 38.

[59] Bauckham, 'Worship', 322–7.   [60] Ibid., 338, n. 42.   [61] Ibid., 330.

[62] Ibid., 329; cf. 330.

[63] Stuckenbruck, 'Refusal' offers the most significant response to Bauckham, 'Worship'.

example, has opened up the possibility that Jewish monotheism before the beginning of Christianity was at least potentially weakened to allow for some kind of binitarian or dualistic position to be held. But recently two scholars have independently promoted the view that, except for a small minority of Jews, strict monotheism *never arrived* in ancient Judaism. That is, the ancient dualism of El and Ba'al/Yahweh never lost its influence through the First and Second Temple periods.

Thus Hayman argues the startling theses that (i) 'it is hardly ever appropriate to use the term monotheism to describe the Jewish idea of God'; (ii) until the philosophers of the Middle Ages there is no discernible progress beyond the basic formulae of Deuteronomy; and (iii) 'Judaism never escapes from the legacy of the battles for supremacy between Yahweh, Ba'al, and El from which it emerged'.[64] The implications of this view for the development of early christology are obvious: since Jews effectively believed in two gods Christianity was able rapidly to develop 'towards the divinization of Jesus'.[65] In similar vein, Barker argues that the worldview of the ancient Israelite religion in which the High God had several Sons of God, one of whom was Yahweh, influenced many in first-century Palestine. Since it was believed that Yahweh manifested himself on earth in human or angelic form or as the Davidic king, it *'was as a manifestation of Yahweh, the Son of God, that Jesus was acknowledged as Son of God, Messiah and Lord'.*[66]

But not all recent scholarship has been heading in the direction of Hayman and Barker. We may note, for instance, Casey's vigorous defence of Jewish monotheism as the bedrock from which Christianity was hewn with the aid of a Hellenistic chisel.[67] The difference between Casey and Barker, for example, is neatly illustrated in their differing responses to Philo's talk of the *Logos* as 'a second god' (*Quaest. in Gn.* ii.62). For Casey this 'indicates that the theoretical limit of Jewish monotheism may appear to be breached by an occasional sentence'.[68] Barker, by contrast, citing *Quaestiones et Solutiones in Genesin* ii.62, states that 'Philo is quite clear what he meant by Logos; he was describing a second

[64] Hayman, 'Monotheism', 2.   [65] Ibid., 14.

[66] Barker, *Angel*, 3 (the italics are Barker's). On heterodox Judaism before the Christian era see also Quispel, 'Ezekiel'.

[67] Casey, *Jewish*.

[68] Ibid., 85; cf. Dunn, *Christology*, 220–8. For an unequivocal statement of the oneness of God in Philo see *Leg. All.* iii.81.

God'.[69] Thus 'Philo shows beyond any doubt that the Judaism of the first Christian century acknowledged a second God'.[70]

The details of the cases advanced by Hayman and Barker in support of each argument need not detain us here since they go beyond the scope of this inquiry. We can, however, make two brief observations in response. First, it is noticeable that the Apocalypse, which offers quite a lot of evidence (in their terms) for Jesus as a second God, *nevertheless* appears to work out its christology in a strongly monotheistic context – a point, as we have seen, which Bauckham underlines. On the one hand, the angel refuses worship and directs John to worship *God* (not God and Jesus, 19.10, 22.9). On the other hand, the worship at the throne 'of God and the Lamb' in 22.1,3 is directed to 'him' – a singular pronoun.[71] Secondly, if, as Barker asserts, 'the great angel' is the second God, it is not clear what she makes of the fact that in the Apocalypse there are at least two 'great angels', Jesus (so to speak in, for example, Apc. 1.13–16) *and* the 'mighty angel' in Apocalypse 10.1. Her case would be better served if Jesus was the *only* 'great angel' in the Apocalypse.[72]

Linked to our discussion so far are the esoteric traditions collectively known as *merkabah* mysticism. *Merkabah* is the Hebrew word for 'chariot' and *merkabah* mysticism may be formally defined in terms of 'an esoteric, visionary-mystical tradition centred upon the vision of God, seated on the celestial throne or Merkabah'.[73] At the heart of this tradition is the exegesis of texts, such as Ezekiel 1, Daniel 7, Isaiah 6, and Exodus 24, which feature visions of the divine throne, or throne-chariot, and its occupant. Its particular relevance to early christology lies in its opening 'the window on a troubling ambiguity in the being of the Jewish God'.[74] Halperin, for example, draws attention to the problem of the living creature with a face like a calf (or ox) and its recall of the worship of the golden calf at Sinai (Ezek. 1.10, Exod. 32).[75] But also perceived as dangerous was reflection on 'the Glory' which led either to its identification as a subordinate, created being (as in

---

[69] Barker, *Angel*, 116. [70] Ibid., 131.
[71] These observations are discussed in more detail in chapter 6.
[72] Cf. Barker, *Angel*, 201–3.
[73] Morray-Jones, 'Transformational mysticism', 1–31. Scholem (*Trends*, 63) points out four mystical preoccupations: (i) God in his aspect as Creator of the Universe; (ii) the vision of the celestial realm; (iii) songs of the angels; and (iv) the structure of the *merkabah*.
[74] Halperin, *Faces*, 449. [75] Ibid.

Gnosticism) or to the identification of a human being with 'the Glory' (as in Christianity).[76]

The relationship between apocalypticism and *merkabah* mysticism has been the subject of much discussion. Gruenwald, for example, has argued that apocalypticism has a close relationship with *merkabah* mysticism.[77] Rowland, admitting the uncertainty of the connection between the two phenomena, draws attention to the common interest shared between them.[78] There is, of course, no doubt that in the case of the Apocalypse itself it shares with *merkabah* mysticism an interest in the divine throne (cf. Apc. 4). But it is not clear that John's throne-vision was influenced by Jewish mystical practice and teaching as opposed to apocalyptic tradition which drew on Ezekiel 1.[79] There is, in fact, a lack of consensus over the dating of the origins of the *merkabah* mysticism which is attested to, reflected upon, and expressed in Jewish literature such as the Talmud and the *Hekhalot* literature.[80] Both sets of texts date from the period after the first century CE. But when did the traditions they attest to originate? Some scholars have argued for origins later than the first century,[81] while others have argued for origins within the first century CE.[82] In short, the problem remains unresolved as to whether the (apparent) parallels between, for instance, the Apocalypse and Jewish rabbinic and mystical writings concerned with the *merkabah* represent the influence of one (set of traditions lying behind the writings) on the other or the mutual interaction of the two.[83] To attempt to settle this

---

[76] Morray-Jones ('Transformational mysticism', 7), who notes the warning against such speculations in *m. Hagigah* 2.1; cf. Quispel, 'Ezekiel'.

[77] Gruenwald, *Apocalyptic*, esp. pp. 29–72.   [78] Rowland, *Heaven*, 340–8.

[79] Scholem (*Trends*, 43) puts the point neatly: no one knows if (e.g.) 1 *Enoch* and the *Apocalypse of Abraham* 'reproduce the essentials of the esoteric doctrine taught by the teachers of the Mishnah'.

[80] For an introduction to these writings see Gruenwald, *Apocalyptic*, 98–234. The 'classic' intersection of apocalyptic and mystical writings is 3 *Enoch*, also known as *Sefer Hekhalot*, dating from the fifth or sixth century CE. For the *Hekhalot* writings in Hebrew see Schäfer, *Synopse*.

[81] Notably, Halperin, *Merkabah*, and *Faces*; Schäfer ('New Testament') 19–35, who argues, *contra* Scholem (*Gnosticism*, 14–19) that *merkabah* mysticism does not provide the background for Paul's famous account in 2 Cor. 12.

[82] Most recently, Morray-Jones ('Merkabah mysticism') who (i) offers a modified version of the hypothesis advanced by Scholem (*Trends*, 40–79, and *Gnosticism*, esp. pp. 14–19, 40), and developed by Gruenwald (*Apocalyptic*, esp. pp. 73–97), while (ii) rejecting (particularly) the case advanced by Halperin.

[83] Halperin, *Faces*, 87–96, from the perspective of one favouring a post-first-century CE origin for *merkabah* mysticism, draws out the significance of the Apocalypse 'as a source for early developments in Jewish *merkabah* exegesis' (p. 87).

issue is beyond the scope of the present project, and consequently we will largely explore the influence of angelology on the christology of the Apocalypse without reference to rabbinic and mystical literature.[84]

We are now in a position to sum up our discussion to this point. A fair amount of research has been undertaken on the christology of the Apocalypse, but only a small portion of this has been related to the question of angelological influence on the christology. Work by Rowland, in the course of examining broader questions concerning the development of apocalypticism, has opened up what appears to be a fruitful line of inquiry, one likely to confirm that the Apocalypse has an 'angelomorphic christology'[85] (rather than an angel christology). Since Rowland has not pursued christological texts in the Apocalypse other than Apocalypse 1.13–16 there would appear to be scope for a contribution to research in this area along the following lines: (i) a re-examination of Apocalypse 1.13–16 with critical response to Rowland; (ii) a wider examination of the influence of angelology on the christology of the Apocalypse.

Terms, aims, and scope

Our aim in this monograph is to investigate the influence of angelology on the christology of the Apocalypse. By 'the christology of the Apocalypse' we mean the portrayal of the form, function, and status of Jesus Christ through accounts of visions and auditions, titles, and acclamations. By 'angelology' we mean talk about angels, especially that which is attested in written material from the OT and from Jewish and Christian apocalypses stemming from the period 200 BCE to 200 CE. Angelology relates to specific propositional statements about angels (e.g. 'one of the seven angels who stand . . . before the glory of the LORD', Tob. 12.15), to stories of angelic involvement in human and heavenly affairs (e.g. Ezek. 9, 3 *Enoch* 16.1–5), and to accounts of angelo-

---

Particularly intriguing is the parallel between the 'sea of glass' (around the divine throne, Apc. 4.6, 15.2) and the warning in *b. Hagigah* 14b, 'do not say, "Water, water"', which appears to be linked to the idea that the sea is the place of chaos.

[84] On *merkabah* mysticism in general, and on its relationship to christological development in the first few centuries CE, see additionally (e.g.) Fossum, 'Jewish–Christian', 260–87; Morray-Jones, 'Transformational mysticism'; Chernus, 'Visions', 123–46; Rowland, 'Visions' (1979).

[85] Rowland, 'Man', 100.

phanies (e.g. Dan. 10.5–6, *Jos. and Asen.* 14.8).[86] We define 'angels' as heavenly beings distinct from God and from human beings, who exist to serve God as messengers, as the heavenly congregation at worship, and as agents of the divine will fulfilling a variety of other functions.[87] By 'the influence of angelology on the christology of the Apocalypse' we mean the shaping and determining of the christology of the Apocalypse by the adoption and adaptation of angelological motifs, images, and concepts.[88] We use the term 'influence' deliberately because it is more general in its meaning than 'dependence'. To look for christological material which *depended* on angelology would be invidious for we would have to determine that John consciously intended to draw on angelology for his portrayal of Jesus. To look for signs of the influence of angelology on the christology of the Apocalypse is to set ourselves not so much an easier task but one which is more amenable to yielding results.[89]

We will begin our task by investigating the 'context' of the christology of the Apocalypse in Jewish and Christian apocalyptic traditions and related writings. That is, we will seek to understand the christology in terms of the angelology prior to and contemporaneous with the Apocalypse, and the angel christology and angelomorphic christology which followed the Apocalypse. The agenda here has been largely set by Rowland, but we will extend the scope of the material which he has considered. This investigation, to be covered in chapters 2–5, begins in chapter 2, with the angelology of three OT writings which have been influential on the Apocalypse: Zechariah, Ezekiel, and Daniel. Angelology in Ezekiel and Daniel is inextricably connected to the theophanies in both books so that inevitably our discussion moves strictly beyond the bounds of 'angelology'. We then consider in chapter 3 the 'principal angels' in apocalypses and related writings outside the OT. Our particular interest is with accounts of angelophanies which (i) have been influenced by passages such as Daniel 7.9 and 10.5–6, and (ii) offer some kind of parallel to the christophany in Apocalypse 1.13–16.

---

[86] 'Angelophanic' refers to appearances of angels, 'theophanic' to appearances of God, and 'epiphanic' to majestic and glorious appearances of any being, whether divine, angelic, or human.

[87] Cf. Carr, *Angels*, 25–43, 127–9; Aune, 'Magic', 488–9.

[88] Cf. Betz ('Problem', 137) describes influences as 'direct adaptation of concepts, traditions, and terminologies'.

[89] Cf. Ruiz, *Ezekiel*, 122–4, for discussion of influence/dependence of the Apocalypse by/on biblical sources.

(By 'principal angel' we mean a leading angel – an 'archangel' like Michael or Gabriel, for instance.[90] Where one angel is superior to all others we will use the term 'chief angel'.)

Epiphanies featuring angels correspond in some instances to epiphanies featuring exalted humans. A link between the two is sometimes explicit in as much as the human is described as 'like an angel' (cf. 1 *Enoch* 106.5–6). In chapter 4 we will consider such accounts and the more general subject of humans who attain to high office within the divine realm in order to understand better the background to the presentation of Jesus Christ in exalted form and status in the Apocalypse. Jesus Christ is called 'the *Logos* of God' in Apocalypse 19.13 while appearing in angelomorphic form, and for this reason we also consider writings in which the *Logos* features as an angelomorphic figure. Finally, in chapter 6 we give further consideration to angel christology. This study takes us into the period after the composition of the Apocalypse but nevertheless remains within the bounds of the 'context' of the christology of the Apocalypse.

In the remaining chapters of the monograph we consider christological material in the Apocalypse itself. Our starting point, in chapter 6, is Apocalypse 1.1 where we find God, Jesus Christ, and an angel connected through their joint participation in the transmission of the revelation to John. We briefly consider the relationships between God and Jesus and between Jesus and the angel in order to clarify certain points about the divine and angelic character of the exalted Jesus. We then consider in four successive chapters the three visions of Christ which are most likely to have been influenced by angelology: Apocalypse 1.13–16, 14.14, and 19.11–16.

Four comments about the investigation need to be made at this point. First, by restricting ourselves to the various passages considered in our study of the relationship between Jesus and the angel and to the visions in Apocalypse 1.13–16, 14.14, and 19.11–16, we do not claim that these are the only christological passages reflecting the influence of angelology. We are confident, however, that to demonstrate such influence on other passages would be a worthy project in its own right.

Secondly, the influence of the OT on the Apocalypse is well known,[91] and thus it is reasonable to consider that the angelology

---

[90] Cf. Segal, *Powers*, 187.
[91] See now Beale, 'Revelation'and literature cited therein.

of the OT, in particular of Zechariah, Ezekiel, and Daniel, may have influenced the christology of the Apocalypse. The influence of Jewish and Christian apocryphal and pseudepigraphal writings on the Apocalypse is less clear.[92] Whatever view may be held of the genre to which the Apocalypse should be assigned,[93] it is indubitable that the Apocalypse includes a number of elements which connect it to apocalyptic literature. For the Apocalypse contains the principal features of this literature: 'the revelation of divine mysteries through visions'[94] and 'mediated revelation, otherworldly realities, and transcendental eschatology'.[95] Whether or not John was directly influenced by writings like the *Similitudes of Enoch* or the *Book of Jubilees*, there are certainly subjects of common interest between the Apocalypse and such writings. A survey of the angelology of the Apocalypse in the next section suggests that one of these common interests was angelology. This does not mean that (say) the angelology of *Jubilees* has influenced the Apocalypse in the sense that John was directly familiar with this work, but it does suggest that considering the angelology of *Jubilees* will enlighten us as to the nature of the angelology with which John was familiar.

Thirdly, notwithstanding the above point, our investigation of the context of the christology of the Apocalypse is inevitably limited: on the one hand, it is important to our overall study that we cover the areas we have just mentioned; on the other, it is important that we consider at least some aspects of these areas in a reasonable amount of detail. This means, however, that we must neglect entirely, or almost entirely, the angelology of the targumic, rabbinic, and Gnostic literature. It also means that we can only make a brief mention of the Hellenistic 'daemon' context of the

[92] Parker ('Scripture', 42–8) finds literary parallels with pseudepigraphal apocalyptic literature but without demonstration of direct literary influence. Charles, i, lxv, finds at least indirect evidence for knowledge of *T. Levi*, 1 *Enoch* (cf. Charles, *APOT*, ii, 180), the *Assumption of Moses*, and, less probably, 2 *Enoch* and the *Psalms of Solomon*. In the light of reassessed datings since the early decades of this century it would be preferable to speak of common knowledge of traditions and motifs found in such works.

[93] Discussion ranges over the categories 'letter' (e.g. Karrer, *Johannesoffenbarung*), 'apocalypse' (e.g. Collins, 'Pseudonymity', Yarbro Collins, 'Early Christian', 70–2), and 'prophecy' (e.g. Mazzaferri, *Genre*); Schüssler Fiorenza (*Justice*, 168–70) amalgamates all three categories; Linton ('Reading', 161) argues for a 'hybrid genre'.

[94] Rowland, *Heaven*, 70.

[95] Collins, 'Jewish', 29; cf. ibid., Introduction, 9; Hanson, *Dawn*, 9–11.

christology,[96] and that we must ignore completely the socio-political context of the christology.[97]

Fourthly, our investigation proceeds on the basis that 'influence' and 'visionary experience' are compatible concepts. It is, of course, theoretically possible that a man named John had absolutely no knowledge of the OT or of apocalyptic and related traditions yet wrote an account of his visionary experiences which coincidentally recalled the language of these writings. It is much more likely, though, that if the Apocalypse represents genuine visions experienced by John then these were influenced by the OT and other traditions. Dreams and visions do not normally take place within a mind which is a *tabula rasa*. The content and structure of a vision may not exactly reflect any previously experienced events or any pattern of ideas and images already stored in the mind; but they will draw on what is already known. We can readily imagine John meditating on passages such as Ezekiel 1, Daniel 7 and 10, and subsequently having a vision which consisted of elements drawn from these familiar passages. Of course John may have had visions which had nothing to do with Ezekiel and Daniel and everything to do with what he ate for lunch. But presumably the visions he would have considered worthy of publication would have been those bearing some resemblance to the visionary tradition with which he and his readers were familiar.[98] Similarly, we can also reasonably suppose that when John wrote down what he 'saw' he attempted to describe it in a way which conformed to familiar visionary tradition.[99] In other words, there was probably an element of interpretation of what he saw. The point we wish to make is that if John had visionary experiences then this is entirely compatible with discussing the possible 'influences' on his mind in terms of the period prior to the experience of a vision and prior to the process of finding the 'right words' to describe such experience.[100] It is not

[96] Betz ('Problem', 134–9) rightly argues that 'extra-Jewish' influences have been significant in the development of apocalypticism; Yarbro Collins ('History') offers a refinement of Betz's thesis. Both articles use as an example the 'angel of the waters' in Apc. 16.4–7. On the Hellenistic context of the Apocalypse see Van Unnik, 'Worthy'; Moore, 'Jesus Christ'; Aune, 'Magic'.

[97] On the socio-political context of the Apocalypse see Aune, 'Matrix'; Beagley, *Sitz*; Downing, 'Pliny's'; Le Grys, 'Conflict'; Klauck, 'Sendschreiben'; Thompson, *Revelation*.

[98] Cf. Beale, *Revelation*, 332–3.

[99] Hartman (*Prophecy*, 105–6), conforming to convention, does 'not exclude a basis of extraordinary experience'.

[100] On visionary experience and its transposition to a literary medium see Hartman,

necessary, therefore, to answer the question whether John had visions, although we are inclined to the view that he did.[101] Of course, if John did not have visionary experiences (or at least did not have visionary experiences relating to Apocalypse 1.13–16, 14.14, and 19.11–16) then we are certainly right to presume that the Apocalypse may be approached as a text which reflects the influence of previous texts and of traditions known to its author.

A number of other points remain to be made about methodology, texts, terms, and other presuppositions. First, we examine texts from a historical-critical perspective. We will have a particular concern with Apocalypse 1.13–16 to discuss the 'history of tradition', that is, to discuss critically suggestions made about developments behind the text and to offer our own proposal concerning this.

Secondly, the author of the Apocalypse is a man named 'John' (Apc. 1.1). There is no consensus as to the identity of this man (i.e. as to whether he was an 'apostle', an 'elder', a 'disciple', or otherwise).[102] We will simply work on the assumption that this author was a Christian prophet familiar with the OT and (as we argue in the next section; see p. 20f.) with Jewish apocalyptic traditions about angels. We habitually refer to the author as 'John', though occasionally as 'the seer'. (Citations of the Gospel bearing the name of John will be in the form 'John 3.16' but other references will be to the 'Fourth Gospel'. To avoid confusion the term 'Johannine' is not used).

Thirdly, we will read the text of the Apocalypse as essentially the work of John himself, in line with the trend in recent scholarly study of the Apocalypse to affirm that it is a unified composition from one hand.[103] This does not mean that John did not incorporate sources, but that the result has not been a clumsy pastiche but a work that expresses what the author wished to say.

Fourthly, with neither expertise in textual criticism nor space to

Prophecy, 102–112; Stone, 'Apocalyptic', 421–7; Bauckham, 'Role', 72; Kim, *Origin*, 216; Jeske ('Spirit', esp. pp. 456, 462–4) argues against ἐν πνεύματι (e.g. 1.10, 4.2) reflecting the ecstatic condition of the writer.

[101] On the genuineness of (some) apocalyptic visions see Russell, *Method*, 158–202; Stone, 'Apocalyptic', 420–8; Rowland, 'Apocalyptic', 173. On visionary experiences in the early church see Dunn, *Jesus*, 177–9, 213–16. On the main features of 'epiphany visions' see Kim, *Origin*, 205–16.

[102] Schüssler Fiorenza, *Justice*, 18–19; Yarbro Collins, *Crisis*, 25–50.

[103] Schüssler Fiorenza, *Justice*, 16 (summarizing modern scholarship); 159–203 (offering her own proposal).

include a detailed discussion of the history of the text of the Apocalypse, we will rely on the authority of the Nestle–Aland (26th) edition, although where relevant we shall not refrain from discussing textual problems. A similar point may be made about the use of *BHS* for the Massoretic text of the OT and, in general, for Rahlfs' *Septuaginta* for the LXX and for Theodotion.[104] We use the NRSV for the English translation of both the NT and OT. In general, we rely on English translations of apocryphal and pseudepigraphal writings. Where appropriate we refer to underlying texts. In an attempt at some kind of consistency we normally work with the English translations provided in *OTP*, *NTA*, and *DSSE* with occasional recourse to other translations such as those in *AOT*. Citations from Philo and Josephus are taken from the Loeb editions of their writings.

Fifthly, we follow the majority of scholars in presuming that the Apocalypse dates from *c*. 96 CE. Although some internal evidence points to a date *c*. 68 CE,[105] the external evidence of Irenaeus is impressive and not easily displaced.[106] A date in the sixties, however, would not greatly affect the course of our discussion.

Sixthly, we tend to refer to Jesus Christ as 'the exalted Jesus' or 'the risen Jesus'. In the Apocalypse 'Jesus' is a frequently used name for Jesus Christ. The use of the adjectives 'exalted' or 'risen' are reminders that we are dealing with the post-resurrection Jesus who is envisaged as dwelling in the heavenly realm.

Finally, there is one set of terms which we must mention, namely, 'divine' and 'divinity'. We will use the adjective 'divine' in a Judaeo-Christian context, principally with reference to God: that is, in descriptions of the activity or throne or form of God. Talk of the risen Jesus in Apocalypse 1.13–16 bearing 'divine characteristics' would mean that the appearance of Jesus incorporates characteristics otherwise associated with the appearance of God, or talk of Jesus claiming 'divine titles' would mean that he claims titles otherwise belonging only to God. When we speak of the 'divinity of Jesus Christ' we will mean that Jesus Christ both has status as God and is essentially distinct from the created order of beings. Occasionally, we will refer to the possibility that (say) a

---

[104] An exception is our extended discussion of Dan. 7.13 LXX on pp. 44–9.

[105] E.g. Robinson, *Redating*, 221–53; Bell, 'Date'; more recently, Gentry, *Before*, 333–7; Moberly ('When', 376–7) argues for the winter of 69–70 CE but allows for publication at a later date.

[106] So, e.g., Sweet, 21–7; Yarbro Collins, *Crisis*, 54–83.

Roman emperor was believed to be 'a divine being'. By this we
will mean that the figure in question was thought to have been
divinized in some sense within the context of Roman religious
belief. Talk of an angel as 'a divine being' will depend on the
context, but essentially an angel as a divine being will mean that
either the angel was believed to be a second god alongside the
God of Jewish and Christian belief or the angel was identified in
some way with God.

The angelology of the Apocalypse

One last task remains before we proceed to explore the apocalyptic
and OT background to the christology of the Apocalypse, namely,
to: (i) set out certain assumptions about angels and angel-like
figures in the Apocalypse; and (ii) demonstrate that the Apocalypse
reflects familiarity with the angelology found in the OT as well as in
Jewish apocalyptic writings. In what follows we do not attempt to
cover every aspect of the angelology of the Apocalypse,[107] or to
relate it to every aspect of angelology outside of the Apocalypse.[108]

The assumptions we will make about the angels and angel-like
figures in the Apocalypse are as follows. First, 'the angels (ἄγγελοι)
of the seven churches' (1.20; cf. 2.1 par.) are heavenly beings rather
than (i) human beings functioning as messengers, church leaders, or
prophets,[109] or (ii) personifications of the life or spirit of the
churches.[110] Briefly, with regard to (i), the impressive symbolism of
the angels as 'stars' and their juxtaposition with the 'seven spirits'
(Apc. 3.1) are inconsistent with understanding the 'angels' as
humans;[111] with regard to (ii), understanding the 'angels' as

---

[107] We know of no monograph on the angelology of the Apocalypse, except for
Michl's work, *Engelvorstellungen*, which deals with the living creatures, the seven
spirits, and the four angels. This was the first of a projected three volumes but we
can find no indication that the other two were published.
[108] For surveys of angels in Jewish, Gnostic, and Christian literature see Michl,
'Engel', 54–258 (pp. 64–84 for specific treatment of angels in Jewish apocalypses); Bietenhard, *Welt*, 102–42; Kaplan, 'Angelology'; and Schäfer, *Rivalität*,
10–32 (for angelology in Apocrypha and Pseudepigrapha) and 41–74 (for
angelology in rabbinic literature). See now Mach, *Entwicklungsstadien* on the
angelology of pre-rabbinic Judaism.
[109] E.g. McNamara, *New Testament*, 198–9. Human 'messengers' (LXX: ἄγγελος)
are mentioned in Hag. 1.13 and Mal 1.1, 2.7, 3.1. On the angels of the churches
as messengers see Kraft, 52.
[110] Cf. Beckwith, 445; Charles, i, 34; Lohmeyer, 18; Swete, 22; Satake, *Gemeindeordnung*, 154.
[111] Cf. Beckwith, 445–6. Note an angelic star in Apc. 9.1–2.

'personifications' seems odd when 'the church' is capable of being addressed in its own right as a body of people.[112] Secondly, 'the seven spirits' (Apc. 1.4, 3.1, 4.5, 5.6) are not angels despite the similarity between their location in 4.5 and the location of the seven angels in 8.2 (ἐνώπιον τοῦ θεοῦ ἑστήκασιν/ἐνώπιον τοῦ θρόνου), respectively. Although controversial, this assumption is well supported by many scholars.[113] Thirdly, we suppose the four apocalyptic horsemen in Apocalypse 6.1–8 to be angelic figures. Although the fourth horseman, 'Death', may be readily understood by modern minds as a personification of death, it is not clear that in the first century CE much if any distinction would have been made between a personification and an angelic figure.

The angelology of the Apocalypse features various significant groups of angels as well as individual angels notable for their status and/or function. In what follows we note these groups and individuals and seek to correlate them with similar angels in the OT and in apocryphal and pseudepigraphal literature.

(i) *Seven angels.* Various groups of seven angels are found in the Apocalypse (e.g. 1.20, 8.2, 15.6–7). Within the OT this feature corresponds to seven 'men' in Ezekiel 9.2 and to seven angels in Tobit 12.15. There is, in fact, a notable parallel between Apocalypse 8.2 and Tobit 12.15: οἳ ἐνώπιον τοῦ θεοῦ ἑστήκασιν (Apc. 8.2), οἳ παρεστήκασιν καὶ εἰσπορεύονται ἐώπιον τῆς δόξης κυρίου (Tob. 12.15; cf. Luke 1.19; 1 *Enoch* 40.2). Seven angels are known in apocalyptic literature (1 *Enoch* 20.3 (Greek Recension; six only in the Ethiopic), 87.1, 90.21; *T. Levi* 8.1).[114] A related feature, unknown in the OT, is the plural 'angels of the presence' (*Jub.* 2.2; 1QSb 4.24–6; 1QH 6.13):[115] the angels who stand before God in Apocalypse 8.2 appear to be such angels. Finally, we note that the trumpet-blowing angels in Apocalypse 8.2 recall *Apocalypse of Moses* 22.1 (cf. 1 Thess. 4.16).

(ii) *Four angels.* Four angels convey the consequences of the first four seals (Apc. 6.1–8), four angels hold back the four winds

---

[112] On the identity of the ecclesial angels, see further Bousset, 200–2; Kraft, 50–2; Lohmeyer, 18; and Hemer, *Letters*, 32.

[113] E.g. Brütsch, i, 46; Prigent, 17; Bauckham, 'Role', 17; Molina, *Espiritu*, 27; Dix, 'Seven', 233; Bruce, 'Spirit', 336. Against: e.g., Allo, 8–9; Lohse, 14; Michl, *Engelvorstellungen*, 138–60.

[114] Cf. seventy angels in *Tg. Yer. I* Gen. 11.7.

[115] A singular 'angel of the presence' appears in Isa. 63.9 MT.

(Apc. 7.1), and four angels are found at the river Euphrates (Apc. 9.14–15). The first group each ride differently coloured horses (recalling Zech. 1.8 and 6.2–3) while the second recalls four chariots interpreted as the four winds (Zech. 6.1–6; cf. Jer. 49.36; Dan. 7.2). Groups of four (arch)angels are specifically mentioned in 1 *Enoch* 9.1, 40.9–10, 54.6, 71.9 and 1 QM 9.15–16. We may note also 'the angels of the spirits of the winds' (*Jub.* 2.2; cf. 1 *Enoch* 60.12, 69.22). The four angels at the river Euphrates may be 'the angels of punishment' (Apc. 9.14–15; cf. 14.10)[116] – a class of angel mentioned in 1 *Enoch* 53.3 and *Testament of Levi* 3.3.

(iii) Holy angels. Ἀγγέλων ἁγίων in Apocalypse 14.10 recall the 'holy angels' (distinguished from the 'angels of the presence') in *Jubilees* 2.2,18. Other references may also be noted: 1 *Enoch* 60.4, 71.9; 2 *Enoch* 1.2; 1 QS 11.8; and *Hermas Visions* 3.4.1–2.[117]

(iv) Michael. 'Michael and his angels' fight with 'the dragon and his angels' (Apc. 12.7). Michael is referred to in Daniel 10.13,21, 12.1, as well as in numerous other texts: for example, 1QM 17.5–8; 1 *Enoch* 20.1, 69.14; 2 *Enoch* 33.10; Jude 9; and *Apocalypse of Abraham* 10.18. Michael quarrelling with the devil is mentioned in, for instance, Jude 9 and *Adam and Eve* 13–16.[118] In other texts a quarrel is described but the angel is not named (e.g. 1QS 3.20–4; *T. Dan* 6.1–3; *As. Mos.* 10.1–2).

(v) The angel with authority over fire. 'The angel who has authority over fire' appears in Apocalypse 14.18 (cf. 8.5, 16.8–9).[119] It is not clear whether the authority of this angel is restricted to the temple[120] or extends over the whole of nature. The 'angel of fire' is not a feature of the OT but is a feature of apocalyptic literature and related writings (e.g. *Jub.* 2.2).[121] The angel of fire is variously identified: Purouel (*Test. Abr.* 13.11); Nathaniel (*Bib. Ant.* 38.3); Gabriel (3 *Enoch* 14.3); and Michael (*Tg. Job* 25.2).

(vi) The angel of the waters. The third bowl angel is 'in charge of the waters' (16.4–5). As with the 'angel of fire', the 'angel of the water(s)' is unknown in the OT but is familiar from other writings. Gabriel, for example, is the angel of the waters in *Tg. Job*

---

[116] Charles, i, 250.
[117] Cf. Tob. 12.15 where, according to the Vaticanus and Alexandrinus recensions, the angels are ἑπτὰ ἁγίων ἀγγέλων. Cf. Michl, *Engelvorstellungen*, 231–2, n. 7.
[118] For a detailed study of Michael, cf. Lueken, *Michael*; and now, Rohland, *Erzengel*.
[119] Cf. Kraft, 205.   [120] Cf. Swete, 188.   [121] Bousset, *Religion*, 371.

25.2. Note also the 'angels . . . in charge of the forces of the waters' (1 *Enoch* 66.2; cf. 60.20–3; 2 *Enoch* 19.4).[122]

(vii)   The angel over the abyss. This angel is known as Abaddon or Apollyon (Apc. 9.11). Abaddon is cited in parallel with Sheol in Job 26.6 and Proverbs 15.11, 27.20. In Job 28.22 Abaddon, along with Death, is personified (cf. Apc. 6.8).[123] Outside the OT we may note the angel Eremiel who is 'over the abyss and Hades' (*Apoc. Zeph.* 6.13), the angel Uriel who is over 'the world and Tartarus' (1 *Enoch* 20.2 (some Greek MSS)), and the assumption of the form of an archangel by Death (*Test. Abr.* 16.6).

(viii)   The angel who refuses to be worshipped. Twice in the Apocalypse an angel refuses to be worshipped by John (19.10, 22.9). This motif is hinted at in Tobit 12.16–22 but explicitly present in *Apocalypse of Zephaniah* 6.12 and *Ascension of Isaiah* 7.21.[124]

This brief survey suggests that the Apocalypse reflects knowledge of angelology both within and outside the OT. This conclusion, along with the 'agenda' set by Rowland's work on the influence of angelology on christology, provides good reason to proceed in succeeding chapters to examine angelology and related subjects in the OT and in apocalyptic and other, non-OT, writings.

---

[122] Cf. Lueken (*Michael*, 52–6) who discusses texts featuring both Michael and Gabriel as the angel of water/fire; Yarbro Collins, 'History'. Note that the very extensive list of angels over nature in 3 *Enoch* 4 has *no* angel of water(s).

[123] Cf. 1QH 3.8–10, where Death is personified as a woman in the throes of labour producing a 'man-child', a 'Marvellous Mighty Counsellor'.

[124] For full discussion of this motif, and for further texts, see Bauckham, 'Worship'.

ANGELIC FIGURES IN ZECHARIAH,
EZEKIEL, AND DANIEL

In this chapter we examine material concerning angels, especially angelophanies, along with other epiphanies. We begin with the Book of Zechariah because one of the angels referred to is the 'angel of the LORD' and this provides an opportunity to consider briefly the earlier parts of the OT where the 'angel of the LORD' is a notable feature. We then proceed to examine relevant material in the Books of Ezekiel and Daniel.

Zechariah

When the word of God came to the prophet Zechariah (1.7) he recorded an encounter with various angelic figures. We set out the first few verses of this account in order to assist our attempt to clarify who these figures are:

> In the night I saw a man (*'yš*) riding on a red horse! He was standing among the myrtle trees in the glen; and behind him were red, sorrel, and white horses. [9] Then I said, 'What are these, my lord?' The angel who talked with me (*hml'k hdbr*) said to me, 'I will show you what they are'. [10] So the man who was standing among the myrtle trees answered, 'They are those whom the LORD has sent to patrol the earth'. [11] Then they spoke to the angel of the LORD (*mlk yhwh*) who was standing among the myrtle trees, 'We have patrolled the earth, and lo, the whole earth remains at peace'. (Zech. 1.8–11)

There are two individual angels here. One is 'the angel who talks with me' (hence referred to as 'the talking angel'). The other is the 'man' or 'angel of the LORD'. No riders for the coloured horses are mentioned so it would appear that they are understood to be equivalent to angels. The talking angel has a role as interpreter of heavenly visions (the so-called *angelus interpres*). In Zechariah 1.9, 1.18–21, 4.1–7, and 5.5–6.8 the talking angel shows and/or interprets various matters to Zechariah. It seems reasonable to presume that when we read in 3.1 that 'he showed me (*wyr'ny*)' the 'he' refers to the talking angel. But in this case what Zechariah is shown is 'the high priest Joshua standing before the angel of the LORD'. There is no reason to think that the angel of the LORD in 1.11 does not equate with the angel of the LORD in 3.1. Consequently, we conclude that the talking angel is distinct from the angel of the LORD.[1]

The role of the talking angel is parallel to that of the angel in the Apocalypse who both reveals and interprets visions (cf. Apc. 17.1–7). It is interesting, therefore, to note a description of this angel which recalls the talking angel, ὁ λαλῶν μετ' ἐμου (Apc. 21.15; cf. ὁ ἄγγελος ὁ λαλῶν ἐν ἐμοί, Zech. 1.9 LXX), and to observe that a function of this angel recalls a function of the talking angel, namely, to measure Jerusalem (Apc. 21.16; cf. Zech. 2.2(6)).

Conceivably, the 'man' (Zech. 1.8) and the 'angel of the LORD' (Zech. 1.11) could be distinct beings. The two different designations suggest that two distinct traditions may have contributed to Zechariah 1.8–11. This would not necessarily mean, however, that two different figures were to be understood since 'man' (*'yš*) is a common designation for an angel (of the LORD) in the OT (cf. Judg. 13.6; Ezek. 9.2; Daniel 10.5).[2] When both figures are described as occupying the same place ('among the myrtle trees', 1.8,11) it is likely that they are meant to be understood as one and the same figure.

What, then, do we learn about the angel of the LORD in Zechariah? First, the angel is a *heavenly being of high (if not the highest) rank*: he leads the equine patrol (1.11), and he commands those standing before him to take off the filthy clothes of Joshua (3.4). Secondly, the angel has a *mediatorial* role. The angel intercedes with God (1.12: although when the answer is given it is to the 'talking angel',1.14; cf. Ezek. 40.3; Hag. 1.13).[3] But in a later scene the angel of the LORD is the mediator when God communicates to a human (3.6–10). The intercessory role of the angel of the LORD shows that he is not to be identified with the LORD. The fact that his

[1] Cf. Meyers and Meyers, *Zechariah 1–8*, 110, 183; Mitchell *et al.*, *Zechariah*, 120.
[2] Cf. R. C. Smith, *Micah-Malachi*, 189–90; Stier, *Gott*, 75.
[3] Cf. Stier, *Gott*, 71–4.

intercession concerns the plight of Jerusalem and Judah is reminiscent of the angel, Michael, who acts as the patron of Israel (Dan. 10.21, 12.1).[4] Thirdly, the angel of the LORD appears to represent the LORD as judge and presider in the divine council (Zech. 3.1–10).[5] In this scene Joshua and Satan appear before the angel of the LORD. Whether or not 3.2 introduces the LORD into it (so the MT and LXX but not the Peshitta which speaks of 'the angel of the LORD'),[6] this scene shows the angel of the LORD as a figure akin to the vizier – the powerful official to whom the supreme ruler delegates rule, authority, and power.[7]

The final reference to the angel of the LORD in Zechariah, 'on that day . . . the house of David shall be like God, like the angel of the LORD, at their head' (Zech. 12.8), recalls the angel in Exodus 23.20–1 whom God promises to send ahead of Israel in their journey through the wilderness. This angel certainly has a vizier-like function since he is delegated the task of leading the people of God on behalf of God and is invested with tremendous authority since God says of him, 'my name is in him'. Although the reference in Zechariah is in a part of the book which may be distinct from chapters 1–6,[8] this section is alluded to a number of times in the Apocalypse.[9] Thus we suggest that John's familiarity with Zechariah most likely extended to the idea of an angel functioning as the representative of God invested with considerable power and authority. Obviously, this raises the question whether this angel may have contributed to the portrayal of Jesus Christ in the Apocalypse, just as the 'talking angel' appears to have influenced the portrayal of one of the angels in the Apocalypse. To this question we shall return in chapter 8.

---

[4] Smith, *Micah-Malachi*, 190.

[5] Cf. Dan. 7.9–10; Job 1.6, 2.1.

[6] That the Peshitta reading represents the original reading is argued for by, e.g., Stier, *Gott*, 77, and Mitchell *et al.*, *Zechariah*, 149, 153. The Peshitta offers a smoothing over of a difficulty, which suggests that it may be a corrective rather than an original reading. On the other hand, 'the LORD' rather than 'the angel of the LORD' could represent an omissive error in transcription.

[7] Stier, *Gott*, 79; cf. Newsom, 'Angels', 251.

[8] This is, for example, the only reference to the angel of the LORD or to any angel outside Zech. 1–6.

[9] E.g. Apc. 21.7, cf. Zech. 8.8; Apc. 3.17, cf. Zech. 11.5; Apc. 11.2, cf. Zech. 12.3; Apc. 1.7, cf. Zech. 12.10–14; Apc. 16.16, cf. Zech. 12.11; Apc. 8.7, cf. Zech. 13.9; Apc. 21.25, cf. Zech. 14.7; Apc. 21.6, 22.1, cf. Zech. 14.8; Apc. 19.6, cf. Zech. 14.9; Apc. 22.3, cf. Zech. 14.11.

Excursus: the angel of the LORD prior to Zechariah

We have argued that the angel of the LORD in Zechariah is an angel
who is distinct from the LORD, though one with a close association
with him. But talk about the angel of the LORD in Zechariah
naturally leads to consideration of other accounts in which a
distinction between the angel of the LORD and the LORD is not so
readily discernible. For example, in the incident when Hagar
encounters the angel of the LORD (*mlk yhwh*) at the spring on the
way to Shur (Gen. 16.7–14), the narrator concludes in this way
after the angel of the LORD has spoken to her: 'So she named the
LORD who spoke to her, "You are El-roi"; for she said, "Have I
really seen God and remained alive after seeing him?"' (Gen.
16.13).[10] While Eichrodt concludes that 'Hagar realizes and states
explicitly that she has seen Yahweh himself',[11] Stier concludes that
she had experienced the help of God through an angel.[12] Discussion
of such passages[13] has included explanations such as (i) the (so-
called) '*Logos*' theory: the angel is the *Logos* or second person of
the trinity; (ii) the 'interpolation' theory: reference to the angel is
added to soften the bold anthropomorphism of a passage; (iii) the
'representation' theory: the angel speaks for the LORD but is not the
LORD; and (iv) the 'identity' theory: the angel is a manifestation of
the LORD himself.[14] We cannot here examine all the issues raised by
these passages,[15] nor can we discuss the explanations just listed. We
will, however, state our position on the matter. In agreement with
Eichrodt we suggest that in some passages the 'angel of the LORD' is
'a specific medium of divine revelation', which exists side by side
with the angel as 'the created messenger of God'.[16] That is, unlike

---

[10] A number of text-critical issues are involved in this verse, and it should be noted
that the meaning of the second clause is uncertain. But the relevant point that
Hagar is believed to have encountered the LORD and not merely an angel is not
affected by these issues.

[11] Eichrodt, *Theology*, ii, 26.

[12] Stier, *Gott*, 35–9. Takahashi, 'Oriental's', 346–8, who speaks about the 'fluctua-
tion or fluidity between God and angels' in the OT.

[13] Cf. Gen. 18.1–33, 21.17, 22.11, 31.11, 32.24–30, 48.16; Exod. 3.2, 14.19; Num.
22.22–35; Judg. 2.1–4, 6.11–24, 13.3–21. Note interpretations of such passages in
other OT writings, e.g., Hos. 12.3–4.

[14] Cf. Heidt, *Angelology*, 95–100; Hirth, *Gottes*, 13–21.

[15] See further Stier, *Gott*, 1–95; Hirth, *Gottes*; Eichrodt, *Theology*, ii, 23–9; Von
Rad, *Theology*, i, 285–9.

[16] Eichrodt, *Theology*, ii, 29. Cf. Dunn, *Christology*, 150, ' 'The angel of Yahweh' is
simply a way of speaking about God'.

the situation in Zechariah, there are occasions when the angel of the LORD is indistinct from the LORD. On these occasions the angel of the LORD is 'a form of Yahweh's self-manifestation which expressly safeguards his transcendent nature', a form in which Yahweh 'can temporarily incarnate himself in order to assure his own that he is indeed immediately at hand'.[17]

In sum: on some occasions in the OT 'the angel of the LORD' is ultimately indistinguishable from the LORD, but on other occasions, especially in Zechariah, 'the angel of the LORD' is distinct from the LORD, yet nevertheless invested with power and authority to represent the LORD.

Ezekiel

The influence of Ezekiel on the Apocalypse in a variety of contexts is certain and uncontroversial.[18] Here we examine accounts of theophanies and angelophanies in Ezekiel which are important for the development of our investigation, especially those found in Ezekiel 1, 8–10, 40, and 43. We examine theophanies, as well as angelophanies since, as we shall see, in some cases it is difficult to distinguish one from the other, and because both seem to contribute to the christophanies in the Apocalypse.

We have already been alerted in chapter 1 to the importance of Ezekiel 1 for *merkabah* mysticism. In the background to the vision of the *merkabah* are passages such as Exodus 24.10 and Isaiah 6.1. In the first of these passages the elders of Israel see 'the God of Israel. Under his feet there was something like a pavement of sapphire stone, like the very heaven for clearness' (Exod. 24.10). Here the detail given is mostly concerned with the surroundings rather than with the form of God.[19] But the use of 'precious stone' imagery is notable as it is a recurring feature of theophanies and angelophanies. In Isaiah 6.1 the prophet begins his account of his vision of God in this way: 'In the year that King Uzziah died, I saw the Lord (*'dny*) sitting on a throne, high and lofty; and the hem of his robe filled the temple.' Once again there is little detail.[20]

These visions may be contrasted with the *more detailed* vision of

---

[17] Eichrodt, *Theology*, ii, 27. On God assuming a form see Barr, 'Theophany', 32.

[18] Cf. Ruiz, *Ezekiel*; Vanhoye, 'L'utilisation'; Goulder, 'Apocalypse'.

[19] Barr, 'Theophany', 32.

[20] See further on these and other *merkabah* texts such as 1 *Enoch* 14 in Gruenwald, *Apocalyptic*, 29–72.

the celestial throne and its occupant in Ezekiel 1. The first part of this account is devoted to 'the living creatures', to the fiery phenomena seen in and around them (e.g. 'fire flashing forth', 1.4; 'sparkled like burnished bronze', 1.6; and 'flash of lightning', 1.14), and to 'the wheels' whose movement they inspire (1.4–21). The second part of this account concerns something above the living creatures which is 'like a dome' (1.22–5). The climax of the vision is then described as follows:

> And above the dome over their heads there was something like a throne, in appearance like sapphire; and seated above the likeness of a throne was something that seemed like a human form. [27] Upward from what appeared like the loins I saw something like gleaming amber, something that looked like fire enclosed all around; and downward from what looked like the loins I saw something that looked like fire, and there was a splendour all around. [28] Like the bow in a cloud on a rainy day, such was the appearance of the splendour all around. This was the appearance of the likeness of the glory of the LORD. When I saw it, I fell on my face, and I heard the voice of someone speaking.
>
> (Ezek. 1.26–8)

Who is the enthroned figure in Ezekiel 1.26–8? At the beginning of his account, Ezekiel says that he has seen 'visions of God' (1.1). At the end, he says that he has seen 'the appearance of the likeness of the glory of the LORD' (1.28). The directness of the first statement is qualified by the tentativeness of the second. But the clear impression is given that the human form on the throne is a manifestation of God himself.[21] The development and content of the vision underline this. The immediate experience is of the living creatures and of the wheels (1.4–21); but then Ezekiel's attention is directed to ascending levels above the living creatures (1.22–8). On the first level is 'something like a dome', on the second level is 'something like a throne', on the third level is 'something like the form of a man'. The fact that (i) there is no higher level, (ii) the figure sits on the likeness of a throne, and (iii) there is a tentativeness in describing the enthroned figure anthropomorphically,[22] suggests

---

[21] Fuhs, *Ezechiel*, 22.
[22] Zimmerli, *Ezekiel* 1, 122, 'The restraint in the description can be seen in the succession of phrases denoting approximate similarity'.

that the enthroned figure which Ezekiel 'sees' is more than an angelic figure of the highest rank.[23] Ezekiel has 'seen' a manifestation of God. But it can scarcely be the case that Ezekiel has seen God in the fullness of his transcendent being. Procksch, for example, points out that Ezekiel has not seen 'the prototype of the divine Glory, but rather the εἰκὼν τοῦ θεοῦ'.[24]

That the manifestation of the LORD should be perceived in human form is hardly surprising for two reasons. First, there are other occasions in the OT when the LORD appears to human beings in human form: Abraham saw the LORD in the form of a man (Gen. 18.1–2), Isaiah saw the LORD '*sitting* on a throne, high and lofty' (Isa. 6.1) – a description indicative of an anthropomorphic figure. Secondly, if humanity is made in the image of God (Gen. 1.26) then there is a certain logic to the manifestation of God taking human form.[25]

The importance for the Apocalypse of the *merkabah* vision in Ezekiel 1 lies mainly in its influence on the theophany in Apocalypse 4. Some influence from Ezekiel 1 is discernible in the christophany in Apocalypse 1, but its minimal influence[26] is all the more striking when we consider the epiphany in Ezekiel 8.2 which gives the impression that the fiery human-like figure on the divine throne can leave the throne and appear before a human being as though an angel. In Ezekiel 8.1–4 the prophet experiences a vision in which a fiery figure appears, who is almost exactly the same as the figure on the divine throne in Ezekiel 1.27: 'I looked, and there was a figure that looked like a human being; below what appeared to be its loins it was fire, and above the loins it was like the appearance of brightness, like gleaming amber' (Ezek. 8.2).

Rowland is not the only scholar to have seen in the developments between Ezekiel and Daniel the hypostatization of the form of God,[27] but one of his particular contributions has been to draw out the significance of Ezekiel 8.2 for the background to the christophany in Apocalypse 1. He has argued that consideration of Ezekiel 1.26–8 and 8.2–4 permits the conclusion that what has

---

[23] Dunn (*Partings*, 218) sees significance in the fact that the description of the enthroned figure in Ezek. 1.26 is very tentative . The descriptions of some glorious figures in apocalyptic literature show greater boldness because 'they were *not* descriptions of God himself'.

[24] Procksch, 'Berufungsvision', 144 (present author's translation).

[25] Procksch, 'Berufungsvision', 148.

[26] Cf. discussion in chapter 8.

[27] Cf. Procksch, 'Berufungsvision', 149; Balz, *Methodische*, 94.

taken place is 'not so much the splitting up of divine functions among the various angelic figures but the separation of the form of God from the divine throne-chariot to act as a quasi-angelic mediator'.[28] According to Rowland this development lies behind both the 'son of man' figure in Daniel 7.13 and the glorious 'man' in Daniel 10.5–6. Of the latter, Rowland makes the point that 'here is the beginning of a hypostatic development similar to that connected with divine attributes like God's word and wisdom'.[29] Since Daniel 10.5–6 figures prominently in the background to Apocalypse 1.13–16, Rowland's proposal suggests that the christology of the Apocalypse is the culmination of the development we have just outlined. Certainly, there are a number of striking similarities to be found between Ezekiel 8.2 and 1.26–7; but there are also a number of interesting discrepancies which must be considered.

First, the figure in Ezekiel 8.2 is 'like the appearance of fire' according to the MT (*dmwt kmr'h 'š*) but 'like a man' according to the LXX (ὁμοίωμα ἀνδρός). On the basis of the LXX reading the apparatus to *BHS* suggests that the MT should read *dmwt kmr'h 'yš*. This suggestion is certainly plausible since the change from an original *'yš* to *'š* is a subtle but satisfactory means of softening the anthropomorphism inherent in the description *dmwt kmr'h 'yš*.[30] But in this case there is a change from *'dm* (1.26) to *'yš* (8.2), which is consistent with the two figures being distinct. Secondly, both figures according to the MT are *dmwt kmr'h*, but according to the LXX the first figure is ὁμοίωμα . . . ὡ εἶδος . . . while the second figure is ὁμοίωμα . . . That is, the LXX maintains the MT's reserve in describing the human form on the heavenly throne, 'a likeness like the image of . . .' (1.26), but appears to lessen the reserve in the case of the second figure, 'a likeness . . .' (8.2). This could reflect the perception that there was a difference between the two figures. Thirdly, in Ezekiel 1.27 the upper part of the figure is described before the lower part, but in 8.2 this order is reversed, and there are differences in the descriptions of each part. With respect to the upper part: in the description of the second figure, (i) *ztr* replaces *'š*, (ii) the order of the first two comparisons is reversed, and (iii) the phrase *byt lh sbyb* is omitted. With respect to the lower part: in the description of the second figure, (i) the comparison *kmr'h 'š* is

[28] Rowland, *Heaven*, 97.   [29] Ibid., 100.
[30] Zimmerli, *Ezekiel 1*, 216.

simply reduced to the word *'š*, and (ii) the phrase *wngh lw sbyb* is omitted.

The apparent reserve when speaking of the hand of the figure (Ezek. 8.3) would certainly be consistent with the fiery figure being an appearance of the LORD. But it is noticeable that the word *tbnyt* is used for 'the form' in 8.3, a word which is not found in Ezekiel 1.22–8.[31] Consequently, the description of the second figure corresponds to an abbreviated and slightly altered version of the first. It is not inconceivable, therefore, that the two figures are distinct, although the differences between the two descriptions scarcely require that we deny the possibility that the two figures are one and the same.

Hurtado has responded to Rowland's proposal by suggesting that it is doubtful Ezekiel 8.2–4 'can support the momentous development Rowland describes'. Hurtado notes that 8.2–4 does not reveal that the figure has separated from the throne of 1.26–8, nor does it describe an empty throne. Rather, the conclusion of the vision in 8.4 implies an identical scene to that found in 1.26–8 and gives 'no indication of the sort of "separation" or "splitting" of God's *kabod* ("glory") from the throne such as Rowland alleges'. Further, it is not the case that Ezekiel 10.4, noted by Rowland as a text which speaks of the glory of the LORD rising above the cherubim,[32] provides support for Rowland's case.[33] Our analysis of Ezekiel 8.2 above lends support to Hurtado's critique of Rowland because we have seen that it is not necessary to conclude that the figure in 8.2 is the same as the figure in 1.27. That the figure in 8.2 is an angel has been plausibly argued for by Zimmerli. He recognizes that the similarity in the descriptions in 1.27 and 8.2 appears to be compelling reason to conclude that the LORD is in view in 8.2, as a number of commentators have done.[34] He argues, nevertheless, that since 'Yahweh otherwise only encounters the prophet visibly in the form of the כבוד (cf. also the Priestly Code), the "man" here must refer to the figure of the heavenly messenger'. The similarity in the appearances of the figures in 1.27 and 8.2 arises, according to Zimmerli, because 'a cliché-like description of a heavenly being is used in 1.27 for Yahweh and in 8.2 for a heavenly messenger'.[35]

---

[31] This is not to deny that *tbnyt* is equivalent to *dmwt*, see further Barr, 'Image', 15–17, 158; Kim, *Origin*, 204–5.

[32] Rowland, *Heaven*, 96, 280.   [33] Hurtado, *God*, 87.

[34] Zimmerli, *Ezekiel 1*, 236, notes Cooke, Herrmann and Fohrer.

[35] Zimmerli, *Ezekiel 1*, 236. Cf. Fuhs, *Ezechiel*, 49.

In favour of this proposal we may make the following observation. In Ezekiel 43.4–5 the 'spirit' and the *kabod* are quite
distinct: 'As the glory of the LORD entered the temple by the gate
facing east, the spirit (*rwḥ*) lifted me up, and brought me into the
inner court; and the glory of the LORD filled the temple.' The
kabod (so to speak) does one thing, the spirit another. They are,
in this passage, distinct beings.[36] In 8.3 the fiery figure appears to
be identified as 'the spirit' (*rwḥ*). In 8.3–4 we observe that (i) the
spirit performs the same action as in 43.4–5 – that is lifting up the
seer, and (ii) the *kabod* is seen *as a result of the spirit's action* in
8.4. This suggests that, as in 43.4–5, the *kabod* and the spirit are
to be distinguished in 8.3–4. In turn, this means that if the spirit
is the fiery figure then the fiery figure is not to be identified with
the *kabod*: the figures in 1.27 and 8.2 are likely, then, to be
distinct.

Even if it were argued that the figures are not distinct it does not
follow that Rowland's proposal carries the day. If the figures in
Ezekiel 8.2 and 1.27 are the same then the figure in 8.2 could be
understood as a full manifestation of the LORD rather than a
bifurcated manifestation as Rowland envisages. Such an event in
general terms would not be without precedent since the LORD
appeared as a 'man' to Abraham in Genesis 18.1–2. On other
occasions, as we have been reminded above, the angel of the LORD
has appeared to humans in a manner which makes him indistinguishable from the LORD.[37] The apparent softening of *'yš* to *'š* in the
MT would then be 'eloquent testimony' to a later Jewish reponse to
the anthropomorphic theophany in Ezekiel 8.2.[38]

In short: the figure in Ezek. 8.2 is difficult to understand. Careful
consideration of this figure does not require the conclusion that it
represents the beginnings of a significant development whereby the
divine *kabod* begins to function separately from the throne of God
as a 'quasi-angelic mediator'. We suggest that it is reasonable to
conclude that the fiery figure in 8.2 is distinct from the *kabod*.

The next epiphany which we consider features seven 'men' of
whom one, a scribe, is clearly the leader (Ezek. 9.2). The consensus among commentators is that the scribe in Ezek. 9.2 is an

---

[36] Ibid., 414.
[37] Cooke, *Ezekiel*, 90; cf. Black, 'Throne-Theophany', 59; Zimmerli, *Ezekiel 1*, 236.
Rowland (*Heaven*) 97, is unsure whether Ezek. 8.2 can be connected with the
angel of the LORD who speaks and acts as though he were God himself.
[38] Black, 'Throne-Theophany', 59. n. 6.

angel.[39] Here is the first occasion in biblical material that we have a reference to a leading group of angels (as all the men are to be understood) which numbers seven.

> And six men came from the direction of the upper gate, which faces north, each with his weapon for slaughter in his hand; among them was a man clothed in linen, with a writing case at his side. They went in and stood beside his bronze altar.
>   (Ezek. 9.2)

In Ezekiel 10.6–8 we have a further occurrence of the *merkabah* vision in which the 'man clothed in linen' interacts with the living creatures. This suggests that there is no reason to think of this man as anything other than a principal angel, possibly the chief angel within the angelology of Ezekiel. We shall demonstrate later (see p. 42) that this man may stand in the background to the glorious 'man' in Daniel 10.5–6, and possibly also in the background to the risen Jesus in Apocalypse 1.13–16.

The next passages to consider occur in the last part of Ezekiel. The introduction to the vision of the temple in Ezekiel 40.1–2 is followed by an encounter with 'a man . . . whose appearance shone like bronze' (*whnh 'yš mr'hw kmr'h nḥšt*, 40.3). This man can scarcely be confused with the LORD since (i) his description as a 'man' lacks the tentativeness which is a feature of Ezekiel 1.26–8, and (ii) the comparison with 'bronze' is not found in Ezekiel 1.26–8.[40] Thus this figure is an example of an angel with a glorious appearance.[41] The description of this figure is important because it appears (as we shall see shortly) to have contributed to the description of the glorious 'man' in Daniel 10.5–6. Finally, we note Ezekiel 43.1–4 where the seer has a further *merkabah* vision, one which is of interest to us because it appears to be the source for John's description of the glorious angel in Apocalypse 18.1–2.

Thus examination of epiphanies in Ezekiel raises a number of issues and points of interest. We have argued that the fiery figure in Ezekiel 1.26 is to be distinguished from the fiery figure in Ezekiel 8.2, and this raises doubts about the course of the development

---

[39] Cooke, *Ezekiel*, 104; Bousset, *Religion*, 368; Black, 'Throne-Theophany', 59; Rowland, *Heaven*, 96. Some rabbinic interpreters identified the man clothed in linen as Gabriel (e.g. *b. Yoma* 77a, *b. Shabbath* 55a).

[40] Zimmerli, *Ezekiel 2*, 348; cf. Cooke, *Ezekiel*, 430, 'he does not possess the splendour of the divine Being'.

[41] Against Kim, *Origin*, 206.

which Rowland sees in the background to the christophany in
Apocalypse 1.13–16. We have also argued that the 'man' in Ezekiel
40.3 is an angel and not an appearance of the LORD.

Daniel

The Book of Daniel, composed between 168 and 165 BCE,[42] at the
height of the crisis for Jewish religion posed by Antiochus Epi-
phanes, is of immense significance for angelology in general and for
the angelology and christology of the Apocalypse in particular.[43] It
introduces the first named angels in the OT – Gabriel (Dan. 8.16,
9.21) and Michael (Dan. 10.13, 21, 12.1). It initiates the idea within
the canonical scriptures that Michael is the angel who guards or
protects Israel (10.21, 12.1) and presents a more detailed description of an angelophany than is found in any other OT book (Dan.
10.5–6).

But it is with the *merkabah* vision in Daniel 7.9–10 that we begin
our reflection on the epiphanies in this book. This epiphany is of
special significance because of its links with part of the description
of the risen Jesus in Apocalypse 1.14.

> As I watched, thrones were set in place, and the Ancient of
> Days (*'tyq ywmyn*) took his throne, his clothing was white
> as snow, and the hair of his head like pure wool; his throne
> was fiery flames, and its wheels were burning fire. [10] A
> stream of fire issued and flowed out from his presence. A
> thousand thousands served him, and ten thousand times
> ten thousand stood attending him. The court sat in judge-
> ment, and the books were opened.   (Dan. 7.9–10)

The Ancient of Days appears not only in resplendent form, but on
a throne with a stream of fire flowing out of his presence and with
myriads of beings standing in attendance to him. In Daniel 7.13
(according to MT and Th.) the 'one like a son of man' comes to the
Ancient of Days and is presented before him. In Daniel 7.13 LXX
the 'one like a son of man' comes *as* the Ancient of Days, and those
present come to him. The final reference to the Ancient of Days
occurs in Daniel 7.22. When 'the horn' made war on the holy ones

---

[42] So most modern commentators.
[43] On the influence of Daniel on the Apocalypse see Beale, *Daniel*.

he prevailed over them (7.21), 'until the Ancient of Days came; then judgement was given for the holy ones of the Most High' (7.22).

The Ancient of Days has been variously identified. Yarbro Collins, for example, proposes that the Ancient of Days was 'a distinguishable manifestation of God as a high angel'.[44] Certainly, the Ancient of Days was understood by some interpreters in the first centuries CE to be an angel. For example, in the *Hekhalot* text, the *Visions of Ezekiel*, the Ancient of Days appears to be identified with the Heavenly Prince of the Third Heaven.[45] But this by no means signifies an overwhelming tendency towards such an identi- fication since it may be counter-balanced by another text, *Sefer ha-Razim*, in which the statement 'He is the Ancient of Days' unequivocally refers to God.[46] The Ancient of Days was most likely widely understood to be God.[47] Emerton has argued, for instance, that whatever may be the mythical background of Daniel 7.9–13, from Maccabean times – that is, when monotheistic doc- trine was a touchstone of Jewish identity – we may presume that the Ancient of Days was understood to be God.[48] The reference to the coming of the Ancient of Days for judgement, for example, recalls texts which speak of the coming of God for judgement (cf. Zech. 14.5; Ps. 96.13; Joel 3.12). Further, the title 'Ancient of Days' is redolent with symbolism which may be properly associated with God, such as longevity, pre-existence, and wisdom. Finally, although it could be argued that the appearance of the Ancient of Days with details given about his clothing and the hair of his head seems to be contrary to the OT precept that no one may see God and live (cf. Exod. 33.20, Judg. 13.22), such a vision is, however, in line with other accounts in the OT. Thus, in both 1 Kings 22.19 ('I saw the LORD sitting on his throne, with all the host of heaven standing beside him') and Isaiah 6.1 ('I saw the Lord sitting on a throne'), there is an implicit suggestion that God may be 'seen' in certain circumstances.

When we inquire as to the understanding of the Ancient of Days which lay in the background to the Apocalypse it is worth noting evidence that in some broadly contemporary Jewish circles Daniel 7.9 was understood to portray God and not the angel of God. Thus

---

[44] Yarbro Collins, 'Tradition', 557.
[45] Cf. Gruenwald, *Apocalyptic*, 140. Kraft, 45, notes that in the Middle Ages the Ancient of Days was a type of Christ.
[46] Morgan, *Sepher*, 84.   [47] Cf. Casey, *Son*, 23.
[48] Emerton, 'Origin', 239. Cf. Goldingay, *Daniel*, 165.

a tradition ascribed to R. Akiba (c. 110–32 CE) interprets the
thrones in Daniel 7.9 as 'One (throne) for Him, and one for David'
(*b. Hagigah* 14a).[49] The first throne is that of the Ancient of Days,
who is clearly understood to be God, while the second is for the
Davidic messiah who is identified with 'one like a son of man'
(Dan. 7.13).[50] Given that John demonstrates familiarity with
merkabah traditions (cf. Apc. 4) in which it is undoubtedly God
who is seated on the throne, and depicts only the *divine* throne
among the various thrones mentioned in the Apocalypse as one
which is surrounded by attendants (Apc. 4–5), it is reasonable to
assume that the epiphany in Daniel 7.9 was understood as a
theophany.

Nevertheless the question might be raised that the conjunction of
both 'the Ancient of Days' and 'the Most High' (*'lywnyn*) in Daniel
7.22 would have led John to believe that two different beings were
implied. That is, on the premise that there was one God only, it is
theoretically possible that John might have distinguished the
Ancient of Days from the Most High.[51] But, given the likelihood
that the Ancient of Days was understood to be God and that 'the
Most High' would be an unusual title to apply to any being other
than God, it is reasonable to suppose that John would have understood the two different titles in the one verse to apply to the one
God. We know that John was a committed monotheist (cf. Apc.
19.10, 22.3–4,9) so he could hardly have been averse to understanding Daniel 7.22 in this way. It is most likely that John
recognized the Ancient of Days to be God appearing in human
form with white hair and clothing. Consequently, for our purposes
Daniel 7.9–10 is important as a theophany which incorporates a
number of images (such as 'snow', 'hair', 'wool', and 'fire') which,
as we shall see, are taken up not only in other theophanies (e.g.
1 *Enoch* 14.20, 46.1) but also in epiphanies of angels and angelomorphic figures (e.g. 1 *Enoch* 106; *Jos. and Asen.* 14.8, 22.7; *Apoc.
Abr.* 11.1–3; and Apc. 1.14).

Our next figure of interest in Daniel is the enigmatic and
mysterious *kbr 'nš* in 7.13 who appears to lie behind the 'one like a
son of man' in Apocalypse 1.13 and 14.14.

---

[49] *b. Sanh.* 38a, 98a.   [50] Segal, *Powers*, 47–8.
[51] Caragounis (*Son*, 75) distinguishes between the Ancient of Days and the Most
High in Daniel 7.22; although in his view the Ancient of Days is God while the
Most High is the Danielic son of man!

> As I watched in the night visions, I saw one like a son of
> man (*kbr 'nš*) coming with the clouds of heaven. And he
> came to the Ancient of Days and was presented before
> him.   (Dan. 7.13)

Two important and interrelated questions arise from this verse.
First, what kind of figure is 'one like a son of man'? Secondly, what
is the identity of the figure? The description 'like a son of man'
suggests a figure who is not actually human and therefore likely to
be angelic.[52] Collins, for example, argues that the figure is angelic
and identifies him as the archangel Michael.[53] Others have argued
that the figure is the angel Gabriel.[54] The accompaniment of the
figure by 'clouds' suggests that the figure has divine status: clouds
are invariably associated with theophanies in the OT (apart from
references to clouds as natural phenomena). Emerton points out
that 'If Dan 7.13 does not refer to a divine being then it is the only
exception out of about seventy passages [i.e. featuring 'cloud(s)'] in
the OT.'[55] Feuillet argues that Daniel 7 has been influenced by
Ezekiel 1 so that the son of man figure in Daniel 7.13 belongs in a
divine category and is effectively an incarnation of the divine glory,
similar to the human-like figure in Ezekiel 1.26.[56] But the correspondence between the son of man in Daniel 7.13 and the 'people
of the holy ones of the Most High' in 7.27 has led others to propose
that the son of man is a symbolic figure representing Israel. Casey,
for example, argues that the figure is 'pure symbol representing the
saints of Israel'.[57]   Black, who interprets the son of man figure in

---

[52] Contrast with the description of the human Abel in angelophanic terms as 'like
unto a son of God' (*Test. Abr.* Rec. A. 12.5).

[53] Collins, *Vision*, 144; Day, *Conflict*, 172–7, who also argues that Michael originates
in the god Baal. Goldingay, *Daniel*, 172, points out that the lack of identity of the
figure is important, 'a facet which interpretation has to preserve', and notes that if
Michael is envisaged in Daniel 7.13 then it is odd that he does not appear at
7.18,22,27.

[54] E.g. Yarbro Collins, 'Tradition', 551; Fossum, *Name*, 279, n. 61; Zevit, 'Implications', 90. Cf. Scherman and Goldwurm, *Daniel*, 206.

[55] Emerton, 'Origin', 232. Cf. Feuillet, 'Le fils', 187, 321; Procksch, 'Berufungsvision', 148–9. Müller, *Messias*, 27, suggests the clouds merely indicate the heavenly
location of the scene. Goldingay, *Daniel*, 171, astutely points out that 'with any of
these approaches, since the one advanced in years stands for God, it is difficult to
attribute the same significance to this second figure'.

[56] Feuillet, 'Le fils', 188–9. Cf. Balz, *Probleme*, 80–94; Delcor, 'Sources', 311. Müller
(*Messias*, 34–5) disputes the thesis that the Danielic son of man originates in
Ezek. 1.26 or Ezek. 9.2.

[57] Casey, *Son*, 39. Cf. Driver, *Daniel*, 88: 'the ideal and glorified people of Israel';
Völter, 'Menschensohn', 173–4: a celestial being who represents Israel.

Daniel 7.13 in corporate terms, suggests he was understood by Daniel as 'nothing less than the *apotheosis* of Israel in the End-Time'.[58] Finally, we note that the apparent link between the Danielic son of man and Israel has led some to ponder the messianic associations of the figure.[59]

The origin of the Danielic son of man is a matter of continuing discussion. We have already mentioned Feuillet's suggestion, for example, that it originates in the fiery human-like figure on the throne in Ezekiel 1.26–8. But it has been pointed out that this passage does not give a reason for there being *two* figures in Daniel 7.13.[60] This problem is resolved if we presume the underlying influence of the Canaanite myth of El and Baal for which parallels with Daniel 7.9–13 can be adduced.[61] Such a presumption, though, faces the difficulty of plausibly explaining why a (by that time) ancient ditheistic myth should have influenced the Book of Daniel, so strict in its adherence to monotheism.[62] Other hypotheses about the origin of the figure have been proposed but we cannot discuss these here.[63]

Even if the origin of the son of man figure does lie in a ditheistic myth or in the *merkabah* vision (or both) it does not follow that either the author of Daniel or his subsequent readers understood the son of man to be a divine figure. Why would Daniel recount a vision in which two apparently divine figures appear? If the author of Daniel had any inkling of the ditheistic connotations of his account it could be argued that he either would have refrained from including it or would have clarified the status of the son of man figure. When other phrases comparable to *kbr 'nš* (Dan. 7.13) are applied to angelic figures in Daniel (e.g. *dmh lbr 'lhyn*, 3.25; *kmr'h gbr*, 8.15; *kdmwt bny 'dm*, 10.16; *kmr'h 'dm*, 10.18) it seems reasonable to conclude that, in fact, an angelic figure is in view.[64] This conclusion is, of course, compatible with the view that the figure also represented Israel in some sense.

---

[58] Black, 'Throne-theophany', 62.
[59] Horbury, 'Messianic'; Rowe, 'Is'. [60] E.g. Rowland, *Heaven*, 97.
[61] E.g. Emerton, 'Origin', 225–42; Day, *Conflict*, 160–7. For criticism of this view see Müller, *Messias*, 35–6; Ferch, 'Daniel 7'; Kim, *Origin*, 208. Colpe, 'υἱός', 415–19, critically reviews arguments for and against, with the conclusion that the Canaanite hypothesis provides 'the closest parallel'.
[62] Cf. Kim, *Origin*, 208, n. 6; Rowland, *Heaven*, 96–7. Day (*Conflict*, 165–6) offers a convincing explanation to overcome this difficulty.
[63] See, for example, discussion in Day, *Conflict*, 157–60, and literature cited there.
[64] Cf. Day, *Conflict*, 167–9; Collins, *Apocalyptic*, 84.

Other important angelic figures are 'seen' or 'heard' in Daniel 7–12. The one of most interest to us is described as follows:

> I looked up and saw a man clothed in linen, with a belt of gold from Uphaz around his waist. [6] His body was like beryl, his face like lightning, his eyes like flaming torches, his arms and legs like the gleam of burnished bronze, and the sound of his voice like the roar of a multitude.
>
> (Dan. 10.5–6)

One of the important questions concerning the figure in Daniel 10.5–6 is whether or not it is an angel. It is conceivable, for example, that such a glorious figure, who strikes fear and awe into Daniel (10.8), and who appears to be superior to Michael (e.g. 10.13), could be an appearance of God.[65] But in Daniel 10.11 we read the statement 'for I have now been sent (*šlḥty*) to you'. This would seem to indicate that the figure who says it is separate from God, who is presumably the sender.[66] But in Daniel 10.10 Daniel describes how 'a hand touched me'. The fact that the hand is not regarded as 'his hand' raises the question whether a different figure from the one in Daniel 10.5–6 touches the prophet and is thus the 'sent one', while leaving open the possibility that the figure in 10.5–6 is an appearance of God. Nevertheless, it seems reasonable to conclude that one figure is present to Daniel throughout Daniel 10.5–15 (noting that the figure in 10.10 is unquestionably present to 10.15 at least). The speech in Daniel 10.11 includes the instruction to 'pay attention to the words I am going to speak to you'. It makes very good sense to think of this instruction as issuing not from a second figure but from the same figure whose words have already impressed themselves upon Daniel as 'like the roar of a multitude' (10.6), and at the sound of whose words Daniel falls into a trance (10.9). It would seem appropriate, therefore, to understand the remarks about sending and coming as applying to one and the same figure in Daniel 10.5–6 and 10.10–15. Similar arguments may be brought forward in favour of the conclusion that just one figure is present to Daniel throughout Daniel 10.5–21.[67] It is not neces-

---

[65] Cf. Goldingay, *Daniel*, 291.

[66] Montgomery, *Daniel*, 420, who makes the point that despite 'the dependence upon Ezek. 1 he cannot be the Deity, for he was "sent"'.

[67] Goldingay, *Daniel*, 291, explains that 'It is not clear how many supernatural beings are involved in the scene [i.e. Daniel 10]' and notes that in '12.5–6 there are two others apart from the man in linen, and so it may also be here'. But nothing

sary to present them here since for our purposes it suffices to show that the one figure is present in Daniel 10.5–15. Consequently, the figure in Daniel 10.5–6 is not an appearance of God but one who has been sent by God. Given that the figure is described as a 'man', which is often an alternative term for 'angel',[68] we conclude that the glorious figure in Daniel 10.5–6 is an angel.

Although the description of this angelophany is unique in the OT since it is more detailed than any other found in there, the language used shows affinity with a number of other passages in the OT. Thus the first part of the description, *whnh 'yš 'ḥd lbwš* (Dan. 10.5), recalls the scribe clothed in linen, *w'yš 'ḥd btwkm lbwš bdym* (Ezek. 9.2). The girding of the man, *wmtnyw ḥgrym bktm 'wpz* (Dan. 10.5),[69] reflects language used in three epiphanic passages in Ezekiel which we have already discussed, *wqst hspr bmtnyw* (Ezek. 9.2), *mtnyw* (Ezek. 1.27, 8.2), as well as recalling *wzhb m'wpz* (Jer. 10.9). 'Beryl', to which the figure's body is compared, *wgwytw ktršyš* (Dan. 10.6), is a feature of the surrounds of the celestial throne in Ezekiel 1, *wm'śyhm k'yn tršyš* (Ezek. 1.16; cf. Ezek. 10.9, 28.13,20; Cant. 5.14). Similar connections can be made for the comparisons of the man's face, *wpnyw kmr'h brq* (Dan. 10.6): *wmn h'š ywṣ' brq* (Ezek. 1.13), and *kmr'h hbrq* (Ezek. 1.14;[70] cf. Nahum 2.5, 3.3; Hab. 3.11); his eyes, *w'ynyw klpydy 'š* (Dan. 10.6): *kgḥly 'š b'rwt kmr'h hlpdym* (Ezek. 1.13; cf. Nahum 2.5); and his arms and legs, *wzr'tyw wmrgltyw k'yn nḥšt qll* (Dan. 10.6): *rglyhm kkp rgl 'gl wnṣṣym k'yn nḥšt qll* (Ezek. 1.7). In the last case there is also a reflection of the description of the angelic figure in Ezekiel 40: *whnh 'yš mr'hw kmr'h nḥšt* (Ezek. 40.3, cf. 9.2). Finally, the description of the voice of the man, *wqwl dbryw kqwl hmwn* (Dan. 10.6), alludes to Isaiah 13.4, *qwl hmwn*, where the reference is to the sound made as the 'LORD of hosts' musters an army for battle. This is interesting since, if Daniel had Ezekiel 1 in mind, then he refrained from drawing on any of the three comparisons provided in Ezekiel 1.24 in connection with the sound of the wings of the living creatures: *kqwl mym rbym, kqwl šdy, kqwl mḥnh*.[71]

---

he says refutes what we have said. Supporters of the argument for one figure in Daniel 10 include Halperin, *Faces*, 76; Charles, *Daniel*, 257, 260.
[68] Cf. Barr, 'Theophany', 37.
[69] Some MSS read *'wpyn*.   [70] BHS Apparatus, following *Tg*.
[71] Montgomery (*Daniel*, 409) sees the Danielic simile as a summary of the three given in Ezek. 1.24.

Although there seems to be a range of influence on the development of the description of the Danielic figure, two parts of this influence are outstanding. First, the opening phrase in Daniel 10.5, *whnh 'yš 'ḥd lbwš bdym*, so clearly recalls the description of the heavenly scribe in Ezekiel 9.2, *w'yš 'ḥd btwkm lbwš bdym*, that it is worth considering the possibility that Daniel believes he is seeing a reappearance of this angel. Secondly, the number of allusions to the living creatures, and to the phenomena closely connected to them, such as the wheels of the throne-chariot, suggests that in Daniel's mind the descriptions of the heavenly scribe and the living creatures have become merged. It is intriguing, therefore, to observe that (i) in Ezekiel 10 we find the man clothed in linen as well as one of the living creatures featuring together in another vision: at one point the two figures actually make contact (10.7); and (ii) in Ezekiel 1 the living creatures are themselves said to have human form: *wmtmkh m'yn dmwt 'dm lhnh* (Ezek. 1.5). Thus in Daniel 10 the vision of the heavenly scribe appears to have been developed through the incorporation of imagery from the living creatures and associated phenomena around the divine throne. The result is a figure of extraordinary majesty and status but with no implication that the figure is anything other than an angel. This explanation of the origin of the glorious 'man' is at variance with those offered by, for example, Rowland and Halperin.

Rowland emphasizes the connection between the glorious 'man' and the human figure seen by Ezekiel on the divine throne. Noting that the word *mtnyw* is common to Ezekiel 1.27 and Daniel 10.5, Rowland argues that 'the more explicit references to the different parts of the angel's body in Dan. x.6 look like a development of the more reserved outlook of Ezek. i.27'.[72] But while the word *mtnyw* is found in Ezekiel 1.27, it is *also found* in Ezekiel 9.2. Given the strong evocation of the figure in Ezekiel 9.2 through the description of the clothing of 'the man' in Daniel 10.5, we must question whether there is any need to suggest a link with Ezekiel 1.27. Moreover, if the fiery figure is in the background to the glorious 'man' then it is strange that there is only *one* word common to Ezek. 1.26–7 and Daniel 10.5–6. In other words, there is not so much reason to suppose that Daniel 10.6 is a less reserved development of Ezekiel 1.27 than that Daniel 10.6 is a more colourful development of Ezekiel 9.2 (albeit using material from Ezekiel 1).[73]

Halperin argues that Daniel 10 is a new 'seeing' of Ezekiel's throne-theophany. He puts forward the view that the alternative description of the 'man' in Daniel 10.16, *kdmwt bny 'dm*, 'seems to correspond to the human-like being who appears at the climax of the *merkabah* vision' in Ezekiel 1.26–8 (cf. *dmwt kmr'h 'dm* in 1.26).[74] The 'monstrosity' in Daniel 10.5–6 corresponds to the 'terrifying multiplicity' which overwhelmed Ezekiel in the first part of Ezekiel 1. By contrast, the 'less intimidating form' in Daniel 10.16–19 corresponds to the form which spoke to Ezekiel in a manner which 'the prophet's humanity could deal with'.[75] With this proposal Halperin rightly recognizes the influence of Ezekiel 1.4–25 on Daniel 10.5–6 but wrongly matches the figure in Daniel 10.16 with the one in Ezekiel 1.26. The latter is seated on the throne and is a manifestation of God, whereas the former is (i) not directly related to the throne in any way, and (ii) appears to be some kind of colleague of Michael (10.13,21). In short, one is a manifestation of God and the other is not. Further, the movement from 'terror' to 'comfort' in Daniel 10 may be analogous to that in Ezekiel 1, but this is scarcely sufficient grounds for understanding Daniel 10 as a re-expression of the throne-theophany.[76] Consequently, we do not find the arguments of Rowland and Halperin persuasive and therefore maintain that the chief background figure for Daniel 10.5–6 is to be found in Ezekiel 9.2 rather than in Ezekiel 1.26.

Finally, we may briefly consider the question of the identity of the figure in Daniel 10.5–6. If we assume that only one figure is present in Daniel 10 then we may presume that John understood that this angel was *not* Michael (cf. 10.13,21). The other great named angel in Daniel is Gabriel (Dan. 8.16, 9.21). There is certainly some similarity between the role of the angel in Daniel 10.12 and that of Gabriel in 9.20–3,[77] and the traditional identification of the angel in Daniel 10.5–6 has, in fact, been

---

[73] In other words, we agree with Rowland in as much as we believe that there was some intentionality in John's use of Ezek. 1; cf. Goldingay, *Daniel*, 291.
[74] Halperin, *Faces*, 76.
[75] Halperin, ibid., does not actually specify which part of the first chapters of Ezekiel he has in mind.
[76] Halperin (ibid., 87–96) sees Daniel 10 as a renewing of the throne-theophany but does not discuss this possibility in connection with Apc. 1.13–16.
[77] Goldingay, *Daniel*, 291; Collins, *Apocalyptic*, 134.

Gabriel.[78] Nevertheless, the angel is not named there, and other possible identifications exist, which could be made: for example, as the figure *who speaks to Gabriel* in 8.16.[79] Thus we see no secure answer to the question of the identity of the angel.

We may sum up our examination of the angelic figure in Daniel 10.5–6 in this way. As originally composed, the vision of the glorious 'man' in Daniel 10.5–6 was the vision of an angel, strongly influenced by the linen-clothed 'man' in Ezekiel 9.2. Both the form of this angel, with its evocation of intimate proximity to the divine throne, and the rank of the figure, as the equal if not the superior of 'prince' Michael, suggest that this angel is the highest angel in the Danielic heavenly hierarchy.[80]

At this point we have covered the three main epiphanies in the Book of Daniel which concern us. Other aspects of the angelology of Daniel must remain uncovered. We now turn our attention to two matters connected with the human-like figure in Daniel 7.13. The first is the question of the LXX version of Daniel 7.13 which appears to equate the human-like figure with the Ancient of Days, and the second is the reappearance of the human-like figure in certain other apocalyptic texts.

Daniel 7.13 LXX

A notable feature of the christophany in Apocalypse 1.13–16 is that imagery is drawn from Daniel 7.9,13 and 10.5–6. An important explanation which has been proposed for this combination suggests that it reflects the influence of the Septuagintal version of Daniel 7.13.[81] It is appropriate at this point, therefore, to examine Daniel 7.13 LXX, but almost inevitably our investigation will involve some discussion of Apocalypse 1.13–16 itself and thus anticipate some of the arguments that are more properly part of chapters 7 and 8.

Whereas in the MT and Theodotion versions of Daniel 7.13, 'one like a son of man' comes *unto* the Ancient of Days, in the LXX 'one

[78] Cf. Montgomery, *Daniel*, 420; Bousset, *Religion*, 377. Charles (*Daniel*, 257–8) argues vigorously that the angel is not Gabriel.

[79] Bampfylde, 'Prince', 129–30.

[80] Charles, *Daniel*, 257: 'not only a supernatural being, but one holding a preeminent dignity amongst such beings'. Bousset (*Religion*, 328) argues that the figure is Gabriel and that originally he was the highest angel though subsequently superseded by Michael.

[81] Rowland, 'Vision', 2.

like a son of man' is said to come *as* or *like* the Ancient of Days.
The relevant versions in full are as follows:

(i) *ḥzh hwyt bḥzwy lyly' w'rw 'm 'nny šmy' kbr 'nš 'th hwh w'd
'tyq ywmy' mṭh wqdmwhy hqrdwhy.*
(Dan. 7.13 MT, *BHS* (1967/77), Aramaic)

(ii) ἐθεώρουν ἐν ὁράματι τῆς νυκτὸς καὶ ἰδοὺ μετὰ τῶν
νεφελῶν τοῦ οὐρανοῦ ὡς υἱὸς ἀνθρώπου ἐρχόμενος καὶ
ἕως τοῦ παλαιοῦ τῶν ἡμερῶν ἔφθασε καὶ προσήχθη
αὐτῷ. (Dan. 7.13 Th.)[82]

(iii) ἐθεώρουν ἐν ὁράματι τῆς νυκτὸς καὶ ἰδοὺ ἐπὶ τῶν
νεφελῶν τοῦ οὐρανοῦ ὡς υἱὸς ἀνθρώπου ἤρχετο καὶ ἕως
τοῦ παλαιοῦ ἡμερῶν παρῆν καὶ οἱ παρεστηκότες
προσῆγαγον αὐτόν.
(Dan. 7.13 according to Ziegler (1954)).[83]

This is Ziegler's reconstruction of MS 88 (see below) on the basis of
ancient witnesses such as Tertullian, Cyprian, and Consultationes,
and with the presumption that ὡς is a corruption of ἕως.[84] Ziegler
did not know of the existence of Pap 967 reading for Daniel 7.13).[85]

(iv) ἐθεώρουν ἐν ὁράματι τῆς νυκτὸς καὶ ἰδοὺ ἐπὶ τῶν
νεφελῶν τοῦ οὐρανοῦ ὡς υἱὸς ἀνθρώπου ἤρχετο καὶ ὡς
παλαιὸς ἡμερῶν παρῆν καὶ οἱ παρεστηκότες παρῆσαν
αὐτῷ.
(Dan. 7.13 according to Codex Chisiasmus (MS 88; Chigi
MS; ninth/eleventh century CE; Origen's Hexapla) and
the Syro-Hexapla = Syh [early seventh century CE])[86]

(v) ἐθεώρουν ἐν ὁράματι τῆς νυκτὸς καὶ ἰδοὺ ἐπὶ τῶν
νεφελῶν τοῦ οὐρανοῦ ἤρχετο ὡς υἱὸς ἀνθρώπου καὶ ὡς
παλαιὸς ἡμερῶ(ν) παρῆν καὶ οἱ παρεστηκότες προσῆγαγον αὐτῷ.
(Dan. 7.13 according to Kölner Teil des Pap. 967
(second/early third century CE)[87]).[88]

---

[82] Ziegler, *Susanna*, 169–70.   [83] Ibid.   [84] Ibid.
[85] Cf. Lust, 'Daniel', 62. Pap. 967 according to Kenyon (*Chester*, 27) has a lacuna
from 7.11–14.
[86] Conveniently found in Rahlfs, *Septuaginta*, ii, 914. This reading can also be
reconstructed from Ziegler, *Susanna*, 169–70.
[87] This date according to Geissen, *Septuaginta-Text*, 18.
[88] Ibid., 108. Lust ('Daniel', 63) argues that this is the original LXX reading.

Our concern here is not with the variants in the translation of 'm
(μετά, ἐπὶ) but with the difference between 'd, ἕως (MT/Th./
Ziegler, respectively) and ὡς (MS 88/Syh./Pap. 967). Whereas the
former means that the 'one like a son of man' came unto 'the
Ancient of Days' with the corollary that the two are distinct figures,
the latter means that 'one like a son of man' came *as* or *like* 'the
Ancient of Days' with the corollary that the two figures might be
identified with each other. (Note that for the remainder of this
monograph 'LXX' with reference to Daniel 7.13 will mean the
textual tradition reflected in MS 88/Syro-Hexapla and Pap. 967
and not the reconstruction by Ziegler.)

We may think of the influence of Daniel 7.13 LXX on the
christophany in Apocalypse 1.13–16 taking place by one of at least
two possible means. On the one hand, Daniel 7.13 LXX may have
contributed to an apocalyptic tradition in which elements from
Daniel 7.9 were combined with elements from Daniel 7.13 and
10.5–6. Subsequently, this tradition influenced the mind of John.
Thus Rowland, for example, reflecting on *Joseph and Aseneth*
14.8–9, *Apocalypse of Abraham* 11.1–3, and Apc. 1.13–16, all of
which include a description of the hair of a glorious figure in terms
of Daniel 7.9, suggests that they all reflect a tradition which was (i)
familiar with the identification implied by the LXX of the human-
like figure with the Ancient of Days, (ii) identified the human-like
figure of 7.13 with an angelic being, and (iii) thus connected 7.13
with the parallel angelophany in Daniel 10.5–6.[89] On the other
hand, John may have been influenced directly by Daniel 7.13 LXX,
in similar fashion to the exegetical tradition outlined above and
with a similar conclusion.

The first observation we can make in response to these explanations is that it is quite possible that the LXX version of Daniel was
influential in the composition of the Apocalypse.[90] Various words
and phrases in Apocalypse 1.13–16, for example, recall the LXX of
both Daniel and Ezekiel, although it is conceivable that the

[89] Rowland, 'Man', 107. Cf. Yarbro Collins, 'Tradition', 551–2.
[90] Thus Beale, 'Reconsideration', 540–3, while recognizing that many scholars
favour the influence of Theodotion (or a related recension), argues that John had
some acquaintance with the LXX; so also Schmidt, 'Semitisms', 602; Trudinger
('Observations'), while arguing forcefully for the influence of Aramaic *Targums* or
similar, does not (e.g. p. 84) rule out minor influence by the LXX. On the
influence of Theodotion on the Apocalypse cf. Salmon, *Introduction*, 548–50;
Charles, i, lxvi–lxviii, sees the influence of LXX and a pre-Theodotionic revision
of the LXX.

explanation for this lies in John coincidentally translating the underlying Hebrew/Aramaic in a similar way to the LXX.[91] We must, of course, recognize that the use of μετά rather than ἐπὶ in Apocalypse 1.7a (which draws on Daniel 7.13) suggests the influence of a Greek recension of Daniel 7.13 closer to the MT and Theodotion than to the LXX,[92] but this does not exclude the possibility that Daniel 7.13 LXX, or something akin to it, was nevertheless also influential in Apocalypse 1.[93]

There are, however, a number of reasons for being cautious about supposing the influence of Daniel 7.13 LXX on the christophany in Apocalypse 1.13–16. First, the dating of Papyrus 967 to the second century CE means that it is quite possible that the variant ὡς παλαιὸς ἡμερῶ(ν) arose later than the composition of the Apocalypse (or, at least, arose 'not early enough to be known by John).[94] Cogent arguments have been made in favour of the explanation that the change from ἕως to ὡς is due to a transcriptional error.[95] It is conceivable, therefore, that the error occurred no earlier than Papyrus 967 itself, that is, no earlier than the second century CE. Even if a two-stage error is supposed,[96] it is conceivable that the first stage did not occur before the composition of the Apocalypse.

Secondly, we must recognize the counter-hypothesis may hold good: that far from influencing texts such as Apocalypse 1.14, Daniel 7.13 LXX may reflect their influence.[97] In other words, it is plausible to suppose that Daniel 7.13 LXX may have arisen in a Christian milieu, one in which a unity between 'one like a son of man' and the Ancient of Days was commonly supposed.[98]

Thirdly, the evidence for the significance of Daniel 7.13 LXX being drawn out in Jewish or Christian texts influenced by Daniel 7 is scarce.[99] Although contemporary texts such as the *Apocalypse of*

---

91 Cf. Yarbro Collins, 'Tradition', 548–52; Trudinger, 'Observations', 85, n. 2; and discussion below, pp. 150–62.

92 Cf. Bousset, 189; Charles, i, 17–18; Grelot, 'Les versions', 386; Montgomery, *Daniel*, 304; Yarbro Collins, 'Tradition', 541, 546.

93 Note that Apc. 14.14 has ἐπὶ τὴν νεφέλην.

94 Montgomery, *Daniel*, 304; Lust, 'Daniel', 66–9.

95 See Montgomery, *Daniel*, 304; Ziegler, *Susanna*, 170, with refutation in Bruce, 'Greek', 25–6. Pace Jeansonne (*Greek*, 96–9) has supported Ziegler against Bruce. Note, however, Rowland, 'Man', 109, n.11, who argues that θαλάσσης, found in some MSS of the LXX for Daniel 10.6, may be a 'theologically motivated change' rather than a textual corruption, and points out that it is found in Pap. 967.

96 Pace Jeansonne, *Greek*, 98.   97 Delcor, 'Sources', 304.

98 Bruce, 'Greek', 26.   99 Dunn, *Partings*, 314, n. 50.

Abraham and *Joseph and Aseneth* may reflect the influence of the LXX variant[100] it is noteworthy that 1 *Enoch* 46, which is strongly influenced by Daniel 7, betrays no sign of the influence of Daniel 7.13 LXX.[101]

A fourth reason for exercising caution is the suggestion by Segal that ὡς παλαιὸς ἡμερῶ(ν) may have originated as a defence against the 'two powers' heresy. That is, ὡς παλαιὸς ἡμερῶ(ν) was understood to mean that 'one like a son of man' and the Ancient of Days were one and the same figure in order to undermine the view that alongside God was a principal angel or exalted messiah.[102] In this case, it is likely that the reading arose in the time of R. Akiba (c. 110–132 CE).[103] Against this suggestion, however, is a point made by Yarbro Collins that the LXX reading need not have arisen from a theological intention.[104] Once in circulation an erroneous reading could have attracted a theological meaning. Thus Daniel 7.13 LXX may not have arisen out of opposition to 'two powers' heresy but simply have been welcomed and promoted by those opposed to this heresy.[105] Segal's proposal also faces the problem of whether ὡς would have been understood as meaning that the two figures were equated.[106]

Finally, in response to the explanations for the influence of Daniel 7.13 LXX on the christophany in Apocalypse 1.13–16 we may legitimately question whether knowledge of Daniel 7.13 LXX would have naturally led to the identification of the Ancient of Days with 'one like a son of man'. It is possible, for example, that the second ὡς could be a temporal and not a comparative particle with the following καὶ understood to introduce a main clause. The last part of Daniel 7.13 LXX would then be rendered 'when (ὡς) the Ancient of Days arrived, then (καὶ) the bystanders were present before him'.[107] This is unlikely, however, since (i) ὡς is never used in a visionary context in Daniel (or in Ezekiel) with a temporal meaning, and (ii) ὡς is already used in the same sentence in Daniel

[100] See discussion in Rowland, 'Man'.   [101] Cf. Swete, 16.
[102] Segal, *Powers*, 201–2, with earlier discussion on the 'dangers' of Daniel 7.9–13 on pp. 34–53. The key rabbinic texts include *Pesiq. R. Piska* 21 100b, *b. Hag.* 14a, and *b. Sanh.* 38b.
[103] Segal, *Powers*, 47–9.
[104] E.g. Lust ('Daniel', 64–9) argues that the intention of the LXX was to identify the two figures in Dan. 7.13.
[105] Yarbro Collins, 'Tradition', 555–7.
[106] Cf. Fossum, *Name*, 319.
[107] Lust, 'Daniel', 65. Cf. Bruce, 'Daniel', 25.

7.13 with a comparative meaning.[108] If the second ὡς is a comparative particle then the question concerning the identification between the Ancient of Days and the human-like figure remains. It is not clear, say, that the presence of the phrase ὡς παλαιὸς ἡμερῶ(ν) in Daniel 7.13 LXX need signify anything more than that the human-like figure comes in a similar manner (e.g. with a host of attendants) or with a similar appearance to the Ancient of Days. It is possible, for example, that 'one like a son of man' was understood to be Michael, that is, 'who is like God?', and accordingly was described as ὡς παλαιὸς ἡμερῶ(ν) because he was deemed to be similar to God in appearance.[109] Furthermore if, as we noted above, it is possible that the Apocalypse reflects the influence of both Daniel 7.13 LXX and Daniel 7.13 Th., then it is conceivable that the latter reading determined the understanding of the former: since two distinct heavenly beings are spoken of in Daniel 7.13 Th., Daniel 7.13 LXX simply means that the exponents of the LXX tradition believed that the two beings were similar in some way(s).

In conclusion, Daniel 7.13 LXX may well have been influential on the development of epiphanies in which details from Daniel 7.9 were combined with details from 7.13 and/or 10.5–6. But there is some doubt as to whether this variant was in circulation early enough to have influenced Apocalypse 1.13–16. In any case, even if it stems from the time before the Apocalypse, this does not of itself guarantee that it was influential in ways outlined above. Consequently, a search for alternative explanations for the incorporation of details from Daniel 7.9 into epiphanies has been justified.

Daniel 7.13 and related apocalyptic visions

It is well known that Daniel 7.13 has influenced texts outside the NT, such as the *Similitudes of Enoch* (= 1*Enoch* 37–71), 4 Ezra, and the Syriac *Apocalypse of Baruch* – all works which may well date from the same period as the Apocalypse itself.[110] In 1 *Enoch*

---

[108] Lust, 'Daniel', 65.

[109] The author is not aware of this connection between Michael and Dan. 7.13 LXX having been made before.

[110] 4 Ezra: *c.* 100 CE (so Metzger, *OTP*, i, 520); Syriac *Apocalypse of Baruch*: *c.* 100–120 CE (so Klijn, *OTP*, i, 617); *Similitudes of Enoch*: Stone and Greenfield ('Pentateuch', 51–60) argue that this document is a contemporary of the Qumran texts (even though absent from them) with final composition in first century CE; Collins ('Son', 451–2) argues that absence from Qumran does not require a date after 70 CE since other pseudepigrapha with undisputed early dates are also

46, for example, the seer has a vision which has a marked similarity
to that found in Daniel 7.9–13:[111]

> At that place, I saw the Head of Days. And his head was
> white like wool, and there was with him another individual,
> whose face was like that of a human being. His counte-
> nance was full of grace like that of one among the holy
> angels. [2] And I asked the one – from among the angels –
> who was going with me, and who revealed to me all the
> secrets regarding the One who was born of human beings,
> 'Who is this, and from whence is he who is going as the
> prototype of the Before-Time?' [3] And he answered me and
> said to me, 'This is the Son of Man, to whom belongs
> righteousness, and with whom righteousness dwells.'
>
> (1 *Enoch* 46.1–3)[112]

It is striking that here the son of man figure is *not* described with
details drawn from Daniel 7.9 and 10.5–6. The Enochic son of man
is more explicitly likened to the angels than is the case with the son
of man figure in the Apocalypse. The Enochic son of man is
comparable to the son of man in the Apocalypse in at least one
respect: both have a weapon coming from their mouths (1 *Enoch*
62.2; cf. Apc. 1.16). It could be that he is understood as a pre-
existent figure (cf. 1 *Enoch* 48.3,6),[113] a possibility that also pertains
to the son of man figure in the Apocalypse.[114] One of the most
striking aspects of the portrayal of the Enochic son of man is that
he appears to be an object of worship (cf. 1 *Enoch* 46.5, 48.5, and
compare with, e.g., the praise of the Lamb in Apc. 5.9–13). As is
the case with the Apocalypse, we must not presume that 'son of
man' is used as a title for this Enochian figure.[115]

absent; Knibb ('Date', 359) argues for a late first-century CE date while Mearns
('Dating', 369) argues for the late 40s CE.
[111] On the two son of man figures see further Muilenberg, 'Son'. Parallels between
the two passages are set out in Beale, *Daniel*, 97–100 and Caragounis, *Son*,
101–2. Casey ('Use', 20–2) argues that Daniel 7.9 has influenced 1 *Enoch* 46.
[112] Isaac, *OTP*, i, 34.
[113] Recently argued by Collins, 'Son', 455; contrast with Manson, 'Son', 183–5, who
argues for 'pre-mundane election' rather than 'pre-mundane existence'; VanderKam, 'Righteous', 179–82.
[114] The white hair of the figure (Apc. 1.14) might symbolize existence from ancient
times, according to Swete, 16; cf. Apc. 1.17, 3.14, 13.8, 22.12–13.
[115] Collins, 'Son', 452. For other informative studies of the Enochic son of man see,
e.g., Collins, 'Representative'; Sjöberg, *Menschensohn*; Casey, *Son*; and now
VanderKam, 'Righteous', 169–91, with further literature cited therein.

In 4 Ezra (= 2 Esdras 3–14), a late first-century apocalypse,[116] the seer records part of a night dream as follows: 'As I kept looking the wind made up something like the figure of a man come up out of the heart of the sea. And I saw that this man flew with the clouds of the heaven' (4 Ezra 13.3 NRSV). The influence of Daniel 7 is clear,[117] the more so because this chapter of Daniel has influenced the preceding chapters in 4 Ezra. The most important versions of 4 Ezra are in Latin and Syriac. In the Syriac the human-like figure is described as '*yk dmwt' dbrns'* which means the original may have been *bn 'dm* or *br 'nš'.*[118] Comparison with the Apocalypse is interesting: the figure that comes up out of the sea is not the 'one like a son of man' but his antitype the beast (Apc. 13.1). In 4 Ezra the human-like figure holds no weapon (4 Ezra 13.9; cf. Apc. 1.16, 14.14, 19.15). But his mouth is associated with judgement, although 'a stream of fire' comes out of his mouth (4 Ezra 13.4,10–11) rather than a sword (cf. Apc. 1.16, 19.15). There is no elaboration of the form of the figure unlike the case in Apocalypse 1.13–16 and 14.14. Other differences may be noted but the impression is reasonably clear that the author of 4 Ezra has incorporated elements from Daniel 7 (and elsewhere) independently of the manner in which John has done so.

In the Syriac *Apocalypse of Baruch* we find another notable example of the influence of Daniel 7 on visionary material (*2 Apoc. Bar.* 53). But neither the vision nor the subsequent interpretation specifically mention a son of man figure. Rather, there is talk of 'my Servant, the Anointed One' (70.9, cf. 72.2).

Recently, Collins has reopened the question of common assumptions being held in the first century CE about the figure in Daniel's vision. Without reaching the conclusion that these assumptions amount to 'a "Son of Man" concept', he argues that anyone speaking in the late first century of a figure reminiscent of Daniel 7.13 'would evoke a figure with distinct traits which go beyond what was explicit in the text of Daniel's vision'.[119] These traits, readily observable in the Apocalypse, include: (i) being an individual (rather than a collective) symbol;[120] (ii) being 'the messiah'; (iii) being pre-existent 'and therefore a transcendent figure of

---

[116] Stone (*Ezra*, 10) argues for the latter part of Domitian's reign (81–96 CE).
[117] Ibid., 384.   [118] Collins, 'Son', 460.   [119] Ibid., 466.
[120] Cf. Black, 'Throne-theophany', 73.

heavenly origin'; and (iv) taking a more active role in the destruction of the wicked than was explicit in Daniel.

Thus the Apocalypse does not stand alone as a work from the period around the turn of the first century which has been influenced by Dan. 7; but the differences between the Apocalypse, the *Similitudes of Enoch*, 4 Ezra, and the Syriac *Apocalypse of Baruch* in their expression of this influence demonstrate that each work presupposed the freedom to restate the earlier vision of Daniel in terms relevant to the situation in which each author lived.

Conclusions

We have reviewed angelological and epiphanic material in the Books of Zechariah, Ezekiel, and Daniel. We have attempted to shed some light on difficult issues, such as the significance of Daniel 7.13 LXX. In the course of our review, we have suggested that aspects of the development behind the christophany proposed by Rowland are open to doubt. In particular, we see the origins of the glorious 'man' in Daniel 10.5–6 lying in the angel introduced in Ezekiel 9.2 as 'a man clothed in linen', rather than in the fiery figure in Ezekiel 1.26–8. Other aspects from Ezekiel 1 have undoubtedly contributed to the portrayal in Daniel 10.5–6 but not in such a way to make us conclude that the 'man' is anything other than an angel. This point is confirmed since the 'man' is 'sent' and therefore is clearly distinct from God. We have also argued that the apparent influence of Daniel 7.13 LXX on the christophany in Apocalypse 1.13–16 is open to doubt. Finally, we have noted that the treatment of Daniel 7 in first-century Jewish and Christian writings implied a freedom to restate the vision of Daniel in a manner relevant to new situations facing the people of God.

3

PRINCIPAL ANGELS

We now turn to accounts of principal angels in apocalypses and related apocryphal and pseudepigraphal writings. Our initial concern is with exalted angels whose appearance more or less parallels that of the risen Jesus in Apocalypse 1.13–16. That is, we consider principal angels who appear in glorious and majestic form: we describe these as 'glorious angels', not because we think they are identified with the *kabod* of God but simply because the extraordinary splendour of their appearance is aptly summed up in the word 'glorious'. We then consider principal angels whose form, glorious or otherwise, is not described. The final issue we consider is the question of angel worship. One question underlying our studies in this chapter is whether or not Jewish and Christian angelology in the period broadly contemporaneous with the Apocalypse itself betray familiarity with the notion that an angel could have divine status.

Glorious angels

Taking our cue from the work of Rowland, already discussed in previous chapters, we begin by considering in detail the angel Yahoel in the *Apocalypse of Abraham*, an unnamed angel in *Joseph and Aseneth*, and the angel Eremiel in the *Apocalypse of Zephaniah*. We then examine more briefly a range of accounts of glorious angels.

In the *Apocalypse of Abraham*, probably dating from late in the first century CE,[1] Abraham meets up with Yahoel who guides him

---

[1] After 70 CE and before *c*.150 CE (Rubinkiewicz, *OTP*, i, 683); possibly later than this (Pennington, *AOT*, 365–7); but Box (*Apocalypse*, xv) dates the *Apocalypse of Abraham* to shortly after 70 CE; Halperin (*Faces*, 103–4) argues that despite some Christian redaction the *Apocalypse of Abraham* may be treated as 'a product of

on his heavenly journey. Two key passages describe this glorious angel:

> The angel he sent to me in the likeness of a man came, and he took me by my right hand and stood me on my feet. And he said to me, 'Stand up, Abraham, friend of God who has loved you, let human trembling not enfold you! For lo! I am sent to you to strengthen you and to bless you in the name of God, creator of heavenly and earthly things, who has loved you. Be bold and hasten to him. I am Iaoel [= Yahoel], and I was called so by him who causes those with me on the seventh expanse, on the firmament, to shake, a power through the medium of his ineffable name in me.'   (*Apoc. Abr*. 10.5–9)

> And I stood up and saw him who had taken my right hand and set me on my feet. The appearance of his body was like sapphire, and the aspect of his face like chrysolite, and the hair of his head like snow. And a kidaris (was) on his head,[2] its look that of a rainbow, and the clothing of his garments (was) purple; and a golden staff (was) in his right hand. And he said to me, 'Abraham.' And I said, 'Here is your servant.'   (*Apoc. Abr*. 11.1–3)[3]

The majestic description of Yahoel recalls both the description of the exalted angel in Daniel 10.5–6 (cf. 'a man', 'His body was like beryl') and the description of the Ancient of Days in Daniel 7.9 (cf. 'his clothing was white as snow, and the hair of his head like pure wool'). Further, the *merging* of these descriptions from Daniel in the one figure parallels the christophany in Apocalypse 1.13–16 which also blends together elements taken from Daniel 7.9 and 10.5–6.[4] The probable dating of the Apocalypse and the *Apocalypse of Abraham* to a common period, however, suggests that it is likely each account is independent of the other and raises the question whether they draw on a common tradition which has blended together elements taken from the theophany in Daniel 7.9 and the

---

early Judaism'; in short: we accept a late first-century date as probable. The oldest known form of the *Apocalypse of Abraham* is in Slavonic.

[2] Rubinkiewicz (*OTP*, i, 694) notes that *kidaris* in the LXX means a 'headdress' (Exod. 39.28) and a 'turban' (Zech. 3.5).

[3] Rubinkiewicz, *OTP*, i, 693–4.   [4] See chapter 8 below.

angelophany in 10.5–6.[5] We have already drawn attention to Rowland's suggestion that the blending of Daniel 7.9 and 10.5–6 in angelophanies reflects the influence of Daniel 7.13 LXX.[6] If the *Apocalypse of Abraham* stems from the same period as the Apocalypse or later then the doubts we have expressed about the influence on Daniel 7.13 LXX similarly apply here.

Yahoel is arguably the chief angel within the angelology of the *Apocalypse of Abraham*.[7] Certainly, no other angel is portrayed in such a glorious manner, or has such power or status. Yahoel has three outstanding characteristics. First, he is 'a power through the medium of his ineffable name in me' (*Apoc. Abr.* 10.9). This suggests that Yahoel is identified with the Exodus angel (cf. 'for my name is in him', Exod. 23.21).[8] Secondly, Yahoel has several impressive functions: (i) to keep the cherubim or living creatures under control; (ii) to teach; (iii) to restrain Leviathan and subdue the reptiles;[9] (iv) to destroy idolators; and (v) to bless God-fearers such as Abraham (*Apoc. Abr.* 10.10–14).[10] Thirdly, Yahoel speaks of Michael as an associate: 'And with me Michael blesses you forever' (*Apoc. Abr.* 10.17). The impression is given that Yahoel is superior to Michael, who is never referred to again in the apocalypse.

We have already noticed that in recent years the status of Yahoel has been debated.[11] Is he an angel, albeit the chief angel? Or, noting his superiority over the living creatures, is he more than this? For example, is Yahoel presented as a figure who is the result of a 'bifurcation' in the being of God?[12] The latter possibility is based primarily on his description as 'a power through the medium of his ineffable name in me' (*Apoc. Abr.* 10.9). This feature is, of course,

[5] Box (*Apocalypse*, 49, n. 6) notes a general resemblance to the christophany in Apc. 1.13–16 but with differences in most details.
[6] See pp. 4–6.   [7] Cf. Segal, *Powers*, 196.
[8] Box (*Apocalypse*, 46, n. 5) draws attention to a similar statement about Metatron in *b*. Sanhedrin 38b.
[9] Some MSS add a reference to a function 'to loosen hell and to destroy those (or he) who wonder at dead things' (Pennington, *AOT*, 376, n. 7; cf. Rubinkiewicz (*OTP*, 694) who includes this in the main body of the text as *Apoc. Abr.* 10.11; cf. Box, *Apocalypse*, 48, n. 1).
[10] Cf. Halperin, *Faces*, 112–13, summing up the functions concerning the living creatures, Leviathan and the reptiles, and hell: '[Yahoel] must suppress the dark and inimical forces of the cosmos.'
[11] Cf. Rowland, *Heaven*, 101–3; Hurtado, *God*, 87–90; Fossum, *Name*, 319.
[12] The term 'bifurcation' in this context refers to the separation of some aspect of the divine being which then takes on an independent or semi-independent life of its own. Cf. discussion in Hurtado, *God*, 85–90.

underlined by the juxtaposition of *Yah* and *El* in his name – indeed 'Yahoel' as a name for God is also found in this apocalypse (*Apoc. Abr.* 17.13).[13] Nevertheless, a number of observations may be made which favour both a clear distinction between God and Yahoel (i.e. the angelic figure in *Apoc. Abr.* 10–11) and an understanding of Yahoel as a being who was *not perceived as* the product of bifurcation within the deity.[14]

First, the figure is described as an 'angel'.[15] Secondly, Yahoel acts in response to God's initiative (e.g. 'I am sent to you', 10.7; 'I am he who is appointed by his command', 10.10). He acts on behalf of God (e.g. 'to bless you in the name of God', 10.7), but he never acts in his own right. Thirdly, at the end of *Apoc. Abr.* 10, Yahoel states, 'And with me Michael blesses you forever' (v. 17). This suggests that whatever great status Yahoel may have, he is a being who belongs to the same ontological category as Michael. That is, he is an angel and not a divine being. Fourthly, Yahoel is clearly depicted as one who *worships God* rather than as one who is worshipped (17.2). The *Apocalypse of Abraham* does not show Abraham attempting to worship Yahoel.[16] Consequently, we can confirm that the angel Yahoel is extraordinarily exalted in status and glorious in form. But we have not found that the treatment of Yahoel in the *Apocalypse of Abraham* blurs a clear distinction between God and the angel; rather, we suggest that with Yahoel speculation about the glorious appearance and exalted rank of an angel *within the bounds of monotheism* was reaching its zenith.[17]

Joseph and Aseneth is better described as a 'romance' than as an 'apocalypse'.[18] It probably comes from the Egyptian Diaspora from a Jewish milieu similar to one from which many Christians were recruited.[19] It was originally written in Greek,[20] most likely

---

[13] Cf. Box, *Apocalypse*, 46, n. 5; Fossum, *Name*, 318; Halperin, *Faces*, 105. A similar composite name, 'Jael', is found in *Adam and Eve* 29 (as a name for God). On the origin of 'Yahoel', see Scholem, *Gnosticism*, 43–55. Fossum (*Name*, 319–20) suggests that Yahoel is the *kabod* of God. Note also magic texts in Naveh and Shaked (*Amulets*, 13, 159–61) dating from talmudic (or later) periods, which barely distinguish between the angel Yeho'el and Yah = God.

[14] Allo, 13.   [15] Cf. *Apoc. Abr.* 10.5; 12.1,2,6; 13.1; 14.10; 15.3; 16.1; 17.3.

[16] Cf. Hurtado, *God*, 87–9.   [17] Cf. Segal, *Powers*, 196.

[18] Cf. Philonenko, *Joseph*, 53–98; Kee, 'Setting', 394–8.

[19] Burchard, 'Importance', 104.

[20] The Greek texts of *Joseph and Aseneth* are referred to as *a*, *b*, *c*, and *d*. The most important are *a* and *d*. Group *a* texts are longer (for critical edition see 'Le livre de la Prière d'Aseneth' in P. Batiffol, *Studia Patristica*, Paris, 1869–90, 1–115); group *b* are shorter (for critical edition see Philonenko, *Joseph*, 128–221; ET in

between the beginning of the last century BCE and the first decades of the first century CE.[21] In the following passage, which we cite in both Greek and English, Aseneth sees a glorious angel:

> ἰδοὺ ἀνὴρ ὅμοιος κατὰ πάντα τῷ Ἰωσὴφ τῇ στολῇ καὶ τῷ στεφάνῳ καὶ τῇ ῥάβδῳ τῇ βασιλικῇ [9]πλὴν τὸ πρόσωπον αὐτοῦ ἦν ὡς ἀστραπὴ καὶ οἱ ὀθαλμοὶ αὐτοῦ ὡς φέγγος ἡλίου καὶ αἱ τρίχες τῆς κεφαλῆς αὐτοῦ ὡς φλὸξ πυρὸς καὶ αἱ χεῖρες καὶ οἱ πόδες αὐτοῦ ὥσπερ σίδηρος ἐκ πυρός.[22]

> [Aseneth looked and saw] and behold a man in every way like Joseph, with a robe and a crown and a royal staff. [9]But his face was like lightning, and his eyes were like sunlight, and the hairs of his head like a flame of fire, and his hands and his feet like iron from the fire.
>
> *(Jos. and Asen.* 14.8–9)[23]

The description of the heavenly figure as 'a man in every way like Joseph' (14.8) is consistent with the fact that he is also described as 'chief of the house of the Most High' (14.7; cf. 15.12) similar to Joseph's position as chief of the house of Pharaoh. It is likely that this figure is in fact Michael, particularly in view of the use of the term ἀρχιστράτηγος (e.g. 14.7). Although there are impressive links between the story of this angel's involvement with Aseneth and the theophany in Ezekiel 1 (cf. 'chariot of fire', *Jos. and Asen.* 17.6),[24] there is no reason to think of this figure as other than an angel. The form of this angel is similar in a number of respects to the angel in Daniel 10.5–6. The faces of both angels are the same, but the descriptions of the eyes are different (cf. 'like flaming torches', Daniel 10.6). The description of the hair of the angel is

---

AOT, 473–503). In *OTP* Burchard presents the ET of his 'preliminary new text': arguing that *d* is a shortened text, Burchard offers a reconstruction which is like *a* for length, like *d* in wording, and leans towards *b* (Burchard, *OTP*, ii, 181; cf. Burchard, 'Importance', 105). Burchard's Greek recension may be found in *DBAT* 14 (1979), 2–53 or in Denis, *Concordance*, 851–9.

[21] Burchard ('Importance', 104) sums up the consensus view as: *Joseph and Aseneth* was written no later than 117–138 CE (the reign of Hadrian), possibly no later than 98–117 CE (the reign of Trajan), and no earlier than 100 BCE. Holtz ('Interpolationen', 67–71), on the basis of features in *Joseph and Aseneth* unparalleled in Jewish literature, argues that Christian interpolations are integral to the oldest attainable text.

[22] Philonenko, *Joseph*, 178. The variations between *a* and *d* are minor here, at least until φλὸξ πυρὸς.

[23] The author's own translation.   [24] Enumerated in Kee, 'Setting', 400–1.

notable. Like those of the risen Jesus and Yahoel, this description draws on Daniel 7.9 but in terms of 'flames of fire' rather than 'wool' or 'snow'. Whether this might be due to a mistaken memory of the contents of Daniel 7.9, or to the desire to distinguish the angel from the Ancient of Days, or otherwise, is unclear. Finally, we have no compelling reason to think that either epiphany in *Joseph and Aseneth* and the Apocalypse is dependent on the other since there is an absence of exact points of comparison between the two figures.

In the *Apocalypse of Zephaniah*, after encountering various mighty angels, Zephaniah experiences the following angelophany, according to this second-century CE apocalypse:[25]

> Then I arose and stood, and I saw a great angel standing before me with his face shining like the rays of the sun in its glory since his face is like that which is perfected in its glory. [12]And he was girded as if a golden girdle were upon his breast. His feet were like bronze which is melted in a fire. [13]And when I saw him, I rejoiced, for I thought that the Lord Almighty had come to visit me. [14]I fell upon my face; and I worshipped him. [15]He said to me, 'Take heed. Don't worship me. I am not the Lord Almighty, but I am the great angel, Eremiel, who is over the abyss and Hades, the one in which all of the souls are imprisoned from the end of the Flood, which came upon the earth, until this day.'   (*Apoc. Zeph.* 6.11–15)[26]

There are, in fact, a number of 'great angels' in this apocalypse. For example, there are 'lords' who sit on thrones seven times as bright as the sun (*Apoc. Zeph.* A).[27] In *Apocalypse of Zephaniah* 4.1–10 Zephaniah walks with 'the angel of the LORD' and sees a multitude of terrifying angels whose 'eyes were mixed with blood' – these angels seem to be under the authority of the angel of the LORD for Zephaniah pleads with him not to give these angels authority over him. One angel is described with his hair 'spread out like the

---

[25] Wintermute, *OTP*, 500: between 100 BCE and 175 CE; Philonenko, *Joseph*, 109: beginning of second century CE. Language: Sahidic, Akhmimic. The title '*Apocalypse of Zephaniah*' may not be appropriate (cf. Bauckham, 'Apocalypses', 100–3) but we follow *OTP*'s practice in the matter. For a brief introduction to the apocalypse (apart from those given in *OTP* and *AOT*) see Himmelfarb, *Tours*, 13–16.

[26] Wintermute, *OTP*, i, 513; cf. K. H. Kuhn, *AOT*, 922–3.

[27] Wintermute, *OTP*, i, 508.

lionesses' (6.8–10) – a later verse identifies this angel as Satan (6.17). References to other great angels are to be found in *Apocalypse of Zephaniah* 7.9, 9.1,3, 10.1, and 12.1.

Elements of the description of Eremiel recall the glorious figure in Daniel 10.5–6 (cf. the description of feet and girdle), although there are variations (e.g. Eremiel's face is like the 'sun' rather than 'lightning'), and omissions (no description of Eremiel's clothing, body, eyes, or voice). With respect to Daniel 7.9, we note that there is no description of the head or hair of Eremiel. Eremiel's appearance stands comparison with that of the risen Jesus in Apocalypse 1.13–16: common elements include golden girdle, face like the sun, and feet like bronze.[28] The second of these common elements cannot be explained in terms of Daniel 10.5–6, which raises the question whether one apocalypse has influenced the other or whether both have drawn on common sources. But the sun-like face of Eremiel is familiar from other writings (e.g. 2 *Enoch* 1.5; *Test. Abr.* Rec. A 12.9, 13.10). Other common features between the two apocalypses, such as an angel's refusal of worship (*Apoc. Zeph.* 6.13; cf. Apc. 19.10, 22.8–9), and an angel in charge of the underworld (*Apoc. Zeph.* 6.13; cf. Apc. 1.18, 9.11), are not sufficiently close to require the conclusion that one is dependent on the other.[29] Although the appearance of Eremiel confuses the seer into thinking that he is in the presence of God the distinction between Eremiel and God is made very clear by Eremiel's denial that he is God and his affirmation that he is a 'great angel' (6.15).

Other accounts of glorious angels, which were a widespread feature of ancient Jewish and Christian apocalyptic and related literature, do not give quite as much detail as in the three accounts we have just considered. Nevertheless, these are well worth considering briefly. In the *Testament of Abraham* Recension A (c. 100 CE?),[30] for example, two archangels serve the patriarch Abel: 'the sun-like angel' (ὁ ἄγγελος ὁ ἡλιόμορφος, 12.9, 13.10) and 'the fiery angel' (ὁ ἄγγελος ὁ πύρινος, 12.10, 13.11).[31] In the same testament, 'Death' manifests itself as a glorious angel wearing a bright robe and having a sun-like appearance and fiery cheeks (ὄψιν

---

[28] For citation of Apc. 1.13–16 see pp. 129–30.
[29] Cf. Bauckham, 'Worship', 325; Himmelfarb, *Tours*, 16.
[30] See p. 78.
[31] Greek from Stone, *Abraham*, 32; cf. parallels with *Apoc. Zeph.* 3.5–9. Sun-like beings are also found in *Test. Abr.* 2.6, 7.5. On the angelology of *Test. Abr.* see Kalenkow, 'Angelology', 153–62.

ἡλιόμορφον . . . τὰς παρειὰς αὐτοῦ πυρὶ ἀστράπτων, 16.8–9; cf. 17.15). In the *Apocalypse of Paul*, a late fourth-century CE document (?),[32] angels are seen 'with faces shining like the sun; their loins girt like girdles'.[33] In the *Similitudes of Enoch* the only extensive description of the form of angels occurs when Enoch ascends to the heavens. He sees 'the sons of the holy angels' treading upon 'the flame of fire; their garments were white – and their overcoats – and the light of their faces was like snow' (1 *Enoch* 71.1).[34] Here the language recalls Daniel 7.9 (more so than 1 *Enoch* 46.1), though without mention of the head or hair of the angels. It is noticeable that the comparison with 'snow' is applied to the face. The value of 2 *Enoch* in the present context is difficult to assess since there is no consensus about its provenance or dating and it could stem from prior to the Christian period or as late as the end of the Middle Ages.[35] Nevertheless, it features an extensive angelology, including an account of two glorious 'men' with faces 'like the shining sun', eyes 'like burning lamps', mouths from which fire comes out, and arms 'like wings of gold' (2 *Enoch* 1.4–5, Short Rec.; cf. 19.1).[36] The longer recension adds that 'their hands were whiter than snow'.[37] In the Gospel of Matthew the angel at the tomb is described as 'like lightning and his clothing white as snow' (Matt. 28.3).[38] Other broadly similar examples of glorious angels are found within the Apocalypse itself (Apc. 10.1–3, 15.6–7). Some accounts of glorious angels express the majestic appearance of the angels in more general terms. Thus in the *Ladder of Jacob*, whose origins may lie in the first century CE,[39] the angel Sariel is 'very beautiful and awesome' (3.3).[40] In 2 Maccabees 3.25–6, a 'rider of frightening mien' on a horse and two 'men . . . remarkably strong, gloriously beautiful and splendidly dressed', come to the rescue of the Jews. In 3 Maccabees 6.18 'two glorious angels of fearful aspect' are seen. The appearance of some angels is described in the

---

[32] Rebell, *Neutestamentliche*, 253. But there is some evidence that the apocalypse was known in the third century CE: see Yarbro Collins, 'Early Christian', 85; Himmelfarb, *Tours*, 18.

[33] Duensing, *NTA*, ii, 764.   [34] Isaac, *OTP*, i, 49.

[35] Andersen, *OTP*, i, 95–7.   [36] Ibid., 107.   [37] Ibid., 106.

[38] Note also with respect to 'snow' imagery *Jos. and Asen.* 5.5: 'four horses white as snow'.

[39] Lunt, *OTP*, ii, 404.

[40] Ibid., 408. Note the distinction in this passage between an earlier theophany and the angelophany, in contrast with *Apoc. Zeph.* 6.11–13, where a theophany is indistinguishable from an angelophany until a clarifying statement is made.

Qumran literature. In 4Q 'Amram[b] 1.13–15, for example, one of the angels mentioned is fearsomely dark, while another has a face like a snake.[41] In 4Q405 23ii the 'spirits' (= 'princes', i.e. angels) are described in terms of 'colours in the midst of an appearance of whiteness' and compared to 'sparkling fine gold'.[42]

From the above survey we can draw out the important observation that the apocalypticists appeared to work freely with imagery although within certain constraints. For example, between Daniel 7.9, 1 *Enoch* 71.1, and 2 *Enoch* 1.5, 'snow' imagery is applied alternatively to clothing, faces, and hands. A traditional image is faithfully retained, but its application is wide ranging. A similar observation can be made about the use of 'fire' and 'sun' imagery.

We may also note that in the angelophanies we have considered descriptive elements, such as comparison with the 'sun', have been used which are not found in Daniel or Ezekiel. A possible source for these could have been the theophany in 1 *Enoch* 14, which may stem from as early as 250 BCE.[43] Two brief citations illustrate the point: 'a lofty throne – its appearance was like crystal and its wheels like the shining sun' (1 *Enoch* 14.18), and 'the Great Glory was sitting upon it – as for his gown, which was shining more brightly than the sun, it was whiter than any snow' (1 *Enoch* 14.20).[44] Interestingly, angelophanies which may have been influenced by this theophany tend to feature the eyes or the face of the angel being compared with the sun. Since 1 *Enoch* 14.21 reports that the face of God itself could not be seen, it would appear that a distinction was being made between angels (with visible faces) and God (with hidden face), even when imagery from the theophany was being used in angelophanies. This observation coheres with earlier ones that despite the fact that theophanic imagery is found in descriptions of glorious angels, none of the angels we have referred to is anything more than an angel. Consequently, we may sum up this section in this way: apocalypticists appeared to work from a 'limited stock of imagery',[45] applied this imagery in a variety of epiphanic contexts, while clearly distinguishing between God and the glorious angels.

---

[41] Cf. Davidson, *Angels*, 290.

[42] *DSSE*, 229. Note also 4Q403 1 ii, where fire imagery predominates, reminiscent of Ezek. 1.

[43] Black, *Enoch*, 151.   [44] Isaac, *OTP*, i, 21.

[45] Dunn, *Christology*, xxiv.

Principal angels without glorious form

We must now consider other principal angels who have a high, if not the highest, status among angels, but whose form is not described (or, at least, not in the detailed way which we have observed above). We do so in order to extend our investigation to the possibility that Jewish and Christian angelology included a principal angel who possessed divine status. Before proceeding to examine various accounts of principal angels, we will draw attention to the varying conceptions of a heavenly hierarchy and of the identity of the highest angel. The following text, for example, gives one conception of the heavenly hierarchy:

> And he will summon all the forces of the heavens, and all the holy ones above, and the forces of the Lord – the cherubim, seraphim, ophanim, all the angels of governance, the Elect One, and the other forces on earth (and) over the water.   (1 *Enoch* 61.10)[46]

Another description is given in *Jubilees* 2.2, which begins with 'the angels of the presence and the angels of sanctification' (described in 2.18 as 'these two great kinds') and goes on to list various angels responsible for aspects of nature.[47] More elaborate hierarchies are found in 2 *Enoch* 8.1–9.15 and 3 *Enoch* 17–29. In some works a hierarchy is implicitly supposed because we are introduced to a group of leading angels with the implication that all other angels belong to a lower rank (e.g. Tob. 12.15). In the *Sabbath Shirot* seven 'sovereign Princes' are mentioned (4Q403 1i 1–29), as well as seven 'deputy Princes' (4Q400 3 ii 2; cf. 4Q405 13 7).[48]

1 *Enoch* 61.10 does not refer to one angel as the chief angel. Some passages in the *Similitudes of Enoch* suggest that Michael was effectively the chief angel (e.g. 1 *Enoch* 60.4, 68.3–5, 69.14–15), while 1 *Enoch* 24.6 explicitly mentions Michael as chief angel. Nevertheless, within the whole of the first Enochian corpus it is groups of leading angels which command attention: either four angels (e.g., 1 *Enoch* 9.1, 40.9, 64.6, 71.9) or seven angels (e.g. 1 *Enoch* 20.3[49]). More explicit references to an angel as chief are found in, for example, *Joseph and Aseneth* 14.7 and 15.12, *Prayer of*

---

[46] Isaac, *OTP*, i, 42.   [47] Wintermute, *OTP*, ii, 55, 56.
[48] Cf. Newsom, *Songs*, 32–3.
[49] Six angels mentioned in Ethiopic, seven in Greek recension.

Joseph, and *Assumption of Moses* 10.2. In *Joseph and Aseneth* 14.7 and 15.12 and *Assumption of Moses* 10.2 the chief angel is unnamed, though likely to be Michael. In the *Prayer of Joseph* the chief angel is 'Jacob-Israel'. In Daniel 10 and *Apocalypse of Abraham* 10 Michael is mentioned but is unlikely to be the chief angel within the conceptions of each apocalypse. Thus there is no consistent identity for the chief angel in the range of literature we are considering.

We now examine some of the more important angels whose form is not described. One outstanding angel is Raphael in the Book of Tobit.[50] Raphael comes to earth in order to help a couple named Tobit and Sarah; but until the moment of his return to heaven Raphael deceives Tobit and Sarah into thinking that he is a human being (Tob. 12.19).[51] Raphael is the 'complete' angel, functioning as guide, revealer, intercessor, healer, exorcist, and tester (cf. Tob. 12.11–20).[52] There are certainly resonances here with the angelology of the Apocalypse: revealing truth is a function of at least one angel in the Apocalypse (cf. Apc. 1.1, 22.6,16), mediating prayer is another (cf. Apc. 8.3), and Raphael, like the trumpet angels, 'stands before' God (Tob. 12.15; cf. Apc. 8.2).[53] But there is nothing which directly connects Raphael with Jesus Christ in the Apocalypse; by contrast, we may observe that Raphael's posing as a human being may have influenced *Ascension of Isaiah* 11.17, where the Beloved feigns feeding at the breast of Mary.[54] For our present purposes the importance of Raphael lies in his example as a heavenly being who successfully conceals his true nature while effectively functioning as a human being. That an angel should descend to earth, appear to be human, and perform such roles as Raphael does is suggestive of a background model for NT christology – one which has not been extensively reflected upon by scholars.[55]

---

[50] Language: Greek. Date: Tob. 1–12 (50–100 BCE), 13–14 (post-70 CE), according to Zimmerman, *Tobit*, 24, 25–7.

[51] See further, Knight, *Disciples*, 104–6.

[52] Segal (*Powers*, 90) suggests that Raphael's function as 'tester' means that he is identified as the angel of the LORD who was sent to test Abraham (Gen. 22.11–18).

[53] In addition to angelological material from Tobit which seems to be reflected in the Apocalypse, we may also note parallels between the visions of Jerusalem in each book (Tob. 13.9–17; cf. Apc. 21.10–21).

[54] Knight, *Disciples*, 104–10.

[55] An exception is Knight, ibid.; cf. Segal, 'Ascent', 1372. On Raphael see Michl, 'Engel', 252–4.

The next angel worth considering is described in a text known as the *Prayer of Joseph*. The main source for this text is Origen, *Commentarii in Johannis* ii.189–90, which means that its *terminus a quo* is 231 CE. However, it has been argued that a first-century CE date for the original text is quite possible.[56]

> I, Jacob, who is speaking to you, am also Israel, an angel of God and a ruling spirit. Abraham and Isaac were created before any work. But, I, Jacob, who men call Jacob but whose name is Israel am he who God called Israel which means, a man seeing God, because I am the firstborn of every living thing to whom God gives life. And when I was coming up from Syrian Mesopotamia, Uriel, the angel of God, came forth and said that I [Jacob-Israel] had descended to earth and I had tabernacled among men and that I had been called by the name Jacob. He envied me and fought with me and wrestled with me saying that his name and the name that is before every angel was to be above mine. I told him his name and what rank he held among the sons of God. Are you not Uriel, the eighth after me? And I, Israel, the archangel of the power of the Lord and the chief captain among the sons of God? Am I not Israel, the first minister before the face of God? And I called upon my God by the inextinguishable name.
>
> (*Pr. Jos.* Fr. A)[57]

It could be that the *Prayer of Joseph* envisages Jacob as a heavenly being who has adopted human form in an attempt to deny the uniqueness of Jesus by presenting another example of a heavenly power descended from God, who becomes a human.[58] But even if this text has been influenced by Christian ideas, the idea of a heavenly being *appearing* to be human was not new to Judaism (cf.

---

[56] E.g. J. Z. Smith, 'Prayer', 26, n. 4, who notes parallelism between the *Prayer of Joseph*, Philo's writings, and other Hellenistic Jewish material (which points not only to a first-century date, but to an Alexandrian provenance); but Smith recognizes the implications of 'eight' archangels which could reflect second-century developments (ibid., 47, n. 52). Dunn (*Christology*, 21) argues that a date for the *Prayer of Joseph* before the second century CE is difficult to maintain on the grounds that it presupposes 'a more developed ranking among the archangels' than is found elsewhere in the first century CE. But it is conceivable that the *Prayer of Joseph* was at the forefront of developments in ranking.

[57] J. Z. Smith, *OTP*, ii, 713 (omitting his italics).

[58] Knight (*Disciples*, 90) counters this idea by noting Origen's silence about any such polemic.

Gen. 18.1–8; Tob. 12.11–15). Hence this example need not be understood solely as a kind of apologetic strategem. It may well represent the possibility that some Jewish circles, even in the first century CE, comfortably accommodated (i) the idea that an angel could take on human form, and (ii) the possibility of pre-existence for a human being.[59]

According to J. Z. Smith it is a 'moot question' whether Jacob-Israel is 'a thoroughly docetic figure . . . [or] an appearance and incarnation of a heavenly power . . . or a heavenly messenger'.[60] Nevertheless, the *Prayer of Joseph* opens up interesting possibilities for the discussion of first-century CE angelology and christology. In particular, it raises the question whether the idea that a heavenly being could become incarnate developed within Jewish angelology independently and (more or less) simultaneously as it developed within early christology.

We have already referred to the archangel Michael. One of his roles was believed to be the protection of Israel. This role may have its roots in an enigmatic text in Deuteronomy:

> When the Most High apportioned the nations, when he divided humankind, he fixed the boundaries of the peoples according to the number of the gods (*bny yšr'l*, MT; ἄγγελων θεοῦ, LXX); [9] the LORD's own portion was his people, Jacob his allotted share.   (Deut. 32.8–9)

This passage has been something of a 'storm-centre' in the debate over the origins of, and adherence to, the monotheism of Israelite religion.[61] Briefly, the LXX implies that responsibility for each nation was given to an angel of God – presupposing *bny 'lwyn*, where the MT has *bny yšr'l*. If the original Hebrew were *bny 'lwyn* instead of *bny yšr'l*, then Deuteronomy 32.8–9 could mean that the LORD was one of the sons of the Most High, that is, the son to whom Israel was assigned. In other words, two divine beings would have been in view: (i) *Elyon* who is superior to (ii) the

---

[59] For an introduction to the *Prayer of Joseph* see Smith 'Prayer'. Note M. Smith ('Account', 743) who finds no less than five Palestinian teachers of the first century CE whose followers believed them to have been an 'appearance or incarnation of a particular supernatural power', and concludes that such belief was 'reasonably common in first century Palestine' (p. 749). A major difficulty with this proposal is its reliance on reading prior reality into later writings.

[60] Smith, 'Prayer', 60–1.

[61] See, e.g., recent discussion about non-monotheistic Israelite religion by Hayman, 'Monotheism', esp. p. 6, and Barker, *Angel*, esp. pp. 4–27.

LORD.[62] That the Hebrew may have actually been *bny ʿl[*, rather than *bny yšr'l* is suggested by a Qumran fragment.[63] Much inevitably remains speculative here: the notion that *Elyon* and 'the LORD' are parallel references to the same being must not be discounted.[64] Deuteronomy is a work noted for its monotheism so that the possibility that it includes a text which denies monotheism needs to be considered carefully.[65] What we can see, however, is that the special role envisaged in Deuteronomy 32.8–9 for the LORD over Israel is transferred to Michael in other writings such as the Book of Daniel.[66] Why and how this should be need not detain us here. What we can recognize is that since Michael takes up a role otherwise belonging to the LORD the high status of Michael within the angelic hierarchy is readily understandable.

Within the Qumran writings the 'Angel of Truth', also known as the 'Prince of Light',[67] has a special role over 'the children of righteousness'. In this the angel is contrasted with his opposite, 'the Angel of Darkness' who rules over 'the children of falsehood' (1QS 3.20–2). In carrying out this role the Prince of Light works in partnership with God: 'The Angel of Darkness leads all the children of righteousness astray . . . But the God of Israel and His Angel of Truth will succour all the sons of light' (1QS 3.20–4; cf. 1QM 13.10, 17.5–8).[68] In texts such as these there is 'a limited form of cosmic dualism' which in no way diminishes the position of God as superior to all angels.[69] Although other texts like 1QH 11.13 refer to the angels as 'the everlasting host', there is no hint or support given to the idea that the angels and God are coeval;[70] rather, God is transcendent over the Angel of Truth. Clearly, the Prince of Light corresponds to the angel Michael in respect of his function as the guardian angel of Israel,[71] but whether the Prince of Light should be identified as Michael continues to be debated.[72] The antipathy between the Angel of Truth/Prince of Light and the

[62] Eissfeldt, 'El', 28–30.
[63] Skehan, 'Fragment', 12–15, esp. p.12; cf. Barker, *Angel*, 5–11.
[64] Cf. Sir. 17.17; *Jub.* 15.31–2.
[65] Mullen, *Divine*, 204, argues for the identification of *Elyon* and the LORD.
[66] Cf. *Ps. Clem.* Recognitions 2.42 and Homilies 18.4. Note *Jub.* 15.32 which denies that any angel has been appointed over Israel.
[67] Davidson, *Angels*, 147.   [68] *DSSE*, 65. Hebrew from TAQ, 10.
[69] Davidson, *Angels*, 309.   [70] Ibid., 290.   [71] Cf. *DSSE*, 53.
[72] Yadin (*Scroll*, 235–6) argues for identification with Michael. Davidson (*Angels*, 148–9) agrees with Yadin, while arguing against identification with Uriel (so Wernberg-Møller, *Manual*, 71). Bampfylde ('Prince', 132–3) argues that since the Angel gives help 'to the kingdom of Michael' (1QM 17.6) he is not Michael. She

Angel of Darkness corresponds to that found in Apocalypse 12.7 where Michael and his angelic army fight against the dragon and his angelic army.[73]

The high status of the Angel of Truth/Prince of Light is mirrored in a passage about Melchizedek in a Hebrew text from Qumran dating from no later than 50 CE.[74]

> For this is the moment of the year of Grace for Melchizedek. [And h]e will, by his strength, judge the holy ones of God, executing judgement as it is written concerning him in the Songs of David, who said, ELOHIM [*'lwhym*] has taken his place in the divine council; in the midst of the gods [*'lwhym*] he holds judgement [Ps. 82.1]. And it was concerning him that he said, '(Let the assembly of the peoples) return to the height above them; EL (god) [*'l*] will judge the peoples [Ps. 7.7–8].'   (11QMelch)[75]

In this fragmentary document, of which we have only included a small part, Melchizedek is a heavenly being of great status, possibly to be identified with Michael,[76] but in any case with the Prince of Light.[77] Notable is the application of *'l* and *'lwhym* to Melchizedek.[78] Normally, these Hebrew words mean 'God' or 'god', but they are not always applied to deities. Note‾that (i) Moses 'as a *'lwhym*' to Aaron (Exod. 7.1); (ii) in some contexts they can mean 'judge',[79] which would be appropriate in this instance since Melchizedek executes the judgements of God; and (iii) in 1 Samuel 28.13, *'lwhym* refers to the ghost of Samuel. In Psalm 82 itself *'lwhym* is used for both 'God' (the Most High, the

---

equates him with the 'Prince of Hosts' in Daniel 8.11 and the 'man' in Daniel 10.5–6.

[73] On parallels between the Apocalypse and Qumran writings see Böcher, 'Johannes-Apokalypse', 3894–7; Comblin, *Christ*, 106–19.

[74] Horton, *Melchizedek*, 73, 80.

[75] *DSSE*, 301 = lines 9–11a of text given in De Jonge and van der Woude, '11Q Melchizedek', 302.

[76] De Jonge and van der Woude (ibid., 305) note that this identification is not made explicit in available Qumran texts; explicit identification is only found in certain medieval Jewish texts; cf. Dunn, *Christology*, 152–3; Horton, *Melchizedek*, 81.

[77] So Bampfylde, 'Prince', 133.

[78] Horton, *Melchizedek*, 75. Carmignac ('Le document') argues that the Qumran author means God, not Melchizedek, when *'lwhym* and *'l* are used in scriptural quotations; cf. response from Delcor, 'Melchizedek', 133–4; Segal, *Powers*, 194. .

[79] *DSSE*, 300.

God of Israel) and for the 'gods' (divine beings subordinate to God; cf. *bny 'lywn*, 82.6) – clearly this psalm expresses a theology which is closer to Israel's early faith than to her later monotheism.[80] Given the unlikelihood that 11QMelch would affirm more than one deity, it seems best to suppose that its author interprets the 'gods' of Psalm 82 to be the angels[81] and that Melchizedek is one of them,[82] albeit their chief. Certainly, there is no reason to think that the author of 11QMelch would have thought of Melchizedek as another divine being alongside the deity.[83] Thus it is extraordinary that Melchizedek is called *'l* and *'lwhym*. Presumably, this is in recognition that Melchizedek's role is analogous to, say, the angel of the LORD on those occasions in the OT when he acts, speaks, and inspires reaction as though it were God actually present.[84] In particular, Melchizedek's role appears to be analogous to the angel who stands in for God in the heavenly council in Zechariah 3.1.

Melchizedek's role in 11QMelch is predominantly *judging*, but in two different texts an angel, described as 'the angel of the presence', has an important role in the *saving* of Israel. Isaiah 63.9, according to one reading, says of Israel:

> In all their distress he was distressed; the angel of his presence saved them (*bkl srtm l' sr wml'k pnyw hwsy'm*); in his love and in his pity he redeemed them; he lifted them up and carried them all the days of old.

This reading corresponds to one pointing of the first five words which we have cited in Hebrew, but with a different pointing another reading is possible, one which corresponds to the LXX:

---

[80] Kselman and Barré, 'Psalms', 540.

[81] Cf. 4Q491 fr.11: 'I [= Michael] am reckoned among the gods' (*'ny 'm 'lym 'thsb*) (*DJD*, and vii, 27).

[82] De Jonge and van der Woude, '11Q Melchizedek', 304, 321–2. Cf. Fitzmyer, 'Light', 37; Milik, '*Milkî-sedeq*', 95–144. On Melchizedek as an angel see also Laubscher, 'Angel', 51. On the early Christian belief that Melchizedek was an angel, rather than a man see De Jonge and van der Woude, '11Q Melchizedek', 323–6.

[83] Cf. Casey, *Jewish*, 93. Contrast 11QMelch with 4Q403 1 i 30–46 which speaks of *'lwhym* (e.g. lines 31, 32, 33), but in a context where the *'lwhym* are urged to praise God. Newsom (*Songs*, 211–12) translates *'lwhym* as 'godlike beings'.

[84] Horton (*Melchizedek*, 77) suggests that *'lwhym* applied to Melchizedek indicates that 'he was regarded as some sort of super-human figure'.

in all their distress. It was no messenger or angel (ἐκ πάσης θλίψεως οὐ πρέσβυς οὐδὲ ἄγγελος) but his presence that saved them.

The variant readings are evidence of a significant debate over whether God acted alone or through an agent.[85] That some Jews believed that God did act through an agent designated the 'angel of the presence' is supported by consideration of a passage from *Jubilees* 48. The *Book of Jubilees* is for the most part a retelling of Genesis 1.1 to Exodus 15.22. It was originally composed in Hebrew, although the only complete text extant is in Ethiopic.[86] Paleographic dating of fragments found at Qumran point to a date prior to 100 BCE.[87] On internal grounds a date between *c.* 163 and *c.* 140 BCE has been proposed.[88] *Jubilees* unveils a developed angelology, with a notable emphasis on angels with responsibility for different aspects of nature (2.2).[89] One angel in particular stands out because of his role as the revealer of the content of the book (1.27, 2.1). This angel is described as 'the angel of the presence who went before the camp of Israel' (1.29).[90] In *Jubilees* 48 this angel retells the story of Exodus 7–14. Of special interest to us are these verses:

> And despite all the signs and wonders, Prince Mastema was not shamed until he had become strong and called to the Egyptians so that they might pursue after you with all the army of Egyptians with their chariots, and with their horses, and with all the multitude of the people of Egypt. [13] And I stood between the Egyptians and Israel, and we delivered them out through the midst of the sea as through dry land. [14] And all the people whom he brought out to pursue after Israel, the Lord our God threw into the middle of the sea . . . [18] And on the fourteenth day we bound him so that he might not accuse the children of Israel . . .   (*Jub.* 48.12–14,18)[91]

[85] Stier, *Gott*, 153–5.   [86] Cf. VanderKam, *Studies*, 95.
[87] Wintermute, *OTP*, ii, 43.
[88] VanderKam (*Studies*, 283) prefers a date between *c.* 163 and *c.* 152 BCE; Wintermute, *OTP*, ii, 44, suggests a date between 161 and 140 BCE.
[89] Wintermute, *OTP*, ii, 55. For Ethiopic text see VanderKam, *Jubilees: A Critical Text*.
[90] Fossum (*Name*, 260) argues that this angel is Michael (on the basis of, e.g., 1 *Enoch* 60).
[91] Wintermute, *OTP*, ii, 139–40.

The angel's description of his own role in foiling the intentions of Mastema takes up an element present in the Book of Exodus itself (cf. 'the angel of God who was going before the Israelite army moved and went behind them', Exod. 14.19); but in *Jubilees* this element is extended. In Exodus 7–14, on a number of occasions, the principal intervening figure on Israel's side is the LORD (e.g. Exod. 11.1, 12.29, 14.21), so that the angel of God seems almost incidental to the action. By contrast, in *Jubilees* the angel acts in partnership with God, and plays a major role in the support of Israel. It is true that the angel nevertheless signifies that the principal actor is still God (e.g. *Jub.* 48.14), but an altogether different impression is conveyed in *Jubilees* from that in Exodus.

Here, then, is an example, well before the Christian era, which represents a belief in God working in partnership with an angel: the angel is central rather than incidental to the action. Whether this kind of view has provoked the antithetical reading of Isaiah 63.9 which asserts that it was 'no messenger or angel but his presence that saved them', or whether it is drawn from the reading of Isaiah 63.9 as 'the angel of his presence saved them', we cannot be sure. Nor is it easy to determine the exact status of the angel in *Jubilees* when 15.32 explicitly expresses the view that God has not appointed an angel over Israel but rules Israel directly.

So what is the significance of *Jubilees* 48? Hayman, for instance, has argued that it is 'just one example of how Jewish angelology reveals a pattern of religion that is anything but monotheistic'.[92] But is this a fair comment? The angel is not worshipped nor is he ever presented as the equal of God. Rather, his equal (and opposite) is Mastema.[93] The angel's use of the first-person plural implies cooperation between God and the angel, but there is no reason to think that this has any implication that the angel actually enjoys divine status.[94]

No survey of 'principal angels' is complete without consideration of Metatron. The texts reporting his existence and activity are all post-first-century CE. 3 *Enoch* (also known as *Sefer ha-Hekhalot*), for example, dates from well past the end of the first century

---

[92] Hayman, 'Monotheism', 8.

[93] Note the parallel situation with God, the Angel of Truth and the Prince of Darkness in Qumran literature discussed above.

[94] Gammie ('Dualism', 368–9) argues that this is 'ethical dualism', reflecting the battle between good and evil in *Jubilees*. Note that Hurtado, *God*, Rowland, *Heaven*, and Barker, *Angel*, fail to discuss the implications of *Jub.* 48.

CE.[95] According to *b. Hag.*15a traditions involving Metatron may
date from early in the second century CE since the visionary
involved in the events it describes, Aher (*alias* Elisha ben Abuya),
lived *c.* 110–35 CE. Whether the story actually dates from such a
period (or even earlier) is another matter.[96] It is not necessary here
to discuss fully all references to Metatron and the many questions
which this controversial figure raises. In what follows we use 3
Enoch to demonstrate briefly why Metatron demands consideration
in a survey of principal angels and to show how Metatron
represents a significant development in speculation about the status
of the chief angel.

According to 3 *Enoch* 1.4 Metatron is God's 'servant, the angel
Metatron, Prince of the Divine Presence'.[97] But he is no ordinary
angel: for example, in 3 *Enoch* 4.2 we are told that Metatron is
Enoch![98] In 3 *Enoch* 8 Metatron is bestowed with qualities such as
wisdom and holiness, while in chapter 9 he is blessed, enlarged in
stature, and given every splendour and brightness. In 10.1 Metatron
receives 'a throne like the throne of glory', and in 10.3–5 the Holy
One appoints Metatron as his vice-regent, as 'a prince and a ruler
over all the denizens of the heights', with the tasks of hearing
whatever any angel or prince has to say in God's presence, and to
command things in the name of God. In 12.5 Metatron is called
'the lesser YHWH', a name which is explicitly connected with the
angel of Exodus 23.21 of whom YHWH said 'My name shall be in
him'.[99] All of these factors contribute to the background of the
following dramatic story.

> At first I [Metatron] sat upon a great throne at the door of
> the seventh palace, and I judged all the denizens of the
> heights on the authority of the Holy One, blessed be he . . .
> ²But when Aher came to behold the vision of the chariot

[95] Alexander, *OTP*, i, 229. Cf. Odeberg, *Enoch*, 41: 'the latter half of the third
century CE'; Gruenwald (*Apocalyptic*, 196) 'compiled . . . probably in the 6th
century CE'.
[96] Segal (*Powers*, 60) argues that the tradition is a 'late addition to the Babylonian
Talmud'. On the origin of Metatron traditions, see Scholem, *Gnosticism*, 43–8;
Odeberg, *Enoch*, 79–146; Gruenwald, *Apocalyptic*, 195–8; Lieberman, 'Metatron'.
[97] Alexander, *OTP*, i, 256.
[98] Gruenwald (*Apocalyptic*, 195) notes that this is the only occasion in *Hekhalot*
literature that Enoch is identified with Metatron, and notes that (p. 200) only in
Tg. Ps.- J. Gen. 5.24 is such identification made elsewhere in midrashic and
talmudic literature.
[99] Cf. *b. Sanh.* 38b.

and set eyes upon me, he was afraid and trembled before me. His soul was alarmed to the point of leaving him because of his fear, dread and terror of me, when he saw me seated upon a throne like a king, with the ministering angels standing beside me as servants and all the princes of the kingdoms crowned with crowns surrounding me. ³Then he opened his mouth and said, 'There are indeed two powers in heaven'. ⁴Immediately a divine voice came out from the presence of the Šekinah and said, 'Come back to me, apostate sons, apart from Aḥer.' ⁵Then 'Anapi'el YHWH, the honoured, glorified, beloved, wonderful, terrible and dreadful Prince, came at the command of the Holy One, blessed be he, and struck me with sixty lashes of fire and made me stand on my feet.   (3 *Enoch* 16.1–5)[100]

The fact that Metatron is identified with Enoch and is called 'the lesser YHWH' suggests that he may represent a fusion of the exalted patriarch Enoch (cf. 1 *Enoch* 71.14) with the angel Yahoel (*Apoc. Abr.* 10).[101] In any case, the speculation about the status of angels and exalted patriarchs such as Yahoel and Enoch has gone beyond the point where their non-divine status is upheld. Although the story specifically emphasizes that there is only one power in heaven,[102] it does so by the device of reporting the speculation of a visionary that there are 'two powers in heaven'. Such an explicit reference to the normally unmentionable possibility for committed monotheists strongly suggests an audience in view which was not upholding the non-divine status of the chief angel. In other words, the story we have cited reflects a situation in which heretical angel speculation was becoming a problem (from a monotheistic perspective). If this speculation developed after Yahoelic and Enochic traditions recorded in the *Apocalypse of Abraham* and the *Similitudes of Enoch* began circulating, then it probably developed from the second century CE onwards, since both works probably stem from no earlier than the mid- to late first century CE.[103]

---

[100] Alexander, *OTP*, i, 268. Cf. *b. Hag.* 15a. The two versions are set out in parallel in Rowland, *Heaven*, 335–6; see also discussion in Gruenwald, *Apocalyptic*, 205–6.

[101] Alexander, *OTP*, i, 244.

[102] Cf. Segal, *Powers*, 102; Odeberg, *Enoch*, 85–6. Note *b. Sanh.* 38b which rejects the notion that Metatron can be worshipped.

[103] Scholem (*Trends*, 44) suggests the merger may have been as late as the third or fourth centuries CE; Gruenwald (*Apocalyptic*, 200) views the exaltation of Enoch

We have so far concentrated our attention on angelology in Jewish apocalypses and related literature. When we turn to the NT (excluding the Apocalypse) we find that angels are very much the subordinates of God. There is no confusion as to whether a given encounter with an 'angel of the Lord' is actually a direct encounter with God. In descriptions of such encounters there is no attempt made to worship the angel, and the title 'the angel of the Lord' does not appear to be applied to any one angel, but is used as a title for distinctive angels of God.[104] In the NT (excluding the Apocalypse) 'angels' (plural) are mentioned on some sixty occasions, so that the idea that angels are an important feature of God's world is well attested. In the light of this observation, it is striking to find that there is so little material concerning the more important angels (e.g. Michael is only mentioned in Jude 9). This paucity suggests that either Jesus was held to have made the role of these angels redundant or that, in view of the glory and exaltation of Jesus to God's right hand, angels were of less importance as mediators between God and humanity.

From our survey we may conclude that principal angels before the end of the first century CE were known to occupy roles as representative of God, and even as (junior) partner to God. But it is probably only beyond this period that an angel was recognized (by some) as a second power alongside God in heaven. We have also observed that angels were believed to function in two ways which corresponded to (developing) early Christian beliefs about Jesus Christ. First, angels could appear to be human, and, in one case, even appear to have become incarnate in an ancient patriarch. Secondly, angels could act in partnership with God, represent God as a kind of vizier, and even be designated 'God'.

The worship of angels?

None of the texts we have examined so far can reasonably be construed as implying that angels were worshipped by Jews prior to the rise of Christianity. The case of Metatron suggests that concomitant developments to the worship of angels, such as the claim

as a polemic against Christianity; Segal (*Powers*, 63–4) sees the origins for the mediating principal angel in the first century CE but cannot demonstrate that this angel was identified with Metatron.

[104] Hirth, *Boten*, 29–30.

that there were 'two powers' in heaven, probably stem from a period later than the first century CE. It is true that a (possibly) late first-century CE document, *Kerygma Petrou*, refers to 'Jews . . . worshipping angels'.[105] But this is likely to be a pejorative characterization of Jewish cultic practice rather than an accurate description of the actual situation.[106] With respect to the well-known reference in Colossians 2.18 to the θρησκείᾳ τῶν ἀγγέλων, we may note that it has been plausibly argued that this refers to the worship performed by angels (cf. the Angel Liturgy at Qumran)[107] rather than to humans worshipping angels.[108]

This and other relevant literature normally cited in support of the claim that angels were worshipped in 'Greco-Roman Jewish Circles' has been examined by Hurtado.[109] He concludes that there is no evidence to imply that the worship of angels was 'a regular part of ancient Jewish cultic practice'. Nevertheless, Hurtado recognizes that it would be unwise to presume that no ancient Jew ever compromised monotheism by participating in the worship of angels.[110] Rainbow, in his review article of Hurtado's book, *One God, One Lord*, agrees with Hurtado's assessment although he questions Hurtado's argument as 'not altogether convincing'.[111] In its place Rainbow offers a different argument which concludes that any angel worship which may have taken place must have been 'a declension from a socially shared ideal'. Rainbow suggests that the fact 'εἷς and μόνος formulae' are reserved for God alone within Judaism (in contrast to pagan applications of these formulae to plural gods and goddesses) corroborates this conclusion.[112] Finally, we may note the important works of Bauckham and Stuckenbruck who both argue that the motif of the angel who refuses to be worshipped was a sign of

---

[105] Schneelmelcher, *NTA*, ii, 100. Idem., 95, dates *Kerygma Petrou* to between 80 and 110 CE.

[106] Hurtado, *God*, 33–4.   [107] Found in Newsom, *Songs*; *DSSE*, 221–30.

[108] Francis, 'Humility', 126–34.   [109] Hurtado, *God*, 28–34.

[110] Ibid., 35.

[111] Rainbow, 'Monotheism', 83, who notes *Bib. Ant.* 13.6 as a text overlooked by Hurtado (though this text scarcely amounts to sufficient reason to reject Hurtado). Also overlooked are those texts in the *Similitudes of Enoch* in which the son of man figure or Chosen One is apparently worshipped (1 *Enoch* 48.5, 62.6,9). The 'worship' could be explained as the worship of an eschatological figure (cf. Rainbow's discussion of this, 'Monotheism', 88, n. 22) or as 'eschatological subjection' of men to God's vicegerent (Bauckham, 'Worship', 339, n. 47).

[112] Rainbow, 'Monotheism', 83, with literature cited in n. 14.

concern that in the increasing acceptance of angelophanies lay the possibility of monotheistic worship being diluted.[113] Significantly for our primary concern in this monograph, both Bauckham and Stuckenbruck argue that within the Apocalypse the refusal of the angel to be worshipped (Apc. 19.10, 22.8–9) is unlikely to be a polemic against an angel cult in Asia Minor.[114]

Conclusions

We have examined a number of angels who conduct the affairs of God not as mere underlings but as powerful ministers within the divine government. We have observed, for example, that some angelophanies are reminiscent of theophanies; that Yahoel has the divine name, while Melchizedek is designated *'lwhym*; and that the angel of the presence, according to *Jubilees* 48, talks of acting with God in terms of 'we'. We have also seen how some angels, such as Raphael and Jacob-Israel, open out the possibility of a powerful angel coming to earth and either feigning human appearance or indwelling a known figure in order to function in the service of God. It is noticeable, however, that the power, majesty, and closeness to God of these angels probably did not result in any of them being worshipped or acclaimed as a second power in heaven before the end of the first century CE. We do not (and cannot) claim that angels were never worshipped or acclaimed by some Jews and Christians on some occasions before 100 CE; but we can observe that such practices seem to have had a minimal impact on the apocalypses and related writings which feature glorious angels of high status. We have also observed that there is no consistent identity for the chief angel. Thus there is no reason to think that one angelic figure was the subject of widespread speculation about sharing in divine status or standing alongside God as an equal. The variety of angels observed in the position of chief angel, and the fact that in some cases four or seven angels form the leading group of angels, suggests that the significance of an apparent dualism between God and one outstanding angel should not be exaggerated.

In short: although glorious in form and exalted in status, the angels we have considered push at the boundaries of monotheism

---

[113] Bauckham, 'Worship', 322–4; Stuckenbruck, 'Refusal', 679–89.
[114] Bauckham, ibid., 327–31; Stuckenbruck, ibid., 692–5.

but in the end do not break it before the second century CE (and even then with a strong and vigorous response). In other words, the angelology which influenced the christology of the Apocalypse was, in all likelihood, an angelology in which an angel was an angel and not a divine being.

4

ANGELOMORPHIC FIGURES

In this chapter we extend our study of the angelological context of the Apocalypse's christology to include the study of figures who may be compared with angels in some way. First, we examine accounts of exalted humans – both those who appear in glorious form like the angels we have just considered in chapter 3 and those who do not have their form described but whose status is comparable with that of the principal angels. Our special interest is in those whose form is similar to the risen Jesus in Apocalypse 1.13–16. Secondly, we consider the *Logos* in writings which speak of him as an angelomorphic figure.

Exalted humans

The first human figure we consider is Adam. In the *Testament of Abraham*, Abraham sees a glorious figure whose appearance 'was terrifying, like the Master's' (11.5). Abraham inquires of Michael as to the identity of 'this most wondrous man' (11.9) and is told that it is 'the first former Adam who is in such glory' (11.10).[1] Specific details of the form of the figure are not given.[2] Speculation of this kind about Adam as the glorious archetypal man has been drawn into discussion of (so-called) Adam christology in recent years.[3] References in texts such as *Adam and Eve* 13–16[4] to the worship of Adam as 'the image of God' have fuelled hypotheses concerning the worship of Adam as a precursor to the worship of

---

[1] E. P. Sanders, *OTP*, i, 888. Note also 4Q504 fr. 8: 'Thou has fashioned A[dam], our [f]ather in the likeness of [Thy] glory' (*DSSE*, 220).

[2] On the *Testament of Abraham* see Nickelsburg, *Studies*.

[3] Cf. Dunn, *Christology*, 98–128, with further refences in notes, pp. 305–15.

[4] M. D. Johnson, *OTP*, ii, 252, dates *Adam and Eve* to the end of the first century CE. This does not preclude its preservation of earlier traditions.

Christ.[5] A tendency to suppose the existence of an 'Adam speculation' or 'Adam myth' in ancient Judaism has been criticized recently
by Levison who argues that diversity, rather than unity, is the
characteristic of portraits of Adam in texts dated between 200 BCE
and 135 CE.[6] The corollary of this conclusion is that caution needs
to be exercised before presuming that worship of Adam was a
widespread phenomenon in pre-Christian Judaism.[7] For example,
Steenburg, who specifically addresses the question of the worship
of Adam as an influence on the worship of Christ,[8] does not
adequately account for the fact that the worship of Adam in *Adam
and Eve* 13 results from God's command rather than from a
perception that Adam was a divine being.

Another early patriarchal figure, Abel, is the subject of one of the
more detailed epiphanic accounts in the *Testament of Abraham*:

> And between the two gates there stood a terrifying throne
> with the appearance of terrifying crystal, flashing like fire. [5]
> And upon it sat a wondrous man, bright as the sun, like
> unto a son of God.[9]

> καὶ ἐν μέσῳ τῶν δύο πυλῶν ἵστατο θρόνος φοβερὸς ἐν
> εἴδει κρυτάλλου φοβεροῦ ἐξαστράπτουν ὡς πῦρ [5]καὶ ἐπ᾽
> αὐτῷ ἐκάθητο ἀνὴρ θαύμαστος ἡλιόρατος ὅμοιος υἱῷ
> θεοῦ.   (*Test. Abr.* Rec. A 12.4–5)[10]

Describing Abel as 'like a son of God' implies that he is like one of
the angels.[11] This may be contrasted with the description of an
angel or heavenly being as 'like a (son of) man' (e.g. Ezek. 1.26;

[5] E.g. Steenburg, 'Worship'. Steenburg *(ibid.*, 95) points out that Hurtado,
God, overlooks the worship of Adam as 'a crucial warrant for the worship
of Christ'. Dunn (*Christology*, 98–128), does not discuss the worship of
Adam.

[6] Levison, *Portraits*, esp. pp. 13–14, 159–60.

[7] The author is grateful to Professor L. Hurtado for drawing his attention to
Steenburg's and Levison's discussions of this matter.

[8] Steenburg, 'Worship', 96–107.

[9] Sanders, *OTP*, i, 889. Date: Sanders (*OTP*, i, 875), *c.*100 CE; Kalenkow,
('Angelology', 157) argues for a second-century CE date; Turner (*AOT*, 394–5)
argues for an original testament dating from the beginning of the first century CE
with Recension B dating from the third century CE, and Recension A from the
sixth century CE.

[10] Greek text from Stone, *Testament*, 28.

[11] Cf. *Asc. Isa.* 9.9. Philo (*Sac.* 5) describes Abraham as one who 'inherited
incorruption and became equal to the angels' (ἴσος ἀγγέλοις γεγονώς).

Daniel 7.13, 10.5,16).[12] The epiphany of Abel, as with some
angelophanies, incorporates theophanic elements. Thus 'a terrifying
throne with the appearance of terrifying crystal, flashing like fire'
may be compared with the throne-theophanies in Ezekiel 1.4–26
and in 1 *Enoch* 14.8–24.[13] The incorporation of such theophanic
elements does not, however, appear to imply divine status for Abel.

In the previous chapters we have already mentioned Enoch.
The considerable speculation about his life which is reflected in
subsequent Enochic literature and elsewhere is due to the extraordinary account in Genesis 5.24 that Enoch did not die but was
simply taken from life on earth by God. In the corpus of writings
known as 1 *Enoch* the patriarch is a central figure, principally as
the seer of the visions revealed therein. But many scholars hold
that the son of man figure first revealed in 1 *Enoch* 46.3 is
subsequently revealed to be Enoch himself in 71.14.[14] Charles,
believing this to be anomalous, suggested an emendation to the
text, but this proposal has been generally thought to be dubious.[15]
Recently, Collins has argued that the supposed identification is
problematic.[16] In brief, he argues that 1 *Enoch* 70.1 makes a clear
distinction between Enoch and the heavenly son of man, and that
the son of man in 71.14, who 'was born in righteousness', is
different from the son of man in 46.3 who 'has' righteousness.
Collins concludes that 'Enoch, then, is a human being in the
likeness of the heavenly Son of Man, and is exalted to share his
destiny'.[17] Thus Collins cautions against readily assuming that
71.14 represents a set of beliefs that a human being could be
exalted to the preeminent position in heaven (i.e. apart from that
held by God). Nevertheless, 3 *Enoch* 4.2 and *Targum Pseudo-
Jonathan* Genesis 5.24 clearly identify Enoch with Metatron,[18]
which suggests that some ancient interpreters knew of a tradition
in which Enoch was exalted to the highest position in heaven.[19]
Finally, we may note that the glorious angelomorphic form of

[12] Cf. Kim, *Origin*, 211–12.   [13] Knight, *Disciples*, 89.
[14] Cf. Collins, 'Son', 453.
[15] Charles, *APOT*, ii, 237; cf. Collins, 'Son', 453.
[16] Ibid., 453–9. Cf. Collins, 'Representative', 111–33; contrast with Casey ('Use', 22–3) who affirms the identity between Enoch and the son of man.
[17] Collins, 'Son', 455–7, citation from p. 457.   [18] Odeberg, *Enoch*, 80.
[19] Cf. 1Qap Gen. 2.20: 'he shared the lot [of the angels]' (so *DSSE*, 253), where Enoch appears to be less than the highest ranked heavenly figure. Note also 2 *Enoch* 22.6: the angelification of Enoch?

Enoch is described briefly in one of the later apocalypses: 'an old man whose face shone like the sun' (*Apoc. Paul* 20).[20]

Noah is another patriarch who takes on radiant form and enjoys great status. The following description in the (so-called) 'Epistle of Enoch' describes his form as a newborn baby:

> And his body was white as snow and red as a rose; the hair of his head as white as wool and his *demdema*[21] beautiful; and as for his eyes, when he opened them the whole house glowed like the sun – (rather) the whole house glowed even more exceedingly. [3]And when he arose from the hands of the midwife, he opened his mouth and spoke to the Lord with righteousness. [4]And his father, Lamech, was afraid of him and fled and went to Methuselah his father; [5]and he said to him, 'I have begotten a strange son: He is not like an (ordinary) human being, but he looks like the children of the angels of heaven to me; his form is different, and he is not like us. His eyes are like the rays of the sun, and his face glorious. [6]It does not seem to me that he is of me, but of angels; and I fear that a wondrous phenomenon may take place upon the earth in his days.' (1 *Enoch* 106.2–6)[22]

The angelic appearance of Noah shocks Lamech and leads him to conjecture whether he is really his son or 'of the angels'. But Enoch is able to reassure Lamech (via Methuselah) that Noah is, in fact, his son (1 *Enoch* 106.7–19). In other words, Noah is a human with angelomorphic form. Various details of Noah's form are familiar from angelophanies and theophanies which we have already discussed. The comparison of the body 'as white as snow', for example, recalls the Ancient of Days in Daniel 7.9 ('his clothing was white as snow'), while the additional comparative image for Noah's body, 'red as a rose', may reflect the fact that this epiphany is about a newborn baby.[23] The description of Noah's hair, 'white as wool', also corresponds to the theophany in Daniel 7.9 ('the hair

---

[20] Duensing, *NTA*, ii, 771.

[21] Isaac, *OTP*, i, 86 note g: 'This Eth. word has no equivalent in English. It refers to . . . what one calls . . . "afro" in colloquial English.'

[22] Ibid. For Greek version (which does not represent the original language of 1 *Enoch* 106) see Black, *Graece*, 43. For reconstructed Aramaic text see Milik, *Enoch*, 207; cf. Fitzmyer, *Genesis*, 167.

[23] Note that the later writing, (*Akhmim* or Greek) *Apoc. Peter* (a secondary edited version of the Apocalypse dating from *c.* 133 CE which is best preserved in Ethiopic), describes the bodies of Moses and Elias as 'whiter than any snow and

of his head like pure wool'). Reminiscence of Daniel 7.9 in the imagery discussed so far would be well complemented by reminiscence of Daniel 10.5–6 in the remainder of the epiphany. But in fact the influence of Daniel 10.5–6 appears to be minimal if not non-existent. The eyes of Noah, for instance, are compared to the 'rays of the sun' (cf. comparison with 'fire' in Daniel 10.6)[24] – 'sun' imagery in 1 *Enoch* 106.2,5 could have been influenced instead by 1 *Enoch* 14.18,20 – and the face of Noah is simply 'glorious' (cf. 'like lightning' in Daniel 10.6). In fact the descriptions of Noah's eyes and face are more similar to that of the glorious angels in *Joseph and Aseneth* and the *Apocalypse of Zephaniah* (cf. 'his eyes were like the light of the sun', *Jos. and Asen.* 14.9; 'his face shining like the rays of the sun in its glory', *Apoc. Zeph.* 6.11).

The dating of 1 *Enoch* 106 makes it unlikely, however, that the description of Noah is dependent on the angelophanies in *Joseph and Aseneth* 14.8–9 and *Apocalypse of Zephaniah* 6.11–15. Some scholars have dated 1 *Enoch* 106 as early as the period prior to 161 BCE[25] but a more likely period of composition is the first century BCE.[26] If the composition was in the earlier period then the similarities between 1 *Enoch* 106.2 and Daniel 7.9 could be due to common dependency on a third source, such as 1 *Enoch* 14.18–20, which includes a comparison with snow. The comparisons 'white as wool', 'white as snow', and 'like the sun' in the description of Noah are, in fact, significant. If they represent the influence of Daniel 7.9 and/or 1 *Enoch* 14.18–20 then these comparisons are applied to a figure who is not divine. Noah is (so to speak) superhuman, but Lamech draws the conclusion that he is angel-like rather than God-like. The significance of the epiphany of Noah is that it cautions against assuming that the presence of comparisons with wool, snow, and sun in the description of an exalted figure carries with it the implication that the figure is divine.[27]

---

redder than any rose' (Duensing, *NTA*, ii, 681). Other parallels between the two accounts may be drawn.

[24] The comparison with the sun may reflect traditions concerning the astral gods, Sunya, Mitra, and Varuna (Gressmann, *Ursprung*, 111).

[25] So Charles, *APOT*, ii, 168. Collins (*Apocalyptic*, 53) suggests pre-160 BCE is plausible, though not certain.

[26] Milik (*Enoch*, 5, 56–7, 59) suggests 100–1 BCE on the basis of fragments found at Qumran. See now Nickelsburg (*ABD*, ii, 512) who assesses the Qumran evidence as indicating a date 'before the middle of the first century BCE'.

[27] For other 'birth legends' of Noah see Josephus, *Ant.* 1.72–108; *Jub.* 4–10; 1Qap Gen. 2; and 1 Q19 fr. 3 (*DJD* i, 84–6). Cf. discussion in Fitzmyer, 'Elect', 371, and

In our examination of the angel Jacob-Israel in the *Prayer of Joseph* (cf. pp. 64–5) we saw that his form is not described. But in *Joseph and Aseneth* the patriarch Jacob appears to Aseneth in angelomorphic form:

> And Aseneth saw him and was amazed at his beauty, because Jacob was exceedingly beautiful to look at, and his old age (was) like the youth of a handsome (young) man, and his head was all white as snow (ἡ κεφαλὴ αὐτοῦ πᾶσα λευκὴ ὡσεὶ χιών), and the hairs of his head were all exceedingly close and thick like (those) of an Ethiopian, and his beard (was) white reaching down to his breast, and his eyes (were) flashing and darting (flashes of) lightning (οἱ ὀφθαλμοὶ αὐτοῦ χαροποιοὶ καὶ ἐξαστράπτοντες), and his sinews and his shoulders and his arms were like (those) of an angel, and his thighs and his calves and his feet like (those) of a giant. And Jacob was like a man who had wrestled with God.   (*Jos. and Asen.* 22.7)[28]

This passage is found in the A (i.e. longer) recension but not in the D (i.e. shorter) recension, and inviting the suggestion that it is an addition to the original story, and thus possibly to be dated after 138 CE – a probable *terminus ad quem* for *Joseph and Aseneth*.[29] Even if this story is part of the original material then the period allowed for its dating makes it possible that this text draws on the Apocalypse and is therefore of less significance for our study. Nevertheless, the description of Jacob appears to be sufficiently different from any of the epiphanies in the Apocalypse for us to conclude that its composition is likely to be independent of the Apocalypse. There are, in fact, a number of interesting features in this epiphany. First, the description of Jacob's head, ἡ κεφαλὴ αὐτοῦ πᾶσα λευκὴ ὡσεὶ χιών, differs from Daniel 7.9 where the clothing of the Ancient of Days is likened to snow (cf. 1 *Enoch* 14.20) and the head is likened to pure wool. The description corresponds more closely to those of Yahoel's head, 'the hair of his

---

VanderKam, *Enoch*, 174–7. Hultgard ('Judentum', 551) relates the birth legends of Noah to the birth of Zarathustra.

[28] Burchard, *OTP*, ii, 238. Greek from Burchard's reconstructed text in Denis, *Concordance*, 857, col. i.

[29] Burchard ('Importance', 104) suggests a *terminus ad quem* no later than 117–38 CE (the reign of Hadrian), but possibly no later than 98–117 CE (the reign of Trajan), and a *terminus a quo* no earlier than 100 BCE.

head like snow' (*Apoc. Abr.* 11.2), and the risen Christ's head and hair, ἡ δὲ κεφαλὴ αὐτοῦ καὶ αἱ τρίχες λευκαὶ ὡς ἔριον λευκὸν ὡς χιών (Apc. 1.14).

Secondly, the description of the eyes of Jacob, 'and his eyes (were) flashing and darting (flashes of) lightning' is reminiscent of Daniel 10.6 ('his face like lightning, his eyes like flaming torches') and Ezekiel 1 – 'fire flashing forth continually' (v. 4) and 'The living creatures darted to and fro, like a flash of lightning' (v. 14; cf. v. 13). Only Ezekiel 1.4 LXX, however, has a common descriptive term ('εξαστράπτον) with *Joseph and Aseneth* 22.7. Since nothing else about the appearance of Jacob suggests the influence of Daniel 10.5–6 it would appear, as in the case of Noah, that the influence of Daniel 10.5–6 on this epiphany is minimal if not non-existent.

Thirdly, the additional detail concerning the thickness of the hair recalls the use of the word *demdema* in the description of Noah's hair (1 *Enoch* 106.2), but otherwise there is no reason to assume that Jacob's description has been influenced by 1 *Enoch* 106. Fourthly, Jacob has a beard, unlike the Ancient of Days, the risen Jesus, Noah, Yahoel, and the angel in *Joseph and Aseneth* 14.8–9. But beards are not unknown on exalted patriarchs (cf. Adam in *Test. Abr.* 11.6). And finally, some parts of the form are clearly influenced by the known wrestling prowess of Jacob.

There is no reason given, however, to think that Jacob here has divine attributes. He is a glorious, impressive-looking man who is compared in part to an angel. The description of Jacob in glorious form is interesting in its own right, but its significance for our project lies in the fact that once again the epiphany of a non-divine figure shares imagery with theophanies (i.e. 'snow' in Dan. 7.9 and 1 *Enoch* 14.20).

Jacob is not the only notable resplendent human figure in *Joseph and Aseneth*. In *Joseph and Aseneth* 5.5–7 Joseph wears magnificent royal robes and a golden crown (cf. 21.5). But a feature worth noting is in 5.4 where the horses pulling Joseph's chariot are described as 'white as snow'.[30] In 18.5–8 Aseneth herself appears in glorious form in the course of preparing to marry Joseph. She also has a golden crown (18.6; cf. 21.5), but the description of her appearance has more in common than Joseph's with the kinds of epiphanic accounts we have been considering. Thus, her robe is

---

[30] Cf. *Jos. and Asen.* 16.8, 'honeycomb . . . white as snow', and 16.18, 'the bees were white as snow'.

'like lightning in appearance' (18.5), she has a 'golden . . . girdle' (18.6; cf. Dan. 10.5), and her face is 'like the sun' (18.8; cf. Apc. 1.16, 10.1).[31] Aseneth's physical transformation symbolizes her conversion to the faith of Israel,[32] and she becomes a creature not dissimilar to an angel (see 20.6).[33] Before we leave *Joseph and Aseneth*, we should note one further feature of the epiphanies recorded there. In the descriptions of the glorious appearances of (i) the angel, (ii) Aseneth, and (iii) Jacob, a different comparison is used in each case for the hair and the eyes. Thus, for the hair we find (i) 'like a flame of fire of a burning torch' (14.9), (ii) 'like a vine in the paradise of God prospering in its fruits' (18.9), (iii) 'all exceedingly close and thick like (those) of an Ethiopian' (22.7); and for the eyes we find (i) 'like sunshine' (14.9), (ii) 'like a rising morning star' (18.9), and (iii) 'flashing and darting (flashes of) lightning' (22.7). Once again, we have an example of the author(s) exhibiting a degree of freedom in the use of epiphanic motifs while operating with a limited stock of imagery.

The next patriarchal figure to concern us is Moses. We cannot here go into all the material which is available about Moses as an exalted human,[34] but in *The Exagoge of Ezekiel the Tragedian* and in the writings of Philo we have sufficient evidence for the belief that Moses attained an extraordinary position in relation to God. In *The Exagoge*, a second-century BCE text,[35] Moses has a vision in which he sees a throne at the top of Mt Sinai:

> 70   Upon it sat a man of noble mien
> 71   becrowned and with a scepter in one hand
> 72   while with the other he did beckon me.
> 73   I made approach and stood before the throne.
> 74   He handed over the scepter and he bade
> 75   me mount the throne and gave to me the crown;
> 76   then he himself withdrew from off the throne.

An interpretation of the vision is then given by Moses' father-in-law:

---

[31] Burchard, *OTP*, ii, 232.
[32] On the transformation of Aseneth see Kee, 'Setting', 404–5.
[33] Cf. Charlesworth, 'Righteous', 136–7.
[34] See, e.g., Meeks, 'Moses', and note that various texts adduced as evidence for the deification of Moses at best incorporate traditions dating from earlier than 100 CE.
[35] Jacobsen, *Exagoge*, 8–13; Robertson, *OTP*, ii, 804.

83 My friend, God gave you this as a sign for good.
84 Would I might live to see the day these things transpire.
85 For you shall cause a mighty throne to rise,
86 and you yourself shall rule and govern men.

(*The Exagoge*, 70–86)[36]

Moses' dream is unique.[37] The apparent replacement of God (i.e. 'a man of noble mien') by Moses is intriguing. It differs, for instance, from Jesus' account in Apocalypse 3.21 that he 'sat down *with* [his] Father on his throne'. It is also different from the example of Abel who sits on a 'fearsome throne', but seems to be the representative of God (and sits on a separate throne) rather than to have replaced God (*Test. Abr.* 12.4–5). Many, but not all, scholars argue that Moses is depicted here as the vicegerent of God.[38] Certainly, the interpretation in lines 83–6 downplays the supreme position of Moses as an exalted patriarch.[39] The assumption of the divine throne is interpreted as the establishment of a great earthly rulership for Moses, as opposed to the transformation of Moses into a divine being.[40] Thus Moses appears to ascend to the divine throne without becoming a divine being. At the least this passage appears to demonstrate that speculation about human ascent to the divine throne dates from well before the Christian era.

Moses occupies a very important place in the aims and intentions of Philo's project to recast the Pentateuch in a manner which engaged with the Hellenistic milieu in which he lived. It is, of course, not possible to provide here more than a snapshot of Philo's treatment of Moses. Of particular interest is Philo's designation of Moses as θεὸς. For example:

> There are still others, whom God has advanced even higher, and has trained them to soar above species and genus alike and stationed them beside himself. Such is

[36] Robertson, *OTP*, ii, 812. For Greek text see Eusebius, *Praep. ev.* 9.28–9.
[37] Jacobsen, *Exagoge*, 90.
[38] So Meeks, *Prophet-King*, 148–9 and 'Moses', 359; Hurtado, *God*, 57–9; contrast with Van der Horst, 'Moses', 21–9; Goodenough, *By Light*, 290–1, but see response by Jacobsen, 'Mysticism', 272–3. Holladay ('Moses', 448–52) argues that Moses is portrayed as *mantis* similar to Apollo and not as king, also with response by Jacobsen, 'Mysticism', 287–9.
[39] Ibid., 273.
[40] For a detailed discussion of the dream and its interpretation see further Jacobsen, *Exagoge*, 89–97. On Jewish traditions about Moses see Jeremias, 'Μωυσης', 849–64.

Moses . . .⁹ . . . He gifted him with no ordinary excellence,
such as that which kings and rulers have, wherewith to
hold sway and sovereignty over the passions of the soul,
but he appointed him as god (ἀλλ᾽ εἰς θεὸν αὐτὸν ἐχειρ-
οτόνει), placing all the bodily region and the mind which
rules it in subjection and slavery to him.   (*Sac*. 8–9)

Again, was not the joy of his partnership with the Father
and Maker of all magnified also by the honour of being
deemed worthy to bear the same title? For he was named
god and king of the whole nation (ὅλου τοῦ ἔθνους θεὸς
καὶ βασιλεύς), and entered, we are told, into the darkness
where God was, that is into the unseen invisible, incor-
poreal and archetypal essence of existing things. Thus he
beheld what is hidden from the sight of mortal nature, and,
in himself, and in his life displayed for all to see, he has set
before us, like some well-wrought picture, a piece of work
beautiful and godlike, a model for those who are willing to
copy it.   (*Mos*. i.158)

Philo does not appear to use the word θεός in connection with
Moses in order to assert that he is another God, a rival or an equal
partner to God, since what Moses has become is entirely dependent
on the power of God (cf. *Mos*. i.148–63). Rather, Moses as 'god
and king of the whole nation' (*Mos*. i.158) seems to be something
akin to the archangel Michael as prince over Israel (cf. Dan. 10.21),
while as 'god [over] all the bodily region and the mind which rules it
in subjection and slavery' (*Sac*. 9) he seems to be an archetypal
good man.⁴¹ Thus Moses is described by Philo as having at least
the kind of elevated honour and heavenly rank which we have just
seen in *The Exagoge*.⁴² In this connection we may also note Sira
45.2 where Moses is described as having been made 'equal in glory
to the holy ones'.

Philo's treatment of Moses appears to demonstrate the extraordinary extent to which a human being could be conceived to be
highly exalted and to enjoy access to the hiddenness of God within
the confines of monotheism. Moses in this context corresponds to
an angelic figure such as Yahoel. Yet we cannot deny that a certain

---

⁴¹ Cf. Abel as the embodiment of holiness in the same passage (*Sac*. 9). In *Det*.
161–2 Philo denies that Moses actually became a god; cf. Hurtado, *God*, 62.
⁴² We cannot here discuss how Philo extends the conception of Moses' exaltedness,
but cf. Segal, *Powers*, 171–2; Goodenough, *By Light*, 199–234.

ambiguity attaches to Moses when seen in Philonic perspective. In
Quaestiones et Solutiones in Exodum 2.40, for example, there is talk
of Moses being 'divinized', we cannot tell what Greek word Philo
originally used or exactly what was meant by this idea.[43]

Before we leave Moses we may note that in a second-century CE
apocalypse Moses is presented in glorious angelomorphic form:

> And behold, there were two men,[44] and we would not look
> on their faces, for a light came from them which shone
> more than the sun, and their raiment also was glistening
> . . . And the other, great, I say, shines in his appearance
> more than hail (crystal) . . . like the rainbow in water was
> his hair.   (Eth. *Apoc. Pet.* 15)[45]

We have adduced examples of exalted humans who appear in
glorious form implicitly or explicitly reminiscent of glorious angels.
By contrast, in the example cited below, we have a description of
Samuel in which his form is said to be theomorphic. The background to this account lies in 1 Samuel 28.13–25 where the
'medium at Endor' reports to Saul that she sees the ghost of Samuel
as '(a) god(s) (*'lhym*, MT; θεοὺς, LXX) coming up out of the
ground'. When Josephus recounts this incident he includes the
following details:

> the woman, beholding a venerable and godlike man (ἄνδρα
> σεμνὸν καὶ θεοπρεπῆ ταράττεται) was overcome and, in
> her terror . . . ³³³ she replied that she saw someone arise in
> form like God (τῷ θεῷ τινα τὴν μορφὴν ὅμοιον).
>   (*Ant.* 6.332–3)

There can be no question here of either the author/redactor of 1
Samuel or Josephus understanding Samuel to be a divine being.
Probably, Josephus is not intending to imply that he knows what
the form of God is; rather, he is interpreting what the woman said –
she sees Samuel in a form of which she associates with God.[46]

In this chapter we have noted humans whose appearance is
described as 'like the angels' or 'like the sons of God' (e.g. Noah in 1
Enoch 106.2–5; Jacob in *Jos. and Asen.* 22.7; Abel in *Test. Abr.* Rec.
A 12.4–5). In the case of Noah, we have observed that his

[43] Cf. Goodenough, *By Light*, 224–9; Segal, *Powers*, 171–2; with evaluation in
Hurtado, *God*, 59–63.
[44] Identified as 'Moses and Elias' in (Ethiopic) *Apoc. Pet.* 16.
[45] Duensing, *NTA*, ii, 680–1.   [46] Cf. Kim, *Origin*, 212–13.

appearance raised the question of whether he was actually an angel, but we saw that the answer given was negative. We must now consider the question of whether humans could not only have an angelomorphic appearance but actually be *transformed* from human beings into another kind of being – in particular, angels or angel-like heavenly beings. In some texts humans are translated to heaven without any reference as to what kind of being they have become (such as Enoch according to Gen. 5.24, Sir. 44.16). Other texts imply, perhaps ambiguously, that certain humans such as Enoch and Moses could be transformed on entry to heaven: we have already mentioned 1 *Enoch* 71.14 which raises the question whether Enoch is merely addressed as 'son of man', or has actually become the heavenly 'Son of Man'.[47] Similarly, Sira 45.2 raises the question whether the description of Moses as 'made equal in glory to the holy ones' implies an underlying belief in Moses' transformation in heaven. In a later text Enoch is transformed into the angel Metatron (3 *Enoch* 4.1–5). In Philo's view Abraham, Isaac, and Jacob join Moses in having been made 'like the angels' (*Sac.* 5–10; cf. *Mos.* 2.290).[48] A similar case is Isaiah who reports how he was transformed and became 'like an angel' (*Asc. Isa.* 9.30 Latin[2]/Slavonic). These six men were, of course, outstanding for either their righteousness or their major roles in God's plans, or both. But there are texts which suggest that all the righteous will become like the angels (e.g. 1 *Enoch* 104.2; 2 *Apoc. Bar.* 51.1,5,10,12; 1QS 11.7–8; 1QH 3.22, 4.24–5, 6.13, 11.12–13; 1QSa 2.3–11; *Herm. Vis.* 2.2.7; *Herm. Sim.* 9.25).[49] In Mark 12.25 Jesus makes the point that the resurrected ones are 'like the angels in heaven', and consequently no longer marry. According to Dunn the notion that such transformation of the righteous takes place 'probably owes something to the belief that Adam/man was "created exactly like the angels" (I Enoch 69.11), "a second angel" (II Enoch 30.11, cf. Gen. 1.26)'.[50] It is noticeable that in most of the examples just given humans do not actually become angels, only 'like angels'.[51] Nevertheless, Charles-

---

[47] Cf. discussion above, p. 79.   [48] Josephus, *Ant.* 3.96–7, 4.326.

[49] See further Segal ('Risen', 304–13) who notes other examples. This important article was unfortunately noticed too late to be fully engaged with in this monograph.

[50] Dunn, *Christology*, 105.

[51] M. Smith ('Ascent') argues that 4QM[a] reflects the influence of 'speculation on deification'. But this stretches the meaning of 'I shall be reclined with the gods' (line 19,35) which implies elevation to the level of the 'gods', i.e. the angels, rather than deification.

worth, surveying a more extensive body of writings than is possible here, concludes that at least as early as 100 CE the concept of humans being transformed into angels was developing in Judaism.[52]

If we depart for a moment from our stated intention to focus on Jewish and Christian literature, we may note that transformation of various kinds of beings (including humans) was certainly a feature of the wider Hellenistic milieu in the first century CE. In a noteworthy passage Plutarch sets forth the doctrine, which he attributes to Hesiod, that there are four classes of beings: 'gods, demigods, heroes . . . and last of all men'. Plutarch further asserts that transmutation between the different classes is possible, both from gods downwards and from humans upwards (*Mor. Def. Orac.* 415a–c).[53] Heroes were both figures who were once considered gods and human figures who came to be worshipped.[54] Two outstanding heroes, who have been the subject of comparison with Christ, are Heracles and Asclepius.[55]

We have noted in respect of angelic transformation that some texts envisaged all the righteous becoming like angels. Tabor makes the point that in the wider Hellenistic context special examples of apotheosis were part of the broader perception that 'the proper goal of human life is to escape the bonds of mortality'.[56] The Apocalypse itself appears to cohere with these observations when, on the one hand, Jesus is entitled ὁ υἱὸς τοῦ θεοῦ (2.18) and, on the other, each believer who 'conquers' is promised by God that αὐτὸς ἔσται μοι υἱός (21.7). Given that John appears to have been familiar with apocalyptic traditions of the kind enshrined in texts such as *Ascension of Isaiah*, *Apocalypse of Abraham*, and 1 *Enoch*, it is reasonable to assume that John was familiar with belief in the idea that humans could be transformed into angel-like beings upon entry to the heavenly realm.

Another aspect of human transformation in the first century CE was the tendency to deify Roman emperors. Thus Vespasian – who

[52] Charlesworth, 'Righteous', 145.
[53] On heroes, gods, and demigods see further, Plutarch, *Pelopidas*, 16; Philo, *Leg.* 78–114; Seneca, *De Benef.* 1.13; for secondary literature see, e.g., Dillon, *Middle*, 317–19.
[54] *OCD*, 506, col. 11. On the worship of Heroes see further Farnell, *Hero Cults*.
[55] The question of the influence of such figures on NT christology cannot detain us here, but see, e.g., Holladay, *Theios*. On Heracles see Knox, 'Christology', 232–47; on Asclepius see Edelstein and Edelstein, *Asclepius*, ii, 132–8; Kee, 'Self-definition', *Miracle*, 78–104.
[56] Tabor, *Things*, 78.

generally refused divine honours – joked before his death 'Vae . . . puto deus fio'.[57] Deification of the emperors was sometimes provisional. For example, deification was proposed for Tiberius by Caligula but was not agreed to because relationships between Tiberius and the senate were strained at the time of his death, while Caligula believed in his own divinity but he was not deified after his death.[58] By the end of the first century, however, deification of the emperor was obligatory and used as a test to identify Christians. The fact that Pergamum was the first centre of the imperial cult in Asia Minor may explain the reference in Apocalypse 2.13 to 'the place where Satan has his throne'.[59] Other chapters in the Apocalypse contain references to the imperial cult: for instance, 4.11 probably stands opposed to the practice of offering praise to the emperor; 'King of kings and Lord of lords' in 17.11 and 19.16 probably 'claims a higher authority than the emperor'; and the 'first beast' in chapter 13 is to be interpreted as the Roman emperor with special reference to the imperial cult.[60] Thus John, writing towards the end of the first century CE, as a Jewish Christian in a province of the Roman empire must have been familiar with a range of beliefs concerning the possibility that humans could be transformed after death into a being of higher status. We cannot be confident, however, that John would have been familiar with the idea that a human could become an angel.[61] More likely he believed that humans could become like the angels, and he must have been aware of the belief in the possibility that humans – especially of royal status – could become divine beings.

Angelomorphic *Logos*

In the previous section we dealt with material which implied that humans could become angels or angel-like creatures. Now we

[57] Suetonius, *Lives*, 8.23.4.
[58] D. L. Jones, 'Christianity', 1026–7. Note R. P. Casey ('Christology', 267) who wonders what 'son of God' would have meant to the centurion at the cross (Mark 15.39), 'since to a pagan the expression would indicate a "hero" of semi-divine, semi-human origin, or, in later times, an emperor'.
[59] Jones, 'Christianity', 1034; cf. Aune ('Form') who argues that the 'letters' to the churches have the form of royal decrees and the function of contrasting Christ and God with the Roman emperor.
[60] Jones, 'Christianity', 1034–5.
[61] In this discussion we have focused on humans becoming angels. On the related question of the transformation of humans into the *kabod* see now Morray-Jones, 'Mysticism'.

consider the case of the *Logos* of God being thought of as an angel
or at least an angel-like being. For one aspect of Jesus as an angel-
like figure in the Apocalypse which we will examine is his appearance in Apocalypse 19.11–16 as the angelomorphic Rider who has
the name 'the *Logos* of God'. We first consider Wisdom 18.15,
which many commentators have cited as background material for
Apocalypse 19.13, and then reflect on Philo's treatment of the
Logos. There is no particular reason to think that John was familiar
with Philo's writings, but we consider what Philo says about the
Logos because it is packed with material concerning the *Logos* as
an angel or, at least, as an angelomorphic being. Finally, we briefly
reflect on the *Memra* of the *Targums* since this has also been
examined in research into the background to Apocalypse 19.13.

In the course of a retelling of the story of the killing of the
Egyptian first-born in the Wisdom of Solomon the following
description of the destroyer (*mšḥyt*) referred to in Exodus 12.23
appears:

> your all-powerful word (λόγος) leaped from heaven, from
> the royal throne, into the midst of the land that was
> doomed, ¹⁶ a stern warrior carrying the sharp sword of
> your authentic command, and stood and filled all things
> with death, and touched heaven while standing on the
> earth.   (Wis. 18.15–16)

The destroyer is portrayed as the *Logos* of God and described in a
manner which resembles that of the angel of the LORD in 1
Chronicles 21.15–16. This angel who is described as both the
'destroying angel' (*ml'k hmšḥyt*, v. 15), and as the 'angel of the
LORD' (*ml'k yhwh*, vv. 15, 16) is sent to destroy Jerusalem (v. 15), is
seen 'standing between earth and heaven' (v. 16), and has a sword
in his hand (v. 16). In other words, the *Logos* recalls the
(destroying) angel (of the LORD) both in appearance and in function,
as described in 1 Chronicles 21.15–16.[62]

In Exodus 12.23–9 the LORD and the 'destroyer' are virtually
indistinguishable (analogous to some appearances of the 'angel of
the LORD'). But in 1 Chronicles 21.15–16 the destroying angel is
distinct from the LORD (since the angel is subordinate to God). In
Wisdom 18.15 the fact that the *Logos* belongs to the 'royal (i.e.
divine) throne' and is not commanded to descend to earth but

⁶² Goodrick, *Wisdom*, 357.

spontaneously leaps down from the throne implies that the *Logos* is not understood as a figure distinct from God.[63] There is no reason, then, to conclude that the *Logos* in Wisdom is understood to be an angel (in the sense of a non-divine being clearly distinguished from God), even though his portrayal draws on an angelic story. With a number of scholars we conclude that in Wisdom 18.15–16 we have a poetic attempt to express God's activity in the world. Talk of the *Logos* in Wisdom involves literary personification rather than the assertion of hypostatic existence.[64] In other words, in Wisdom 18.15–16 the *Logos* is spoken of as an angelomorphic figure without the implication that the *Logos* is an angel.

Since Philo's writings can be almost certainly dated before 50 CE,[65] they form a valuable record of at least one stream of Jewish thought prior to the composition of the Apocalypse.[66] One of the most frequently cited Philonic passages in connection with the background to christology is the following:

> But if there be any as yet unfit to be called a son of God, let him press to take his place under God's Firstborn, the Word (λόγον), who holds the eldership among the angels, their ruler as it were (ὡς ἂν ἀρχάγγελον). And many names are his, for he is called, 'the Beginning' (ἀρχή), and the Name of God and His Word, and the Man after his image and 'he that sees', that is Israel.   (*Conf.* 146)[67]

In this passage the relationship of the *Logos* to God is a little vague: is he an archangel, a creature separate and distinct from God, or is he (so to speak) the visible face of God? In support of an affirmative answer to the first alternative we might cite *Quis Heres* 205, for example, where the *Logos* is described as one who 'pleads with the immortal as suppliant for the afflicted mortality and acts as ambassador of the ruler of the subject'. This role is the *Logos*' 'special prerogative' and involves standing between creature and

---

[63] Note that in the parallel case of the portrayal of *Sophia* the situation is more ambiguous: in Wis. 9.4 *Sophia* 'sits by your throne' (not 'on' it!), but in 9.10 God is urged to send *Sophia* 'from the throne of your glory'.

[64] So Dunn, *Christology*, 163–76, 213–20; Goodrick, *Wisdom*, 358; and Gregg, *Wisdom,* xxxviii–ix, 'the Logos . . . a rhetoric-poetical personification of the Divine will and energy'.

[65] Goodenough, *Philo*, 2.

[66] Goodenough (*By Light*, 80) argues that Philo is as close to the Sadducees as Paul is to the Pharisees.

[67] Cf. *Mig. Abr.* 174–5.

Creator. The *Logos* appears to be a *mediator between God and creation*.[68] Nevertheless, more competent authorities than the present writer have considered what Philo has to say about the *Logos* and have concluded that the *Logos* is inseparable from God. Thus Dunn argues that although some references, such as *Quis Heres* 205, *Quaestiones et Solutiones in Exodum* ii.94 and *Quod Deus* 138, suggest Philo thought of the *Logos* as a being entirely distinct from God,[69] consideration of the whole panoply of references to the Logos yields the conclusion that 'the Logos of God is God in his self-revelation'.[70] In passages such as *De Confusione Linguarum* 146 an expression like 'God's Firstborn, the Word' is a manner of speaking about God in his self-revelation and not a declaration that God has begotten or created a being who in some real sense has a separate existence from God.

Winston draws this conclusion about the Philonic *Logos*: 'The Philonic Logos is thus not literally a second entity by the side of God acting on his behalf, nor is it an empty abstraction, but rather a vivid and living hypostatization of an essential aspect of Deity, the face of God turned toward creation.'[71] One passage in particular bears these conclusions out with the aid of a vivid metaphor:

> Why, then, do we wonder any longer at His assuming the likeness of angels, seeing that for the succour of those that are in need He assumes that of men? Accordingly, when He says 'I am the God who was seen of thee in the place of God' (Gen. xxxi.13), understand that He occupied the place of an angel only so far as appeared, without changing, with a view to the profit of him who was not yet capable of seeing the true God. 239 For just as those who are unable to see the sun itself see the gleam of the parhelion and take it for the sun, and take the halo round the moon for that luminary itself, so some regard the

---

[68] Dunn (*Christology*, 294, n. 6) comments that *Quis Her*. 205–6 'should not be taken as any more than a typically Philonic allegorical identification of the Logos with Moses'.

[69] Ibid., 220, who also notes *Cher*. 36; *Sac*. 119; *Agr*. 51; *Conf*. 146; *Quaest. in Gn*. ii.62.

[70] Ibid., 230; cf. Casey, *Jewish*, 84: 'The *logos* effectively functions as the aspect of God by which people know him'; Sandmel, 'Philo', 24: 'The Logos . . . is the immanent facet of the transcendent *To On*.'

[71] Winston, *Logos*, 49–50; cf. Tobin, 'Logos', 351: '[Logos] was not a straightforward description of a being other than God. It was a real aspect of the divine reality through which God was related, although indirectly, to the universe.'

image of God, His angel the Word, as His very self (οὕτως καὶ τὴν τοῦ θεοῦ εἰκόνα, τὸν ἄγγελον αὐτοῦ λόγον, ὡς αὐτὸν κατανοοῦσιν). ²⁴⁰ Do you not see how Hagar, who is the education of the schools, says to the angel 'Thou art the God that didst look upon me'? (Gen. xvi.13); for being Egyptian by descent she was not qualified to see the supreme Cause.   (*Som.* i.238–40)⁷²

Here Philo argues that God assumes the likeness of angels as a gracious gesture to the spiritually immature. The consequence is that some folk, such as Hagar, mistakenly conclude that to have seen the angel is to have seen God's 'very self'. This mistake is analogous to believing that the parhelion is the sun or the lunar halo is the moon. Philo distinguishes between 'the image of God' and God's 'very self'. Yet, continuing the analogy with the parhelion and the lunar halo, the distinction between the image of God and the very self of God does not involve separation. The parhelion is intrinsically linked to the sun and the lunar halo to the moon. To see the image of God may be quite different from seeing God in his essential being, but it is not to see a separate being from God.

In *De Somniis* i.238–40 the 'image of God' is 'His angel the Word'. When God assumes the likeness of angels he expresses himself as the *Logos*. The *Logos* is the manifestation of God and the form of the *Logos* is the form of an angel. It would appear that the *Logos* for Philo is not an angel, but the *Logos* can appear angelomorphically. Conversely, in relation to God the *Logos* is not God in his essential being but God's self-revelation.⁷³ In other words, the *Logos* is not a true intermediary being (in the sense of a being who is neither God nor part of humanity) but a means of communication between God and humanity. Nevertheless, *De Somniis* i.238–40a makes the point that the *Logos* was capable of being misunderstood. Not every ancient interpreter of the *Logos* had the acumen of Philo (or of Dunn and Winston)! When discussing *De Somniis* i.226–41 and *Quaestiones et Solutiones in*

---

⁷² Wolfson ('Angel', 96) states that 'Philo never calls the Logos an angel'. Barker ('Imagery', 87) rightly says that this statement is incredible; she cites *Conf.* 146, but we may also note *Leg. All.* iii.177; *Conf.* 28; *Quis Her.* 205; *Som.* i.239; *Cher.* iii.35; *Mut.* 87; *Mig. Abr.* 173.

⁷³ Thus Philo distinguishes between 'Him who is truly God' signified by the arthrous title ὁ θεός, and 'His chief Word' who has the anarthrous title θεός (*Som.* i.229–30). Cf. Casey, *Jewish*, 84–5.

Genesin ii.62 ('the second God, who is His Logos (πρὸς τὸν δεύτερον θεόν, ὅς ἐστιν ἐκείνου λόγος)'), Segal rightly observes that

> It takes but a small leap of the imagination, based on Philo's discussion of those 'incapable of forming any conception of God whatsoever without a body' [*Som.* i.236] to suspect that there were others in Philo's day who spoke of a 'second god' but who were not as careful as Philo in defining the limits of the term.[74]

This is a very important point for it reminds us that, despite the conclusions reached in our preceding discussion of the *Logos* in Wisdom and in Philo's writings, we cannot rule out the possibility that the *Logos* of God in a text such as Apocalypse 19.13 is an angelic figure separable and distinct from God.

Conceptually related to the *Logos* is the *Memra*, although it has as much to do with the name of God as with the word of God. Thus Hayward defines *Memra* as 'God's 'HYH, His Name for Himself expounded in terms of his past and future presence in Creation and Redemption'.[75] This means that the *Memra* is not to be understood as an intermediary being who is distinct from God. Thus Segal argues that

> *Memra, yekara,* and *shekinah* [as] used in the targumim and midrash . . . are never clearly defined as independent creatures. It rather appears that rabbinic concepts of *memra, shekinah, yekara* avoid the implications of independent divinity and are possibly meant to combat them.[76]

Although there are important distinctions to be made between the *Memra* and Philo's *Logos*, which seems to have been developed without knowledge of *Memra*-theology,[77] the *Memra*, which is often translated as 'Word', is sometimes held to have influenced *Logos*-christology such as that found in the Fourth Gospel.[78] With respect to Apocalypse 19.13, Hayward has argued that, as Wisdom

---

[74] Segal, *Powers*, 163; see further discussion, pp. 23, 163–6.
[75] Hayward, *Memra*, 147.   [76] Segal, *Powers*, 182–3.
[77] Hayward, *Memra*, 137–9; cf. Sandmel ('Philo', 40) who argues that the use of *Memra* in the *Targum*s is not so much to bridge the gap between man and deity as to introduce a gap: 'The *memra* is to be classified with euphemism, not with philosophic constructs.'
[78] E.g. Hayward, 'Holy name'; McNamara, '*Logos*'.

18.14–16 is probably using 'Targumic *Memra*-theology', it follows that 'the similarity of [the *Logos* of God in Apc. 19.13] with that of the *Wisdom* writer . . . makes it probable that the *Memra* is in the background, especially as God's Name is expounded in *Memra*-fashion elsewhere in the work [i.e. Apc. 4.8,10]'.[79] Hayward draws attention to the parallel between the *Logos* of God going forth to effect redemption of the faithful at the end of time and *Targum Neofiti* I Exodus 12.42,[80] where the *Memra* goes out to accomplish redemption for Israel on the last night of the old age.[81] Thus some sort of parallel can be established between Jesus as the *Logos* of God in the Apocalypse and the *Memra*, and there may be an indirect influence from *Memra*-theology via Wisdom 18.15. The question of the relevance of the *Targum*s to NT study remains an open one, and it is beyond the scope of this monograph to attempt to resolve it.[82] What we may profitably note is that if *Memra*-theology lies behind Jesus as the *Logos* of God then it constitutes support for the idea that Jesus in the Apocalypse is not conceived as a figure completely separate and distinct from God but as one who is ultimately indistinguishable from God.

Conclusions

We have extended our discussion of the angelological context of the christology of the Apocalypse to include angelomorphic figures such as exalted humans and the *Logos*. We have seen in our representative, but not exhaustive, survey of texts featuring exalted humans that such figures were depicted in glorious form similar to the form of the glorious angels. Just as we observed that the inclusion of theophanic imagery in the descriptions of glorious angels did not mean that such angels were divine beings, so also with the inclusion of theophanic imagery in the descriptions of exalted humans such as Abel and Noah. Similarly, as in the case of the principal angels, there was talk of these figures having exalted status, with the term θεὸς, for example, applied to Moses. As with the angel Yahoel, this kind of talk raises the question whether the

---

[79] Hayward, *Memra*, 120–1. Note that McNamara (*New Testament*, 230–3) does not discuss the origin of the *Logos*-name when he examines the targumic background to Apc. 19.11–16.

[80] Cf. Diez Macho, *Neophyti 1*, ii, 77–9, 441.   [81] Hayward, *Memra*, 132–3.

[82] See, e.g., Tobin ('Logos', 352) on problem of dating of the *Targum*s with respect to their relevance to NT questions.

boundaries of monotheism were broken prior to 100 CE within Jewish circles. The answer appears to be no. At the most, humans such as Abel and Moses represent God as a vizier-like figure, or, in the case of Enoch in 1 *Enoch*, he may have been identified with the greatest heavenly figure apart from God. We have also noted material which demonstrates the widespread belief in the possibility of human transformation in the milieu in which the Apocalypse was composed.

With respect to the *Logos*, we have argued that God in his self-revelation sometimes appeared in the likeness of an angel. A certain ambiguity, however, is integral to presentations of the *Logos* in Wisdom and in Philo's writings so that it would not be inconceivable that some conceptions of the *Logos* held that he was a separable and distinct angelic figure alongside God. We have also briefly considered the *Memra*, particularly with respect to Apocalypse 19.13, and noted that if the *Memra* lies behind Apocalypse 19.13 then we must consider that Jesus as the *Logos* is, in some ultimate sense, indistinguishable from God.

5

ANGEL CHRISTOLOGY

An investigation into the influence of angelology on christology inevitably raises the question of whether the result is an 'angel christology' or an 'angelomorphic christology'. We have already briefly reviewed the main contributions this century to the discussion concerning the possibility of angel christology and angelomorphic christology within the NT and noted that angel christology is not widely agreed to be present within its pages.[1] In this chapter we review various texts not found in the NT, which refer to Christ in angelic or angelomorphic terms. We aim to extend our knowledge of the possible conclusions that we might draw concerning christology in the Apocalypse which has been influenced by angelology.[2] It is beyond the scope of this chapter to survey exhaustively all the available material on angel christology and angelomorphic christology.[3]

Early angel(omorphic) christology

The writings of Justin, who died in 165 CE, are (i) among the earliest Christian documents in which a christological interpretation of the OT angelophanies and theophanies is found, and (ii) the only known texts of the first and second centuries CE in which such an interpretation is explicitly found.[4] Typical of this interpretative approach is the following passage:

> Now the Word of God is His Son, as we have said before. And he is called Angel (ἄγγελος) and Apostle; for he declares whatever we ought to know, and is sent forth to

[1] See pp. 3–4.
[2] Barbel (*Christos*, 286) notes six varieties; while Trigg ('Angel', 37) notes four.
[3] See Barbel, *Christos*, 47–180, Daniélou, *Theology*, 117–45, and Trigg, 'Angel', for fuller studies.
[4] Traketellis, *Pre-Existence*, 59.

declare whatever is revealed . . . being of old the Word, and appearing sometimes in the form of fire (ἐν ἰδέᾳ πυρός), and sometimes in the likeness of angels (ἐν εἰκόνι ἀσωμάτων); but now, by the will of God, having become man for the human race. (*Apol.* i.63)[5]

Here three different aspects of Christ as an 'angel' are found: (i) Christ has the title 'Angel' (ἄγγελος), derived from Isaiah 9.5 LXX (καὶ καλεῖται τὸ ὄνομα αὐτοῦ Μεγάλης βουλῆς ἄγγελος);[6] (ii) Christ functions as an angel or messenger because he 'declares whatever we ought to know'; and (iii) Christ sometimes appeared 'in the likeness of angels' – specifically in the form of the 'angel of the LORD' in the OT. Nothing here suggests that Justin believed that ontologically Jesus Christ had the nature of an angel.[7] Bakker, however, has observed that while giving Christ the title 'Angel' did not necessarily *imply* his identification with one of the angels, nevertheless 'as the title "Angel" conveyed the whole cyclus of conceptions implied in it, the *danger* of Jesus being identified with an angel generally, or even with a special angel was not imaginary'.[8] In another passage Justin appears to court this very danger with an apparent implication that he worshipped angels: 'But both Him, and the Son who came forth from Him and taught us these things, and the host of the other good angels who follow and are made like to Him, and the prophetic Spirit, we worship and adore' (*Apol.* i.6).[9] But since elsewhere Justin gives no hint of such a practice (e.g. *Apol.* i.13,16,61), it has been suggested that there may be some carelessness in Justin's expression, which could be remedied by supposing that he meant to say either 'the Son . . . taught us *about* these things and *about* the host of the other good angels', or 'the Son . . . taught us *and* the host of other good angels . . . *about these things*'.[10] Yet we cannot be sure that Justin was careless; he may have meant what he said, however anomalous and inconsistent it appears to be.[11]

Nevertheless, *Apology* i.6 is something of a conundrum since, on

---

[5] ANCL, ii, 61.   [6] *Dial.* 76. Cf. Lueken, *Michael*, 76.

[7] Cf. Traketellis, *Pre-Existence*, 63.

[8] Bakker, 'Christ', 257; Cf. Werner, *Formation*, 140.

[9] ANCL, ii, 11. Cf. *Dial.* 100.   [10] So Trollope, *Justini*, i, 28–9.

[11] So Trollope, *Justini*, i, 27. Commenting on *Apol.* i. 6, Bauckham ('Worship', 335) notes that 'there were probably early Christian circles in which a general neglect of the limits of monotheism in worship accompanied the emergence of the worship of Jesus'.

the one hand, the implication of 'the other good angels' is that the Son is one of the angels and, on the other, the fact that the angels 'are made like to Him' appears to imply that the angels are changed in some way to make them conform to the Son. Goodenough has argued that because there is a similarity between Christ and the angels which goes beyond that of function – relating to matters such as origin, nature, and character – Justin was prompted to make his statement in *Apology* i.6 'to the great discomfort of later Christian Apologists'.[12] He has also argued that the confusion inherent in Justin's position, between the *Logos* as unique and distinct from the angels, and the *Logos* as essentially similar to the angels is 'entirely Philonic'.[13] In other words, in the writings of Justin we have evidence that Christ was talked of in explicitly angelic terms in the first decades after the composition of the Apocalypse. Christ was entitled 'Angel', seen to function in an angelic manner, and perceived to have appeared as an angel to humankind. Possibly, though the evidence is ambiguous, Christ was even thought to actually to be an angel.

With Origen (c.185–254 CE) we are moving more than a century away from the composition of the Apocalypse. However, his contribution to angel christology is worth considering as it highlights what is *not* said in the Apocalypse. In *De principiis* i.3.4, Origen passes on an interpretation he has received concerning the two seraphim in Isaiah 6.3, namely, that they are Christ and the Holy Spirit. Nothing in the Apocalypse betrays familiarity with this interpretation. Similarly, as in the case of Justin, the expression ἄγγελος μεγάλης βουλῆς found in Isaiah 9.5 LXX influenced the christology of Origen (cf. citation below),[14] but not the christology of the Apocalypse.[15] Origen envisages Jesus Christ functioning as an 'angel' (e.g. *Comm. Joh.* i.277), but it is his 'dispensational' interpretation of the angelic Christ which most interests us:[16]

The Saviour, therefore, in a way much more divine than

---

[12] Goodenough, *Justin*, 156, cf. 192–3.

[13] Ibid., 157; cf. 114–15, 117; note, e.g., *Conf.* 146, τὸν ἀγγέλων πρεσβύτατον, ὡς ἂν ἀρχάγγελον, and *Som.* i. 239, τὸν ἄγγελον αὐτοῦ λόγον. Such 'confusion' is also witnessed to in the *Shepherd of Hermas*: see discussion on pp. 106–8. On the probable influence of Philo on Justin see also Traketellis, *Pre-Existence*, 47, 53–92; Segal, *Powers*, 224; and compare *Dial.* 56.1/*Mut.*15 and *Dial.* 56.4,10/*Mos.* i.66.

[14] Cf. Trigg, 'Angel', 37–42.

[15] In fact there is no trace of the influence of Isa. 9.5 in any form in the Apocalypse.

[16] So Trigg, 'Angel', 44.

Paul, has become 'all things to all', that he might either 'gain' or perfect 'all things'. He has clearly become a man to men, and an angel to angels (γέγονεν ἀνθρώποις ἄνθρωπος καὶ ἀγγέλοις ἄγγελος). [218] No believer will have any doubt that he became a man; and we may be convinced that he became an angel if we observe the appearances and words of the angels when [some angel appears with authority] in certain passages of Scripture when the angels speak. For example, 'An angel of the Lord appeared in the fire of a burning bush. And he said, I am the God of Abraham, and of Isaac, and of Jacob.' But also Isaias says, 'His name shall be called angel of great counsel' (ἄγγελος μεγάλης βουλῆς). [219] The Saviour, therefore, is first and last, not that he is not what lies between, but it is stated in terms of the extremities to show that he himself has become 'all things'. But consider whether the 'last' is man, or those called the underworld beings, of which the demons also are a part, either in their entirety or some of them.   (*Comm. Joh.* i. 217–19)[17]

Origen suggests that Jesus becoming 'an angel to angels' is not simply a feature of the past before his becoming a man (cf. Justin, *Apol.* i.63), but also a feature of his (post-exaltation) ministry. For Trigg this 'dispensational' interpretation means 'the Son's taking on angelic nature corresponds to taking on human nature in the Incarnation'.[18] In other words, Origen supposes that Jesus is not an angel,[19] but he believes that he had the ability temporarily to become one.

Tertullian (c. 160–post 220 CE), who was also familiar with the title 'Angel of Great Counsel', may be mentioned as an example of an early Christian theologian who was suspicious of angel christology. In the process of affirming that as the 'Angel of Great Counsel' Christ held the office of messenger, Tertullian vigorously denied the belief that Christ was an angel like Gabriel or Michael (*de carne Christi* 14). Talbert suggests that Tertullian's 'distaste for angel christology derives in large measure from its docetic implications'.[20] But this distaste was not shared by everyone: a number of

---

[17] Translation from Heine, *Origen* (vol. 80), 76–7.   [18] Trigg, 'Angel', 37.
[19] Origen explicitly denies this in *Contra Celsum* v. 53; *Comm. Matt.* xiii.26; cf. Trigg, 'Angel', 45–7.
[20] Talbert, 'Redeemer', 434.

ancient writers refer to the Ebionites' view of Jesus as an angel. A notable example is Epiphanius:[21]

> And [the Ebionites] say that for this reason Jesus was born of the seed of man and was chosen and that he therefore was called Son of God according to the election because Christ descended upon him from above in the form of a dove. [4] They do not say that he was born of God the Father but that he was created as one of the archangels (and even higher) and that he is Lord over the angels as also over everything the Almighty has created
>
> (*Pan.* 30.16.3–4)[22]

Here we find an angel christology, in which Jesus does not simply look like an angel or function like an angel, but is said to have been created as one of the highest archangels. Daniélou argues that Christ is identified here with Michael.[23] Schoeps argues that the Ebionites were 'adoptionists' in the sense that they believed that Christ was an angelic being who entered Jesus at baptism.[24] We may also note here the expression of a christology in which Christ reappears throughout the ages.[25]

Another group of early Jewish Christians who seem to have promoted an angel christology in which Christ was an angel were the Elkesaites (a movement which may have had its beginnings in the reign of Trajan, early in the second century CE).[26] In similar vein would appear to be the views lying behind the *Testament of Solomon*, which probably began as a Jewish document in the first century CE and was extended and developed by a Christian author in the third century CE.[27] Thus, 'I said to him, "By what angel are

---

[21] Klijn and Reinink (*Evidence*, 13, n. 1) date this report before 428 CE.

[22] Ibid., 189. Cf. Epiphanius, *Pan.* 30.17.6, 19.4.1, 53.1.9; Irenaeus, *Adv. haer.* 1.26 (Cerinthus taught that Christ was a spiritual being who descended upon Jesus); and Tertullian, *De carne Christi* 14: 'So then, even as he is made less than the angels while clothed with manhood, even so he is not less when clothed with an angel. This opinion could be very suitable for Ebion who asserts that Jesus is a mere man' (Klijn and Reinink, *Evidence*,109).

[23] Daniélou, *Theology*, 125–6.   [24] Schoeps, *Theologie*, 80–2.

[25] So Klijn and Reinink (*Evidence*, 73) who note that this conception is only found in Epiphanius' accounts of the Ebionites and the Elkesaites, and that it has a number of variations: cf. Epiphanius, *Pan.* 30.3; 53.1.8; Hippolytus, *Ref. omn. haer.* 9.14.2; 10.29.

[26] Hippolytus, *Ref. omn. haer.* 9.13.4; cf. Klijn and Reinink, *Evidence*, 55–6.

[27] Whittaker, *AOT*, 735; Duling, *OTP*, i, 942. *Testament of Solomon* is extant only in Greek.

you thwarted?" He said, "By the one who is going to be born from a virgin and be crucified by the Jews" ' (*Test. Sol.* 22.20).[28] In this passage Christ is apparently an angel but no indication is given whether this angel christology is dispensational or functional in character.[29]

The *Epistula Apostolorum*, a second-century CE document, possibly of Egyptian provenance,[30] envisages Christ appearing in the form of the angel Gabriel. In the passage cited below it is not so much a case of Christ being identified with Gabriel, but of Christ taking 'the form of Gabriel in his function as messenger of God'.[31] Thus,

> 'Do you know that the angel Gabriel came and brought the message to Mary?' And we said to him, 'Yes, O Lord'. And he answered and said to us, 'Do you not remember that I previously said to you that I became like an angel to the angels?' And we said to him, 'Yes, O Lord'. And he said to us, 'At that time I appeared in the form of the archangel Gabriel to (the virgin) Mary and spoke with her, and her heart received (me); and she believed and laughed; and I, the Word, went into her and became flesh; and I myself was servant for myself, and in the form of the image of an angel; so I will do after I have gone to my Father.'
>
> (*Ep. Apost.* 14)[32]

An important apocalypse from a similar period of composition as the Apocalypse of John is the apocalypse known as the *Ascension of Isaiah* (or the *Martyrdom and Ascension of Isaiah*). This is a composite document consisting of a Jewish apocalypse, often called 'The Martyrdom of Isaiah' (chs. 1–5), and a Christian apocalypse often called 'The Ascension of Isaiah' (chs. 6–11). To make matters confusing, the Jewish part may itself be composite, incorporating a

---

[28] Duling, *OTP*, i, 984; cf. Whittaker, *AOT*, 749: 'born of a virgin, since angels worship him, and who is to be crucified by the Jews'. Duling, *OTP*, i, 984 note a, cites MSS P and Q as providing an even longer version of this verse.

[29] Charlesworth ('Righteous', 144) suggests that it is difficult to decide whether 'Jesus' portrayal here as an angel is the result of angelic transmogrification or is the disclosure of a primordial (preearthly) form'.

[30] Rebell, *Neutestamentliche*, 119; Duensing, *NTA*, i, 191; Ehrhardt, 'Judaeo-Christians', 368.

[31] Talbert, 'Redeemer', 433. See further on *Ep. Apost.* C. Schmidt, *Gespräche*; with response from Ehrhardt, 'Judaeo-Christians', 367–71. Daniélou (*Theology*, 131) notes a parallel to *Ep. Apost.* 14 in *Sib. Or.* 8.456–61.

[32] Duensing, *NTA*, i, 198–9.

Christian addition (3.13–4.22).[33] The entire document is found only in Ethiopic, although this is probably a translation of a Greek original.[34] Fragments are found in Greek, and partial versions in Latin and Slavonic.[35] The dating of the apocalypse is not easy to determine: fragments found for both parts suggest a *terminus ad quem* of *c.* 350 CE for the complete document.[36] Knibb suggests a date of *c.* 100 CE for *Ascension of Isaiah* 3.13–4.22 and a date between 100 and 200 CE for 6–11.[37] Recently, Knight has argued for a date before the end of the first century CE for the whole document.[38] If this is so then a comparative study between the *Ascension of Isaiah* (as we will refer to the whole document) and the Apocalypse would be well worthwhile. Here we can only note two important similarities between the two: both describe Jesus as the object of worship alongside God (Apc. 5.13, 22.1–4; *Asc. Isa.* 7.17) and both describe the refusal of an angel to be worshipped (Apc. 19.10, 22.9; *Asc. Isa.* 7.21).[39]

In a recent study of the christology of the *Ascension of Isaiah*, Knight argues that two particular strands in Jewish angelology were influential. The first, reflected in a variety of other apocalypses, supplied the idea of God ruling through a vizier, and is reflected in the ambiguous position of the Beloved (i.e. Jesus Christ) as both subordinate to God (*Asc. Isa.* 9.40) and worshipped by the angels (e.g. *Asc. Isa.* 7.17, 9.27–32, 10.16–19).[40] The second, the story of the descent of Raphael in the Book of Tobit, influenced the 'descent narrative' of the Beloved in *Ascension of Isaiah* 10.17–31.[41]   Although (i) the Beloved is described as worshipping God in the company of other angels (*Asc. Isa.* 9.40–2), and (ii) in this same passage one of the angels is 'the angel of the Holy Spirit', a description which calls to mind passages in Origen (where the two seraphim in Isaiah 6.3 are interpreted as Christ and the Holy Spirit: *De principiis* i.3.4) and in Hippolytus (where the Elkesaites are said to teach that there were two angels of giant dimensions, 'the son of God' and 'the Holy Spirit': *Ref.*

---

[33] Barton, *AOT*, 780.   [34] Ibid., 781.

[35] All found conveniently in parallel columns in Charles, *Ascension*, 83–139. Additionally, fragments are found in Sahidic and Akhmimic.

[36] Barton, *AOT*, 780–1.   [37] Knibb, *OTP*, ii, 149–50.

[38] Knight, *Disciples*, 53, 160–1. Cf. Daniélou (*Theology*, 12–13) who dates the whole work to the 80s; Robinson (*Redating*, 240, n. 98) dates it to the 60s.

[39] See further Bauckham, 'Worship'.

[40] Knight, *Disciples*, 95–103.   [41] Ibid., 104–10.

omn. haer. 9.13.2–3),[42] two observations tell against Jesus being an angel. First, as noted above, the Beloved is worshipped by the angels.[43] Secondly, the Beloved is temporarily *transformed into* the form of an angel according to two passages, 9.27–31 and 10.17–31. In the first of these, Isaiah sees one 'whose glory surpassed that of all' (9.27), and who is worshipped by all the righteous and the angels (9.28–9). Verse 30 then reads (according to the Ethiopic): 'And he was transformed and became like an angel.'[44] But according to the 'Latin[2]' and 'Slavonic' MSS, it reads: 'And I was transformed again and became like an angel.'[45] The Latin[2] and Slavonic version of *Ascension of Isaiah* 9.30 suggests that it was Isaiah who was transformed, presumably so that he is drawn into the angelic chorus. The word 'again', absent in 9.30 (Eth.), recalls 7.25 where Isaiah says that he is being transformed as he goes up from heaven to heaven. While the sentiment of *Ascension of Isaiah* 9.30 (Lat.[2] and Sl.) coheres with 7.25, this reading is more readily explained as a correction to the idea that the Beloved becomes an angel than the converse. Support for the Ethiopic reading appears to be given in *Ascension of Isaiah* 9.33 where it says of the angel of the Holy Spirit that 'his glory was not transformed'.[46] Implicitly, the non-transformation of the Holy Spirit is being compared with the transformation of the Beloved. Some commentators and translations (e.g. *AOT*) read 'my glory' instead of 'his glory', but there is no textual support for this in the Ethiopic, Latin, or Slavonic versions.[47] We can also observe in support of the Ethiopic reading

---

[42] The 'angel of the Holy Spirit' has led to conjecture that this might be Gabriel. Daniélou (*Theology*, 127), noting *Asc. Isa.* 11.4, argues for identification with Gabriel, and suggests (pp.129–30), that 2 *Enoch* 21.3–22.5 presents Gabriel performing similar functions to the angel of the Holy Spirit in *Asc. Isa..* Bauckham ('Worship', 334) disagrees. Cf. Charles, *Ascension*, 20.

[43] Bauckham ('Worship', 334) sees elements of angel christology in the background to *Asc. Isa.* but argues that its christology is better defined in terms of worship – where Christ is sharply distinguished from the angels – than in terms of angel christology. On the christology of *Asc. Isa.* see further Werner, *Formation*, 122–3, 132; and summary of recent debate between Pesce and Simonetti in Knight, *Disciples*, 74–5.

[44] Knibb, *OTP*, ii, 171.

[45] Barton, *AOT*, 805. Note that *AOT*'s reading is in the main body of the text with the alternative as a footnote, whereas the reverse is the case with *OTP*'s reading.

[46] Knibb, *OTP*, ii, 172.

[47] Charles (*Ascension*, 66–7) recognizes that the Ethiopic, Latin[2], and Slavonic MSS for 9.33 support the Ethiopic for 9.30 but argues that all are corrupt and that, e.g., 'transfiguravit' in 9.33 is 'a primitive error'. His argument for this is not convincing.

that (i) the Beloved becoming 'like an angel' fits with the subsequent portrayal of him as worshipping alongside the 'angel of the
Holy Spirit' and the other angels in *Ascension of Isaiah* 9.40–2, and
(ii) the Beloved is explicitly described as being transformed into
angelic form in *Asc. Isa.* 10.17–31. Thus the correct reading of
Ascension of Isaiah 9.30 suggests that the Beloved is transformed
and becomes like an angel. Knibb explains that this was 'for the
sake of Isaiah',[48] meaning that only in this form could Isaiah take
in the vision of the Beloved (cf. 9.37 where the vision of the 'Great
Glory' overwhelms the prophet). It seems likely, therefore, that
Ascension of Isaiah 9.30 (Eth.) represents a tradition which could be
at least as old as the turn of the first century CE in which Christ is
transformed into an angel as a *concession* to the humanity of the
seer. Far from viewing Christ as an angel, this tradition would
appear to involve a belief that Christ was akin to God in the sense
that, like God, he was beyond the comprehension of human beings.

The second passage describing transformation into angelic form
is *Asc. Isa.* 10.17–31 where the Beloved takes up angel-like form as
he descends through the heavens to earth. So successful is this
disguise that the angels do not recognize him. For our purposes it is
not important to determine more precisely the angelomorphic
character of the christology represented in passages such as these in
the *Ascension of Isaiah*. What is important is that in the *Ascension
of Isaiah* we have, possibly contemporaneously with the Apocalypse, an expression of a christology in which (i) Jesus Christ
temporarily appears like an angel, and (ii) the angelomorphic
Christ appears more closely aligned with the one God than with the
created order.

The next writing we consider, the *Shepherd of Hermas*, which
could be contemporaneous with the Apocalypse but more likely
stems from the second century CE,[49] refers to Jesus on a number of
occasions in angelic terms: for example, τοῦ σεμνοτάτου ἀγγέλου
(*Herm. Vis.* 5.2; cf. *Herm. Mand.* 5.1.7); τοῦ ἁγίου ἀγγέλου (*Herm.
Sim.* 5.4.4); ὁ ἔνδοξος ἄγγελος (*Herm. Sim.* 7.1–3); ὁ ἄγγελος
κυρίου ἐκεῖνος (*Herm. Sim.* 7.5).[50] Thus the christology of the

---

[48] Knibb, *OTP*, ii, 171, n. o2.

[49] Rebell, *Neutestamentliche*, 267: *c.* 140–155 CE; Robinson, *Redating*, 352: *c.* 85 CE.

[50] Cf. *Herm. Sim.* 8.1.2; 8.2.1. Daniélou (*Theology*, 119) points out that ἔνδοξος
ἄγγελος and σεμνότατος ἄγγελος applied to the *Logos* is a characteristic feature
of the *Shepherd of Hermas*. On the angelology of the *Shepherd of Hermas* see
Carr, *Angels*, 143–4.

Shepherd of Hermas appears to be closer to a full-blown 'angel christology' than to an 'angelomorphic christology'. Particularly interesting in connection with this point is *Hermas Similitudes* 8.3.3: 'And the great and glorious angel is Michael (ὁ δὲ ἄγγελος ὁ μέγας καὶ ἔνδοξος Μιχαὴλ), who has power over this people and governs them.' Since in *Hermas Similitudes* 9.1.3 the 'glorious angel' is the Son of God,[51] the author either apparently envisages two equivalent glorious angels, Michael and Christ, or he identifies Michael with Christ.[52] But there is no evidence elsewhere in the *Shepherd of Hermas* to suppose that the angel Michael is thought of as an equivalent figure to Christ. As leader of the angels Christ takes up a function of Michael so that it is conceivable that Michael has been identified with Christ. Charlesworth, however, points out that identical functions do not automatically lead to identity and 'transference of traditions associated with Michael to expressions about Christ does not justify the equation of Michael and Christ'.[53] Various solutions have been proposed for the problem raised by *Hermas Similitudes* 8.3.3. Werner, for example, simply identifies Michael with Christ.[54] Daniélou argues that once the seven archangels were understood as six archangels with the *Logos* as their leader (cf. *Herm. Sim.* 9.12.7–8) it was natural that the name of the chief archangel in Jewish tradition, Michael, should be applied to the *Logos*.[55] Pernveden argues that *Hermas Similitudes* 8.3.3 signifies a functional identity rather than a personal identity between the Son of God and Michael: that is, we find an angel functioning instead of the Son of God. In support of this argument we may note *Hermas Mandates* 5.1.7 where justification is attributed to an angel. The explanation given by Pernveden for passages such as *Hermas Similitudes* 8.3.3 and *Hermas Mandates* 5.1.7 is that a 'gradually delegated authority' exists in which Michael, for example, stands between the Son of God and humankind as mediator. Consequently, neither *Hermas Similitudes* 8.3.3 nor *Hermas Mandates*. 5.1.7 justify talk of 'an angel-christology in

---

[51] Cf. *Herm. Sim.* 9.12.7–8: 'The glorious man, said he, is the Son of God.'
[52] E.g. Collins, 'Son', 66. Cf. Longenecker, *Christology*, 26, n. 5.
[53] Charlesworth, 'Righteous', 150, n. 27.
[54] Werner, *Formation*, 135.
[55] Daniélou, *Theology*, 124. Cf. Barbel, *Christos*, 230. Pernveden (*Concept*, 62–3) cautions against readily assuming that in *Herm. Sim.* 9.12.7–8 Christ is the seventh angel since some Jewish material refers to only six archangels (cf. 1 *Enoch* 20 (Eth.)). Carr (*Angels*) 144, following Hippolytus, *Eis ton Daniel* iv.36, suggests that Ezek. 9.2 is influential in this regard.

the true meaning of the term'.[56] Finally, we note Moxnes who argues that there is one supreme angelic figure who is 'the son of God, Christ' but that the problematic texts should not be interpreted as 'dogmatic statements about Christ'.[57] For our purposes the resolution of the problem need not detain us. In the present context the *Shepherd of Hermas* is significant in that it provides evidence for a christology which at the least came within a hair's breadth of being an angel christology not many decades after the composition of the Apocalypse.

Correspondence of some kind between Jesus Christ and Michael is, in fact, a feature of other texts. First, we consider the *Testaments of the Twelve Patriarchs*. The date of the *Testaments* is problematic. In their present form they may date from the second century CE.[58] But in this form they have almost certainly been influenced by Christian ideas.[59] The original texts date from after the time of the LXX (*c.* 250 BCE), and may have been composed in the reign of John Hyrcanus (137–107 BCE).[60] Thus the *Testaments*, despite Christian redaction, may witness to pre-Christian developments in Jewish angelology. Of special interest for our discussion are these two passages:

> Draw near to God and to the angel that intercedes for you, because he is the mediator between God and men for the peace of Israel. He shall stand in opposition to the kingdom of the enemy.   (*T. Dan* 6.2)[61]

> And he said, 'I am the angel that intercedes for the nation of Israel, so that no one may destroy them completely for every evil spirit is ranged against them.'[7] And afterwards I woke up, and I blessed the Most High and the angel that intercedes for the nation of Israel and all the righteous.
>   (*T. Levi* 5.6–7)[62]

Longenecker has argued that in these texts there 'seems to be a transposition from the Jewish theme of the intercession of the angel

---

[56] Pernveden, *Concept*, 60–2.
[57] Moxnes, 'God', 50.   [58] De Jonge, *AOT*, 512.
[59] De Jonge, 'Christian', 195–246; *ibid.*, 'Once More', 311–19; Braun, 'Testaments', 516–49.
[60] Kee, *OTP*, i, 777–8.   [61] Kee, *OTP*, i, 810.
[62] De Jonge, *AOT*, 528 (following the *editio maior* of M. De Jonge). We cite this version because it illustrates Longenecker's point in contrast to Kee, *OTP*, i, 790, which follows the critical edition of R. H. Charles.

Michael for the nation Israel to the Jewish–Christian theme of the mediatorship of Christ'.[63] The reason for this conclusion is because 'Israel' has been enlarged here to 'men' and 'all the righteous' in general (cf. 1 Tim. 2.5),[64] and because the opposition is not simply from 'the enemies of Israel', but from 'the kingdom of the enemy'.[65] Thus these texts, if they have been redacted according to Christian principles, may bear witness to the influence of a 'primitive Christian angel-christology'.[66] The link between Christ and Michael appears to be explored in later material such as the Pseudo-Clementine writings (*Homilies* 18.4, *Recognitions* 2.42).[67] In the former the 'Son' takes up 'the Hebrews as his portion' (cf. Michael as patron angel of Israel) and in the latter Christ is 'one among the archangels who is greatest'. According to Daniélou, this means that the Son of God is identified with Michael.[68]

Finally, we note that angel christology largely died out after the fourth century CE. This was mainly because it was an intrinsically subordinationist christology and was incompatible with the development of the *homoousian* doctrine which culminated in the Trinitarian orthodoxy of Nicea.[69] It also came to have Arian associations. Beyond the fourth century, therefore, there has been little adherence to angel christology.[70]

Conclusions

Reviewing some of the texts which speak of Jesus Christ as an 'angel' in the first Christian centuries, we have seen that a number of possibilities were expressed. Perhaps most frequent was the application of the title 'Angel (of Great Counsel)' to Christ. In

---

[63] Longenecker, *Christology*, 26; he also cites in respect of the identification of Michael with Christ Hermas, *Herm. Sim.* 8.3.3 and 2 *Enoch* 22.4–9 (which passage Daniélou (*Theology*, 124–5) describes as 'unskilful christianisation').

[64] Cf. De Jonge, 'Christian Influence', 246, n. 1.

[65] Daniélou, *Theology*, 125. Cf. 1QM 17.5–8.

[66] Hollander and De Jonge, *Testaments*, 291.

[67] Date: before 360 CE (*NTA*, ii, 534).

[68] Daniélou, *Theology*, 126–7. [69] Werner, *Formation*, 137.

[70] Daniélou, *Theology*, 117. Werner (*Formation*, 137) notes traces of the development of angel christology in the Paulicians, Bogomils, and medieval Catharists – and in the writings of one E. W. Hengstenberg in the nineteenth century. For discussion of references to Christ as 'angel' in the liturgy see Barbel, *Christos*, 269–84. Note also references to 'Christ, Michael, Gabriel' on amulets and in inscriptions connected with Syrian Christianity in the fourth century: cf. Lueken, *Michael*, 118; Werner, *Formation*, 136; and Barbel, *Christos*, 262–9.

some cases Christ *functions* as an angel, in others he becomes an angel *temporarily*, analogously to his becoming the human Jesus. In *Ascension of Isaiah* 9.30 'the Beloved' appears to be transformed into an angel as a concession to Isaiah who otherwise could not look on him. A 'full-blown' angel christology was clearly denied by some such as Tertullian and Origen, but others such as the Ebionites and Elkesaites appeared to have subscribed to the belief that Jesus Christ was created an (arch)angel. In some writings the relationship between Michael and Christ is ambiguous.

In other words, talk of Jesus as an angel in the first centuries CE, outside the NT, largely fell under the category of 'angelomorphic christology'. That is, Jesus was not generally understood actually to be an angel; rather, he was (i) frequently entitled 'Angel', (ii) sometimes perceived to be like an angel in function, and (iii) occasionally recognized as having temporarily taken up the form of an angel.

Summary of investigation

In this and the previous three chapters we have all too cursorily surveyed material concerning angels, angelomorphic figures, epiphanies, and angel or angelomorphic christologies. In chapter 2 we examined angelology and epiphanies in Zechariah, Ezekiel, and Daniel. One of the main functions of this examination was to review aspects of Rowland's proposal concerning the background to the christophany in Apocalypse 1.13–16. We argued that there was good reason to doubt that: (i) the figure in Ezekiel 8.2 represented a bifurcation in the deity; (ii) the figure in Daniel 10.5–6 represented a development through Ezekiel 1.26–8 and 8.2–4; and (iii) Daniel 7.13 LXX had influenced the combination of Danielic texts in Apocalypse 1.13–16. Positively we argued that the figure in Daniel 10.5–6 represented a development of the angel in Ezekiel 9.2.

In chapter 3 we examined principal angels with glorious form and/or exalted status. We argued that the presence of theophanic imagery in an angelophany was not necessarily a sign that the angel concerned was a being of divine status. We had already seen in Zechariah that the angel of the LORD occupied the position of God's vizier and we found a number of other examples of this. But in no case before the second century CE did this clearly and unmistakably lead to the infringement of monotheism. Examining the subject of the worship of angels we could not rule out the occurrence of this practice before the second century CE, but we argued that if it did occur then it was unlikely to have influenced the worship of Jesus in the Apocalypse. In sum: an angel was an angel and if the limits of monotheism were broken through angelological speculation before the end of the first century CE then this was probably not significant for the christology of the Apocalypse.

With respect to exalted humans in chapter 4 we reached similar conclusions. Theophanic imagery in the description of angelomorphic humans did not mean that they were divine, nor, in the case of Moses, did the application of the word θεός mean that Moses had been deified. Just as angels could appear to be human (e.g. Raphael, Jacob-Israel), so humans could become like angels, in line with conceptions about transformation in the wider Hellenistic milieu. Conversely, with the *Logos* we found transformation in a different direction: the self-revelation of God could be manifested in the form of an angel.

In the present chapter we have seen that Jesus as an 'angel' in the first Christian centuries could mean a number of things, most of which were to do with Jesus being like an angel as opposed to him being an angel, that is, a created, non-divine heavenly being. We saw that ideas were held about the transformation of Jesus Christ into an angelic figure: for example, Jesus became like an angel so that Isaiah could look on him (*Asc. Isa.* 9.30 Eth.), and Jesus became an angel in order to minister to angels (Origen, *Comm. Joh.* i.277). With the results of our investigation so far in mind we can turn to consider the question of the influence of angelology on the christology of the Apocalypse.

6

GOD, JESUS, AND THE ANGEL

We turn our attention in this chapter to the christology of the Apocalypse, and in particular to the relationships between (i) Jesus and God and (ii) Jesus and the angel who makes known the revelation (hence, the revealing angel). This investigation is a prerequisite for the following chapters in which we consider the visions in Apocalypse 1.13–16, 14.14, and 19.11–16. The first verse of the Apocalypse introduces us to Jesus Christ in conjunction with God and the revealing angel, and gives us a lead into this stage of our investigation.

> Ἀποκάλυψις Ἰησοῦ Χριστοῦ ἥν ἔδωκεν αὐτῷ ὁ θεὸς δεῖξαι τοῖς δούλοις αὐτοῦ ἃ δεῖ γενέσθαι ἐν τάχει, καὶ ἐσήμανεν ἀποστείλας διὰ τοῦ ἀγγέλου αὐτοῦ τῷ δούλῳ αὐτοῦ Ἰωάννῃ.　　　　　　　　　　(Apc. 1.1)

Here Jesus Christ is located in a 'chain of transmission'[1] which begins with 'God' and ends with 'his servants'. The central links in the chain are 'Jesus Christ', 'his angel', and 'John'. John and the servants reside on earth. God, Jesus Christ, and the angel are located in heaven. This verse raises the question of where Jesus stands in relationship to God. For example, following the linking of the revelation to both Jesus Christ and God, does the singularity of the sender of the angel signify that Jesus stands with God in some kind of unity as the authority behind the angel? Or, is Jesus to be considered as a distinct subordinate of God, and, if so, is Jesus equivalent in heavenly rank, or superior to, the angel?

---

[1] Cf. Boring, 64–67; Sweet, 57–8.

God and Jesus Christ in the Apocalypse

In chapter 1 we noted that a few interpreters of the Apocalypse have argued that there is nothing which requires the conclusion that Jesus Christ is understood to be divine.[2] But most interpreters have drawn the conclusion that the evidence is strongly in favour of the divinity of Jesus Christ in the Apocalypse.[3] Karrer, for example, while recognizing that there are subordinationist components in the christology of the Apocalypse concludes that the emphasis is not on subordination but on the coordination, if not identification, of Jesus Christ as God's Son with God.[4] In general terms, the argument for the divinity of Jesus Christ in the Apocalypse rests on two observations: (i) Jesus the Lamb is worshipped (Apc. 5) and (ii) the relationship between Jesus and God tends towards a unity. Since the majority position supports the conclusion that Jesus is divine within the Apocalypse we briefly rather than exhaustively consider these matters. We first consider the worship of Jesus in the Apocalypse.

There is no doubt that worship in the Apocalypse is constrained in the direction of a single object of worship. Not once but twice, in Apocalypse 19.10 and 22.9, an angel spurns John's attempts to worship him and exhorts him to 'worship God' (τῷ θεῷ προσ-κύνησον). In Apocalypse 22.3–4 the heavenly worshippers gather around the (singular) 'throne of God and of the Lamb'. Both here and in the great vision of the open heaven in Apocalypse 4 and 5 there is only one throne as the object of worship. In that vision we notice, on the one hand that God is worshipped in a hymn (4.11) which is closely paralleled by a hymn to the Lamb (5.12) and, on the other, the culmination of the worship in 5.8–13 is the addressing of a hymn to 'the one seated on the throne and to the Lamb' (5.13). When we also observe that the four living creatures and the twenty-four elders fall down before the Lamb (5.8) and that only the Lamb – of all beings in heaven and on earth – has been adjudged 'worthy' (5.2–5), the implication seems clear: Jesus the Lamb is worshipped

---

[2] See p. 2.

[3] E.g. Brütsch, iii, 87; Allo, 331; Prigent, 354; Lohse, 105; Ritt, 117; Roloff, 211; Swete, 303; Mounce, 393; Beasley-Murray, 339 (all references relating to discussion of Apc. 22.13); Caird, 290; Bauckham, *Theology*, 63; Comblin, *Christ*, 15. A recent restatement of the 'non-divine' position by Casey (*Jewish*, 141–3) does not do justice to the worship of the Lamb in Apc. 5, and omits discussion of the crucial text, 22.13.

[4] Karrer, *Johannesoffenbarung*, 148–9.

in the view of the Apocalypse. But this worship only allows for a
fleeting impression that Jesus is a second object of worship. The
worship of Jesus is within the bounds of monotheism. The high
point of the heavenly worship is the 'joint worship of God and
Christ, in a formula in which God retains the primacy'.[5] As the
object of worship in the Apocalypse we may appropriately conclude
that Jesus Christ is divine.[6]

Reflection on the worship of Jesus in the Apocalypse leads
naturally to the second observation which supports the divinity of
Christ, namely, the unity of Jesus Christ and God. (By 'unity' we
simply mean that the relationship between Jesus and God is
characterized by a closeness that tends to a singularity so that, for
example, together they share one throne and are spoken of in terms
of a singular pronoun.) We have seen that the worship of Jesus in
Apocalypse 5 is the worship of one who is distinguished from
creatures and conjoined with the Creator. Jesus is bound with God
in such a manner that together they form a single object of worship.
There are, in fact, other observations which we can make supporting the apparent unity between Jesus and God.

The first set of these develops the idea of the singular throne 'of
God and of the Lamb' and the second concerns the use of common
titles between God and Jesus. In Apocalypse 21.22–22.6 God and
the Lamb are referred to both together and separately. John sees no
temple in the new Jerusalem and explains ὁ γὰρ κύριος ὁ θεὸς ὁ
παντοκράτωρ ναὸς αὐτῆς ἐστιν καὶ τὸ ἀρνίον (21.22). The city has
no need for sunshine or moonlight since ἡ γὰρ δόξα τοῦ θεοῦ
ἐφώτισεν αὐτήν, καὶ ὁ λύχνος αὐτῆς τὸ ἀρνίον (21.23). Only those
'who are written in the Lamb's book of life' will enter the city
(21.27). The river of the water of life which flows through the city
flows ἐκ τοῦ θρόνου τοῦ θεοῦ καὶ τοῦ ἀρνίου (22.1). Apocalypse
22.3–4 is worth citing in full since it refers not only to the throne of
God and of the Lamb but also to the worship which takes place
around it. Significantly, singular pronouns are used with respect to
the object of worship:

> καὶ ὁ θρόνος τοῦ θεοῦ καὶ τοῦ ἀρνίου ἐν αὐτῇ ἔσται, καὶ
> οἱ δοῦλοι αὐτοῦ λατρεύσουσιν αὐτῷ ⁴ καὶ ὄψονται τὸ
> πρόσωπον αὐτοῦ, καὶ τὸ ὄνομα αὐτοῦ ἐπὶ τῶν μετώπων
> αὐτῶν.   (Apc. 22.3–4)

[5] Bauckham, 'Worship', 330–1, citation from p. 331.
[6] Sweet, 127.

Two further references interest us in relation to these verses. In Apocalypse 22.5 the seer states that there will be no need for the light of lamp or sun 'for the Lord God will be their light'. Then in 22.6 the seer is addressed with words which include reference to 'the Lord, the God of the spirits of the prophets'. The most important question raised by these references concerns the referent of the singular pronouns in Apocalypse 22.3–4. Does '*his* servants . . . worship *him* . . . *his* face . . . *his* name' refer to God, or to the Lamb, or to God and the Lamb? It is scarcely conceivable that the Lamb alone would be the referent, which leaves us to consider that either God is in view or God and the Lamb together. Sweet, for example, favours the former arguing that 'for all his associating the Lamb wholly and equally with God, John's final picture . . . is of God alone'.[7] By contrast, Beasley-Murray, perhaps too hastily dismissing the former, argues for the latter: 'God and the Lamb are viewed as a unity in so real a fashion that the singular pronoun alone is suitable to interpret them.'[8]

Given the monotheistic beliefs which shaped John's theology it is not surprising that references to 'God and the Lamb' should not be sustained (e.g. in 22.5,6). But the fact that there are *several* references to 'God and the Lamb' in the culmination of the vision of the new Jerusalem, and that they are made in conjunction with 'the temple' and 'the throne', suggest that Beasley-Murray is essentially correct: within the Apocalypse God and the Lamb are viewed in such a manner that they are understood as a unity.[9] It is a little implausible to suppose that as the heavenly worshippers bow before 'the throne of God and of the Lamb' – the same throne which elsewhere is described as the one on which the Son sits with the Father (3.21) and the Lamb is at the centre (7.17) – they distinguish between God and the Lamb as the object of their worship. It is far more plausible to suppose that they worship God and the Lamb as a unity. Thus consideration of the final part of the vision of the new Jerusalem lends added support to an implication

[7] Sweet, 312; cf. Beckwith, 766.
[8] Beasley-Murray, 332; cf. Holtz (*Christologie*, 202–3) who sees a similar characteristic in Apc. 11.15.
[9] On singular pronouns (possibly) referring to God and Christ and singular verbs with God and Christ as (possible) subjects in the Apocalypse see Bauckham, 'Worship', 330–1 (with note on Apc. 6.17 as a possible exception), 339, n. 51; Holtz, *Christologie*, 202–3; and Stuckenbruck, 'Refusal', 690–1.

of the worship of Jesus in Apocalypse 5, namely, that the relationship between Jesus Christ and God tends towards a unity.

We now consider the question of common titles shared between
Jesus and God. It is as well to begin by noting several ways in
which Jesus is distinguished from God within the Apocalypse.
First, Jesus is ὁ υἱὸς τοῦ θεοῦ (Apc. 2.18), while God in relation to
Jesus is πατρὶ αὐτοῦ (Apc. 1.6), πατρός μου (Apc. 3.21). Secondly,
Jesus is God's χριστὸς (Apc. 11.15, 12.10; cf. 20.6). Thirdly, God is
ὁ παντοκράτωρ (Apc. 1.8), a title which is never applied to Jesus.[10]
These distinctions, however, should not be pressed too far. When
Jesus refers to 'my Father' it is in the context of a declaration that
he has sat with his Father on his throne (Apc. 3.21). This sharing of
the divine throne is reflected, as we have seen, in other statements
in the Apocalypse so that Jesus is τὸ ἀρνίον τὸ ἀνὰ μέσον τοῦ
θρόνου (7.17), and the divine throne is described as ὁ θρόνος τοῦ
θεοῦ καὶ τοῦ ἀρνίου (22.3). On three occasions when Jesus is
described as '[God's] Anointed' in the Apocalypse it is in the
context of sharing in divine privilege and power (11.15, 12.10,
20.6). If Jesus is not entitled ὁ παντοκράτωρ it is nevertheless the
case that in speeches attributed to him he takes up predicates
otherwise belonging only to God. In Apc. 22.12–13, for example,
we find the following statement:

> Ἰδοὺ ἔρχομαι ταχύ, καὶ ὁ μισθός μου μετ' ἐμοῦ ἀποδοῦναι
> ἑκάστῳ ὡς τὸ ἔργον ἐστὶν αὐτοῦ. ¹³ ἐγὼ τὸ ἄλφα καὶ τὸ ὦ,
> ὁ πρῶτος καὶ ὁ ἔσχατος, ἡ ἀρχὴ καὶ τὸ τέλος.
>
> (Apc. 22.12–13)[11]

There can be little doubt that these are the words of Jesus since (i)
the phrase Ἰδοὺ ἔρχομαι ταχύ recalls Jesus' words ἔρχομαι ταχύ in
2.16 and 3.11, and (ii) in 22.20 the words ναί ἔρχομαι ταχύ are
followed by the response, Ἀμήν, ἔρχου κύριε Ἰησοῦ'.[12] There is no
reason to suppose that the subject of 22.13 is different from that of
22.12. Whether the speaker is Jesus or an angel speaking for Jesus

[10] See further on the distinction between God and Christ in Holtz, 'Gott', 262–3.
[11] There is no justification for the claim by Charles, ii, 219, that v. 12 follows v. 13.
[12] In Apc. 22.7 we find ἰδοὺ ἔρχομαι ταχύ following the speech of the angel in 22.6,
which raises the question whether the angel or Jesus speaks these words. Note
also ἔρχομαι σοι (2.5), which is to be attributed to Jesus, and ἔρχομαι ὡς
κλέπτης (16.15), which also comes from Jesus. On the significance of ἰδοὺ
ἔρχομαι ταχύ as a counter to contemporary magical practice, see Aune, 'Magic',
491–3.

is immaterial for the point we wish to make.[13] Turning to the
content of Apocalypse 22.12–13 we find that the statement concerning the intention to repay, ὁ μισθός μου μετ᾽ ἐμοῦ ἀποδοῦναι
ἑκάστῳ ὡς τὸ ἔργον ἐστὶν αὐτοῦ, combines OT prophecy about
God's coming in judgement (Isa. 40.10, 62.11) with proverbial
wisdom about God's repaying all according to their deeds (Prov.
24.12).[14] As with many of the statements in the Epilogue (i.e. Apc.
22.6–21), there is a strong echo of an earlier statement in the
Apocalypse, δώσω ὑμῖν ἑκάστῳ κατὰ τὰ ἔργα ὑμῶν (2.23). Thus
the exalted Jesus declares that he is coming in judgement but his
judgement is no less or more than God's judgement. In the
eschatological future God and Jesus are identified together as the
coming judge.

If the emphasis in Apocalypse 22.12 is eschatological then there
is a balancing protological declaration in 22.13 when Jesus makes
the astonishing claim in verse 13: ἐγὼ τὸ ἄλφα καὶ τὸ ὦ, ὁ πρῶτος
καὶ ὁ ἔσχατος, ἡ ἀρχὴ καὶ τὸ τέλος. Two of these titles recall 'I
am' statements made by God earlier in the Apocalypse: ἐγώ εἰμι τὸ
ἄλφα καὶ τὸ ὦ (1.8, 21.6), and ἐγώ (εἰμι) τὸ ἄλφα καὶ τὸ ὦ, ἡ ἀρχὴ
καὶ τὸ τέλος (21.6).[15] The remaining title recalls Jesus' own
statement in 1.17: ἐγω εἰμι ὁ πρῶτος καὶ ὁ ἔσχατος (cf. 2.8). The
context of the last-mentioned title – the appearance of the risen
Jesus to John – could imply that Jesus, being the first to rise from
the dead (cf. Apc. 1.5), is 'first and last' with respect to the church
(cf. Col 1.18). Nevertheless this title, as with the others, has divine
connotations, for the statement in Apocalypse 1.17 itself takes up
two 'I am' sayings attributed to God in Isaiah: ʾny rʾšwn wʾny ʾḥrwn
(Isa. 44.6 MT) and ʾny rʾšwn ʾp ʾny ʾḥrwn (Isa. 48.12 MT). When we
also consider that in Apc. 22.13 'the first and the last' is parallel to
'the Alpha and the Omega' and 'the beginning and the end', it
would appear that its application to Jesus Christ extends beyond
his relationship to the church. For 'the Alpha and the Omega' and
'the beginning and the end' applied to God speak of the eternal life
of God from which all things originate and in which all things find
their fulfilment. The implication of Apocalypse 22.13 is that Jesus

[13] Beckwith, 776; cf. Swete, 302–3; Vanni, 'Dialogue', 358; Hartman, 'Form', 147;
Giblin, *Revelation*, 218; Boring, 'Voice', 344; Ritt, 116–17; Roloff, 211; W. Scott,
446.
[14] Beckwith, 776; Beasley-Murray, 338; Bauckham, *Theology*, 64.
[15] Charles, ii, 220 draws attention to the Orphic roots of ἡ ἀρχὴ καὶ τὸ τέλος; cf.
Beasley-Murray, 339; Aune, 'Magic', 489–91.

Christ participates in the eternal being of God. In other words, when acting both as agent of creation (cf. 3.14) and as eschatological judge (cf. 22.12) Jesus Christ is not simply equated with God at the level of *function* but shares in the very being of God.[16]

This point can be made in another way: our review above of the worship of Jesus which brought out the strictly monotheistic character of the Apocalypse means that we can scarcely conclude that Apocalypse 22.12–13 signifies that Jesus is another god. Just as the worship of Jesus in the Apocalypse is the worship of Jesus conjoined with God in a unity, so the 'I am' statements signify that Jesus is '[included] in the eternal being of God'.[17] The unity envisaged between God and Jesus Christ goes beyond the matter of function to the level of being. Thus Apocalypse 22.13 effectively constitutes a declaration affirming the divinity of Jesus Christ. To suggest this is the case in the Apocalypse is, of course, to imply that an apocalyptic theologian in the first century *was beginning to make some sense* of a two-in-one approach to understanding the being of God in relation to Jesus Christ.[18] This is not to say, though, that the Apocalypse already enshrines a viewpoint which approximates to the later christology of Nicea and Chalcedon.[19] For this reason we must take care with our description of the relationship between God and Jesus Christ in the Apocalypse. When referring to this relationship we will speak of 'the unity between God and Jesus Christ'. With this expression we will have in mind the above discussion and mean that, in the relationship between God and Jesus Christ, there is a participation in the being of God such that Jesus can speak as the divine 'I am', and that together God and Jesus Christ form one object of worship. We do not mean to imply that the Apocalypse is implicitly closer to the later christology of the patristic period than it is. Nevertheless, we affirm that in the Apocalypse Jesus Christ is understood to be divine, and in some sense to relate with God in a unity.

Two important implications need to be noted before we proceed

---

[16] Cf. Bauckham, *Theology*, 54–8, 62–3.

[17] Bauckham, *Theology*, 58. Cf. Brütsch, iii, 87; Allo, 331; Prigent, 354; Lohse, 105; Ritt, 117; Roloff, 211; Michl, *Engelvorstellungen*, 181.

[18] For the purposes of the present discussion we simply ignore discussion of the Spirit in the Apocalypse. Bauckham (*Theology,* 109–18) is an excellent starting point for such a discussion.

[19] Swete, clviii. Bauckham (*Theology*, 61–2) suggests that the distinctive way John presents his christology has obscured the significance of his work in the development of theology towards the later patristic understanding.

further. First, that the christology of the Apocalypse recognizes the pre-existence of Christ, perhaps most clearly expressed in the self-descriptive phrase, 'the beginning of God's creation' (3.14). Secondly, and consequent upon the first, the christology of the Apocalypse is not about the exaltation of a human Jesus of Nazareth to become a heavenly being, so that we do not have to reckon with the possibility that the figure in Apocalypse 1.13–16 is merely an exalted, angelomorphic human. In the chapters that follow we will work with the understanding, at least *pro forma* since we cannot undertake further discussion of important issues associated with these implications here, that our task involves drawing out the significance of the divine Jesus Christ appearing in angelic form.

Jesus Christ and the revealing angel

We return to Apocalypse 1.1 to consider the relationship between Jesus Christ and the revealing angel. We first examine some pertinent matters which arise from Apocalypse 1.1 and its immediate context, and then trace the appearances and auditions of the angel through the remainder of the Apocalypse. The opening verse of the Apocalypse introduces us to the four key characters in the dramatic revelation that follows: God, Jesus Christ, the revealing angel, and John. Our concern is primarily with Jesus and the angel. In Apocalypse 1.1 Jesus Christ is both the *Offenbarungs-mittler* since he acts on behalf of God, and the *Offenbarer* since the revelation which is revealed bears his name.[20] Although it has been argued that τοῦ ἀγγέλου refers to Jesus as God's 'messenger',[21] nevertheless this does not make good sense of the fact that an angel is involved in the transmission of the revelation later in the Apocalypse (e.g. 17.1), nor does it make sense if God and Jesus Christ together send the 'angel'. We conclude with the vast majority of scholars that τοῦ ἀγγέλου refers to an angel in the sense of a created heavenly being distinct from Jesus Christ. Angels as

---

[20] Pesch, 'Offenbarung', 17–18. Boring ('Voice', 356) helpfully distinguishes between God as the 'ultimate source', the angel as the 'intermediate source', and Jesus Christ as the 'definitive source'. Cf. Karrer, *Johannesoffenbarung*, 98. The genitive at the beginning of Apc. 1.1 is subjective: the revelation belongs to Jesus Christ, so Charles, i, 6; Kraft, 20; Beckwith, 418; opposed are, e.g., Ford, 373 and Pesch 'Offenbarung', 17.

[21] Schmitt, 'Christologische', 262.

mediators and interpreters of divine revelation are, in fact, familiar
figures in apocalyptic literature (e.g. *Jub.* 1.27; *Jos. and Asen.* 14.14;
Asc. Isa. 6.13; 4 Ezra 4.1; Daniel 8.15; 1 *Enoch* 1.2, 43.3, 72.1; 5Q
15; cf. 1QH 18.23).[22] In Apocalypse 1.1 it is not immediately clear
who the referent of αὐτοῦ is in the expression διὰ τοῦ ἄλλέλου
αὐτου τω δούλω αὐτου Ἰωάννῃ. On the one hand, if Jesus is the
subject of ἐσήμανεν ἀποστείλας then it is possible that αὐτου
refers to him and, looking ahead, we can note that in Apocalypse
22.16 Jesus speaks of sending 'my angel'. On the other hand, it is
also possible to understand the verse as saying that Jesus made the
revelation known by sending it through the angel of God to John,
the servant of God. A further possibility is that, as Lohmeyer
argues, in the ambiguity ('Schwebenden') of the meaning of αὐτου
'the fundamental unity of God and Christ comes to characteristic
expression'.[23] This makes sense in the context of a 'superscription',
that is, an introduction added after the completion of the rest of the
book. For it would then be taking up the fact that elsewhere in the
Apocalypse, as we have argued above, God and Christ are presented as a unity. Given that at the end of the book the sending of
the angel is ascribed to both God (22.6) and Jesus (22.16) this last
possibility is to be preferred. The first three verses of the Apocalypse are likely to be a superscription. This is suggested by the
words ἐμαρτύρησεν (v. 2) and γεγραμμένα (v. 3) which imply that
the author is writing with his completed work before him.[24] Nevertheless, from a narrative-critical perspective Apocalypse 1.1–3 is
the first part of the book to be read (or heard). Thus it sets up an
expectation that the angel will be mentioned again in those parts of
the work which refer to the process of receiving the revelation. Our
next concern is to track down the appearances and auditions of this
angel in the Apocalypse.

The obvious place to look for this angel would appear to be
Apocalypse 22.6, for here an angel is referred to in a similar way to
Apocalypse 1.1: ὁ κύριος ὁ θεὸς τῶν πνευμάτων τῶν προφητῶν
ἀπέστειλεν τὸν ἄγγελον αὐτοῦ δεῖξαι τοῖς δούλοις αὐτοῦ ἃ δεῖ
γενέσθαι ἐν τάχει. Whether the speaker is the angel himself,[25] or
another (e.g. Jesus Christ),[26] need not concern us here. The role of
the angel is δεῖξαι τοῖς δούλοις αὐτοῦ ἃ δεῖ γενέσθαι ἐν τάχει. In

[22] Cf. Davidson, *Angels*, 311.
[23] Lohmeyer, 6; cf. Holtz, *Christologie*, 202.
[24] Beckwith, 417–23, esp. p. 421; Kraft, 18.
[25] Beckwith, 772.   [26] Charles, ii, 217.

Apocalypse 1.1 the same expression is found but it is associated with the intentions of God expressed through Jesus Christ. Thus in Apocalypse 22.6 the action of the angel is described in a way which indicates that it fulfils the purpose of God. At this point Jesus is out of view (unless he is the speaker). In 22.16, however, where Jesus is the speaker, we find a reference to an angel which is different from 22.6 yet appears to share a common concern with the transmission of the revelation: Ἐγὼ Ἰησοῦς ἔπεμψα τὸν ἄγγελόν μου μαρτυρῆσαι ὑμῖν ταῦτα ἐπὶ ταῖς ἐκκλησίαις. The fact that Jesus 'sends' this angel suggests that the angel is a subordinate of Jesus. There are instances in which an angel 'sends' another angel (e.g. 1 *Enoch* 60.4) or an angel commands another angel to do something (e.g. Apc. 14.18) so that 22.16 by itself does not signal that Jesus is co-equal with God as the superior to the angel. But having authority over the angel is consistent with our previous conclusion that Jesus and God form a unity in the Apocalypse.[27] The use of μαρτυρῆσαι in 22.16, rather than δεῖξαι as in 22.6 and 1.1, raises the question whether the angel in 22.16 is the same angel as the one referred to in 22.6 and 1.1. The difference in verbs could be explained, however, in terms of the frequent association between Jesus and μαρτ-root words in the Apocalypse.[28]

There are, in fact, other differences between the descriptions of the angel in 22.6 and 22.16: (i) a different verb for 'sending' is used (πέμπω, v. 16; cf. ἀποστέλλω, v. 6); (ii) ταῦτα (v. 16) is the content of the angel's testimony instead of ἃ δεῖ γενέσθαι ἐν τάχει (v. 6); and (iii) there is no mention of 'servants' (δοῦλοι) as the recipients of the angel's testimony in verse 16 (cf. ὑμῖν ... ἐπὶ ταῖς ἐκκλησιαις). These differences, however, are not necessarily significant. Although the two verbs for 'sending' can be distinguished in meaning they are effectively synonyms.[29] Ταῦτα could refer to the content of 22.14–15,[30] but it is found in 22.8 where John describes himself as ὁ ἀκούων καὶ βλέπων ταῦτα meaning that he has heard and seen ἃ δεῖ γενέσθαι ἐν τάχει (22.6).[31] It is reasonable, therefore, to suppose that ταῦτα in 22.16 equates with ἃ δεῖ γενέσθαι ἐν τάχει in 22.6 (and 1.1). The addressees of the angel's testimony, ὑμῖν ... ἐπὶ ταῖς ἐκκλησίαις, appear to involve a

[27] Beasley-Murray, 342; Giblin, *Revelation*, 219.
[28] Apc. 1.2,5,9; 12.17; 19.10; 20.4; 22.20.
[29] Rengstorf ('ἀποστέλλω', 405) notes that in the Fourth Gospel πέμπειν is always used of the sending of the Spirit by Jesus.
[30] So Vanni, 'Dialogue', 358–9.   [31] Swete, 300.

twofold group: ὑμῖν referring to John and his fellow servants the prophets,[32] and ἐπὶ ταῖς ἐκκλησίαις referring to all the other Christians in Asia Minor.[33] Such a twofold group is consistent with τοῖς δούλοις in 22.6. Thus there is no intrinsic reason to deny that the references to a revealing angel in Apocalypse 22.6 and 22.16 pertain to the same angel. That there is only one such angel is confirmed by 1.1 which only envisages one angel acting as intermediary between God/Jesus and John/servants.[34] According to Apocalypse 1.1, 22.6, and 22.16 this angel is a key link in the chain of transmission. The expectation raised in 1.1 that the reader will subsequently find clear indications that the angel participates in the transmitting of the revelation to John contrasts with the fact that we never find a scene in which God or Jesus send an angel to John. Nevertheless, it is possible to see signs of the presence of the revealing angel in the narrative apart from the three verses so far considered. In what follows we demonstrate where these occasions arise.

When John first sees the open heaven before him (Apc. 4.1–2a) he hears the voice of a guide who says something which corresponds closely to the description of the revealing angel's activity in 22.6: ἀνάβα ὧδε, καὶ δείξω σοι ἃ δεῖ γενέσθαι μετὰ ταῦτα (4.1). The speaker is unlikely to be God himself since (i) characteristically, God does not speak in the Apocalypse (with the exception of 1.8, 21.5–8), and (ii) there is no reason to think that God would introduce John to the vision of God. The speaker could be Jesus[35] since he has just been speaking (having completed dictation of the seventh ecclesial letter in 3.22), yet two observations indicate that this possibility should also be discounted. First, the description of the speaker as ἡ φωνὴ ἡ πρώτη ἣν ἤκουσα ὡς σάλπιγγος suggests a new speaker is in view and not Jesus who has just been speaking.[36] (This point is overlooked by those who argue that since

[32] Aune, 'Prophetic circle', 111; Beckwith, 777: 'it is best explained as referring to the prophets in general'.

[33] Here ἐπὶ with the dative means 'for', so Beckwith, 777, who notes Eph. 2.10: ἐπὶ ἔργοις ἀγαθοῖς. That ἐπὶ ταῖς ἐκκλησίαις has a general reference to Christians is implied by its correspondence with ἐπὶ λαοῖς καὶ ἔθνεσιν καὶ γλώσσαις καὶ βασιλεῦσιν πολλοῖς, Apc. 10.11 (Swete, 305).

[34] In theory the ἄγγελος in Apc. 22.16 could be John (so, Schmitt, 'Christologische', 262), but in practice this term is never used of John in the Apocalypse.

[35] So, e.g., Prigent, 82.

[36] Charles, i, 108, argues that ἡ φωνὴ ... λέγων is an editorial addition but recognizes that if the voice in 1.10 is that of an angel then it could also be the case here.

ἡ φωνὴ ἡ πρώτη ἣν ἤκουσα ὡς σάλπιγγος refers back to the figure in 1.10–11 it must be Jesus.[37] Logically, of course, if the speaker in 4.1 is *not* Jesus then neither is the speaker in 1.10–11.)

Secondly, the dramatic impact of the opening to the second part of the heavenly vision (5.1–5) is heightened if the pretence is maintained that Jesus is absent throughout the vision prior to this point.[38] While it is possible that the speaker in 4.1 could be one of the numerous anonymous voices that are heard throughout the Apocalypse (e.g. 14.13a) or even the Spirit (e.g. 14.13b), the words the speaker uses are so clearly echoed in 22.6 (cf. 17.1–3, 21.9–10) that it makes good sense to conclude that the speaker is the revealing angel.[39]

One consequence of our conclusion that 4.1 represents an occasion when the revealing angel is present to John is that he is also present in 1.10–11, where John first hears the φωνὴν μεγάλην ὡς σάλπιγγος (1.10).[40] This conclusion is not uncontroversial. It contrasts, for example, with an important study by Charlesworth on 'the voice' in Apocalypse 1.10–13 in which he argues that τὴν φωνὴν in 1.12 is a christological term adapted from Jewish talk about hypostases. But it is noteworthy that Charlesworth (i) does not consider the identity of 'the voice' from the perspective of Apocalypse 4.1, and (ii) recognizes that in some instances in Jewish literature 'the voice' is to be identified as an angel.[41] That the angel is the voice in 1.10 is controversial also in the sense that 1.10–13 can quite naturally be read in such a way that only one figure is understood to be present audibly and visibly to John, that is, Jesus, the 'one like a son of man'. But it is quite plausible to recognize two figures in 1.10–13: we have already observed in Zechariah 1.8–13 that the focus of attention switches backwards and forwards between the 'angel of the LORD' and 'the angel who talked with me'. Similarly, we may suppose a switch in Apocalypse 1.10–13: while 'the voice' in 1.10–12 is an angel yet as John turns to 'see the voice'

---

[37] E.g. Beckwith, 495.

[38] Cf. Bousset, 243; Charles, i, 108.

[39] Holtz, *Christologie*, 110, n. 3; Swete, 13; Lohse, 34; Roloff, 40.

[40] Holtz, *Christologie*, 110, n. 3; Lohmeyer, 14; Lohse, 18; Roloff, 40; Karrer, *Johannesoffenbarung*, 104, n. 66. Against: Allo, 11; Prigent, 25; Loisy, 77; Beckwith, 436, 495; Bousset, 193; Farrar, 65.

[41] Charlesworth, 'Jewish roots', 32; cf. P. Kuhn (*Offenbarungsstimmen*, 115) who recognizes that in some instances in apocalyptic tradition 'the voice' is an angel, e.g., *Apoc. Abr.* 19.1. Unfortunately, Kuhn has nothing to say about Apc. 1.12.

$(1.12)^{42}$ he sees Jesus as 'one like a son of man' (1.13). Thus we conclude that after the initial mention of the revealing angel in 1.1 this angel is implicitly present in the narrative in Apocalypse 1.10 and 4.1. In both cases a significant part of the revelation begins to be disclosed to John and it is quite plausible that the revealing angel should be part of the proceedings.

The next possible occasion where the revealing angel is present in the narrative is in Apocalypse 10.1 where a 'mighty angel' appears holding a 'little scroll' and commissions John to 'prophesy again'. Although the description of this angel has nothing directly in common with the descriptions given in Apocalypse 1.1, 1.10, 4.1, 22.6, and 22.16, there does not seem to be any decisive reason against understanding this angel to be the revealing angel.^{43} Jesus himself is described in different ways in the Apocalypse, and since 1.1 mentions only one revealing angel it is likely that the angel in 10.1 is *the* revealing angel.

The revealing angel apparently features next in the narrative in Apocalypse 17.1 when an angel – one of the bowl angels – appears. This angel says that he will 'show' (δείξω) John certain things and is present throughout 17.1–18, and reappears in 19.9–10.^{44} In 21.9 an angel, also described as 'one' of the bowl angels, appears and also says that he will 'show' (δείξω) John certain things. Again, since only one revealing angel is referred to in 1.1 we may presume that one and the same bowl angel is meant. This angel is present with John through to at least 22.5, is referred to by John in 22.8, and certainly speaks with him in 22.9–11, if not in 22.6.^{45} Disagreement over the identity of the speaker occurs with a number of verses in Apocalypse 22.6–21. Thus, for example, there is considerable diversity over the identity of the speaker in 22.14–15. Suggestions have included the revealing angel,^{46} John,^{47}

^{42} We agree with Charlesworth ('Jewish roots', 20–5) when he argues that this is the correct translation of βλέπειν τὴν φωνὴν (so NIV, contrast NRSV, NEB: 'to see whose voice'). Cf. W. Shakespeare, *A Midsummer Night's Dream*, Act 5, sc.1: 'I see a voice'.

^{43} See the argument given in Bauckham (*Theology*, 80–2) and Brighton (*Angel*, 111–22, 181–92). We disagree, however, with Bauckham's assertion (p. 82; cf. Bousset, 182; Pesch, 'Offenbarung', 21), that the revealing angel 'does not appear in the book until 10.1'.

^{44} The 'he' in Apc. 19.9–10 can only be an angel. On the revealing angel in Apc. 17–22 cf. Giblin, 'Correlations', 495.

^{45} Note the verb δείκνυμι used with reference to this angel in 21.10 and 22.1, 22.8.

^{46} Vanni, 'Dialogue', 358–9.

^{47} Beckwith, 776: 'The speaker may be Christ, but probably the Apocalyptist.'

Jesus,[48] a spokesman for the community,[49] and a process of modulation in which the voice of the angel fades into the voice of Jesus.[50] We do not intend to resolve these disagreements here.[51] Rather, we will simply note those places where the angel as speaker has been supported: namely Apocalypse 22.6,[52] 22.7,[53] 22.9–11,[54] and 22.14–15.[55]

Apocalypse 22.6–7 is probably significant for the relationship between Jesus and the angel and thus worth examining in a little detail. We have already considered 22.6 in terms of the description it gives of the revealing angel. Here we look at the question of the significance of the angel as the one who (possibly) speaks these words. On the one hand, if the speaker changes from the angel in 22.6 to Jesus in 22.7,[56] then Jesus and the angel function closely together. The sudden interjection of Jesus into the dialogue would then mirror the sudden change from the angel to 'one like a son of man' according to our interpretation of 1.10–13.[57] Using a thespian analogy we can envisage Jesus 'waiting in the wings' – his main part is coming up shortly in 22.12–16 – and at the concluding words of the angel in 22.6, ἐν τάχει, he 'throws his voice' with the apt rejoinder, καὶ ἰδοὺ ἔρχομαι ταχύ. It is the angel who is 'on stage', however, and John is confused by the collocation of the voice of Jesus and the presence of an angel whose appearance is reminiscent of the risen Jesus.[58] He falls down to worship only to be rebuked in

---

[48] Hartman, 'Form': 'Christ, the speaker of vv. 12–16 . . .'

[49] Giblin (*Revelation*, 218): 'vv.14–15 are best assigned . . . to a spokesman for the community'.

[50] Boring, 'Voice', 344, 358; cf. Farrar, 225 (on 22.10–15): 'one inspired utterance runs on – it is John's, the angel's, Christ's'.

[51] On the question of the attributions of the speeches in Apc. 22.6–21 see further Vanni, 'Dialogue' (with response from Aune, 'Intertextuality', 147); Boring, 'Voice'; Gaechter, 'Original sequence'; Hartman, 'Form'; Giblin, *Revelation*, 218; Rissi, *Future*, 84.

[52] Vanni, 'Dialogue', 357; Hartman, 'Form', 145.

[53] Ibid.; Loisy, 389. Note that some discern two speakers in 22.7: e.g. Vanni ('Dialogue', 357) who attributes 22.7a to Jesus and 22.7b (the beatitude) to the angel.

[54] Vanni, 'Dialogue', 357; Hartman, 'Form', 146; Giblin, *Revelation*, 218.

[55] Vanni, 'Dialogue', 358–9.

[56] Note the change from the third person, εἶπεν, in 22.6 to the first person, ἔρχομαι, in 22.7, and the words, καὶ ἰδοὺ ἔρχομαι ταχύ, which are characteristic of Christ, so Vanni, 'Dialogue', 357; cf. Roloff, 209; Allo, 329; Ritt, 115.

[57] A similar interruption may be found in 16.15; cf. Caird, 207–8.

[58] Giblin, *Revelation*, 217–18, 'His impulse (v. 8) to worship the angel, a matter on which he had already been corrected (19:10), becomes more intelligible here as a somewhat confused response to the two speakers in vv. 6–7'. On the (in)signifi-

such a way that he is in no doubt that it is the angel and not Jesus who stands before him! On the other hand, if the angel continues speaking throughout 22.6–7 then he can scarcely be held to be announcing his own coming with the words καὶ ἰδοὺ ἔρχομαι ταχύ. Rather, the angel would be speaking on behalf of Jesus, suggesting that he acts as representative for Jesus, analogous to the angel of the LORD in certain situations in the OT.[59]   Nevertheless we must also recognize that it has been argued that Jesus is the speaker throughout 22.6–7,[60] in which case 22.6–7 contributes little to our understanding of the relationship between Jesus and the angel.

The apparent absence of the revealing angel in the main body of the narrative of the Apocalypse has led some scholars to posit a 'synchronic' interpretation of Apocalypse 1.1.[61] That is, the revelation is given by God, Jesus, and the angel who each speak for the other in an essentially non-hierarchical process of transmission. The more traditional 'diachronic' interpretation may be upheld, however, if we recognize that the revealing angel is implicitly present in the main body of the narrative, especially at 4.1 and 10.1, which are highly significant in the story of the unfolding of the revelation to John.

Having traced out the presence of the revealing angel in the Apocalypse, and having noted one or two instances in which the angel and Jesus work very closely together, we can attempt an answer to the question of the relationship between the exalted Jesus and the revealing angel. In the light of Apocalypse 1.1 and 22.16 we first note that Jesus is the superior of the angel: Jesus joins with God as the *sender* of the angel; the angel is subordinate to God and Jesus. But we may also observe that there is a degree of *functional equivalence* between Jesus and the angel. In Apocalypse 1.1, for instance, both Jesus and the revealing angel function as intermediaries between God and John. If the angel gives the command to write down what John 'sees' (1.11) then the similar command given by Jesus (1.19) is a further example of functional equivalence. The angel in Apocalypse 10 also shares a similar function to Jesus since both commission John for his prophetic task. Comparison between Apocalypse 22.16 and 22.20 suggests another instance in which

cance of the angel's appearance see Stuckenbruck, 'Refusal', 693. We suggest the angel's appearance plays a greater role in the attempt of the seer to worship than Stuckenbruck allows.
[59] Hartman, 'Form', 145.   [60] Charles, ii, 217.
[61] E.g. Boring, 'Voice', 350–6.

Jesus and the angel function equivalently. In 22.16 the revealing angel's function is characterized by the use of μαρτυρῆσαι. In 22.20 John records a statement and its response: Λέγει ὁ μαρτυρῶν ταῦτα· ναί, ἔρχομαι ταχύ. Ἀμήν, ἔρχου κύριε Ἰησοῦ. The statement, ναὶ, ἔρχομαι ταχύ, echoing by now familiar words of Jesus (cf. 2.16, 3.11, 22.12) and its response which specifically names Jesus, imply that ὁ μαρτυρῶν is Jesus.[62] This designation, of course, coheres with titles given elsewhere in the Apocalypse for Jesus: ὁ μάρτυς ὁ πιστός (1.5) and ὁ μάρτυς ὁ πιστὸς καὶ ἀληθινός (3.14).

In 22.16 the matters to which the revealing angel testifies are described with the word ταῦτα. Thus describing Jesus in 22.20 as ὁ μαρτυρῶν ταῦτα suggests a further example of a functional equivalence between Jesus Christ and the revealing angel: both act as witnesses to the 'things' of God. The functional equivalence between the angel and Jesus, however, raises the question why this is so since a certain redundancy appears to be the result. One possible answer is that the doubling up between Jesus and the angel serves at least two important purposes. On the one hand, if only the angel were involved in the transmission of the revelation John's readers could have lost any sense of the direct involvement of their risen Lord in their time of trial. By portraying the Lord of the church in a similar role to the angel the readers were reminded that their Lord was close at hand in their hour of need. On the other hand, if only the exalted Jesus mediated the revelation then the readers might conceivably have thought that the risen Jesus was an angel. By juxtaposing Jesus and the angel yet distinguishing between them (e.g. never designating Jesus as ἄγγελος; demonstrating that the Lamb could be worshipped but not the angel) John sets up a point of comparison which cautions against the conclusion that Jesus was actually an angel. Some sense therefore can be made of the relationship between Jesus and the revealing angel which is paradoxically characterized by status differentiation and functional equivalence.[63]

---

[62] Beckwith, 779; Giblin, *Revelation*, 220; Hartman, 'Form', 148.

[63] Stuckenbruck ('Refusal', 695) rightly suggests that John did not remove the analogues between Christ and the angels because 'an angelophanic Christology was part of the author's (and readers') *Vorstellungswelt*'. We see this suggestion as compatible with our own view on the matter.

Conclusions

The opening words of the Apocalypse present Jesus Christ in relationship to both God and the angel of the revelation. Examination of relevant passages throughout the remainder of the Apocalypse suggests the exalted Jesus is bound with God in a unity. No encouragement is given to those inclined to believe Jesus to be a second god. Rather, there is a strict adherence to monotheism – but a monotheism which allows for Jesus to be included with God as the object of worship and which envisages Jesus sharing the divine throne with God. We have not attempted to assess the extent to which John may have understood the theology and christology represented in the Apocalypse in terms which anticipated later developments in patristic thought but we have noted that the christology of the Apocalypse recognizes the pre-existence of Christ. However, the exalted Jesus who, united with God, sends the revealing angel is nevertheless comparable to this angel in sharing the function of unveiling the revelation to John and his fellow servants. Jesus and the revealing angel appear to work closely – on occasion there is even a barely perceptible switch between the two as the subject of the action. We have proposed an explanation for an apparently unnecessary doubling up in terms of a pastoral motive (Jesus comes close to his church) and a christological motive (to prevent Jesus being identified as an angel). These observations concerning the relationship between Jesus Christ and God and the revealing angel will be returned to in the course of the next four chapters in which we focus on the three visions found in Apocalypse 1.13–16, 14.14, and 19.11–16.

7

APOCALYPSE 1.13–16 (PART A)

In Apocalypse 1.9–20 we have an account of the commissioning of John to write down 'the revelation of Jesus Christ' (1.9–20). The account of this commissioning is dominated by the appearance of an exalted figure whose form is described in some detail (1.13–16). The figure goes on to speak words which identify him with the risen Jesus Christ: 'I was dead, and see, I am alive forever and ever' (1.18).[1] Thus John is the recipient of a christophany. This christophany has, of course, been the subject of a great deal of study.[2] In this chapter and the next we confine ourselves to reflection on the christophany in keeping with our overall aim. Although the christophany is often related to its presumed background, it has not been compared in depth with the other epiphanies in the Apocalypse (that is, with the angelophanies, and with the theophany in Apc. 4). Accordingly, in this chapter we compare the christophany with the other epiphanies. In practice we consider not only Jesus in relation to the angels and to God but also in relation to the living creatures and to the elders. The results of this investigation will be useful for our discussion in the next chapter of the christophany in the light of its background.

First of all we review the text of Apocalypse 1.12b–16:

> καὶ ἐπιστρέθας εἶδον ἑπτὰ λυχνίας χρυσᾶς ¹³καὶ ἐν μέσῳ
> τῶν λυχνιῶν ὅμοιον υἱὸν ἀνθρώπου ἐνδεδυμένον ποδήρη
> καὶ περιζωσμένον πρὸς τοῖς μαστοῖς ζώνην χρυσᾶν. ¹⁴ἡ
> δὲ κεφαλὴ αὐτοῦ καὶ αἱ τρίχες λευκαὶ ὡς ἔριον λευκὸν ὡς
> χιὼν καὶ οἱ ὀφθαλμοὶ αὐτοῦ ὡς φλὸξ πυρὸς ¹⁵καὶ οἱ πόδες
> αὐτοῦ ὅμοιοι χαλκολιβάνῳ ὡς ἐν καμίνῳ πεπυρωμένης

---

[1] No commentator disputes this.

[2] See commentaries for symbolic significance of the details of Christ's appearance; for a detailed form-critical analysis of the expanded passage, 1.9–20, see Karrer, *Johannesoffenbarung*, 139–47; Holtz, *Christologie*, 116–28.

καὶ ἡ φωνὴ αὐτοῦ ὡς φωνὴ ὑδάτων πολλῶν, [16]καὶ ἔχων ἐν τῇ δεξιᾷ χειρὶ αὐτοῦ ἀστέρας ἑπτὰ καὶ ἐκ τοῦ στόματος αὐτοῦ ῥομφαία δίστομος ὀξεῖα ἐκπορευομένη καὶ ἡ ὄψις αὐτοῦ ὡς ὁ ἥλιος φαίνει ἐν τῇ δυνάμει αὐτοῦ.

No major textual critical matters arise from this passage. The phrase ὅμοιον υἱὸν ἀνθρώπου is interesting for its 'strange defiance of grammar'.[3] Except in Apocalypse 14.14 where this phrase recurs, John consistently uses the dative after ὅμοιον (e.g. 1.15, 2.18, 4.3: nineteen times in all). Beckwith concludes that this grammatical oddity is evidently intended.[4] Mussies argues that because *k-* formed a single word with the following substantive in Hebrew and Aramaic then this might account for 'the idea that ὅμοιον and its complement had to show grammatical concord'.[5] Ozanne proposes that ὅμοιον υἱὸν ἀνθρώπου represents a feature known as '*kap veritatis*' and should be translated as 'the very Son of Man' or 'the Son of Man himself'.[6] But this begs the question why John did not simply use ὁ υἱὸς τοῦ ἀνθρώπου. On any reckoning, ὅμοιον υἱὸν ἀνθρώπου is the equivalent of *kbr 'nš*.

Jesus and the angels

In the Apocalypse the form of most angels is entirely neglected by John. We are given no clues in phrases such as 'Michael and his angels' (12.7) as to what constitutes their form. Some angels have a certain object with them, such as a trumpet (e.g. 8.7) or a sickle (e.g. 14.17), which suggests that these creatures must have at least one limb! In the case of the trumpet-angels they presumably have legs and feet since they *stand* before God (8.2), and the blowing of trumpets suggests that they have hands, arms, and mouths.[7] But two angels (Apc. 10.1, 18.1) and one group of angels (15.6–7) are described in sufficient detail to warrant discussion of their form in comparison to the risen Jesus in Apocalypse 1.13–16.[8] Relating these appearances to the christophany in particular and to the

---

[3] Swete, 15.   [4] Beckwith, 437.   [5] Mussies, *Morphology*, 139.
[6] Ozanne, 'Language', 7–8.   [7] Cf. Michl, *Engelvorstellungen*, 189, n. 6.
[8] We reject Barker, 'Temple', 72, when she attempts to interdict critical reading of angelophanies: it is simply wrong to assert that 'the same angel is intended in each case'.

christology of the Apocalypse in general has been a neglected feature of christological research.[9]

The first of these angels is the subject of Apocalypse 10, and its form is described in 10.1–3. It is worth citing this passage in full for the sake of the discussion which follows. We then consider this angel in terms of its background before comparing it with Jesus Christ in the context of the Apocalypse.

Καὶ εἶδον ἄλλόν ἄγγελον ἰσχυρὸν καταβαίνοντα ἐκ τοῦ οὐρανοῦ περιβεβλημένον νεφέλην, καὶ ἡ ἶρις ἐπὶ τῆς κεφαλῆς αὐτοῦ καὶ τὸ πρόσωπον αὐτοῦ ὡς ὁ ἥλιος καὶ οἱ πόδες αὐτοῦ ὡς στῦλοι πυρός, ²καὶ ἔχων ἐν τῇ χειρὶ αὐτοῦ βιβλαρίδιον ἠνεῳγμένον. καὶ ἔθηκεν τὸν πόδα αὐτοῦ τὸν δεξιὸν ἐπὶ τῆς θαλάσσης, τὸν δὲ εὐώνυμον ἐπὶ τῆς γῆς, ³καὶ ἔκραξεν φωνῇ μεγάλῃ ὥσπερ λέων μυκᾶται. καὶ ὅτε ἔκραχεν, ἐλάλησαν αἱ ἑπτὰ βρονταὶ τὰς ἑαυτῶν φωνάς.

(Apc. 10.1–3)

As ἄλλόν ἄγγελον ἰσχυρὸν the angel in this passage is the successor to the 'mighty angel' who appears in Apocalypse 5.2.[10] Like the glorious angel in 18.1 the mighty angel in 10.1 is seen καταβαίνοντα ἐκ τοῦ οὐρανοῦ. Being wrapped in a cloud (περιβεβλημένον νεφέλην) and having a rainbow over his head (καὶ ἡ ἶρις ἐπὶ τῆς κεφαλῆς αὐτοῦ) is unique to this angel within the angelology of the Apocalypse (cf. the heavenly woman, περιβεβλημένη τὸν ἥλιον, 12.1). No other angel has a voice 'like a lion roaring', though there are several references to angels crying out with a φωνῇ μεγάλῃ (cf. 7.2, 14.7,9,15, 19.17; ἰσχυρᾷ φωνῇ, 18.2). The possession of a sun-like face (τὸ πρόσωπον αὐτοῦ ὡς ὁ ἥλιος) and fiery legs (καὶ οἱ πόδες αὐτοῦ ὡς στῦλοι πυρός) recall the appearance of the risen Jesus (ἡ ὄψις αὐτοῦ ὡς ὁ ἥλιος φαίνει ἐν τῇ δυνάμει αὐτοῦ, 1.16; οἱ πόδες αὐτοῦ ὅμοιοι χαλκολιβάνῳ ὡς ἐν καμίνῳ πεπυρωμένης, 1.15). We may also note that the association of this angel with 'cloud' corresponds to associations with 'cloud(s)' for Jesus Christ in Apocalypse 1.7 and 14.14.

[9] E.g. Rowland (*Heaven*, 102) only discusses the christological aspect of one angelophany (Apc. 10.1). Brighton (*Angel*, 199–203) discusses the christological significance of the angel in 10.1, and Gundry, 'Angelomorphic', argues for a 'Jesuanic' identification between Jesus and the angels in Apc. 7.2; 8.3; 10.1; 14.18; 18.1,21; 20.1; and 22.6.

[10] A few witnesses, e.g., P 2053 𝔐^k, omit ἄλλον which could be an attempt to equate the mighty angels in 5.2 and 10.1; cf. Allo, 120.

Some elements of the angelophany recall angelophanies and epiphanies in other writings which we have already discussed: (for example) 'a *kidaris* (was) on his head, its look that of a rainbow' (*Apoc. Abr.* 11.2);[11] 'his face shining like the rays of the sun in its glory' (*Apoc. Zeph.* 6.11;[12] cf. 1 *Enoch* 106.2; *Jos. and Asen.* 14.8; Daniel 10.6); αἱ χεῖρες καὶ οἱ πόδες αὐτοῦ ὥσπερ σίδηρος ἐκ πυρός (*Jos. and Asen.* 14.9; cf. Daniel 10.6; *Apoc. Zeph.* 6.11; Ezek. 1.27, 8.2); 'the angel of the LORD standing between earth and heaven' (1 Chron. 21.16; cf. Wis. 18.16).

The angelophany also recalls various theophanies: 'around the throne is a rainbow (ἶρις) that looks like an emerald' (Apc. 4.3); 'like the bow (τόξου, LXX)[13] in a cloud on a rainy day, such was the appearance of the splendour all around' (Ezek. 1.28);[14] 'you have wrapped yourself with a cloud (ἐπεσκέπασας νεφέλην, LXX) so that no prayer can pass through' (Lam. 3.44; cf. Exod. 19.9, 20.21; Ps. 96(97).2). In general terms, the appearance of the angel compares favourably with the Psalmist's impression of the appearance of the LORD in Psalm 104.1–3: 'You are clothed with honour and majesty, wrapped in light as with a garment . . . you make the clouds your chariot' (cf. Isa. 19.1). Other details in the angelophany also have theophanic associations. Thus the loud voice of the angel may be linked to the thundering voice of the LORD against the Philistines (1 Sam 7.10) and the leonine roar of the LORD in Hosea 11.10 (cf. Amos 3.8). And the sun-like face of the angel recalls the description of God's glory in Habakkuk 3.4: 'The brightness was like the sun.'[15] The description of the angel setting his feet on the land and the sea is not found elsewhere in angelophanies prior to the Apocalypse, although its implication that the angel is of immense size recalls the angel of the LORD which David sees standing by the threshing floor of Ornan the Jebusite (1 Chron. 21.16).[16] The resting of the right foot on the sea gives the

---

[11] Rubinkiewicz, *OTP*, i, 694.   [12] Wintermute, *OTP*, i, 513.

[13] Cf. Ezek. 1.4 (ὁ ἑβραῖος), where ἶρις is used rather than ἠλέκτρου, and discussion below, p. 134.

[14] Cf. Gen. 9.13 (the rainbow of the covenant). In connection with the 'clothing' of the angel cf. *Odes Sol.* 4.7–8.

[15] Ford (p. 162) speaks of 'hints at a theophany' in the appearance of the angel. For a full discussion of the details of the form of the mighty angel see Brighton, *Angel*, 80–122 and Ford, 161–3. Other relevant biblical passages worth noting are Exod. 14.19, 24; 33.9; and Sir. 24.4

[16] Brighton (*Angel*, 141–4 and 166–7) finds no pertinent antecedent figure in Jewish material for an angel of great size. But he overlooks 1 Chron. 21.16 and Wis.

impression that the sea is as stable as the land to the angel – a reversal of the usual connotations of the sea in Jewish tradition as a place of chaos.[17] If this is so then the sea is comparable to the 'sea of glass' in front of the divine throne (Apc. 4.6; cf. 15.2), and just possibly we have another element in the account of the angelophany which draws on theophanic tradition. The conjunction of 'sea' and 'earth' is an idiom for the 'whole world',[18] which also underlines the majesty of this angel.

It follows from this analysis that the mighty angel in Apocalypse 10.1 stands firmly in the tradition of the principal angels. But the angelophany in 10.1–3 does not reproduce any one angelophany. Indeed it extends the tradition with its own blend of angelophanic and theophanic elements.[19] Within the Apocalypse itself this angel is notable since no other angel carries explicit images connoting the visible and audible presence of God such as the rainbow, the cloud, and the leonine voice, and no other angel so closely resembles Jesus Christ. There are four features of the angel's appearance which bear further consideration. First, the association of the rainbow with the angel is intriguing. The word ἶρις is also used in Apocalypse 4.3 to describe the immediate surrounds of the divine throne. This fact alone suggests that the rainbow imagery in 10.1 is a theophanic element in the description. Nevertheless, the rainbow has other associations with God. In Genesis 9.11–17 the rainbow is a sign of God's *mercy*, of his covenant never again to flood the earth to destroy it (cf. τὸ τόξον μου τίθημι ἐν τῇ νεφέλῃ, v. 13 LXX).[20] In Ezekiel 1.28 the *glory* of God is described as 'like the bow in a cloud on a rainy day' (ὡς ὅρασις τόξου, ὅταν ᾖ ἐν τῇ νεφέλῃ ἐν ἡμέρᾳ ὑετοῦ, LXX). There is no reason why we should deny that the angel represents God in both these aspects.[21] Interestingly, Apocalypse 4.3 and 10.1 do not use the word τόξον found in Genesis 9.13 LXX and Ezekiel 1.28 LXX. The goddess of the rainbow and one of the messengers of the gods was Ἶρις (e.g. Homer, *Iliad* 8.398; Vergil, *Aeneid* 10.73), so that John, who was not averse to blending Jewish and pagan material together into his

---

18.16. Later *Hekhalot* writings such as *Shiʿur Qomah* are concerned with the size of the divine body, cf. Cohen, *Shiʿur*, 9.
[17] Swete, 124.   [18] Lohmeyer, 82; cf. Exod. 20.4,11; Ps. 69.34.
[19] Cf. Lohmeyer, 81; Kraft, 147.
[20] Cf. Caird, 125, Ford, 161–2; Allo, 120; Brütsch, i, 394.
[21] Brighton, *Angel*, 100.

work,[22] may have chosen ἶρις for this reason.[23] However, the use of ἶρις in 4.3 reflecting strongly the influence of Ezekiel 1 raises the question why τόξον was not employed. One explanation, put forward many years ago,[24] but rarely discussed,[25] is that ἶρις derives from Ezekiel 1.4 according to a version known as 'the *Hebraios*' and attested in Origen's *Hexapla*.[26] Ezekiel 1.4 records the beginning of the prophet's call-vision where he sees a stormy wind with a great cloud that is surrounded by brightness and flashing light. In the middle of it, according to the *Hebraios* version, was a light 'like the appearance of a rainbow' (ὡς ὅρασις ἴριδος; cf. ὡς ὅρασις ἠλέκτρου, LXX). No corroborating evidence for either explanation is at hand. In any case, each explanation is consistent with the thought that the angel comes as a distinguished representative of God and the rainbow illustrates this.

Secondly, the fact that the angel descends from heaven wrapped in a cloud also has definite theophanic connotations. In texts such as Exodus 19.9 and 33.9 'cloud' is the means by which God becomes present with his servant Moses while preserving the hiddenness of his essential being. In texts such as Lamentations 3.44 and Psalm 104.3, 'cloud(s)' are used by God to separate himself from humanity and for the purpose of movement. The *conjunction* of 'rainbow' and 'cloud' in 10.1 recalls Ezekiel 1.28,[27] where both images are part of the description of the *kabod*. Yet we must also allow that in other OT texts 'cloud(s)' are associated with beings other than God (e.g. Dan. 7.13; Exod. 14.19–20), and that in the Apocalypse 'cloud' is used as a vehicle for the two (creaturely) witnesses of God to ascend to heaven (11.12). Thus, although 'cloud' is a theophanic element incorporated into the description of the angel, it is not necessarily indicative that the angel is divine. Rather, similar to the 'rainbow', it signifies the close association between the angel and God. The angel acts on behalf of God just as the angel of God went before the Israelites

---

[22] Most noticeably in Apc. 12, cf. Yarbro Collins, *Combat*, 57–83; Court, *Myth*, 106–21.

[23] Brighton, *Angel*, 101; cf. Charles, i, 115.

[24] Montgomery, 'Education', 75.

[25] E.g. Halperin, *Faces*, 526, notes it, but Brighton, *Angel*, and most commentators overlook it.

[26] The citation from the *Hebraios* translation is in Field, *Hexaplorum*, ii, 768 (in full: φῶς γὰρ ἐν μέσῳ αὐτοῦ, ὡς ὅρασις ἴριδος, καὶ αὕτη διειδὴς ἦν ἐν μέσῳ αὐτῶν).

[27] Kraft, 147.

(Exod. 14.19; cf. 23.20) in exactly the same way as God himself did (Exod. 13.21, 14.24).[28]

The third feature which commands our attention is the resemblance of the mighty angel to the glorious 'man' in Daniel 10.5–6. In Apocalypse 10.5–6 the angel raises his right hand and swears by God that 'There will be no more delay'. This action closely reflects the action of 'the man clothed in linen' in Daniel 12.7:

> Then the angel whom I saw standing on the sea and the land raised his right hand to heaven [6]and swore by him who lives forever and ever, who created heaven and what is in it, the earth and what is in it, and the sea and what is in it: 'There will be no more delay, [7]but in the days when the seventh angel is to blow his trumpet the mystery of God will be fulfilled, as he announced to his servants the prophets.'   (Apc. 10.5b–7)

> The man clothed in linen, who was upstream, raised his right hand and his left hand toward heaven. And I heard him swear by the one who lives forever that it would be for a time, two times, and half a time, and that when the shattering of the power of the holy people comes to an end, all these things would be accomplished.   (Dan. 12.7)

In both Apocalypse 10.5b–6 and in Daniel 12.7 the angel raises his right hand to heaven and swears by the living, eternal God. Although passages such as Deuteronomy 32.40 may be in the background here, other observations suggest that Daniel 12 is in view in Apocalypse 10. Both passages feature angels, and both are concerned with scrolls (Apc. 10.2, 8–10; Daniel 12.4; cf. 10.21). Also, in Apocalypse 11.2–3, a period of time is mentioned concerning the desecration of the temple and the holy city: 'forty-two months' or 'one thousand two hundred and sixty days', which is drawn from Daniel 12.7 ('time, times, and a half' which equates to forty-two months) and 12.11 ('one thousand two hundred and ninety days'). The 'man clothed in linen' in Daniel 12.7 can only be the angel in Daniel 10.5–6.[29] This angel has 'a face like lightning' and 'legs like the gleam of burnished bronze' so that there is some resemblance to the mighty angel in Apocalypse 10. Moreover, the

---

[28] Ibid. understands the angel as an 'Engel des Herrn'. Cf. Ford, 163; Brighton, *Angel*, 79–93.

[29] Montgomery, *Daniel*, 475.

mighty angel in Apocalypse 10 commissions John for prophetic ministry just as the angel in Daniel 10 commissions Daniel for ministry as guardian of the truth. At the very least these observations suggest that the vision of the mighty angel in Apocalypse 10 draws on the vision of the 'man clothed in linen' alongside the other sources we have already mentioned.[30] The significance of this observation will be elucidated in the next chapter.

With the preceding discussion in mind, we now consider the mighty angel in relation to Jesus Christ. In both form and function the angel resembles the risen Jesus who, like the angel, commissions John in Apocalypse 1.13–16.[31] In general terms, both have a glorious appearance about which specific details concerning the clothing, head, face, legs, and voice of each figure are given; in particular, the faces of both are compared with the sun. The resemblance between the two figures has led some interpreters to equate them. Thus the Elkesaites, for example, are reported as holding the view that Christ is a power whose length is '96 miles' and whose breadth is '24 miles'.[32] Others certainly have understood the angel to be Jesus Christ,[33] even in the present century.[34] But the description of the angel in Apocalypse 10.1–3 has no one component which exactly resembles those of the christophany in Apocalypse 1.13–16: for example, although both faces are 'like the sun', different words are used for the face of each figure (ὄψις, πρόσωπον).[35] Nor is there any descriptive detail in the rest of chapter 10 which is suggestive of the angel being Jesus: for example, the angel does not speak alone and on his own authority but is supplemented by a voice from heaven (10.4) and he swears by God (10.6), unlike Jesus in 1.17–20, who speaks with the sovereign

---

[30] Cf. Charles, i, 259.

[31] Brighton (*Angel*, 161) argues that the first commissioning in Apc. 1.9–20 is for the revelation to the seven churches while the object of the second is 'all nations' (10.11).

[32] So Epiphanius, *Pan.* 19.4.1; cf. 30.17.6; 53.1.9; Hippolytus, *Ref. omn. haer.* 9. 13.2–3. Daniélou (*Theology*, 121) argues that the colossal stature of the *glorious angel* is characteristic of Jewish–Christian teaching, cf. *Herm. Sim.* 9.6.1.

[33] E.g. Primasius, Bk. 3, 'Dominum Christum descendentum de caelo'; Victorinus, 88–9; Augustine, 2430–1. Ruperti Tuitensis, 1006, accepts that the angel is Christ but denies that this is the nature of Christ, rather this is his *officium*.

[34] E.g. Scott, 219; Kraft, 147; Gundry, 'Angelomorphic', 663–8; Brighton (*Angel*, 5) also cites J. Wellhausen, *Analyse der Offenbarung Johannis*, Berlin: Weidmannische Buchhandlung, 1907, 14; cf. Rowland, *Heaven*, 102: 'it is not easy to differentiate between [the angel in Apc. 10.1] and the risen Christ who appears to John on the island of Patmos'.

[35] Cf. Bergmeier, 'Buchrolle', 236.

'I am'. In fact, since the figure is clearly understood as an ἄγγελος (10.1, 5, 8, 10), a term never used of Jesus in the Apocalypse, it is unlikely that the mighty angel in Apocalypse 10 is meant to be Jesus.[36] Furthermore, it is noticeable that John does not fall down in awe or to attempt to worship the angel in Apocalypse 10. Presumably, at this point he was well aware that he was in the presence of a creaturely angel notwithstanding the theophanic elements in his appearance.

This observation undermines recent attempts to interpret the angelophany in Apocalypse 10 as 'an angel-theophany'[37] or as an appearance of the exalted Jesus (since in Apc. 1.17 John falls at the feet of the risen Jesus).[38] In our view, then, the mighty angel in Apocalypse 10.1 is glorious in a manner which suggests that he comes as some kind of plenipotentiary of God. His appearance recalls a wide range of theophanies and angelophanies, including the angelophany in Daniel 10.5–6, but the angel is an appearance of neither God nor Jesus Christ.[39] Yet the points of similarity between the angelophany and the christophany raise the question whether the angel comes as the representative of Jesus Christ. Giblin, for instance, suggests that although the angel is identified with neither God nor the risen Jesus, with his sun-like face and fiery legs 'he seems to be a stand in for the Lord'.[40] This proposal faces the difficulty that, with the glorious angels of apocalyptic literature in mind, there seems to be no reason to link the angel specifically to Jesus – with respect to the sun-like face and fiery legs the angel is simply a typical glorious angel. Nevertheless, the angel can be thought of as the angel of God *and of Jesus* since, as we have seen above,[41] this angel is likely to be the revealing angel.

---

[36] Cf. Arethas, 635–42; Andreas, 306; Swete, 124; Bousset, 307–8; Caird, 125–6; Charles, i, 258–9; Lohse, 50; Prigent, 151; Allo, 120; Loisy, 194: 'un ange est un ange'; Dunn, *Christology*, 156, who overstates the distinction between Christ and the angels in the Apocalypse; and Brighton, *Angel*, 184–6, who notes the lack of godly fear in the response of the seer to the angelophany. Gundry ('Angelomorphic', 663–8) overlooks the point that against the wider context of glorious angels, the angel in Apc. 10.1 is not unusual and thus there is no need to press the resemblance to the exalted Jesus to the conclusion that the angel is Jesus.

[37] Brighton, *Angel*, 79. In any case, 'angel-theophany' is a confusing term.

[38] Gundry, 'Angelomorphic', 663–8. Gundry's attempts to identify other angels in the Apocalypse with Jesus are unconvincing.

[39] The outstanding form of the angel in Apc. 10.1 undermines the claim that the Apocalypse is 'anti-angel', so Boring, 'Voice', 338.

[40] Giblin, *Revelation*, 109. Cf. Brighton, *Angel*, 79; Kraft, 147; Caird, 125–6.

[41] See p. 124.

We must bring our discussion of the mighty angel in Apocalypse 10 in relation to Jesus Christ to a close. Clearly, this angel stands in the tradition of the glorious angels we have studied in earlier chapters. Despite a certain similarity between the two, this angel is not Jesus Christ. If the angel is the revealing angel then it is the angel of God and of Jesus Christ. The mixture of theophanic and angelophanic imagery associated with the appearance of the angel underlines this conclusion. His presence in the narrative indicates that the conception of the heavenly world in the Apocalypse is broad enough to include alongside Jesus glorious angels with similar form and function. It also indicates familiarity with the conclusion drawn above that angelophanies and epiphanies of angelomorphic figures incorporated theophanic imagery without the corollary that the figure concerned was divine.

The next detailed angelophany in the Apocalypse involves not one but seven angels. These angels may be called the 'bowl angels' since they pour out the seven bowls of God's wrath. They appear to the seer in the following form: ἐνδεδυμένοι λίνον[42] καθαρὸν λαμπρὸν καὶ περιεζωσμένοι περὶ τὰ στήθη ζώνας χρυσᾶς (Apc. 15.6). Whether these angels are a reappearance of the trumpet angels (Apc. 8.2–11.19) need not detain us here.[43] Our concern is with the relationship of these angels to other mighty angels and to the exalted Jesus of the Apocalypse. Although the form of the bowl angels does not include as many details as the mighty angel in Apocalypse 10, the role of these angels as agents of the judgement of God, the fact that one of the angels is the angel of the revelation (Apc. 17.1, 21.9),[44] and that the group consists of seven angels all indicate that these are angels of high rank. The clothing of the angels as described in Apocalypse 15.6 implies links with glorious angels described in other apocalyptic writings (*Apoc. Zeph.* 6.12; 1 *Enoch* 71.1; Ezek. 9.2; Daniel 10.5). The appearance of the seven bowl angels also calls to mind the appearance of Jesus in the christophany in Apocalypse 1.13: ἐνδεδυμένον ποδήρη καὶ περι-

---

[42] So N–A[26]; also Swete, 195; Lohmeyer, 129; Bousset, 394. A C 2053 2062 have λίθον (cf. Ezek. 28.13). Some witnesses, e.g. 𝔓[47] (ℵ) 046, have λίνουν. Charles, ii, 38, suggests βύσσινον (cf. 19.14).

[43] One interesting question is whether there are two groups of angels or one group appearing twice. If there are two groups it is conceivable that one group consists of deputies to the other group, by analogy with the seven 'deputy princes' mentioned in 4Q400 3 ii 2, cf. 4Q405 13 7.

[44] The equation bowl angel = revealing angel = mighty angel (Apc. 10.1) is possible.

εζωσμένον πρὸς τοῖς μαστοῖς ζώνην χρυσᾶν. The differences between these angels and the exalted Jesus are slight with respect to this aspect of the more detailed description of the latter: the robes of the angels are described with more precision, and different words are used for 'chest'.[45] The resemblance between Jesus and the bowl angels may account for John's attempt in Apocalypse 19.10 and 22.9 to worship the bowl angel who functions as the revealing angel.

The next relevant angelophany in the Apocalypse involves a single angel who comes down out of heaven to proclaim the fall of 'Babylon':

> Μετὰ ταῦτα εἶδον ἄλλον ἄγγελον καταβαίνοντα ἐκ τοῦ
> οὐρανοῦ ἔχοντα ἐξουσίαν μεγάλην, καὶ ἡ γῆ ἐφωτίσθη ἐκ
> τῆς δόξης αὐτοῦ. ²καὶ ἔκραχεν ἐν ἰσχυρᾷ φωνῇ λέγων.
>
> (Apc. 18.1–2a)

The description of this angel appears to draw on Ezekiel 43.2 which describes the coming of the 'glory of God' from the east. The impressive sound associated with this coming is noted, *kqwl mym rbym* (cf. ἐν ἰσχυρᾷ φωνῇ, Apc. 18.2) and the earth is illuminated by the glory, *wh'rṣ h'yrh mkbdw* (cf. καὶ ἡ γῆ ἐφωτίσθη ἐκ τῆς δόξης αὐτοῦ, Apc. 18.1). The description of this angel as having 'great authority' begs the question: How did John know this? One possible surmise is that he drew his conclusion from features of the angel's appearance which symbolized authority in much the same way as the purple robes and golden staff of Yahoel (*Apoc. Abr.* 11.3), and the robe, crown, and royal staff of the angel in *Joseph and Aseneth* 14.8 symbolised their authority. But it may have been that John recognized the authority of the angel because of his generally glorious appearance – an appearance he describes in terms which reflect most directly not the traditions concerning glorious angels but the description of the appearance of the *kabod* itself (cf. Ezek. 43.1–2).[46] The appearance of this angel differs from the risen Jesus, the mighty angel in Apocalypse 10.1,[47] and various other principal angels in having a glorious appearance *without*

---

[45] For an explanation for the correspondence in appearance between Christ and the bowl angels see Stuckenbruck, 'Refusal', 695.

[46] So Charles, ii, 95; Ford, 296; Swete, 223: 'so recently has he come from the Presence that in passing he flings a broad belt of light across the dark Earth'.

[47] Brighton (*Angel*, 193) however, makes the point that the angel's glory might light up the whole earth because he is of immense size.

physical characteristics being described, such as a shining face and fiery legs.[48] Even the description of the angel's voice, ἐν ἰσχυρᾷ φωνῇ, differs from that of the exalted Jesus (ἡ φωνὴ αὐτοῦ ὡς φωνὴ ὑδάτων πολλῶν, Apc. 1.15) and from most other angels (ἐν φωνῇ μεγαλῇ, Apc. 5.2; 7.2; 10.3; 14.7,9,15; 19.17). In another context, one which was not dominated by Jesus Christ, the mighty angel in Apocalypse 10.1, and the bowl angels in 15.6–7, this glorious angel would surely be considered a quite extraordinary and unique figure. In particular, it would be tempting to identify this angel as the visible *kabod* of God (especially in the light of the links between Apc. 18.1 and Ezek. 43.2). Yet in the Apocalypse this outstanding angel is not unique: he is one of a number of glorious angels. Just as the rainbow over the head of the angel in Apocalypse 10.1 does not mean that he is divine, we need not conclude that the angel in 18.1 is the *kabod* of God itself. Rather, this angel shines gloriously as a sign of the divine authority with which he is sent on his mission into the world.[49]

Consideration of the mighty and glorious angels of the Apocalypse leads us, therefore, to see that if Jesus is greater than the glorious angels in the Apocalypse then he is very great indeed, because the form of these angels, in which angelophanic and theophanic elements are adopted, adapted, and blended together, indicates that they are of the highest status before God. Conversely, the resemblance between Jesus and these angels suggests that the form of the risen Jesus in Apocalypse 1.13–16 is typically angelic (a point we will pursue further in chapter 8). Also important for later discussion is the observation that theophanic imagery in the angelophanies in Apocalypse 10.1 and 18.1 does not require the conclusion that these angels are anything other than angels.

Jesus, the living creatures, and the elders

Having considered the figure of the exalted Jesus in comparison to the glorious angels in the Apocalypse we now look at two sets of beings who, if not actually angels, are like angels in various respects, and who command our attention here because of their

---

[48] Cf. the general descriptions of glorious figures such as Adam (*Test. Abr.* 11.10) and Sariel (*Ladd. Jac.* 3.3).

[49] The same point could be made in respect of Moses whose glory had to be veiled (Exod. 34.29–35) but whose status as a (mere) human being was not thereby altered.

exalted status as those privileged to exist in and around the divine throne. The first set of beings are the 'living creatures' who surround the throne (e.g. Apc. 4.6). Of all heavenly beings the living creatures live in closest proximity to the throne and for this reason it is worthwhile comparing Jesus Christ who is also closely associated with the divine throne (e.g. 7.17). Each creature has six wings (4.8), and sings, day and night, an acclamation to God (4.9). Each recalls an earthly creature: the first, a lion; the second, an ox; the third, a human face; and the fourth, a flying eagle (4.7). As the vision of heaven unfolds before John's eyes he sees 'Around the throne, and on each side of the throne (Καὶ ἐν μέσῳ τοῦ θρόνου καὶ κύκλῳ τοῦ θρόνου) . . . four living creatures (ζῷα) full of eyes in front and behind' (Apc. 4.6). That the form of these creatures owes a considerable debt to the four living creatures of Ezekiel's call-vision (cf. Ezek. 1.4–25) and to the cherubim of Ezekiel 10.10–14 is affirmed by most, if not all, commentators on the Apocalypse.[50] But there are notable differences between the two conceptions of the living creatures. Since for our present purpose these differences are not of special significance, we will simply give the most obvious ones.

First, the living creatures in Ezekiel *each* have four faces (human, ox, lion, eagle, 1.6,10; cherub, human, lion, eagle, 10.14), whereas in the Apocalypse each living creature only has one face in a simplification of the scheme he has received from Ezekiel.[51] Secondly, whereas in Ezekiel 1.6 the appearance of the living creatures is described as 'of human form', in the Apocalypse the forms of the living creatures are taken from the types of faces in Ezekiel 1.6 so that in three cases they appear to have the form of an animal (lion, ox, flying eagle). Only in one case is the face of the creature 'like a human face' (Apc. 4.7), but we are left uncertain as to whether this means the creature as a whole has human form. Thirdly, the living creatures, according to Ezekiel, are associated with movement in terms of wheels (1.15–21) and lie *under* the divine throne (1.22). The impression is given of a (so-called) throne-chariot, and not simply a throne as in Apocalypse 4 where the living creatures are stationary, and their main function in the

---

[50] E.g. Beckwith, 500–2; Sweet, 120; Caird, 64; Swete, 69–70; Lohmeyer, 45–6; Kraft, 99. For an extended treatment of the four living creatures, with special attention to their background in Ezekiel, see Michl, *Engelvorstellungen*, 5–111.
[51] Cf. Charles, i, 121. Note that in *Apoc. Abr.* 18.4–5 traces of the more complex scheme of Ezekiel remain.

heavenly vision is to praise God (Apc. 4.9; cf. 5.13–14, 7.1–12, 19.4).[52] The praise of the living creatures, involving the use of the Trisagion (Apc. 4.8), recalls the call-vision of Isaiah, in which six-winged seraphs are seen in attendance *above* the throne, and they are heard to praise God using the Trisagion (Isa. 6.2–3).

Thus the living creatures in the Apocalypse seem to be a blending of the seraphim of Isaiah and the cherubim of Ezekiel.[53] This conclusion is confirmed by the observation that the living creatures in the Apocalypse are neither above nor below the divine throne, but 'around the throne and on each side of the throne' (4.6). Halperin suggests that, since the living creatures in the Apocalypse are 'full of eyes all around' (4.8; cf. the *'wpnym* in Ezek. 1.18, 10.12) and since a similar Trisagion is attributed in the *Similitudes of Enoch* to the 'cherubim, seraphim, ophannim' (1 *Enoch* 39.12, 71.7), the living creatures are 'composite of all three orders'.[54] In the Apocalypse the living creatures not only praise God: they hold 'a harp and golden bowls full of incense, which are the prayers of the saints' (5.8) and command the four apocalyptic horsemen (6.1,3,5,7).[55] One of the living creatures gives the seven bowl angels 'seven golden bowls full of the wrath of God' (15.7). In these ways the living creatures function like the angels.

One important question raised by the living creatures is how they can be both ἐν μέσῳ τοῦ θρόνου and κύκλῳ τοῦ θρόνου (Apc. 4.6). Does this mean that (say) two living creatures are 'in the middle of the throne' and two are on an imaginary circle running around the throne?[56] Or does it mean that all four living creatures are on an imaginary line running around the throne in such a way that each is positioned opposite the middle of each side of the throne?[57] Recently, Hall has offered a way out of

---

[52] Cf. Bietenhard, *Welt*, 62.

[53] Cf. Swete, 71; Lohmeyer, 46; Bousset, 250. Note 1 *Enoch* 72.8–13 in which four of the archangels are closely associated with the Head of Days.

[54] Halperin, *Faces*, 91.

[55] Ibid., 92, argues that these actions represent the darker side of the living creatures.

[56] Note Kraft, 98, who suggests that 'throne' means both 'heaven' and 'the divine throne' (cf. Ps. 33.14), so that Apc. 4.6 means that the four living creatures are in the middle of heaven and around the throne.

[57] Cf. Swete, 70, who suggests 'the figures are so placed that one of the ζῷα is always seen before the Throne, and the other on either side of it and behind, whether stationary or moving round in rapid gyration' (cf. Ezek. 1.12–13). Lohmeyer (p. 45) is against the idea that each creature is in the middle of each side of the throne.

something of a scholarly *impasse* over this question by proposing that, in addition to other sources, John draws on Exodus 25.17–22 and 37.6–9 for his model of the heavenly throne. In Exodus 25.17–22 Moses commands the craftsmen to make cherubim for each end of the mercy-seat, to be 'of one piece' with the mercy-seat. The mercy-seat, as part of the ark of the covenant, was later interpreted as God's throne (Jer. 3.16–17). Solomon sat on such a throne, although lions are featured instead of cherubim (1 Kings 10.18–19). Thus the 'raw materials for interpreting the living creatures as part of God's heavenly throne' were in place before the Common Era. In Jewish literature through the next ten centuries there is evidence of the conception that the living creatures were not distinct from the divine throne (as in Ezekiel) but constituent parts of it (e.g. Josephus, *Ant.* 3.137; *Pirqe R. El.* 4). Hall concludes that in this light ἐν μέσῳ τοῦ θρόνου καὶ κύκλῳ τοῦ θρόνου is 'a perfectly natural way to describe the position of the living creatures'. Just as the legs, arms, and back of a chair are within the space taken up by the chair, so the living creatures are ἐν μέσῳ τοῦ θρόνου, which he translates as 'within the space taken up by the throne'. Likewise, the living creatures are κύκλῳ τοῦ θρόνου, just as a chair is surrounded by legs, arms, and back. The living creatures are nevertheless *living* creatures so they are not described as 'affixed' or 'sculpted' on the divine throne.[58]

We cannot examine the merits of this explanation in detail, but its importance lies in the point it makes that it is conceivable that the living creatures were understood as integrally associated with the divine throne. If this explanation is correct, then it sheds light on the position of the Lamb in Apocalypse 5.6 where he appears ἐν μέσῳ τοῦ θρόνου καὶ τῶν τεσσάρων ζῴων καὶ ἐν μέσῳ τῶν πρεσβυτέρων. Charles has plausibly pointed out that ἐν μέσῳ . . . ἐν μέσῳ is equivalent to the Hebrew *byn . . . byn*, which would mean that the Lamb was between the throne and the living creatures on the one hand and the elders on the other.[59] But a Greek reader without knowledge of Hebrew would presumably have inferred, in the light of Apocalypse 3.21, 7.17 and 22.1,3, that the Lamb was on the throne *in the midst* of the living creatures. Hall's explanation suggests the latter interpretation is, in fact, likely to be correct.[60] Whether or not it is correct, it is undoubtedly true

[58] Hall, 'Living', 609–12.   [59] Charles, i, 140.   [60] Hall, 'Living', 612–13.

that the description ἐν μέσῳ τοῦ θρόνου gives an impression of the close, intimate proximity of the living creatures to the presence of God on his throne.[61] The living creatures, then, are extraordinary creatures who exist in the closest proximity to the divine throne short of being placed in the midst of it. Yet it is noticeable that they are inferior to Jesus for they bow down before the Lamb (5.8) and worship him (5.12). Since on the one hand Jesus Christ sits at the very centre of the divine throne, in a Father–Son relationship (7.17, 3.21) and on the other Jesus the Lamb is worshipped by the most exalted of all heavenly beings apart from God, it would appear that the divinity of Jesus Christ within the Apocalypse is underscored by comparative study of Jesus and the living creatures.

The next set of exalted heavenly beings we must consider are the twenty-four elders whom John sees in the vision of the open heaven in Apocalypse 4. The elders occupy twenty-four thrones which surround the divine throne, and each are 'dressed in white robes, with golden crowns on their heads' (4.4). The main function of the elders appears to be worshipping God: whenever the living creatures acclaim God the elders fall before him and worship him by casting their crowns and singing a song of praise (4.10–11, cf. 5.14, 11.16–18, 19.4). The elders also acclaim the Lamb in song (5.12). Some functions are shared with the living creatures: like them, the elders also hold harps and bowls of incense (5.8), and they share with them the acclamation in the rejoicing over the marriage of the Lamb (19.4). One of the elders functions as the *angelus interpres* (7.14). Thus, even if they are not angels, the elders are attributed with angelic functions.[62] The question of the identity of the elders (angels? OT heroes? priests? patriarchs and apostles?) need not detain us here.[63] In sum: similar to the case of the living creatures, we find that although the elders have high status (since they sit on thrones and wear crowns) Jesus Christ has even greater status (since the elders acclaim him in song).

---

[61] Cf. Halperin (*Faces*, 157–93) on speculations in some Jewish circles about the ox-like creature as a second power in heaven.

[62] Gruenwald, *Apocalyptic*, 66.

[63] For a detailed discussion of the elders see Satake, *Gemeindeordnung*, 137–50; for discussion of the elders and parallels in rabbinic and *Hekhalot* literature see Gruenwald, *Apocalyptic*, 64–7, with the conclusion that the elders function as elders but enjoy a privilege accorded to the just and not the angels, namely, sitting in heaven.

The christophany and the theophany

The appearance of the risen Jesus in Apocalypse 1.13–16 apparently mixes both angelophanic and theophanic elements. Exploring these elements in the light of their background is our task in the next chapter. If the appearance of the risen, divine Jesus incorporates theophanic elements we might expect this to be underlined by reminiscences of the theophany in Apocalypse 4. In this section we seek to determine whether or not this is so. Accordingly, we compare the christophany and theophany as follows. First, we consider 'location'. The encounter with Jesus appears to take place on earth. By contrast, at the beginning of the theophany John sees a door open in heaven, hears an invitation to ascend (Apc. 4.1), and finds himself, if not in heaven, then close by looking in (cf. 'there in heaven stood a throne', 4.2). The comparison of locations gives the impression that Jesus is able to move between heaven and earth, whereas God remains in heaven. This impression is confirmed in as much as we never find God in the Apocalypse outside heaven. Rather, God is always seated on the divine throne in heaven (Apc. 4.2; cf. 4.3, 9,10), which is located in the centre of the thrones of the twenty-four elders (4.4).[64] It was the first thing which John noticed when he looked into heaven (4.2). But when John first encountered the risen Jesus there was no connection with any throne (cf. 1.10–20).

Secondly, we compare the forms of Jesus and of God. The form of the risen Jesus includes the following features: (i) anthropomorphism ('like a son of man', 1.13); (ii) comprehensive detail (references to hair, head, eyes, face, clothing, hands, legs, mouth, and voice, 1.13–16); (iii) influence of Daniel 7.9 in Apocalypse 1.14; and (iv) description of the voice with a report of Jesus' speech (Apc. 1.15,17–20). By contrast, the form of God has the following features: (i) veiled anthropomorphism (see further comment below); (ii) sparse detail: reference to the hand in Apocalypse 5.1, and to a likeness to precious stones in 4.3; (iii) no influence from Daniel 7.9;[65] and (iv) no description of the voice of God with no speech attributed to God. The veiled anthropomorphism in Apocalypse 4 is worth noting. We may assume that the form of God in

---

[64] Cf. Hurtado, 'Revelation' on the significance of the elders for the throne vision.
[65] Beale (*Daniel*, 154–228) argues that Apc. 4 is modelled on Dan. 7. But the argument is unsustainable in view of the dominance of Ezek. 1–3 in the background to Apc. 4–5. In any case there is no influence from Dan. 7.9 on Apc. 4.3.

Apocalypse 4–5 was implicitly understood in anthropomorphic terms since God is described as the one 'seated' on the throne, and John sees 'the *right hand* of the one seated on the throne' (5.1). When John actually describes the form of God, however, he simply says 'the one seated there looks like jasper and carnelian' (ὅμοιος ὁράσει λίθῳ ἰάσπιδι καὶ σαρδίῳ, 4.3). When so many details demonstrate the strong influence of the throne-vision in Ezekiel 1 on Apocalypse 4,[66] it is particularly striking that in 4.3 John departs from the script (so to speak) which provides an explicit anthropomorphic manifestation of God (*dmwt kmr'h 'dm*, Ezek. 1.26).[67] By describing the form of God in terms of precious stones, John appears to be deliberately avoiding explicit anthropomorphism in his account of the theophany.[68] Interestingly, although Daniel 10.6 uses mineral imagery in its description of the body of the glorious angel John omits this from his vision of the risen Jesus.[69]

Thirdly, we may note that there is no comparable throne-vision for Jesus Christ in the Apocalypse. Although there is an explicit reference to a throne for Jesus in Apocalypse 3.21 this throne is never actually 'seen' in the heavenly visions in the Apocalypse.[70] Thus comparison of the christophany and the theophany throws up a number of differences. Particularly interesting are the observations that (i) in the theophany John appears to draw on a detail from the angelophany in Daniel 10.5–6 which is absent in the christophany (i.e. the use of mineral imagery), and (ii) in the christophany John appears to draw on the theophany in Daniel 7.9 but does not do so for the theophany in Apocalypse 4. On the one hand, these observations support the conclusion we have drawn attention to previously that epiphanic imagery was shared between theophanies and angelophanies. On the other hand, these observa-

---

[66] No commentator disputes this.

[67] Halperin (*Faces*, 89): 'John turns the human-like shape of Ezekiel's God into a blur of colour.' Charles, i, 113, says 'no form is visible'; and (p.115) argues that the rainbow contributes to the veiling of the one on the throne. Cf. Kraft, 96. Rowland (*Heaven*, 99) draws attention to Ezek. 28.13 where 'the king of Tyre' is covered with precious stones including ἴασπιν and σάρδιον. But if Ezek. 28.13 is part of the developing 'heavenly man' tradition then it admits no direct parallels to Apc. 4.3 (or to Dan. 10.5–6) where mineral imagery is also found.

[68] Cf. Black, 'Throne-theophany', 59, n. 6.

[69] Some manuscripts of the LXX compare the 'body' to θαλάσσης, notably Pap. 967.

[70] Unless it is the 'great white throne' of Apc. 20.11 or the 'cloud' on which 'one like a son of man' sits in Apc. 14.14 which may be a kind of mobile throne.

tions suggest that John distinguished between the theophany and the christophany. In fact, there are no shared images between the theophany and the christophany.[71] The impression is given that the *form* of the exalted Jesus and that of God are sharply distinguished. A question which then arises is whether or not the appearance of the exalted Jesus is illustrating something other than his divine status.[72] A possible answer to this question will be developed in succeeding chapters.

Conclusions

Comparing the risen Jesus to the glorious angels, the living creatures, and the elders in the Apocalypse shows that, in certain respects, Jesus is similar to each, although also distinct. In the particular case of the form of Jesus there is a degree of similarity with the form of the mighty angel in Apocalypse 10.1–3 and the bowl angels in Apocalypse 15.6–7. The form of the exalted Jesus would appear to be consistent with that of a glorious angel. This conclusion is consistent with the observation that the form of Jesus appears to be sharply distinguished from the form of God in Apocalypse 4.3. Yet we have no reason to question our supposition that Jesus Christ in the Apocalypse is divine and in fact this is confirmed through comparison of Jesus and the living creatures. Great though the living creatures are, they do not occupy the centre of the divine throne and they themselves bow the knee to Jesus the Lamb. The full significance of our findings in this chapter needs to be drawn out and this we attempt to do in the following chapters.

[71] Cf. Büchsel, *Christologie*, 32.
[72] In contrast to, e.g., Farrar (p. 66): 'The Jesus of the Resurrection . . . is not seen as the Man of Nazareth transfigured but as the Divine Glory personified.'

8

APOCALYPSE 1.13–16 (PART B)

In the previous chapter we examined the christophany in Apocalypse 1 in comparison with epiphanies found elsewhere in the Apocalypse. In this chapter we examine the christophany in the light of epiphanies in the OT and apocalyptic and related writings. Our particular focus in this examination will be the angelophanic and theophanic background to the christophany, in order to draw out the significance of the angelophanic and theophanic elements in the christophany. To keep our focus on our goal we will not attempt to offer an exhaustive examination of every aspect of the christophany which in any case would only repeat what is already available in the best commentaries.

The setting of the christophany

Although our main interest is in the form of the risen Jesus in Apocalypse 1.13–16, there are in fact possible angelological influences on Apocalypse 1.12–13a worth considering. Why does John 'see' the risen Jesus in the midst of the seven lampstands (Apc. 1.12–13a)? A good deal of attention has been paid to the origin of the 'seven lampstands',[1] which almost certainly draws on Zechariah 4.1–2.[2] But what might lie behind the placing of Jesus *in the midst* of the seven lampstands? John's familiarity with the Books of Ezekiel and Daniel suggests influence from passages such as Ezekiel 1 where the living creatures in human form are seen in the middle of fire (1.4), and Daniel 3.25(92) where Nebuchadnezzar sees 'four men unbound, walking in the middle of the fire'.[3] But texts such as

---

[1] McNamara (*New Testament*, 192–9) reviews the main lines of inquiry before offering his own hypothesis concerning the influence of *Tg. Yer. I* Exod. 39.37.

[2] E.g. Farrar, 65, who draws attention not only to the mention of the lampstand there but also to the fact that John 'sees' the lampstand.

[3] Beale, *Daniel*, 159.

these do not provide an explanation for why John specifically sees Jesus in the midst of *seven lampstands*. We suggest a possible explanation which draws on the Book of Zechariah which, as we have just seen, is a likely source for the image of the seven lampstands.

We have already discussed the angelology of the Book of Zechariah noting that John was familiar with it. We saw that Zechariah has a vision of a figure variously styled 'a man' (1.8) or the 'angel of the LORD' (1.11). We also saw that alongside this angel is another one which we designated 'the talking angel' (1.9). Parallels were noted between the talking angel of Zechariah and the (so designated) revealing angel of the Apocalypse.[4] Since the talking angel works closely with the angel of the LORD in Zechariah 1 and since (arguably) the revealing angel works closely with 'one like a son of man' in Apocalypse 1, it would appear worth considering whether there is, in fact, any other correspondence between the angel of the LORD and the risen Jesus. We may observe, for example, that Zechariah sees the former 'standing among the myrtle trees in the glen' (*whw' 'md byn hhdsym 'šr bmṣlh*, Zech. 1.8). In Zechariah 1.11, where 'the man' is identified as 'the angel of the LORD', the same observation is repeated with a slight variation, *whwh h'md byn hhdsym*. Thus both the angel of the LORD in Zechariah 1 and the risen Jesus in Apocalypse 1 are seen 'in the midst' of something (cf. ἐν μέσῳ τῶν λυχνιῶν, Apc. 1.13). There is no particular connection between myrtle trees and lampstands,[5] so it would appear that the myrtle trees have been replaced by lampstands to develop further John's symbolic scheme.[6] The risen Jesus in the midst of the lampstands nevertheless echoes the earlier scene in which the angel of the LORD is in the midst of the mytle trees. Other connections between the angel of the LORD and Jesus can be made. In general terms, both figures may be compared as

[4] See p. 25.
[5] Myrtle symbolized divine generosity (Isa. 41.19, 55.13) and peace (Zech. 1.8–11), and was used to construct booths at the Feast of the Tabernacles (Neh. 8.15). Lampstands, especially the seven-branched *menorah* of the Tabernacle (Exod. 25.37; 37.17–24; 39.37; 40.4; Lev. 24.2–4; Num. 8.2) or of the post-exilic Temple, are not without arboreal connotations. Note, however, that the *menorah* in the Tabernacle had cups shaped like almond blossoms (Exod. 25.31–40).
[6] Cf. Ford, 382; Beckwith, 437; Swete, 15; Sweet, 71; Caird, 24: 'whereas Israel was represented by a single candelabra with seven lamps, the churches are represented by seven separate standing lamps . . . each local congregation . . . is the church universal in all its fullness'.

the vizier of God in the perception of Zechariah and John, respectively. In particular, the angel of the LORD has responsibility for 'patrolling' the earth in common with Jesus the Lamb (Zech. 1.8, 10; cf. Apc. 5.6). Consequently, it seems possible that John saw a correspondence between Jesus and the angel of the LORD as presented in Zechariah. The initial vision of the angel of the LORD portrays him in the midst of a grove of myrtle trees. We suggest that this picture may have been transformed into the initial setting of the risen Jesus 'in the midst of seven golden lampstands' in Apocalypse 1.12–13a.

The christophany against its OT background

We begin considering the christophany in the light of its background in Daniel, Ezekiel, and other OT texts by comparing Apocalypse 1.13–16 with Daniel 10.5–6, the epiphanic account which most closely corresponds to it. The variations between the two accounts will serve to introduce the other OT texts which have influenced the christophany. In the citation of Apocalypse 1.13–16 below all words which appear directly to reflect the influence of Daniel 10.5–6 in the Hebrew are in bold type; words which may have been influenced by Daniel 10.5–6, but more probably draw on other sources, are underlined.

> καὶ ἐν μέσῳ τῶν λυχνιῶν ὅμοιον υἱὸν ἀνθρώπου **ἐνδεδυμένον ποδήρη** καὶ **περιζωσμένον πρὸς τοῖς μαστοῖς ζώνην χρυσᾶν**. ¹⁴ἡ δὲ κεφαλὴ αὐτοῦ καὶ αἱ τρίχες λευκαὶ ὡς ἔριον λευκὸν ὡς χιὼν καὶ **οἱ ὀφθαλμοὶ αὐτοῦ** <u>ὡς φλὸξ πυρὸς</u> ¹⁵καὶ **οἱ πόδες αὐτοῦ ὅμοιοι χαλκολιβάνῳ ὡς ἐν καμίνῳ** πεπυρωμένης καὶ ἡ φωνὴ αὐτοῦ ὡς φωνὴ ὑδάτων <u>πολλῶν</u>, ¹⁶καὶ ἔχων ἐν τῇ δεξιᾷ χειρὶ αὐτοῦ ἀστέρας ἑπτὰ καὶ ἐκ τοῦ στόματος αὐτοῦ ῥομφαία δίστομος ὀξεῖα ἐκπορευομένη καὶ **ἡ ὄψις αὐτοῦ ὡς ὁ ἥλιος** φαίνει ἐν τῇ δυνάμει αὐτοῦ.   (Apc. 1.13–16)

> ⁵*w'š' 't 'yny w'r' whnh 'yš ' ḥd lbwš bdym wmtnyw ḥgrym bktm 'wpz* ⁶*wgwytw ktršyš wpnyw kmr'h brq w'ynyw klpydy 'š wzr'tyw wmrgltnyw k'yn nḥšt qll wqwl dbryw kqwl hmwn.*
> (Dan. 10.5–6 MT)

In the citations of Greek versions of Daniel 10.5–6 below, words which are also found in Apocalypse 1.13–16 are underlined:

καὶ ἦρα τοὺς ὀφθαλμους μου καὶ εἶδον καὶ ἰδοὺ
ἄνθρωπος εἷς ἐνδεδυμένος βύσσινα καὶ τὴν ὀσφὺν περι-
εζωσμένος βυσσίνῳ, καὶ ἐκ μέσου αὐτοῦ φῶς, ⁶καὶ τὸ
σῶμα αὐτοῦ ὡσεὶ θαρσις, καὶ τὸ πρόσωπον αὐτοῦ ὡσεὶ
ὅρασις ἀστραπῆς, καὶ οἱ ὀφθαλμοὶ αὐτοῦ ὡσεὶ λαμπάδες
πυρός, καὶ οἱ βραχίονες αὐτοῦ καὶ οἱ πόδες ὡσεὶ χαλκὸς
ἐξαστράπτων, καὶ φωνὴ λαλιᾶς αὐτοῦ ὡσεὶ φωνη
θορύβου.   (Dan 10.5–6 LXX)

καὶ ἦρα τοὺς ὀφθαλμους μου καὶ εἶδον καὶ ἰδοὺ ἀνὴρ εἷς
ἐνδεδυμένος βαδδιν καὶ ἡ ὀσφὺς αὐτοῦ περιεζωσμένη ἐν
χρυσίῳ Ωφαζ, ⁶καὶ τὸ σῶμα αὐτοῦ ὡσεὶ θαρσις, καὶ τὸ
πρόσωπον αὐτοῦ ὡσεὶ ὅρασις ἀστραπῆς, καὶ οἱ ὀφθαλμοὶ
αὐτοῦ ὡσεὶ λαμπάδες πυρός, καὶ οἱ βραχίονες αὐτοῦ καὶ
τὰ σκέλη ὡς ὡσεὶ ὅρασις χαλκοῦ στίλβοντος, καὶ ἡ φωνὴ
τῶν λόγων αὐτοῦ ὡς φωνὴ ὄχλου.   (Dan 10.5–6 Th.)

The amount of material in bold type in the citation of Apocalypse
1.13–16 demonstrates that the background is dominated by the
description of the glorious man in Daniel 10.5–6. Most of the
imagery directly mirrors that found in Daniel 10.5–6. Some
imagery, however, reflects a merging of motifs from Daniel 10.5–6
and other sources. For example, both epiphanies make reference to
the eyes of the figure but the comparison in Apocalypse 1.14, ὡς
φλὸξ πυρὸς, most directly reflects Daniel 7.9 (LXX/Th.) rather
than 10.5–6 (ὡσει λαμπάδες πυρός, LXX/Th.). Nevertheless, φλὸξ
is a possible translation of *lpyd*.[7] Similarly, reference to the voice of
Jesus corresponds to a reference in Daniel 10.6 to the sound of the
words of the man, although the actual comparison of the voice of
Jesus, ὡς φωνὴ ὑδάτων πολλῶν,[8] draws most directly on Ezekiel
1.24/43.2, *kqwl mym rbym*. We may also note that in both Daniel
10 and Apocalypse 1 the faces of the figures are mentioned. But in
the former the face is compared with 'lightning' whereas the face of
the exalted Jesus is compared with 'the sun' (καὶ ἡ ὄψις αὐτοῦ ὡς ὁ
ἥλιος φαίνει ἐν τῇ δυνάμει αὐτοῦ, Apc. 1.16).[9] An immediate
reminiscence is to the transfiguration of Jesus as reported in
Matthew's gospel (καὶ ἔλαμψεν τὸ πρόσωπον αὐτοῦ ὡς ὁ ἥλιος,
Matt. 17.2). But the added detail that the shining is 'with full force'

---

[7] Yarbro Collins, 'Tradition', 549.
[8] Cf. variant πληθους λαλοῦ in MS 143, Apc. 1.15 (cited in Beale, *Daniel*, 160, n.18).
[9] Elsewhere in the NT ὄψις is only found at John 7.24, 11.44.

also recalls the ending of the Song of Deborah in which the wish is expressed that the friends of the LORD would be 'like the sun as it rises in its might' (*w'hbyw kṣ't hšmš bgbrtw*, MT; καὶ οἱ ἀγαπῶντες αὐτὸν ὡς ἔξοδος ἡλίου ἐν δυνάμει αὐτοῦ, LXX (Vaticanus); Judg. 5.31).[10]

Whereas our citation of Apocalypse 1.13–16 is full of bold type reflecting the influence of Daniel 10.5–6, comparison with Daniel 10.5–6 LXX and Daniel 10.5–6 Th. suggests the influence has been from the Hebrew rather than the Greek. For example, John follows neither Greek version in his description of the robe of Jesus (ποδήρη, Apc. 1.13, rather than βύσσινα/βαδδιν), although it is possible that John is reflecting the influence of Ezekiel 9.2 LXX (cf. ἐνδεδυκὼς ποδήρη). In his description of the chest band of Jesus John uses περιζωσμένον which is also found in Daniel 10.5 LXX/Th, but he uses ζώνην (cf. Ezek. 9.2 LXX) rather than βυσσίνῳ (Dan. 10.5 Th.), and μαστός rather than ὀσφὺς (Dan. 10.5 LXX/Th.). Similarly, with the description of the feet of Jesus (Apc. 1.15):[11] here an additional clause, ὡς ἐν καμίνῳ πεπυρωμένης, is found in Apocalypse 1.15, which has no basis in Daniel 10.5–6. Beale suggests that this echoes a phrase found in Theodotion's rendering of the story of the three men consigned to the furnace, καμίνου τοῦ πυρὸς τῆς καιομένης (Dan. 3.26(93)).[12] Perhaps such an echo is to be heard but the similarity of the two expressions does not necessitate the conclusion that John was familiar with Theodotion.[13] The additional clause could be readily explained as an extension of the imagery in Daniel 10.6 or as an image in keeping with the emphasis on fiery imagery in Ezekiel 1 (especially vv. 4, 7, 13, and 27).

John follows the pattern of the description in Daniel 10.5–6, but not exactly; and he omits and adds to the pattern.[14] Thus John, like

---

[10] When most of the background material to Apc. 1.13–16 is taken from Ezekiel and Daniel it is notable that John draws on Judg. 5.31 for his description of the face of Jesus. John knew about stars functioning as divine agents (cf. Apc. 8.10–11; 9.1) and his attention may have been drawn to Judg. 5.31 via Judg. 5.20: 'The stars fought from heaven.' Cf. Beale, *Daniel*, 163.

[11] Intriguing here is the use of χαλκολίβανον rather than χαλκὸς (Dan. 10.6 LXX/Th.) – the latter is used by John elsewhere, cf. Apc. 18.12. The derivation and exact meaning of χαλκολίβανον are a matter of conjecture, although it probably refers to 'a high-quality metal alloy of the copper, bronze, or brass type' (Hemer, *Letters*, 111).

[12] Beale, *Daniel*, 161; cf. Farrar, 67.

[13] See Thompson, 'Sociological', 102–8, esp. p. 107; cf. Mussies, *Morphology*, 352–3.

[14] Farrar, 67.

Daniel, envisages a man-like figure, but describes him as 'one like a son of man' rather than as 'a man'. John, like Daniel, describes the clothing, girding, feet (= legs), eyes, voice (= sound of his words), and face of the glorious figure appearing before him. But John omits mention of the arms and the body of the figure; he adds a description of 'the hair and the head' of the figure; and he varies the order in which the aspects of the form are mentioned (Apocalypse: man, clothing, girding, eyes, feet, voice, face; Daniel: man, clothing, girding, face, eyes, legs, voice).[15] John also describes the risen Jesus as having a sword in his mouth and holding seven stars in his right hand, details which are not found in Daniel's vision. The variety in order of elements between the two accounts suggests that John is not mechanically following Daniel 10.5–6.

Another issue arising from comparison of Apocalypse 1.13–16 and Daniel 10.5–6 is the omission of 'the body' of Jesus. The reason for the omission of any reference to the body of the risen Jesus is not clear. Holtz has explained the absence as a solution to a problem in the Danielic vision: in the earlier vision the body of the 'man' *and* the garment covering the body are described. This confusing state of affairs is remedied by replacing the description of the body with the description of the head and hair of Jesus.[16] Rowland points out that reference to the body of the 'man' is absent in the Peshitta of Daniel 10 and suggests that both here and in apocalyptic texts such as Apocalypse 1.13–16 the absence is due to reverential reasons, analogous to the reluctance in texts such as 2 *Enoch* 22.1–3[17] to describe details of a theophany.[18] Another possible explanation, arising from our discussion in the previous chapter, is that John wished to avoid confusion between the appearance of God and the appearance of Jesus. In describing the form of God in Apocalypse 4.3, John uses the imagery of precious stones (ὅμοιος ὁράσει λίθῳ ἰάσπιδι καὶ σαρδίῳ; cf. Daniel 10.6 LXX/Th.: ὡσεὶ θαρσις). Thus to compare the body of Jesus with a precious stone would only blur the distinction between the appearance of God and the appearance of the risen Jesus.

Another difference between the visions in Apocalypse 1 and Daniel 10 worth noting is that the Danielic figure says that he has been 'sent' to Daniel (Dan. 10.11), but the exalted Jesus does not

---

[15] For a fuller form-critical comparison between Apc. 1 and Daniel 10 see Karrer, *Johannesoffenbarung*, 139–47, esp. p. 144.

[16] Holtz, *Christologie*, 117.

[17] Andersen, *OTP*, i, 136.   [18] Rowland, 'Man', 105.

say this to John.[19] This is a suggestive feature of the christophany when we consider other information given about Jesus Christ in the Apocalypse. If Jesus shares the throne of God (cf. Apc. 3.21, 7.17), then it would be natural that he comes as a figure coordinate with, rather than subordinate to God. In this case we would not expect an indication that Jesus had been sent.

There are similarities in the response of each seer to the respective epiphanies. John falls down, as though dead, at the feet of the exalted figure who appears before him (Apc. 1.17). The figure reaches out his right hand, touches John and says to him 'do not be afraid' (μὴ φοβοῦ, 1.17). A similar set of events follows the epiphany in Daniel 10.5–6, but other events are present in that account. The common features are by no means unique to these two accounts of epiphanies (cf. Daniel 8.18; 4 Macc. 4.10; Matt. 28.4; Luke 24.5; Acts 9.4–6; *Test. Job* 3.1–5.2; *Jos. and Asen.* 14.3–15.10). This suggests that John sees his experience as part of a continuing epiphanic tradition, and not simply as a repetition of Daniel's experience.

Finally, the sword coming out of the mouth of Jesus (Apc. 1.16) is both entirely independent of any epiphany in the OT and clearly dependent on 'messianic' texts such as Isaiah 11.4 and 49.2.[20] Whatever else we may say about the risen Jesus from an angelological perspective, he is clearly understood in the Apocalypse as the *Christ* or *Messiah* (cf. 1.1,2; 11.15; 12.10; 20.4, 6). Thus we may sum up our discussion to this point as follows: the angelophany experienced by Daniel in Daniel 10.5–6 plays a significant role in the account of the christophany experienced by John in Apocalypse 1.13–20. Yet the influence of this angelophany is not of the kind that John slavishly copies every detail provided by it. Some differences, such as comparing the face of Jesus with the 'sun' rather than with 'lightning', do not appear to be christologically significant. But others, such as the lack of reference to Jesus having been 'sent', appear to underline the status of the risen Jesus as a being in a coordinate relationship to God rather than the subordinate relationship of the glorious 'man' in Daniel 10.5–6.

---

[19] There is only one figure experienced by Daniel in Daniel 10 as we have argued above, pp. 40–1.

[20] Cf. Beale,*(Daniel,* 162–3) on the use of these texts in passages elsewhere in the Apocalypse, featuring allusion to both Zechariah and Daniel. Among apocalyptic texts featuring a heavenly son of man see 1 *Enoch* 62.2, 4 Ezra 13.4, 10–11, for other references to the mouth as a weapon of judgement.

The next focus for our discussion is the second greatest influence on the christophany, Daniel 7.9, which is exclusively reflected in Apocalypse 1.14 where every word except for the phrase καὶ οἱ ὀφθαλμοὶ αὐτοῦ reflects the influence of Daniel 7.9:

> ἡ δὲ κεφαλὴ αὐτοῦ καὶ αἱ τρίχες λευκαὶ ὡς ἔριον λευκὸν ὡς χιὼν καὶ οἱ ὀφθαλμοὶ αὐτοῦ ὡς φλὸξ πυρός.
>
> (Apc. 1.14)

> *ḥzh hwyt 'd dy krswn rmyw w'tyq ywmyn ytb lbwš ktlg ḥwr wš'r r'š k'mr nq' krsyh šbybyn dy nwr glglwhy nwr dlq.*
>
> (Dan 7.9 MT)

In the following citations of the Greek versions of Daniel 7.9 we have underlined those words which also appear in Apocalypse 1.14:

> ἐθεώρουν ἕως ὅτε θρόνοι ἐτέθησαν καὶ παλαιὸς ἡμερῶν ἐκάθητο ἔχων περιβολὴν <u>ὡσεὶ χιόνα</u> καὶ τὸ τρίχωμα τῆς <u>κεφαλῆς αὐτοῦ ὡσεὶ ἔριον λευκὸν</u> καθαρόν ὁ θρόνος <u>ὡσεὶ φλὸξ πυρός</u>. (Dan 7.9 LXX)

> ἐθεώρουν ἕως ὅτου θρόνοι ἐτέθησαν καὶ παλαιὸς ἡμερῶν ἐκάθητο καὶ τὸ ἔνδυμα αὐτοῦ <u>ὡσεὶ χιὼν λευκόν</u> καὶ ἡ <u>θρὶξ</u> τῆς <u>κεφαλῆς αὐτοῦ ὡσεὶ ἔριον</u> καθαρόν ὁ θρόνος αὐτοῦ <u>φλὸξ πυρός</u> οἱ τροχοὶ αὐτοῦ πῦρ φλέγον. (Dan. 7.9 Th.)

Although the description of the head and hair in Apocalypse 1.14 is undoubtedly influenced by Daniel 7.9, it is by no means the case that the model provided by the Daniel text has been slavishly followed. Most notably, Daniel 7.9 refers to an enthroned figure, but there is no hint in Apocalypse 1 that the risen Jesus is enthroned. Whereas Daniel 7.9 speaks of 'the hair of his head' and uses a singular noun for 'hair', Apocalypse 1.14 refers to 'his head and the hairs'. In Apocalypse 1.14 the head and hairs of Jesus are likened to 'white wool' (cf. 'pure wool', MT/Th.; 'pure white wool', LXX) and to 'snow', yet the latter comparison in Daniel 7.9 is applied to the garment of the Ancient of Days. There is no mention of the eyes of the Ancient of Days in Daniel 7.9; reference to the eyes of the exalted Jesus draws instead on the example of the figure in Daniel 10.5–6. But the form of the comparison which is applied to the eyes appears to draw on the description of the throne in Daniel 7.9 and not on the description of the eyes in 10.5–6.[21]

The descriptive detail ὡς χιὼν in Apocalypse 1.14, which is drawn from the description of the robe of the Ancient of Days, is somewhat awkwardly placed in the description of the head and hair. Moreover, since we have already been told that the hair and head are λευκαὶ ὡς ἔριον λευκὸν, this description seems to be redundant. If a visionary experience lies behind Apocalypse 1.13–16 then the inclusion of ὡς χιὼν is a sign that John is interpreting his experience: the hair is not just described as white with an appropriate comparison to clarify the degree of whiteness, its whiteness is described in such a way that it recalls the whiteness found in Daniel 7.9.[22] On the face of it, John has transferred the description of the throne of the Ancient of Days to the description of the eyes of the exalted Jesus, ὡς φλὸξ πυρὸς (Apc. 1.14; cf. Daniel 7.9 LXX/Th.). But we cannot be sure that John had either Greek version of Daniel 7.9 in mind,[23] so that it is possible that his description of the eyes, which is a satisfactory translation of *w῾ynyw klpydy ʾš* (Dan. 10.6), only coincidentally reflects the description of the divine throne. Nevertheless, when so much else in Apocalypse 1.14 is drawn from Daniel 7.9 it is likely that this comparison is also drawn from there.

What John does not do is extensively model the risen Christ on the Ancient of Days. Christ is not enthroned, nor accompanied by a retinue of heavenly figures. His garment (already described in 1.13) does not reflect that of the Ancient of Days. John describes the 'eyes' of his figure with material drawn from Daniel 7.9, even though the eyes of the Ancient of Days are not mentioned there. Rather, John draws on Daniel 7.9 to furnish imagery for his description of the risen Christ. Some of this is additional to what was available in Daniel 10.5–6 (where there is no mention of either the head or the hair of the figure). But the comparison ὡς φλὸξ

---

[21] Note that the fiery character of heavenly beings goes back much further than Daniel 7.9/Dan. 10.5–6. In Exod. 3.2, for example, the angel of the LORD appears to Moses 'in a flame of fire out of a burning bush'.

[22] Charles, i, 28, says that ὡς χιὼν is 'manifestly a marginal gloss'. It is awkward, but its inclusion can be explained as we have just done.

[23] If John knew of a Greek version of Daniel 7.9 then it is likely that it was the LXX. Thus, with Apc. 1.14 first and Daniel 7.9 second for each equation: (i) ὡς ἔριον λευκὸν = ὡσεὶ ἔριον λευκὸν (LXX, Th. omits λευκὸν), (ii) ὡς φλὸξ πυρὸς = ὡσεὶ φλὸξ πυρός (LXX, Th. omits ὡσεὶ).

πυρὸς appears to be drawn from Daniel 7.9 when a descriptive image was already available from 10.6.

We turn now to the first phrase in the description of the exalted Jesus in Apocalypse 1.13. Given the influence of Daniel 10.5–6 on the christophany, we might expect Jesus to be described as ἄνθρωπος or ἀνὴρ, but in fact he is described as ὅμοιον υἱὸν ἀνθρώπου. For many scholars this expression has recalled in the first instance the description of the Danielic son of man in Daniel 7.13: *kbr 'nš*, MT (cf. ὡς υἱὸς ἀνθρωπου LXX, Th.). In favour of an allusion to Daniel 7.13 is the fact that prior to the christophany John indisputably draws on Daniel 7.13 and links Jesus Christ with this verse. In Apocalypse 1.7 John prophesies about the 'pierced one', that is, Jesus. The opening words of the prophecy, Ἰδοὺ ἔρχεται μετὰ τῶν νεφελῶν, recall the manner of the coming of the Danielic son of man in Daniel 7.13, *'m 'nny šmy*.[24] It is true that the Danielic son of man is not specifically referred to in Apocalypse 1.7. That is to say, it is conceivable that John simply uses an expression derived from Daniel 7.13 without any implication that he is doing so because he thinks that the human-like figure there is linked in some way to Jesus Christ. It is possible, for example, that the prophecy in Apocalypse 1.7, which is an amalgam of Daniel 7.13 and Zechariah 12.10, had become a traditional form by the time of the composition of the Apocalypse.[25]

Nevertheless, there is reason to think that John does see a connection between the risen Jesus and the Danielic son of man, for in Apocalypse 1 there are two motifs *other than those found in 1.7*, which resonate with motifs found in Daniel 7. First, Jesus Christ is entitled ὁ ἄρχων τῶν βασιλέων τῆς γῆς (Apc. 1.5). This rank places him in a similar position to the Danielic son of man who is given 'dominion and glory and kingship', so that 'all peoples, nations, and languages should serve him' (Dan. 7.14). Secondly, John's self-reference as a brother and companion to his readers ἐν τῇ θλίψει καὶ βασιλείᾳ καὶ ὑπομονῇ ἐν Ἰησοῦ (Apc. 1.9) resonates with some of the concerns of Daniel 7. There we find the 'holy ones

---

[24] Lohse, 'Menschensohn', 82–3; R. B. Scott, 'Behold', 127–32.
[25] Cf. Beale (*Daniel*, 155): 'Matthew 24.30 may have suggested the combination to John but it is also possible that he made a free rendering'; Beale further suggests (pp. 155–6) that the combination may reflect interest in the equation 'stone' (cf. Daniel 2.34–5) = 'son of man' (Dan. 7.13) and the 'stone' in Zech. 12.3–4. Other texts which may be cited in connection with Apc. 1.7 include *Barn.* 7.9–10; *Did.* 16.6. Cf. Bousset, 189–190; Kraft, 35–6.

of the Most High' receiving the kingdom (Dan. 7.18; cf. Daniel 7.27) in the context of tribulation (Dan. 7.21, where they have war made against them by 'the horn').[26]

Moreover, these observations pertain only to the links between Apocalypse 1 and Daniel 7. But there are a number of other allusions elsewhere in the Apocalypse to Daniel 7,[27] so that it would be most remarkable if the influence of the Danielic son of man on the portrayal of the risen Jesus were non-existent. We might also note in this connection a point made by Rowland concerning Apc. 14.14 where the expression ὅμοιον υἱὸν ἀνθρώπου is also to be found: the fact that in 14.14 the phrase is linked with ἐπὶ τὴν νεφέλην makes a connection between 14.14 and Daniel 7.13 almost certain. It would be strange, therefore, if there were no such connection in the parallel case in 1.13.[28] Casey has promoted an argument against the conclusion that the expression ὅμοιον υἱὸν ἀνθρώπου is an allusion to Daniel 7.13. He has argued that the difference between ὅμοιον υἱὸν ἀνθρώπου (Apc. 1.13, 14.14) and ὡς υἱὸς ἄνθρωπου (Dan. 7.13 LXX, Th.) is not insignificant. He suggests that John does not have the Danielic son of man in mind. His reasoning is twofold. First, that ὅμοιον is standard usage in visionary material. Secondly, that for a writer of semitic Greek such as John, terms equivalent to *bar enash* and *ben adam* are normal language when referring to 'a man'. Hence ὅμοιον υἱὸν ἀνθρώπου does not by itself point to any particular text. If anything, Casey suggests, this phrase refers to Daniel 10.16 Th., ὡς ὁμοίωσις υἱοῦ ἀνθρώπου (cf. LXX: ὡς ὁμοίωσις χειρὸς ἀνθρώπου; MT: *kdmwt bny 'dm*).[29]

Casey's point that ὅμοιον υἱὸν ἀνθρώπου does not point to any one text by itself is indisputable. The expression coheres closely with a number of variant phrases used in Ezekiel and Daniel, as we can observe by citing the following texts in Greek: ὁμοίωμα ἀνθρώπου (Ezek. 1.5 LXX); ὁμοίωμα ὡς εἶδος ἀνθρώπου (Ezek. 1.26 LXX); ὁμοίωμα ἀνδρὸς (Ezek. 8.2 LXX); ὡς υἱὸς ἀνθρώπου (Dan. 7.13 LXX = Th.); ὡς ὅρασις ἀνθρώπου (Dan. 10.18

---

[26] Cf. Beale, *Daniel*, 173; Holtz, *Christologie*, 110. Beale (ibid., 156, 158) also notes a parallel between Daniel 7.11 LXX (ἐθεώρουν τότε τὴν φωνὴν ... ὧν ... ἐλάλει) and Apc. 1.12 (βλέπειν τὴν φωνὴν ἥτις ἐλάει).

[27] Beale ('Revelation', 318) notes that the greatest number of Danielic allusions come from Daniel 7.

[28] Rowland, 'Man', 104.

[29] Casey, *Son*, 144.

LXX = Th.); ὡς ὁμοίωσις υἱοῦ ἀνθρώπου (Dan. 10.16 Th.).[30]
Casey's argument, however, is not convincing. There is no particular reason to deny that ὅμοιον υἱον ἀνθρώπου is a satisfactory
translation of the underlying Aramaic of Daniel 7.13.[31] Even if
John knew of a Greek version of this verse such as the LXX or
Theodotion, there seems to be no reason to deny that his rendering
is a fair alternative to these versions, coming as it does from the
hand of one who almost never reproduces his sources exactly.[32] But
the most important objection to Casey's argument is the fact it is
impossible in the light of our observations above to accept that
there is no allusion to the Danielic son of man in Apc. 1.13. When
Casey himself accepts that Apocalypse 1.14 has been influenced by
Daniel 7.9,[33] it is difficult to accept that Apocalypse 1.13 has not
been influenced by Daniel 7.13. Casey rightly draws attention to the
possibility that ὅμοιον υἱον ἀνθρώπου has been influenced by
Daniel 10.16 Th., but the question remains why John does not
strictly follow the example of Daniel 10.5 Th. and simply describe
Jesus as ἀνήρ.

Finally, the latter part of the first century saw an upsurge in
meditation on Daniel, as evidenced in 4 Ezra, the Syriac *Apocalypse
of Baruch*, and passages such as Apocalypse 1.7 and 1.13–16. It
seems reasonable to presume, against Casey, that for John this
process included reflection on the mysterious and extraordinary
human-like figure in Daniel 7.13. A mediating point, however, can
be made in the light of the above discussion. That is, given that the
glorious 'man' of Daniel 10 and the human-like figure in Daniel
7.13 lie in the background to the christophany, it is possible that
ὅμοιον υἱον ἀνθρώπου is best understood as a kind of hybrid
formula which combines ὡς υἱος ἀνθρπου/*kbr 'nš* and ὡς ὁμοίωσις
υἱοῦ ἀνθρώπου/*kdmwt bny 'dm* in an attempt to signify that both
Danielic figures lie in the background to the christophany.[34] We

---

[30] Cf. Karrer, *Johannesoffenbarung*, 142.

[31] Even if, as Casey (*Son*, 148) argues, the term consists of 'two semitisms'.

[32] Charles, i, 36, for example, has pointed out that John uses ὅμοιον synonymously
in meaning and construction with ὡς, since elsewhere in the Apocalypse (except
14.14) ὅμοιον is found with the dative. But see comment by Karrer, *Johannesoffenbarung*, 142, n. 27.

[33] Casey, *Son*, 146.

[34] Beale (*Daniel*, 159) argues that Daniel 3.25(92) Th. (ἐν μέσῳ τοῦ πυρός . . . ὁμοία
υἱῷ) is in the background (cf. Apc. 1.13: ἐν μέσῳ τῶν λυχνιῶν ὅμοιον υἱὸν). His
confidence in John's familiarity with Theodotion is not sufficiently underpinned.
Nevertheless, he recognizes that Dan 10.16 and 7.13 are also in mind.

also concur with the increasing consensus that the expression ὅμοιον υἱὸν ἀνθρώπου is not to be interpreted as equivalent to the title ὁ υἱὸς τοῦ ἀνθρώπου[35] found in the NT gospels.[36] Thus it is likely that the expression ὅμοιον υἱὸν ἀνθρώπου in Apocalypse 1.13 is an allusion to the mysterious 'one like a son of man' in Daniel 7.13. In addition to forging a link with Daniel 7.13, it also serves to indicate that the risen Jesus is a heavenly being in the tradition of the heavenly beings who are described as human-like in Daniel, Ezekiel, and apocalyptic literature. The use of ὅμοιον rather than ὡς may reflect the influence of the figure in Daniel 10.5–6,16 on the christophany alongside the figure in Daniel 7.13.

Our next concern is with passages from the Book of Ezekiel, which most probably lie in the background to the christophany. Two descriptive phrases in Apocalypse 1.13, for example, appear to recall the clothing of the heavenly scribe described in Ezekiel 9.2. While the description of the clothing of Jesus, ἐνδεδυμένον ποδήρη (Apc. 1.13), recalls the description of the clothing of the glorious 'man' in Daniel 10.5, it also calls to mind the clothing of the heavenly scribe in Ezekiel 9.2.[37] The link with the latter is highlighted by the LXX, which uses a virtually identical Greek phrase to Apocalypse 1.13 (in contrast to Daniel 10.5 LXX, Th.). But since we have reason to question whether John was familiar with the LXX we cannot be certain, from a linguistic point of view that he particularly had the heavenly scribe in mind.[38] We must remember that the description of the clothing in Daniel 10.5 in Hebrew is the same in Ezekiel 9.2: *lbwš bdym* (Dan. 10.5) = *lbš bdym* (Ezek. 9.2). Thus it is quite possible that John's own rendering of this phrase in Greek is only coincidentally the same as

---

[35] E.g. Müller, *Messias*, 157; Lohse, 'Menschensohn', 86–7; Casey, *Son*, 144–5. Contrast with Longenecker (*Christology*, 86, n. 103); NRSV which has 'one like the Son of Man' in Apc. 1.13; and Charles, i, 27.

[36] This is not to deny that the inclusion of ὅμοιον υἱὸν ἀνθρώπου in the description of the risen Jesus may allude in passing to the son of man sayings in the gospels. The primary allusion goes behind the gospels to the human-like angelic and divine beings who appear in Ezekiel and Daniel; and of these beings the son of man in Daniel 7.13 is particularly in view (*contra* Vos, *Synoptic*, 146).

[37] Cf. Rowland, 'Man', 107.

[38] Sometimes this description of Jesus' clothing is thought also to refer to his priestly character (so Lohmeyer, 15; Holtz, *Christologie*, 118; cf. Exod. 28.4; 29.5; Josephus *Ant.* 3.159). But Charles, i, 27, correctly notes that this is not necessarily the case: 'the long robe used here is simply as an Oriental mark of dignity'; cf. Büchsel (*Christologie*, 32); Kraft, (p. 45) sees a link here with Wis. 18.24; he attributes the robe mentioned there to 'the end-time leader, the divine Logos' – but 18.24 surely refers to Aaron (cf. Num. 17.11–26).

that found in Ezekiel 9.2 LXX. Nevertheless, it is noticeable that Apocalypse 1.13 also describes a chestband around Jesus, τοῖς μαστοῖς ζώνην, incorporating a word ζώνην, which is also used in Ezekiel 9.2 LXX – ζώνη σαπφείρου ἐπὶ τῆς ὀσφύος αὐτου – but not in Daniel 10.5 LXX/Th. However, apart from the fact that we have reason to doubt that John was familiar with the Greek version of Ezekiel 9.2, ζώνην is a common word[39] the use of which could be accounted for in a number of ways. The fact that the man clothed in linen in Ezekiel 9 marks the foreheads of the human inhabitants of Jerusalem with a *tau* on their foreheads (*whtwyt tw 'lmshwt*, 9.4) may be significant. The Hebrew letter *tau* resembles a cross and thus the placing of this mark on the foreheads of those who were to be saved could have been construed by a Christian reader of Ezekiel such as John as an anticipation of the saving work of Christ on the cross.[40] Even if John made no such connection, it is possible that passages from Ezekiel are in the background to the christophany simply because this book is influential throughout most of the Apocalypse. In chapter 7 above, for example, we remarked on the influence of Ezekiel on the theophany in Apocalypse 4, and on the angelophanies in 10.1–3 and 18.1–2.

Another possible connection between the christophany and Ezekiel worth considering involves the description of the voice of the exalted Jesus in Apocalypse 1.15: καὶ ἡ φωνὴ αὐτοῦ ὡς φωνὴ ὑδάτων πολλῶν. This description resembles the description of (i) the sound of the wings of the living creatures who surround the divine throne in Ezek. 1.24, *kqwl mym rbym*, and (ii) the sound of the *kabod* coming from the east in Ezekiel 43.2, *wqwlw kqwl mym rbym*.[41] The fact that John had an alternative image available in his dominant source (*kqwl hmwn*, Daniel 10.6) raises the question whether some special significance is to be attached to this description of the voice of Jesus. Although possible, we should note that this need not be so since the detail could simply reflect the fact that John's mind was steeped in the language of the theophanies and angelophanies of Daniel and Ezekiel, so that ὡς φωνὴ ὑδάτων πολλῶν was a comparison which readily sprang to mind rather than a carefully chosen image full of theological intent.

---

[39] E.g., in the NT it is found in Matt. 3.4, 10.9; Mark 1.6, 6.8; and Acts 21.11.

[40] Cooke (*Ezekiel*, 106–7) cites Jerome as an ancient Christian who proposed this interpretation.

[41] Note that Ezek. 1.24 LXX is ὡς φωνὴν ὕδατος πολλοῦ, while Ezek. 43.2 is καὶ φωνὴ τῆς παρεμβολῆς ὡς φωνὴ διπλασιαζόντων πολλῶν.

Nevertheless, the use of this particular description is interesting. First, to the extent that the comparison draws on the description of the living creatures in Ezekiel 1.24, the process in Daniel 10.5–6 is continued, in which the description of the scribe in Ezekiel 9.2 is supplemented with details from the description of the living creatures and the environs of the divine throne. Secondly, the description of Jesus' voice alludes to the living creatures and to the *kabod* itself, underlining the exalted status of the risen Jesus in the Apocalypse. The possibility that the risen Jesus is identified with the *kabod*, however, must not be unduly stressed since we have already seen that Ezekiel 43.2 has influenced the description of the angel in Apocalypse 18.1–2 without the corollary that the angel has been identified with the *kabod*.[42] That is, the description of the voice of the risen Jesus takes us to the theophanies in Ezekiel 1 and 43, but this does not mean that the christophany is essentially different in character from the angelophanies in Daniel 10.5–6 or Apocalypse 18.1–2.

Thus, the christophany read against its OT influences reveals a diverse background. For our purposes, the key points are: (i) the dominant influence of the angelophany in Daniel 10.5–6; (ii) the strong influence of the theophany in Daniel 7.9; and (iii) the influences of angelophanies in Daniel 7.13 and Ezekiel 9.2, and (possibly) theophanies in Ezekiel 1.24 and 43.2. This combination of texts suggests a continuation of the process which we have discerned behind Daniel 10.5–6, where the vision of an angel has its roots in an earlier angelophany (Ezek. 9.2) supplemented by other epiphanic details. In other words, the christophany appears to all intents and purposes to be an angelophany or the epiphany of an angelomorphic being. Such a conclusion coheres with our suggestion in the previous section that John saw a correspondence between Jesus Christ and the angel of the LORD in Zechariah 1.8.

The christophany against its extra-OT background

We have considered the christophany in terms of its OT epiphanic background. Now we turn to examine it in comparison with epiphanies from outside the OT. First, for convenience, we recite Apocalypse 1.13–16, and then recite the most relevant parts of the

---

[42] See above, p. 139.

epiphanies we have already considered in chapters 3 and 4 which offer at least a reasonably close comparison with the christophany.[43]

καὶ ἐν μέσῳ τῶν λυχνιῶν ὅμοιον υἱὸν ἀνθρώπου ἐνδεδυμένον ποδήρη καὶ περιζωσμένον πρὸς τοῖς μαστοῖς ζώνην χρυσᾶν. [14]ἡ δὲ κεφαλὴ αὐτοῦ καὶ αἱ τρίχες λευκαὶ ὡς ἔριον λευκὸν ὡς χιὼν καὶ οἱ ὀφθαλμοὶ αὐτοῦ ὡς φλὸξ πυρὸς [15]καὶ οἱ πόδες αὐτοῦ ὅμοιοι χαλκολιβάνῳ ὡς ἐν καμίνῳ πεπυρωμένης καὶ ἡ φωνὴ αὐτοῦ ὡς φωνὴ ὑδάτων πολλῶν, [16]καὶ ἔχων ἐν τῇ δεξιᾷ χειρὶ αὐτοῦ ἀστέρας ἑπτὰ καὶ ἐκ τοῦ στόματος αὐτοῦ ῥομφαία δίστομος ὀξεῖα ἐκπορευομένη καὶ ἡ ὄψις αὐτοῦ ὡς ὁ ἥλιος φαίνει ἐν τῇ δυνάμει αὐτοῦ. (Apc. 1.13–16)

... and the aspect of his face like chrysolite, and the hair of his head like snow and the clothing of his garments (was) purple; and a golden staff (was) in his right hand.
(*Apoc. Abr.* 11.2)[44]

Then I arose and stood, and I saw a great angel standing before me with his face shining like the rays of the sun in its glory since his face is like that which is perfected in its glory. [12]And he was girded as if a golden girdle were upon his breast. His feet were like bronze which is melted in a fire. (*Apoc. Zeph.* 6.11–12).[45]

ἰδοὺ ἀνὴρ ὅμοιος κατὰ πάντα τῷ Ιωσηφ τῇ στολῇ καὶ τῷ στεφάνῳ καὶ τῇ ῥάβδῳ τῇ βασιλικῇ [9]πλὴν τὸ πρόσωπον αὐτοῦ ἦν ὡς ἀστραπὴ καὶ οἱ ὀφθαλμοὶ αὐτοῦ ὡς φέγγος ἡλίου καὶ αἱ τρίχες τῆς κεφαλῆς αὐτοῦ ὡς φλὸξ πυρὸς καὶ αἱ χειρες καὶ οἱ πόδες αὐτοῦ ὥσπερ σίδηρος ἐκ πυρός. (*Jos. and Asen.* 14.8–9)[46]

... the hair of his head as white as wool ... as for his eyes, when he opened them the whole house glowed like the sun ... He is not like an (ordinary) human being, His eyes are like the rays of the sun, and his face glorious.
(1 *Enoch* 106.2–5)[47]

[Jacob] ... and his head was all white as snow (ἡ κεφαλὴ

---

[43] An alternative table of comparison may be found in Rowland, 'Man', 102–3.
[44] Rubinkiewicz, *OTP*, i, 693–4.   [45] Wintermute, *OTP*, i, 513.
[46] Philonenko, *Joseph*, 178.   [47] Isaac, *OTP*, i, 86.

αὐτοῦ πᾶσα λευκὴ ὡσεὶ χιών) . . . his eyes (were) flashing and darting (flashes of) lightning (οἱ ὀφθαλμοὶ αὐτοῦ χαροποιοὶ καὶ ἐξαστράπτοντες).   (*Jos. and Asen.* 22.7)[48]

Other briefer examples of glorious angels and exalted humans whose form at least in a general sense compares with the form of the risen Jesus may be noted. For example:

- ὁ ἄγγελος ὁ ἡλιοωμορφος (*Test. Abr.* Rec. A 12.9, 13.10);
- ὁ ἄγγελος ὁ πύρινος (*Test. Abr.* Rec. A 12.10, 13.11);
- 'Death' as a glorious angel: ὄψιν ἡλιόμορφον . . . τὰς παρειὰς αὐτοῦ πυρὶ ἀστράπτών (*Test. Abr.* Rec. A 16.8–9; cf. 17.15);
- ἀνὴρ θαύμαστος ἡλιόρατος ὅμοιος υἱῷ θεοῦ (*Test. Abr.* Rec. A 12.4–5);
- angels who tread upon 'the flame of fire; their garments were white – and their overcoats – and the light of their faces was like snow' (1 *Enoch* 71.1);[49]
- two glorious 'men' with faces 'like the shining sun', eyes 'like burning lamps', mouths from which fire comes out, and arms 'like wings of gold' (2 *Enoch* 1.4–5, Shorter Rec.).[50]

Although 1 *Enoch* 14 features imagery such as 'snow', it is not done in connection with the hair or head of the form of God (14.20), and, in contrast to the christophany, the face of God cannot be seen (14.21): consequently, we have omitted it from our survey. We also argue that 1 *Enoch* 46.1 ('his head was white like wool') need not be separately considered in this context since it is essentially a repetition of Daniel 7.9. Two important points follow from this survey. First, the christophany is not unique when it includes details found in the theophany in Daniel 7.9: it is a feature of at least four other epiphanies of angels and exalted humans. Secondly, with the exception of the 'sword in the mouth', the elements of the christophany correspond to elements found in angelophanies and epiphanies of angelomorphic figures: human-like form, wearing a robe and a girdle, white head and hair, fiery eyes, burnished feet, voice, holding something in the hand, and a sun-like face. Of these elements only the description of the voice, which is found in Daniel 10.6 though with a different comparison applied, is not found in the epiphanies we examined in chapters 3 and 4. In other words, in

---

[48] Burchard, *OTP*, ii, 238.
[49] Isaac, *OTP*, i, 49.   [50] Andersen, *OTP*, i, 107.

the context of epiphanies in apocalyptic and related writings
outside the OT the christophany compares favourably with angelophanies and with epiphanies of angelomorphic figures. This observation, of course, coheres with our conclusion in the previous
chapter that the christophany is more closely aligned with the
angelophanies in the Apocalypse than with the theophany in
Apocalypse 4, and it coheres with our conclusion to the previous
section of this chapter. It seems appropriate, therefore, to speak of
the risen Jesus in Apocalypse 1.13–16 as a figure who is like the
angels in form and to refer to this figure as the angelomorphic
Jesus.

The angelomorphic Jesus in Apocalypse 1.13–16

The angelomorphic character of the christophany in Apocalypse
1.13–16 needs further exploration. What, for example, is the
relationship between our affirmation of the divinity of Jesus Christ
in the Apocalypse and the angelomorphism of Apocalypse 1.13–16?
Can we say more about possible influences on the combination of
images in the description of the christophany? The key verse for
this further exploration is 1.14. Mostly, the contents of 1.14 are
understood in terms of a connection with the Ancient of Days: the
usual implication of the imagery shared with Daniel 7.9 being that
Jesus Christ shares in the divinity of the Ancient of Days.[51] Many
readers have come to the Apocalypse with a prior belief in the
divinity of Christ and consequently have assumed that the resemblance to the Ancient of Days is a reflection of this fact.[52] Our
argument so far suggests that such an approach overlooks a
number of possible alternative explanations of the significance of
Apocalypse 1.14. Bauckham, for example, has listed four reasons
for the description of the white head and hair of Christ, the first,
second, and fourth of which constitute such alternatives:[53] (i) 'an
attempt to share John's visual impression of the resplendent Son of
Man'; (ii) 'a conventional item in literary descriptions of heavenly
beings'; (iii) a reflection of 'John's high christology' because this
feature belongs to the Ancient of Days; and (iv) 'a symbol of
Christ's [eternal] pre-existence'. These reasons are not mutually

---

[51] Brütsch, i, 86; W. Scott, 441; Lohse, 18; Roloff, 43.
[52] Yarbro Collins, 'Tradition', 553.
[53] Bauckham, 'Figurae', 109–10.

exclusive. The first two cohere well with our examination thus far. In the first case, recalling our discussion in chapter 1 of visionary experiences and their origin and interpretation, it seems quite plausible to suppose that Apocalypse 1.14 reflects the influence of Daniel 7.9 as part of the seer's stockpile of images, but without the requirement that images from Daniel 7.9 could only be applied to manifestations of the deity. In the second case, we have noted a number of epiphanies which, like Apocalypse 1.14, reflect the language of Daniel 7.9 and this suggests that there may well have been an element of conventionality about the inclusion of such imagery. We cannot rule out Bauckham's fourth alternative, but there is no particular reason to suppose that this was an intended meaning.[54]

It is not our intention to exclude the possibility that John may have intended to draw attention to the divinity of Jesus Christ by the inclusion of details from Daniel 7.9. But we argue that this possibility is far from certain. On the one hand, we have noted other more or less similar epiphanies where such details are included but no divine status for the figure involved is implied. On the other hand, we have argued in the previous chapter that the theophany in Apocalypse 4 and the christophany in Apocalypse 1 share no common details and thus the christophany may not be illustrating the divinity which on other grounds we believe the exalted Jesus shares with God in the Apocalypse.[55]

In connection with the possible illustration of Christ's divinity in Apocalypse 1.14 we need also to comment further on the idea that Apocalypse 1.13–16 reflects the influence of Daniel 7.13 LXX, which appears to identify the human-like figure with the Ancient of Days. We have already discussed a number of questions concerning the influence of Daniel 7.13 LXX on the christophany (see pp. 44–9) and have come to the conclusion that the evidence for such influence is by no means overwhelming. We have also argued that if such an influence was present in 1.13–16 it is likely that it was an expression of the belief that 'one like a son of man' and the Ancient

---

[54] Cf. Allo, 13; Prigent, 28; Swete, 16, who notes that this was the view of ancient commentators such as Andreas, but argues that the idea should not be pressed since white hair 'suggests decay whereas Jesus Christ is unchangeable'.

[55] Thus when Beale ('Revelation', 321), in the context of discussion about intentional use of the OT, says that 'the Son of Man is clearly portrayed as a divine figure in Revelation 1' our point is that this is by no means clear: the risen Jesus appears like angelic figures in other contemporary texts.

of Days were similar in appearance, rather than that they were identified together as two manifestations of the one being. Consequently, if Daniel 7.13 LXX has influenced the christophany in Apocalypse 1 then it is not necessarily an indication that Apocalypse 1.14 is illustrative of his divinity.[56] Such influence is consistent with the supposition that Apocalypse 1.13–16 portrays an angelomorphic figure. But, with less than overwhelming evidence for the influence of Daniel 7.13 LXX on the description of the christophany, then it is important to consider whether there is an alternative explanation for the combination of material from Daniel 7.9 with material from Daniel 7.13 and 10.5–6.

Before putting forward our own suggested explanation, we may consider alternatives proposed by Rowland and Yarbro Collins. Rowland notes an alternative to his own preferred hypothesis involving Daniel 7.13 LXX. Having argued that there are close connections between Daniel 10.5–6 and Ezekiel 1,[57] Rowland suggests that as a consequence of links between Daniel 10.5–6 and descriptions of theophanies being recognized, details from these theophanies 'contributed to the later use of Dan 10.5f'.[58] Rowland does not elaborate and the explanation we will shortly propose effectively provides the missing exposition. Yarbro Collins argues that, while the Danielic son of man is Michael from the point of view of the composition of the Book of Daniel, it does not follow that John made this identification. She suggests that the designation of the revealing angel as a 'man' in 8.15 (cf. ἀνθρώπου, LXX) may have indicated that this angel, identified as Gabriel, was the same angel as in 7.13. The similarity in revealing functions between this angel and the angel in Daniel 10 may have suggested that the angel in Daniel 10 was also Gabriel. In turn, this means that the angels in Daniel 7.13 and 10.5–6 were identified and this would explain 'why elements from Dan 7:13 and Dan 10:5–6 are conflated to describe the heavenly being of Rev 1:12–16'.[59]

Further, the Ancient of Days was 'a distinguishable manifestation of God as a high angel', and probably identified with Gabriel by John with the consequent conflation of Daniel 7.9, 13, and 10.5–6 in Apocalypse 1.13–16.[60] We have already discussed the possibility that the Ancient of Days was interpreted as an angel and

---

[56] See pp. 48–9.   [57] E.g. Rowland, 'Vision', 3.
[58] Rowland, 'Man', 106.
[59] Yarbro Collins, 'Tradition', 551.   [60] Ibid., 557–8.

concluded that this was unlikely from the perspective of the Apocalypse.[61] But we also dispute the first part of Yarbro Collins' proposal as we have outlined it. For this approach overlooks the fact that John is just as likely to have read Daniel 7.16 and made a connection with 8.16.[62] In the former Daniel seeks out 'one of the attendants' to explain the vision to him; in the latter Gabriel is commanded to go to Daniel to interpret the vision. It seems as reasonable to presume that if John identified Gabriel with one of the figures in Daniel 7 then it was with one of the attendants as it was with 'one like a son of man'. But if the figure in Daniel 7.16 is Gabriel then he cannot be 'one like a son of man' who is certainly not 'one of the attendants'.[63]

Another explanation is possible which involves the epiphany of the angelomorphic Noah in 1 *Enoch* 106.2–6. This epiphany occurs in a text undoubtedly older than the Apocalypse, dating from no later than 1 BCE, and conceivably as early as 161 BCE.[64] It is, of course, possible that this text has been influenced by Daniel 7.9, on the supposition of a date of composition for the latter of *c.* 165 BCE. Or the former might share with Daniel 7.9 a common indebtedness to 1 *Enoch* 14.[65] In any case, there is no reason to presume the influence of Daniel 7.13 LXX, since Noah is not linked in any way to the Danielic son of man. Our explanation begins, then, with the existence of the epiphany of Noah as a glorious being who has a body as white as snow, hair as white as wool, and eyes like the sun.

Four points about 1 *Enoch* 106.2–6 are significant in the present context. First, it provides a model of a glorious figure of comparable stature to the glorious 'man' in Daniel 10.5–6 (i.e. they are both very impressive figures even though there are few common details between them). Secondly, the description of Noah includes images, such as 'white hair', which are not found in Daniel 10.5–6. Thirdly, 1 *Enoch* 106 is indisputably older than the Apocalypse, unlike Daniel 7.13 LXX. Fourthly, the influence of 1 *Enoch* 106.2–6 directly or indirectly on epiphanies such as Apocalypse 1.13–16 (and 10.1) is by no means inconceivable, given that it shares 'sun' imagery with these epiphanies, a feature absent in the epiphanies in Ezekiel and Daniel. That is, it is conceivable that Apocalypse 1.16 where the face of Jesus is like the sun shining in

[61] See pp. 36–7.   [62] Day, *Conflict*, 171–2.
[63] Zevit ('Implications', 490) is confusing on this point.
[64] See above, p. 81.   [65] See above, p. 81.

full force, and Apocalypse 10.1, where the face of the angel is like the sun, reflect the influence of 1 *Enoch* 106.5 ('His eyes are like the rays of the sun').

Consequently, the existence of the epiphany of Noah in 1 *Enoch* 106 from long before the time of the Apocalypse is an important element in a possible explanation as to why the christophany is broader in its range of images than those supplied by Daniel 10.5–6. Such an explanation does not presuppose that John actually knew 1 *Enoch* 106, only that John was familiar with apocalyptic tradition influenced by that text. This explanation has the significant advantage of providing a specific example of an epiphany which includes white hair, comparison with snow, and comparison with the sun. In the christophany the actual language used to describe the risen Jesus is mainly drawn from Daniel and Ezekiel. Our explanation complements this observation by providing the model of a glorious figure whose appearance included elements found in Daniel 7.9 and 10.5–6. An obvious shortcoming, though, is the lack of evidence for the influence of 1 *Enoch* 106 on the Apocalypse, other than the similarity of details between the epiphanies of Noah and Jesus. Nevertheless in the context of considering the merits of an alternative explanation based on the influence of Daniel 7.13 LXX, this shortcoming does not constitute a serious objection since there is a comparable lack of evidence for the influence of Daniel 7.13 LXX. (Noting that the question of the influence of the Septuagintal text of Daniel on the Apocalypse – for which there is some evidence – is distinct from the question of the influence of the version of Daniel 7.13 LXX as found in Pap. 967.) A notable implication of our explanation is that the inclusion in Apocalypse 1.13–16 of details found in Daniel 7.9 need not imply that the divine status of the risen Jesus was being illustrated since similar elements are found in a non-divine figure such as Noah.

A consensus appears to be forming around the view that Daniel 7.13 LXX is the key to the conflation of Daniel 7.9,13, and 10.5–6 in Apocalypse 1.13–16.[66] But this consensus appears to be forming without the exercise of due caution over the question of whether Daniel 7.13 LXX was early enough to have been an influence on Apocalypse 1.14 or over the question of the meaning of Daniel 7.13 LXX. We argue that this need for caution is sufficient to warrant consideration of a further possible explanation in which the key to

---

[66] In addition to Rowland and Yarbro Collins, note also Aune, 'Prophecy', 421.

the conflation is the influence of 1 *Enoch* 106. A significant advantage of this is that 'sun' imagery, which is not found in epiphanic accounts in either Ezekiel or Daniel, is found in 1 *Enoch* 106.2–5. The importance of 1 *Enoch* 106 has been overlooked by scholars such as Hurtado, Rowland, and Yarbro Collins in their discussion of the christophany. A significant corollary of our suggested explanation is that it resonates strongly with our conclusion in this and the previous chapter that the christophany is typically angelophanic.

Since we have argued that the Jesus of the christophany appears in the form of an angel and have observed that he carries out a similar function to an angel then the question arises whether the christophany reflects a belief that Jesus was an angel. Two factors, however, count against this possibility. First, and foremost, is the lack of the designation ἄγγελος for the risen Jesus. If we compare Apocalypse 1.13–16 with Apocalypse 10.1, for example, where both passages feature glorious beings, the sharpest distinguishing feature is that the term ἄγγελος is not applied in the former case, suggesting that John distinguishes between Jesus and the angels. Secondly, the combination of Jesus' divine status and the sharp distinction in the Apocalypse between the angels and God (cf. Apc. 19.10, 22.9) indicates that an angel christology is unlikely. Nevertheless, with respect to Daniel 10.5–6 it might be argued that the strong influence of this passage on the christophany suggests an identification between the exalted Jesus and the angel who commissioned Daniel. But one crucial observation we have made is that the 'man' in Daniel 10.5–6 also reappears in 12.7–8 and the latter account is taken up in Apocalypse 10. As we have distinguished between Jesus Christ and the mighty angel in Apocalypse 10 it would appear that the story of one angel in Daniel has influenced the descriptions of two beings in the Apocalypse. This implies that neither Jesus nor the mighty angel has been identified with the 'man' in Daniel 10.5–6. Rather, the information supplied in Daniel has simply contributed to the descriptions of two different figures. In other words, it would appear that in this case the 'man' in Daniel 10 and 12 is not the *object* of interpretation, but the *means* of interpretation for John.[67] Dan. 10.5–6, for example, has not been reinterpreted in Apocalypse 1.13–16, so that the risen Jesus is a

---

[67] Cf. Yarbro Collins ('Review', 735) commenting on the failure of Beale (*Daniel*, 319) to make this distinction properly.

reappearance of the 'man'; rather, it has contributed to the vision of the risen Jesus.[68] This point is reinforced by the observation that, while details from Daniel 10.5–6 dominate Apocalypse 1.13–16, there is very little in the latter which is an exact reproduction of the former. In short: it is unlikely that Apocalypse 1.13–16 implies that Jesus is identified with the angel in Daniel 10.5–6.[69] It would appear correct, therefore, to conclude that the risen, angelomorphic Jesus is not actually an angel in the context of Apocalypse 1. This conclusion is consistent with the fact that nowhere in Apocalypse 1 (or in the rest of the Apocalypse) is Jesus ever designated or entitled ἄγγελος. Our observations about the similarity between Jesus and the angels in the Apocalypse in terms of form and function have always been accompanied by observations that Jesus is distinct from the angels. We have no reason to believe that Jesus was perceived to be an angel. At the most, he was an angelomorphic being according to his presentation in Apocalypse 1.13–16.

We have argued in chapter 6 that in the Apocalypse Jesus is a divine being to the extent that: (i) he belongs with God as the object of heavenly praise (5.13, 22.1–4); (ii) he shares the divine throne (3.21, 7.17, 22.1–3); and (iii) he is identified with God in a series of 'I am' statements (22.13). Jesus Christ in the Apocalypse lies 'on the divine side of the line which monotheism must draw between God and creatures'.[70] *Inter alia*, we have noticed above that the divinity of Jesus in respect of Apocalypse 1.13–20 is supported (though not required) by the fact that there is no reference to Jesus having been 'sent' – in contrast to the glorious 'man' in Daniel 10.11 (and to Yahoel in *Apoc. Abr.* 10.7). We can also observe what the exalted Jesus has to say in Apocalypse 1.17–18. When Jesus speaks in 1.17–18 John hears the following words:

> μὴ φοβοῦ· ἐγώ εἰμι ὁ πρῶτος καὶ ὁ ἔσχατος 18 καὶ ὁ ζῶν, καὶ ἐγενόμην νεκρὸς καὶ ἰδοὺ ζῶν εἰμι εἰς τοὺς αἰῶνας τῶν αἰώνων καὶ ἔχω τὰς κλεῖς τοῦ θανάτου καὶ τοῦ ᾅδου.

At first sight these statements are commensurate with Jesus' status as some kind of exalted, angel-like, human being. To die and to be alive simply refers to Jesus' resurrection. To have the key to Death and Hades is to have an authority attributable elsewhere in the

---

[68] Cf. Kretschmar, *Studien*, 222.
[69] Contrast Hippolytus, *Eis ton Daniel*, iv.36.4–6.
[70] Bauckham, 'Worship', 335.

Apocalypse to an angel (e.g. 9.1, 20.1; cf. *Apoc. Zeph.* 6.13). The statement ἐγώ εἰμι ὁ πρῶτος καὶ ὁ ἔσχατος could be interpreted in terms of Jesus' relationship to the church as, for example, the 'first-born from the dead' (cf. Apc. 1.5; Col 1.18).[71] But our discussion above (see pp. 117–18) suggested that ἐγώ εἰμι ὁ πρῶτος καὶ ὁ ἔσχατος must be interpreted in the light of 22.13: it is not simply a statement about Jesus in relationship to the church but one about Jesus in relationship to the whole of creation and history. It is a statement which expresses the unity of Jesus Christ with God. In this light we may then understand the power over Death and Hades as a divine prerogative.[72] Likewise, the statement that Jesus is ὁ ζῶν may be seen as a further alignment of Jesus Christ with God.[73] The conjunction of ὁ ζῶν with εἰς τοὺς αἰῶνας τῶν αἰώνων recalls, for example, 'He who lives forever created the universe' (Sir. 18.1),[74] and the description of God in the Apocalypse itself, τῷ ζῶντι εἰς τοὺς αἰῶνας τῶν αἰώνων (Apc. 4.9,10, 10.6, 15.7).

It would appear, then, that in Apocalypse 1.13–20 John 'sees' an angelomorphic figure but 'hears' one who participates in the eternal being of God. The angelomorphism of the divine Jesus at first sight seems somewhat strange and paradoxical, begging for some kind of explanation. At this point, however, our study of angel christology in chapter 5 becomes highly relevant. We saw there the implication of the Ethiopic reading of *Ascension of Isaiah* 9.30 – that Jesus was transformed into an angel-like figure so as not to overwhelm Isaiah, and that Jesus evaded recognition by the angels through angelo-morphic transformation (*Asc. Isa.* 10.17–31) – and we observed that Justin (*Apol.* i.63) and Origen (*Comm. Joh.* i. 217–19) both talk about Jesus taking up angelic form temporarily for specific purposes. Also, in *Testament of Abraham* 16.8–9, 'Death' manifests itself in the form of an archangel. We suggest that, in the Apocalypse, Jesus appears as an angelomorphic figure as a temporary measure, analogously to these examples. Jesus is not an angel but

---

[71] Note that Uncial A offers πρωτότοκος as an alternative to πρῶτος.

[72] E.g. *Tg. Yer. I* Deut. 28.12; *Tg. Yer. I* Gen. 30.22; cf. Aune ('Magic', 484–9) who argues for the influence of the goddess Hekate.

[73] Cf. Swete, 19. Note that God as *'l ḥy* (θεὸς ζῶν), *ḥy yhwh* (ζῇ Κύριος), or *ḥy 'ny* (ζῷ ἐγώ) in the OT: Deut. 32.40; Josh. 3.10; Ps. 41(42).3, 83(84).3; Isa. 49.18; Jer. 5.2; Hos. 1.10 (2.1); and as θεὸς ζῶν or ὁ θεὸς ὁ ζῶν in Matt. 16.16, 26.63; Acts 14.15; Rom 9.26; 2 Cor. 3.3, 6.16; 1 Thess. 1.9; 1 Tim. 3.15, 4.10; Heb. 3.12, 9.14, 10.31; 1 Pet 1.23.

[74] Cf. Daniel 4.34; 12.7; 1 *Enoch* 5.1.

he takes up the form of an angel temporarily in order to fulfil certain roles.

Two observations about this interpretation of the christophany can now be made. First, when John takes some trouble to underline the fact that there is only one God (see especially Apc. 19.10, 22.9, and 22.3–4, where singular pronouns are used, even though both God and the Lamb are in view),[75] then the angelomorphic appearance of Jesus devoid of imagery found in the theophany in Apocalypse 4.3 underlines the oneness of God. Secondly, given that the true form of God is veiled from human sight (Apc. 4.3), it is understandable that Jesus does not appear in a manner which illustrates his divinity. Rather, Jesus is seen in ways which are accessible to human vision, and cohere with his roles and functions. In broad terms, in the Apocalypse Jesus as the saviour-messiah appears as the Lamb, and as the commissioning agent of the revelation he appears as an angelic figure. An obvious (partial) analogy is with the incarnation. On the one hand, to interact with humanity on earth Jesus becomes a human being (cf. 'the Word became flesh', John 1.14); on the other, to lead heavenly forces and to work alongside heavenly agents in a manner visible to the church, the exalted Jesus becomes like an angel. Our proposal is not, of course, completely analogous with the incarnation since we are not suggesting that Jesus actually becomes an angel, rather that he takes on the form of an angel and functions like an angel. There are obvious resonances here with the angelomorphic christology of the *Ascension of Isaiah* and with the 'dispensational' angel christology of Origen.[76] But in *Commentarii in Johannis* i.217–19 Jesus becomes an angel for the sake of the angels, whereas in the Apocalypse Jesus is presented as an angelic figure for the sake of his church.

Conclusions

We have set ourselves the task of investigating the influence of angelology on the christology of the Apocalypse. Our study of Apocalypse 1.13–16 has determined that angelology has influenced

---

[75] Cf. Bauckham ('Worship', 331): 'John is evidently reluctant to speak of God and Christ together as a plurality. Their "functional unity" [Holtz, *Christologie*, 202] is such that Christ cannot be an alternative object of worship, but shares in the glory due to God.' Cf. Beasley-Murray, 332; Holtz, *Christologie*, 202.

[76] See above, pp. 100–1, 104–6.

the vision of Jesus Christ. In appearance Jesus is like an angel. Each element of his form recalls the form of other glorious angels and angelomorphic beings. The form of the Ancient of Days is also recalled, but when Apocalypse 1.14 is read against the background of a number of epiphanies which feature similar imagery it is questionable that the divinity of Jesus Christ is being illustrated. Also questionable in respect of Apocalypse 1.14 is the explanation for the conflation of elements from Daniel 7.9,13 and 10.5–6 in terms of the influence of Daniel 7.13 LXX. We consider this to be far from an assured result and have proposed an alternative explanation based on 1 *Enoch* 106.2–6.

In other words, we are suggesting that the christophany is more akin to an angelophany than to a theophany. When examined in the context of the Apocalypse itself, the epiphanic tradition of the OT, and the epiphanic tradition of apocalyptic and related writings outside the OT, the form of the risen Jesus in Apocalypse 1.13–16 is effectively the form of an angel, and the christology of 1.13–16 is appropriately described as an 'angelomorphic christology'. Our view contrasts, for example, with Caird who says that 'John has seen the risen Christ, clothed in all the attributes of deity'.[77] We would say instead that John has seen Christ clothed in all the attributes of a glorious angel. Although the exalted Jesus appears in angelomorphic form, this is not a diminishment of his divine status within the Apocalypse. Recalling observations drawn from the study of angelology and angel christology, we have suggested that Jesus takes on angelomorphic form temporarily. We now proceed to study 'one like a son of man' in Apocalypse 14.14 with a view to determining whether what is said there corroborates our findings so far.

[77] Caird, 26.

9

APOCALYPSE 14.14

We continue our investigation of the influence of angelology on the christology of the Apocalypse by examining the human-like figure in Apocalypse 14.14. Although many commentators identify this figure as Jesus Christ not all do so because in 14.15 the next figure in a sequence of seven figures is described as ἄλλος ἄγγελος which raises the possibility that the figure in 14.14 is not the risen Jesus but an angel. Consequently, we must first carefully weigh up the identity of the human-like figure. We must also consider the possibility that if the human-like figure is the risen Jesus then ἄλλος ἄγγελος implies that he is an angel.

Preliminary issues

Καὶ εἶδον, καὶ ἰδοὺ νεφέλη λευκή, καὶ ἐπὶ ἣν νεφέλην καθήμενον ὅμοιον υἱὸν ἀνθρώπου, ἔχων ἐπὶ τῆς κεφαλῆς αὐτοῦ στεφανον χρυσοῦν καὶ ἐν τῇ χειρὶ αὐτοῦ δρέπανον ὀξύ. [15]καὶ ἄλλος ἄγγελος ἐξῆλθεν ἐκ τοῦ ναοῦ κράζων ἐν φωνῇ μεγάλῃ τῷ καθημένῳ ἐπὶ τῆς νεφέλης· πέμψον τὸ δρέπανόν σου καὶ θέρισον, ὅτι ἦλθεν ἡ ὥρα θερίσαι, ὅτι ἐξηράνθη ὁ θερισμὸς τῆς γῆς. [16]καὶ ἔβαλεν ὁ καθήμενος ἐπὶ τῆς νεφέλης τὸ δρέπανον αὐτοῦ ἐπὶ τὴν γῆν καὶ ἐθερίσθη ἡ γῆ.   (Apc. 14.14–16)[1]

The phrase ἄλλος ἄγγελος in 14.15, one of six occurrences in 14.6–20, is intriguing. In 14.8,9,17,18 this expression occasions no difficulty per se, since the angels referred to clearly follow the appearance of a previous angel, and thus are appropriately described as ἄλλος ἄγγελος. Our previous discussion of the phrase ὅμοιον υἱὸν ἀνθρώπου has shown that it is similar to other

---

[1] There is no major text-critical issue affecting this passage.

expressions used with reference to angelic figures. It would be quite reasonable, therefore, to construe ἄλλος ἄγγελος in 14.15 as meaning 'another angel, following the appearance of an angel described as a human-like figure'. We must then ask whether ἄλλος ἄγγελος in 14.15 necessarily implies that the figure in 14.14 is an angel (with the further implication either that the figure is not the exalted Jesus or that the exalted Jesus is an angel). The answer to this question would be appear to be negative, however, since there are instances in the Apocalypse of angels being described as ἄλλος with no immediate predecessor in view. For example, in the case of ἄλλον ἄγγελον ἰσχυρὸν in 10.1 its predecessor is ἄγγελον ἰσχυρὸν in 5.2.[2] More pertinently, the first angel in the sequence in 14.6–20 is ἄλλος ἄγγελος, which appears to have no predecessor immediately in view. The nearest previous reference to angel(s) is in 12.7, where Michael and the dragon and their armies of ἄγγελοι fight each other. A number of explanations for ἄλλος in 14.6 have been proposed: for instance, that ἄλλος in 14.6 is a stylistic device,[3] or that ἄλλος ἄγγελος means 'again, an angel',[4] or 'another, an angel',[5] or that it is referring to 'die aktualisierende Stimme Gottes'.[6] Whatever the explanation, the point remains that 14.6 provides a relevant example of 'another angel' with no apparent immediate predecessor. The absence of ἄλλος from 14.6 in some texts[7] could be explained by the awkwardness of its presence in the original text and, in fact, its originality is well supported.[8]

If ἄλλος ἄγγελος in 14.15 does not necessarily imply that the human-like figure in 14.14 is an angel, can we advance a plausible case for a previous angel to whom ἄλλος refers? In fact, it has been argued that a plausible referent for ἄλλος in 14.15 is the angel in 14.9.[9] This possibility has been denied by Charles since 14.6–11 and

---

[2] Cf. discussion in Bousset, 383, and Holtz, *Christologie*, 130, n. 2, concerning (possible) previous angels.

[3] Holtz, *Christologie*, 130, n. 2; Lohmeyer, 123.   [4] Ibid., 121.

[5] Charles, ii, 12; cf. Beckwith, 655; with refutation by Holtz, *Christologie*, 129, n. 3.

[6] Van Schaik, 'Apk', 221–5, citation from p. 222. The principal objection to this explanation and to the previous one is that elsewhere in the Apocalypse ἄλλος ἄγγελος means 'another angel'.

[7] E.g. 𝔓⁴⁷ ℵ 𝔐 sa.

[8] Ἄλλος ἄγγελος in 14.6 is supported by, e.g., ℵ² A C P 051, 1006. Cf. Beckwith, 655; Holtz, *Christologie*, 130, n. 2; Metzger, *Textual*, 751. The suggestion by Weiss (cited in Beckwith, 666 and Van Schaik, 'Apk', 218) that 14.6 was originally ἄλλον ἀετόν (cf. similarities between 14.6 and 8.13 where an ἀετός also flies in mid-heaven announcing a message) has no textual support that we are aware of.

[9] E.g. Swete, 185; Beckwith, 662.

14.14–20 are 'quite distinct visions'.[10] But even if the visions are
distinct this is scarcely a reason to deny that ἄλλος could refer back
to 14.9. The bounds of possibility are not stretched by supposing
(on this hypothesis) that when the two visions were conjoined
ἄλλος was added to 14.15. This could have been done, for example,
to lend a semblance of continuity to 14.6–20 as a whole, or to
match each angel in the second vision with each angel in the first.
Bousset also denied (what we might call) the '14.9 solution'. He
argued that in Apocalypse 14.14–20 the author has reworked an
apocalyptic source which was concerned with a '*Weltgericht*' into
one concerned with a '*Vorgericht*', in the process downgrading the
'*Weltrichter*' to the rank of the angels,[11] and consequently adding
ἄλλος to ἄγγελος in 14.15 in the original material.[12] This
approach, however, is questionable on the grounds that it is
difficult to understand why John or a redactor wishing to down-
grade the human-like figure to the level of the angels did not
redesignate the human-like figure accordingly.[13]

Van Schaik describes the '14.9 solution' as the simplest but most
improbable solution.[14] But this comment is an unelaborated and
unwarranted judgement. For at least two reasons we may, in fact,
argue that 14.9 supplies the antecedent angel to the ἄλλος ἄγγελος
in 14.15. First, all the angels mentioned in 14.6–20 are involved in
one way or another with the judgement of God.[15] The three angels
in 14.6–9 *announce* the judgement. (Even the holy angels in 14.10,
who are not part of the series of angels in 14.6–20, watch the
punishment of the condemned.) The three angels in 14.15–20 act to
carry out the judgement – two give commands and one wields the
sickle. In this sequence the angel in 14.15 is 'another angel', the
next after the angel in 14.9. Secondly, that each of the six angels
should be described as ἄλλος ἄγγελος could result from conforma-
tion to a traditional pattern. The ἄλλοι ἄγγελοι in 14.6–20 plus the
human-like figure make a group of seven heavenly figures.[16] On the
one hand, a group of *seven* conforms to the ancient idea that there
was a leading group of seven heavenly beings, describing the six

---

[10] Charles, ii, 21. With Vos (*Synoptic*, 144) and Holtz (*Christologie*, 128) we reject
 Charles, ii, 18–19, when he proposes that vv. 15–17 are an interpolation made by
 someone who regarded the figure in 14.14 merely as an angel.
[11] Bousset, 391.   [12] Ibid., 389.
[13] Van Schaik, 'Apk', 218; cf. Beckwith, 667–8; Kraft, 192.
[14] Van Schaik, ibid., 218.   [15] Beckwith, 662–3.
[16] Müller, *Messias*, 197.

angels in the same way underlines the mostly homogeneous nature of the group.[17] On the other hand, a group of six leading angels is not unknown (cf. 1 *Enoch* 20 (Eth.)) and describing each angel as ἄλλος ἄγγελος would be consistent with the possibility that John envisages six archangels accompanying 'one like a son of man'. In other words, the angel in Apocalypse 14.15 is ἄλλος ἄγγελος in order to conform the leading figures in the vision(s) in 14.6–20 to a traditional Jewish pattern. Accordingly, the angel in 14.15 is the next angel after the one in 14.9. Therefore, in our view, there is no need to suppose, on the basis of Apocalypse 14.15, that the human-like figure in 14.14 is an angel, and the expression ἄλλος ἄγγελος in 14.15 may be plausibly explained in terms of the angel in 14.9.

Another matter in Apocalypse 14.14–20 which may appropriately be considered at this point is the theme of judgement symbolized by the harvest and the vintage. 'One like a son of man' and one of the angels each have a sickle in order to gather the crop. In 14.15 the human-like figure is told to 'reap, for the hour to reap has come, because the harvest of the earth is fully ripe'. He swings his sickle 'and the earth was reaped' (14.16). An angel appears with a sickle and is told to reap, but this time it is in terms of gathering 'the clusters of the vine' (14.18). The angel gathers 'the vintage of the earth' and throws it into 'the great winepress of the wrath of God' (14.19). The winepress is then trodden and an extraordinary amount of blood flows for 'two hundred miles' (14.20). The material here has been the subject of an ongoing debate. Important issues raised include the following: (i) the meaning of the symbolism: for example, both harvest and vintage symbolize the ingathering of the elect;[18] the harvest symbolizes the ingathering of the elect but the vintage symbolizes the judgement of the unrepentant nations;[19] the harvest symbolizes the one judgement on good and bad alike, while the vintage represents the vengeance of God on the wicked[20] and (ii) the history of the tradition: for example, 14.15–17 is an interpolation;[21] 14.14–20 is a reworked apocalyptic source which downgrades a '*Weltrichter*' to an angel;[22] 14.14–19 is

---

[17] The difference between the first group of three ἄλλοι ἄγγελοι and the second group, whereby the angels of the second group are not described with ordinal numbers, suggests that two groups of angels are in view. But this does not negate the possibility that an overall group with two parts is in view.

[18] Caird, 191–4.

[19] Lohmeyer, 129; Holtz, *Christologie*, 134–5; Vos, *Synoptic*, 151; Bauckham, *Theology*, 94–8.

[20] Beckwith, 661–5.   [21] Charles, ii, 18–19.   [22] Bousset, 389.

the reworking of synoptic gospel traditions;[23] 14.14–20 represents
the development of early christological tradition independently of
the synoptic gospels.[24]

As far as we can see, issue (i) has little bearing on the identity of
'one like a son of man' in 14.14. Whatever interpretation is placed
on the harvest and vintage nothing requires that the human-like
figure be identified either as Christ or as an angel. Issue (ii) has
some bearing on the question of the identity of the figure. If, for
example, John has incorporated a Jewish source involving angels
then it is possible that 'one like a son of man' in 14.14 is an angel.
Nevertheless, we must always ask with this kind of issue whether
the source material is determinative for the interpretation of the
resulting composition.[25] We must determine the nature of the
human-like figure according to the text as presented by John rather
than according to the (presumed) history of tradition behind the
text.

Finally, in this introductory part of the chapter we note that the
text in the background to the angel's command in Apocalypse
14.15 is undoubtedly Joel 3.13 (= 4.13 MT): 'Put in the sickle, for
the harvest (*qṣyr*) is ripe. Go in, tread, for the winepress is full. The
vats overflow, for their wickedness is great.'[26] In Apocalypse 14.15
the only words in the angel's message which have no analogy with
Joel 3.13 are 'for the hour to reap has come' (ὅτι ἦλθεν ἡ ὥρα
θερίσαι).[27] In 14.18 the angel is told to gather in the grapes which
are ripe. This expands on Joel 3.13 where no mention is made of
'grapes', or 'clusters of the vine', or the grapes being ripe. Joel 3.13,
in fact, appears to combine two harvests – grain and grape – in one
illustration of judgement.[28] Who says the words in Joel 3.13 to
whom is a little uncertain. Joel 3.11 ends with a request to God,
'Bring down your warriors, O LORD' but 3.12 ends, so it would
seem, with God speaking, 'for there I will sit to judge all the
neighbouring nations'. Consequently, when 3.13 begins with the
words 'Put in the sickle' it is not immediately obvious whether this
is *a request to God* to begin his judgement or *an instruction given by*

---

[23] Vos, *Synoptic*, 144–52; with refutation in Yarbro Collins, 'Tradition', 562–6.
[24] Ibid., 566–8.
[25] Cf. Gaechter ('Original', 485): 'you can never trust John to endorse [parallel ideas in the OT] even if he should borrow from their imagery'.
[26] Almost certainly the Hebrew rather than the LXX version is used by John; cf. Lohmeyer, 128.
[27] Holtz, *Christologie*, 131.   [28] Cf. ibid., 133, n. 2. Bauckham, *Theology*, 95.

God for his people on earth to enact the judgement for God. This point will be taken up in our discussion below (see pp. 189–92).

The vision in Apocalypse 14.14

With the underlying purpose of determining the identity of 'one like a son of man' in Apocalypse 14.14 we will examine the vision in detail. The introduction to the appearance of the figure in 14.14, Καὶ εἶδον, καὶ ἰδοὺ νεφέλη λευκή, is similar to the introduction to the appearance of the Lamb on Mount Zion in 14.1: Καὶ εἶδον, καὶ ἰδοὺ τὸ ἀρνίον.[29] By contrast we may observe that the corresponding opening to the appearance of the first ἄλλος ἄγγελος is the briefer formula, Καὶ εἶδον ἄλλον ἄγγελον (14.6). Elsewhere in the Apocalypse εἶδον alone is frequently found in connection with visions of all kinds of beings,[30] but εἶδον with ἰδοὺ is found only at the beginning of the following visions: (i) the vision of the open heaven (4.1); (ii) the visions of the first, third, and fourth apocalyptic horsemen (6.2,5,8); (iii) the vision of the great international crowd before the throne and before the Lamb (7.9); (iv) the vision of the Lamb on Mount Zion (14.1); (v) the vision of 'one like a son of man' (14.14); and (vi) the vision of the apocalyptic Rider (19.11). Thus the introductory formula to Apocalypse 14.14 is found on most other occasions to introduce a vision which features (i) either explicitly or implicitly the divine throne (4.1, 7.9), or (ii) Jesus as the Lamb (7.9, 14.1) or as the Rider (19.11). The exception are the three visions featuring apocalyptic horsemen.[31] Consequently, although we cannot state a rule such that 'Καὶ εἶδον, καὶ ἰδοὺ is normally used in visions concerning either God or Jesus Christ or both together', the use of this phrase in 14.14 is consistent with the identification of 'one like a son of man' in 14.14 with the risen Jesus.[32]

At the beginning of the vision of the human-like figure John sees a νεφέλη λευκή. Elsewhere in the Apocalypse we find Jesus 'coming with the clouds' (1.7), the mighty angel in 10.1 is 'wrapped in a cloud' as he comes down from heaven, and the 'two witnesses' go up to heaven 'in a cloud' (11.12). In each case, as in 14.14,

---

[29] Van Schaik, 'Apk', 225, n. 21.
[30] E.g. Apc. 1.12; 5.1,6; 6.1; 7.1; 8.2; 10.1; 13.1,11; 15.1; 17.3; 18.1; 20.1,11; 21.1.
[31] With, e.g., Rissi ('Rider', 416) we hold that the first horseman in Apc. 6.2 is an anti-Christ figure.
[32] Cf. Holtz, *Christologie*, 131, n. 3.

'cloud' is associated with a figure coming from or going to heaven. Clearly, the presence of the cloud in the vision is not by itself an indicator of identity since in the context of the Apocalypse it is associated with diverse figures. In the OT 'cloud(s)' are often associated with the presence or activity of God (e.g. Exod. 19.9; Ps. 96(97).2,[33] 103(104).2) so that we must keep in mind the idea that Apocalypse 14.14 is a theophany. With respect to the possibility that the figure on the cloud might be identified as the exalted Jesus who is associated with 'clouds' in 1.7, it is noticeable that there are three specific contrasts between Apocalypse 1.7 and 14.14: τῶν νεφελῶν/νεφέλη λευκή; ἔρχεται/no reference to 'coming'; and μετὰ τῶν νεφεῶν/ἐπὶ τὴν νεφέλην. None of these differences precludes the identification of the figure as Jesus, but they do allow for the possibility that the figure is different from the one envisaged in 1.7, that is, other than Jesus.

John does not simply see 'a white cloud', he also sees a figure ἐπὶ τὴν νεφέλην καθήμενον. The seatedness of the figure is notable because John continues to refer to the figure in terms of this observation: τῷ καθημένῳ ἐπὶ τῆς νεφέλης (14.15), and ὁ καθήμενος ἐπὶ τῆς νεφέλης (14.16). Nowhere else in the Apocalypse is a figure seated on a cloud. References to seated figures include God sitting on his throne (4.2 *et al.*), Jesus sitting on his throne (3.21) and on a horse (19.11), a rider on a horse (6.5), and heavenly figures seated on thrones (4.4, 20.4). In background material we may note (i) Ezekiel 1 where the chariot-throne lies in the midst of 'a great cloud with brightness around it' (Ezek. 1.4); (ii) Sira 24.3, where *Sophia* speaks of how 'my throne was in a pillar of cloud';[34] and (iii) Vergil, *Aeneid* 9.638–40, where Apollo is sitting on a cloud.[35] It is in the synoptic gospels, however, that we find material intriguingly similar to Apocalypse 14.14. Thus,

> ὄψεσθε τὸν υἱὸν τοῦ ἀνθρώπου ἐκ δεξιῶν καθήμενον τῆς
> δυνάμεως καὶ ἐρχόμενον μετὰ τῶν νεφελῶν τοῦ οὐρανοῦ
> (Mark 14.62; cf. ἐπὶ τῶν νεφελῶν, Matt 26.64)

[33] Swete (p. 185) suggests that the 'white cloud' in 14.14 is 'not the dark storm-cloud which to the Hebrew mind suggested the inscrutable mystery of unrevealed Deity . . . but the symbol of light and blessing'.

[34] Cf. Holtz (*Christologie*, 130, n. 1) who notes that neither Dan. 7.13 nor 4 Ezra 13.1–3 nor Mark 13.26 *par.* offer an analogy to the human-like figure coming as one *seated* on a cloud. But Yarbro Collins ('Tradition', 564) points out that the son of man sits on his throne of glory in 1 *Enoch* 69.27 (cf. 55.4, 61.8, 62.3).

[35] Noted by Casey, *Son*, 148.

and

> τὸν υἱὸν τοῦ ἀνθρώπου ἐρχόμενον ἐν νεφέλῃ μετὰ
> δυνάμεως καὶ δόξης πολλῇ.   (Luke 21.27)

The multiple references in Apocalypse 14.14–16 to the figure as 'one who is seated on the cloud' draws attention to the significance of the cloud. Describing the figure in this way also recalls the frequent reference in the Apocalypse to God as 'the one seated on the throne' (4.2,9,10; 5.1,7,13; 6.16; 7.10,15; 19.4; 21.5). It seems at least possible that the 'cloud' is a kind of throne. When we observe that in another judgement scene John sees θρόνον μέγαν λευκὸν καὶ τὸν καθήμενον ἐπ' αὐτόν (Apc. 20. 11) then it seems quite probable that the cloud is, in fact, a form of throne. Noting that in Apocalypse 1.7, 10.1, and 11.12 cloud(s) are associated with movement between earth and heaven, it is plausible to suppose that a 'cloud' rather than a 'throne' is seen because the scene is one in which heavenly figures have come close to the earth, close enough for a swing of the sickle to effect judgement. A further point can then be made: if the cloud is effectively a throne, we can understand why a single cloud is seen rather than the plural clouds of Apocalypse 1.7 if the occupant is, in fact, the exalted Jesus.[36]

Nevertheless, the possibility remains that the occupant is an angel given the association between 'cloud' and 'angel' in Apocalypse 10.1. One conceivable factor against the human-like figure being an angel is the rabbinic tradition that angels could not fold their legs and hence could not sit.[37] But there appears to have been at least one exception to this 'rule' in a contemporary apocalypse, since *Ascension of Isaiah* 7.21 gives the impression that an angel sat on a throne in each of the six heavens below the seventh and highest heaven.[38] Another factor against the figure being an angel is the improbability that an angel would be referred to as 'one seated on the cloud' when this description, as we have just noted above, is akin to the description of God as the 'one seated on the throne'. In the light of other instances in the Apocalypse of the exalted Jesus sharing in the titles of God (e.g. 1.18) and the throne of God (e.g. 7.17), it would seem more likely that the occupant of the cloud was Jesus rather than an angel. We must also keep in mind the gospel

---

[36] Vos (*Synoptic*, 146–7) draws attention to Luke 21.27 where the son of man comes ἐν νεφέλῃ.

[37] Cf. Gruenwald (*Apocalyptic*, 60, 66–7) who cites *Bereshit Rabbah* as a source.

[38] As Gruenwald (ibid., 60) recognizes.

references noted above which tend, on the presumption of some
familiarity with gospel tradition by the seer, to favour an identification of the seated, human-like figure with the exalted Jesus.[39]

The next phrase in Apocalypse 14.14, ὅμοιον υἱὸν ἀνθρώπου,
has a quite definite reminiscence within the Apocalypse to the risen
Jesus (1.13). The simplest explanation for the use of this phrase is
that the two figures are identical.[40] For several reasons, however,
we should not quickly accept this explanation. First, ὅμοιον υἱὸν
ἀνθρώπου recalls other phrases applied to various heavenly figures
in the OT. As we saw in the previous chapter (see pp. 157–60), this
fact has led some scholars to conclude that ὅμοιον υἱὸν ἀνθρώπου
is a typical apocalyptic turn of phrase which signifies a human-like
being and could be simply intended to designate an angelic being.
Consequently, it is possible that while ὅμοιον υἱὸν ἀνθρώπου
recalls the description of Jesus in Apocalypse 1.13, it does so only
in the sense that Jesus and the figure in 14.14 are *similar kinds of
human-like beings*.

Secondly, the fact that the next detail in the description of the
figure's form also directly mirrors a detail in the description of the
form of the twenty-four elders suggests that no one detail was
intended as an indicator of the figure's identity (ἔχων ἐπὶ τῆς
κεφαλῆς αὐτοῦ στέφανον χρυσοῦν; cf. ἐπὶ τὰς κεφαλὰς αὐτῶν
στεφάνους χρυσοῦς, 4.4). Rather, John may have 'borrowed'
details from here and there within his 'stock of imagery',[41] so that it
is merely coincidental that one detail mirrors a detail in the
description of the risen Jesus. In our discussion in chapter 7
concerning the bowl angels, we noted a similarity between the
description of their form and the description of the form of the
exalted Jesus (Apc. 15.6; cf. 1.13). No scholar, however, as far as
we are aware, has suggested that this means that Jesus is one of the
bowl angels.

Thirdly, it is possible that if John did wish to emphasize a link
between the figure in 14.14 and the exalted Jesus by his use of the
phrase ὅμοιον υἱὸν ἀνθρώπου then it was merely a link, and not an
identity, between the two figures which was signified. If the figure in
question is meant to be identified as Jesus through the provision of
a detail also found in Apocalypse 1.13–16 it is surprising that there

[39] Vos, *Synoptic*, 146–9.
[40] Small variations of ὅμοιον and υἱὸν in some witnesses do not affect this point.
[41] Dunn, *Christology*, xxiv.

are *no other* details which link this appearance to the christophany in 1.13–16 (and to other aspects of the portrayal of Jesus in the Apocalypse). In this respect we may contrast the figure in 14.14 with the apocalyptic Rider in 19.11–16 where (i) two details (eyes like flames of fire, sword in mouth, 19.11,15) link the figure with the exalted Jesus in Apocalypse 1.13–16, and (ii) other details connect the figure with the portrayal of Jesus elsewhere in the Apocalypse (e.g. rule with a rod of iron, 19.15, cf. 2.26–8, 12.5; the name 'King of kings and Lord of lords', 19.16, cf. 17.14). In short, the use of the phrase ὅμοιον υἱὸν ἀνθρώπου in the description of the figure in 14.14 does not necessarily mean that the figure is Jesus Christ and is consistent with the possibility that the figure is an angel.

There is no doubt that the use of the phrase ὅμοιον υἱὸν ἀνθρώπου in the description of the figure draws on Daniel 7.13. Even though there are obvious differences with Daniel 7.13 (e.g. singular 'cloud' here versus 'clouds' in Dan. 7.13), the conjunction of 'cloud' and 'one like a son of man' means that it is highly probable that Daniel 7.13 is being alluded to here.[42] Vos has argued that the allusion is distant with the immediate source for Apocalypse 14.14 lying in the 'gospel tradition' (i.e. Mark 14.62 *par.*).[43] But this argument is difficult to sustain when ὅμοιον υἱὸν ἀνθρώπου is preferred to ὁ υἱὸς τοῦ ἀνθρώπου.[44] The use of the former expression suggests that, whatever knowledge of the synoptic gospel tradition John may have had, Daniel 7.13 was firmly in mind as well.

In the course of our discussion of the phrase ὅμοιον υἱὸν ἀνθρώπου we noted that Apocalypse 14.14 shares a descriptive detail with the account of the twenty-four elders, that is, ἔχων ἐπὶ τῆς κεφαλῆς αὐτοῦ στέφανον χρυσοῦν (cf. 4.4).[45] Undoubtedly, the human-like figure (and the elders) wears a golden crown as a sign of his heavenly rank.[46] The fact that the locusts in 9.7 have on their heads ὡς στέφανοι ὅμοιοι χρυσῷ suggests that the wearing of golden crowns is considered by John to be a general mark of

---

[42] *Contra* Casey (*Son*, 148) who does not allow for a *cumulative* case for dependency on Daniel 7.13.

[43] Vos, *Synoptic*, 146–7.

[44] Yarbro Collins ('Tradition', 563–6) offers an extensive refutation of Vos' proposal.

[45] This correlation seems to undermine Müller (*Messias*, 193–7) who argues that Apc. 14.14–20 is a Jewish source untouched by John. In turn this has implications for Müller's understanding of the christology of the Apocalypse: cf. Holtz, *Christologie*, 244–5; Lohse, 'Menschensohn', 85, n. 8; De Jonge, 'Use', 280.

[46] Satake, *Gemeindeordnung*, 144.

majesty rather than a particular insignia of the elders.[47] The human-like figure, of course, sits on a throne-cloud so it is not inconceivable that the figure is one of the elders. Nevertheless, there is no clear indication as to why one of the elders should have the role which the human-like figure has, and it seems unlikely that 'one like a son of man' is one of the elders. Crowns are a feature of contemporary apocalypses and testaments,[48] but references to 'golden crowns' appear to be restricted to *Joseph and Aseneth* where both Joseph and Aseneth wear them (*Jos. and Asen.* 5.5, 18.5, 21.5). Crowns (though not described as 'golden') are linked in the Apocalypse with the theme of conquering (2.10, 3.11, 6.2) so that it is possible that the human-like figure wears a crown because he has 'conquered'. In this case, the figure in Apocalypse 14.14 would most probably be Jesus Christ, who has conquered (cf. 3.21 where 'conquering' is linked with possession of a 'throne'), unlike the angels who are never directly associated with this theme.[49]

The final part of the description of the human-like figure in Apocalypse 14.14 concerns the hand: ἔχων . . . ἐν τῇ χειρὶ αὐτοῦ δρέπανον ὀξύ. This part of the description provides no clue as to the identity of the figure. It does, however, lead to an observation about the functional similarity between the human-like figure and one of the other angels. First, both figures are spoken to in a similar way: (to the son of man figure) πέμψον τὸ δρέπανόν σου καὶ θέρισον . . . (14.15); (to the angel) πέμψον σου τὸ δρέπανον τὸ ὀξὺ καὶ τρύγησον . . . (14.18). Secondly, both figures act similarly in response to their instructions: ('one like a son of man') ἔβαλεν ὁ καθήμενος ἐπὶ τῆς νεφέλης τὸ δρέπανον αὐτοῦ ἐπὶ τὴν γῆν καὶ ἐθερίσθη ἡ γῆ (14.16); (the angel) ἔβαλεν ὁ ἄγγελος τὸ δρέπανον αὐτοῦ εἰς τὴν γῆν καὶ ἐτρύγησεν τὴν ἄμπελον τῆς γῆς . . . (14.19). In other words, 'one like a son of man' has a sickle in his hand, he is commanded to use it, and he uses it. All of which is replicated in the case of one of the angels who also feature in the vision. Clearly, a functional similarity between 'one like a son of man' and an angel is consistent with the conclusion that the former is himself an angel. But, as we have seen in previous chapters, elsewhere in the Apocalypse we find Jesus Christ functioning like an angel.

Our discussion of each part of the vision of the human-like figure

---

[47] Trebilco, *Jewish*, 110.
[48] E.g. *Test. Abr.* Rec. A. 7.5; *T. Levi* 8.2; *T. Ben* 4.1; *Pss. Sol.* 2.2; *3 Apoc. Bar.* 6.2; *Apoc. Esdras* 6.17; *T. Job.* 6.21.
[49] Charles, ii, 20.

in Apocalypse 14.14 has shown that no one aspect requires that the figure be identified in a particular way. One important conclusion we can draw is that the form of the figure seems to be a result of John's own conception whatever sources may have influenced him. 'One like a son of man' in Daniel 7.13 does not sit on a cloud holding a sickle nor does he wear a golden crown. No principal angel that we are aware of in background texts sits on a cloud holding a sickle. Conversely, we have been able, with each aspect of Apocalypse 14.14, to find a fairly close parallel within the Apocalypse itself. This suggests that 14.14 is a passage whose form and content has been shaped by John himself whatever sources may lie behind it.

The identity of the figure in Apocalypse 14.14

Many, indeed most, commentators identify the figure as Jesus,[50] but a number do not, preferring to understand the figure as an angel.[51] Nothing we have discussed so far suggests that we need to look outside these two possibilities for the identity of the figure.[52] In what follows we develop our detailed examination in the previous section and weigh the arguments for the figure as an angel and for the figure as Jesus Christ. It is true that there is little in Apocalypse 14.14 which points clearly to the figure being an angel, since no angel in the Apocalypse is described as seated on a cloud, as wearing a golden crown, or as ὅμοιον υἱὸν ἀνθρώπου. However, an angel does have a sickle (14.17), and 'cloud' is associated with an angel (10.1). The wearing of golden crowns by the elders (who are often understood as angelic creatures) suggests that in principle the angelology of the Apocalypse could incorporate an angel wearing a golden crown.

There are a number of examples outside the Apocalypse of angels being described in similar terms to ὅμοιον υἱὸν ἀνθρώπου (e.g. Daniel 10.16). Nevertheless the argument in favour of angelic

---

[50] E.g. Charles, ii, 19; Lohse, 78; Prigent, 233; W. Scott, 305; Brütsch, ii, 180; Allo, 222; Farrar, 166–7; Holtz, *Christologie*, 129–30; Lohse, 'Menschensohn', 85.

[51] E.g. Kraft, 197; Ritt, 77; Loisy, 273; Kiddle, 285; Coppens, 'Mention', 229; Casey, *Son*, 148–9.

[52] We do not envisage God as a possible identity for the human-like figure on the grounds that in Apc. 4.3 John takes the trouble to obscure the anthropomorphism of the being on the divine throne as portrayed in the original *merkabah* vision of Ezekiel (cf. Ezek. 1.26–27). In Apc. 14.14 the figure is unmistakably anthropomorphic and therefore unlikely to be a manifestation of God.

identification faces this difficult question: What kind of angel would be depicted in such impressive terms as the human-like figure in Apocalypse 14.14? An obvious answer to this question is: An angel of similar status to the mighty angel in Apocalypse 10.1.[53] This mighty angel, we may recall, was marked by theophanic imagery such as 'cloud' and 'rainbow' and christophanic imagery such as 'sun-like face' and 'fiery legs'. The figure in 14.14 is also marked by theophanic (cf. 'seated on a white cloud', 14.14) and christophanic (cf. 'like a son of man', 14.14) imagery. In particular, we could think of ὅμοιον υἱὸν ἀνθρώπου as simply an element in the description of the risen Jesus in Apocalypse 1.13–16 which has been selected to link the angel to Jesus in a similar manner to the sun-like face of the mighty angel in 10.1 (cf. 1.16). In other words, ὅμοιον υἱὸν ἀνθρώπου can be understood as a direct link to Jesus (and not just a general indicator that an angel is being described, *pace* Casey), but without the implication that the figure is thereby to be identified as Jesus.

One objection to this response is the observation that the mighty angel in Apocalypse 10.1 is noticeable for having christophanic characteristics which are *similar to* but not *the same as* those of the risen Jesus. Both figures have a sun-like face, but different language is used in each case, as we have observed above. John links this angel to Jesus yet distinguishes between them. In 14.14 ὅμοιον υἱὸν ἀνθρώπου is exactly the same phrase used in 1.13 and thus the human-like figure is not clearly distinguished from Jesus. Furthermore, since John carefully designates majestic heavenly figures such as the one in 10.1 as an 'angel' it is curious that in 14.14 he fails to do this but offers the phrase ὅμοιον υἱὸν ἀνθρώπου. In the context of the Apocalypse, where the only other occurrence refers to Jesus, the use of this phrase is misleading if the figure in 14.14 is an angel. Why not say that John saw an 'angel' seated on the cloud? In our estimation, therefore, there are a number of important difficulties involved with the suggestion that the figure in Apocalypse 14.14 is an angel, unless the figure is the exalted Jesus and the exalted Jesus is an angel.

While recognizing as we have done that ὅμοιον υἱὸν ἀνθρώπου does not necessitate the conclusion that the figure is Jesus Christ, the fact remains that the only other occurrence of this expression in the Apocalypse is in the description of the risen Jesus (1.13). The

---

[53] Cf. Brütsch, ii, 182; Loisy, 273.

argument for the figure in 14.14 being Jesus thus begins from the fact that ὅμοιον υἱὸν ἀνθρώπου is also found in the description of the risen Jesus in 1.13. It gathers strength from the observation made above that the introduction to the vision in 14.14 recalls the introductions to other visions of Jesus, particularly at the beginning of Apocalypse 14. A further key observation is that not only is the figure described as ὅμοιον υἱὸν ἀνθρώπου but it is also seen with a cloud. This association recalls Daniel 7.13 which, as we have seen, is applied by John to Jesus in Apocalypse 1.7 and 1.13. In the light of this application it seems entirely reasonable to presume that John understood the vision of the human-like figure seated on the white cloud to be a vision of Jesus.[54]

Finally, the description of the figure as 'one seated on a cloud' suggests that the cloud is a kind of throne and the occupant is one who may appropriately be described in similar terms to God. While it is true that elders are seated on thrones and have golden crowns there is no other reason to think that the figure is one of the elders. Jesus, however, shares the throne of God (3.21, 7.17) – the God who is often referred to as 'the one seated on the throne' – and it makes sense to identify the 'one who sits on the cloud' as the exalted Jesus. Cumulatively, therefore, the evidence points strongly in the direction of an identification of the human-like figure in Apocalypse 14.14 with the risen Jesus.

We must nevertheless consider at least three problems with this identification. First, if the figure is Jesus, why is there not a further characteristic to make the conclusion sure? We noted above that in Apocalypse 19.11–16 there is more than one characteristic to link the Rider to earlier appearances of Jesus. Why then, if the figure in Apocalypse 14.14 is Jesus, do we not find one further characteristic to confirm this? A possible answer, however, is that although the figure is Jesus and not an angel, nevertheless John was not averse to portraying Jesus *as though he were an angel*. In other words, there is deliberate ambiguity in the description. We shall consider this possibility in more detail below. The second and third problems have been clearly expressed by Morris in his commentary on the Apocalypse.[55] The second problem is that the command issued by the angel in 'rather peremptory terms' in Apocalypse 14.15 is

[54] Contrast with Casey, *Son*, 148–9.
[55] Morris, 184. Lohse ('Menschensohn', 87) makes much of the 'divine authority' of the figure in 14.14 , but offers no discussion of these problems.

difficult to reconcile with the identification of the human-like figure as Jesus. Morris recognizes that the command could be understood as one which comes from God with the angel as 'no more than a messenger'. In the synoptic gospels and in Acts Jesus does not know the time of the end since this is the prerogative of the Father (e.g. Mark 8.32; Acts 1.7),[56] yet when due allowance is made for this it remains curious, according to Morris, that the exalted Christ is commanded in such a fashion as occurs in 14.15. In short: it is strange that Jesus should be commanded by an angel. The third problem is that it is 'more than curious' that one who shares his Father's throne requires an angel to inform him of his Father's will. Ignorance on the part of the incarnate Jesus about the time of the end is explicable, but ignorance on the part of the Lamb who is seen in the midst of the throne (7.17) is not.[57] In sum: there are two connected problems to consider: (i) the fact that if the figure is Jesus then he is ordered by an angel and (ii) the content of the order suggests a certain ignorance on the part of Jesus.

Morris' analysis of the angel commanding the figure on the cloud, however, contains within it the seeds of a reply to the point he makes. In particular, the role of the angel as an intermediary is worth considering further. We noted above that a certain ambiguity hangs over the question of the speaker in Joel 3.13 (which lies behind Apc. 14.15). Is the speaker God or is it the prophet? Does 'Swing the sickle' amount to a command from God to Judah to act in judgement on his behalf or to a request from Judah through the prophet to God to carry out his judgement? If Joel 3.13 were interpreted in the latter way then the angel in Apocalypse 14.15 could be understood not as a messenger from God but as a messenger from the believers in Asia Minor. That is, the angel, who 'comes from the temple', brings a request from struggling Christians for the judgement to begin. In this regard it is interesting that the first two angels in 14.15–20 come from the 'temple' and the third from the 'altar'. For it is at the altar that the 'prayers of the saints' are offered up by an angel to God (8.3–4).[58] It is true that this interpretation still leaves us with an angel commanding Jesus but the difficulty is lessened because that angel is no longer an intermediary between God and Jesus with the impression given that Jesus is subordinate to both.

---

[56] Cf. Beckwith, 663; Sweet, 186; Vos, *Synoptic*, 150.
[57] Morris, 184.   [58] Cf. Allo, 222–3.

Since Joel 3.13 is ambiguous we must also consider the alternative interpretation, that the angel is a messenger of God and delivers a *command* to an apparently *ignorant* Jesus Christ?[59] The explanation that the situation here is akin to those occasions in the gospels and in Acts when Jesus states that not even he knows the time of the end has been rightly questioned by Morris. The command is given in a manner which begs the question: Would the exalted Jesus be spoken to in that way? And the apparent ignorance of Jesus begs the question: Would the heavenly Jesus – the intimate of the divine throne – not be privy to his Father's will? An explanation for the angel issuing a divine command to Jesus, however, is readily available. By giving an angel this role rather than (say) simply having God command Jesus, John provides a role for an angel so that the number of angels in 14.6–20 reaches six, and the number of heavenly beings becomes a group of seven. In this role the angel could be understood as an alternative to the hypostatic voice of God.[60] The problem of the peremptory character of the command is perhaps best explained as a matter of style. The angel's words are what they are because they follow the model provided in Joel 3.13. From a literary-critical perspective the sharpness of the command could also be understood as a device to attract the reader's attention. The point of the command is not to galvanize 'one like a son of man' into action but to alert the reader to the imminence of the harvest.[61]

The major problem is, in fact, the apparent ignorance of Jesus as to the time of harvest. The important observation to make is that although the apparent ignorance concerns the time of the harvest (cf. ἦλθεν ἡ ὥρα θερίσαι, v. 15) the time is itself linked to the *readiness* of the crop to be harvested (cf. ὅτι ἐξηράνθη ὁ θερισμὸς τῆς γῆς, v. 15). The use of ἐξηράνθη is interesting because it conveys the idea of fruit or grain on the verge of withering, thus signifying 'that the precise moment has come for reaping'.[62] We suggest that the time of the harvest is not envisaged as a fixed point in history which God has known ahead of time, but a time which depends on various factors.[63] That is, factors which (so to speak) affect the ripening process of the harvest. We do not propose to develop this point in detail but offer as a supporting observation

---

[59] Cf. Prigent, 233–4.
[60] Holtz, *Christologie*, 132–3; but disputed by Müller, *Messias*, 190; cf. Ford, 246.
[61] The author is indebted to Professor A. J. M. Wedderburn for this point.
[62] Swete, 186.   [63] Cf. ibid.

the response to the cry of the souls under the altar in Apocalypse 6.9–11. When the souls cry out 'how long will it be before you judge and avenge our blood on the inhabitants of the earth?' (6.9) the answer is given that they must wait 'until the number would be complete both of their fellow servants and of their brothers and sisters who were soon to be killed as they themselves had been killed' (6.11). In other words, the time of the judgement is dependent on human factors such as the level of the intensity with which the persecution of Christians is pursued. We suggest, therefore, that in 14.15 a similar situation prevails. The ripening of the harvest is contingent on the action of human agents of the beast. This raises the possibility that Jesus' ignorance could be explained in terms of his absence from heaven at the time when it becomes known that the number is complete, that is, that the harvest is ripe. It follows that Jesus' ignorance of the time for harvest need not pose a problem along the lines of 'how can one so close to God not know the mind of God'. Rather, Jesus' ignorance can be understood as a result of his being separated from God at the point at which God concludes that the harvest should be cut. Apocalypse 14.14–16 appears to be just such an occasion. Jesus as the human-like figure is clearly in closer proximity to earth than to heaven. On the one hand, the angel comes from the 'temple', that is, heaven,[64] which implies that Jesus is no longer there and, on the other hand, Jesus is close enough to earth to reap it with his sickle.[65]

Thus the solution to the problem of Jesus' apparent ignorance lies in understanding Jesus to be actually separate from the divine throne at this point. So long as this separation is understood as *temporary* there is no contradiction between the general assumption in the Apocalypse that Jesus Christ is associated with God 'in the midst of' the divine throne and the particular event in which an ignorant Jesus is commanded by an angel. Since the knowledge of the time for harvest is *contingent* on human factors (relating to the suffering inflicted upon the church) the ignorance of Jesus is understandable. In Apocalypse 14.14 the situation of Jesus is analogous to that of a commando dropped behind enemy lines awaiting the final order to proceed with his mission – a final order which depends on the assessment of data received back in HQ.

---

[64] Beckwith, 663.

[65] Minear ('Cosmology') does not deal with the relation between heaven and earth which is presupposed here; we do not see that his important study on the cosmology of the Apocalypse rules out our explanation.

Accordingly, Apocalypse 14.15 is the account of the passing on of this order. Consequently, the difficulties with identifying 'one like a son of man' in Apocalypse 14.14 with Jesus Christ are not insuperable and this identification is to be preferred to that in which 'one like a son of man' is an angel. Nevertheless, 'one like a son of man' has a number of angelic characteristics.

The angelomorphic Jesus in Apocalypse 14.14

In the previous chapter we argued that Jesus *temporarily assumes the form of an angel* when he is seen by John at the beginning of the narrative of the revelation which he receives. With respect to Apocalypse 14.14 we have observed that there are a number of features which suggest that although distinct from the angels, 'one like a son of man' is presented as though he were an angel. First, 'one like a son of man' appears in the middle of a series of six angels, making in all a series of seven heavenly beings. Secondly, he is succeeded by an angel described as ἄλλος ἄγγελος (14.15) giving the impression that Jesus is an angel.[66] Thirdly, he performs a similar function to one of the angels. Fourthly, his appearance as 'one like a son of man' is similar to angels and angelomorphic figures in other apocalyptic literature. Fifthly, the wearing of a crown recalls the appearance of the elders who, if not angels, are angelomorphic figures.

One response to this presentation of Jesus has been to recognize that there are 'traces of an angel-christology' here.[67] Bauckham suggests that Apocalypse 14.14–15 '*seems* to imply that Christ can be called an angel'. But he argues that this has been 'reduced to relative insignificance by the sharp theological distinction between Christ and angels'.[68] It is true that there is a distinction between Jesus Christ and the angels in the Apocalypse in as much as angels offer praise to the Lamb in heavenly worship (5.9–12), whereas worship offered to angels in heaven is absent and human attempts to worship an angel are vigorously rejected (19.10, 22.9). Nevertheless, Bauckham's point assumes that the distinction between Christ and the angels is continuous throughout the narrative. We have argued above that Apocalypse 14.14 represents a change in the situation of Jesus: he is separate from the divine throne and he

---

[66] Bauckham, 'Worship', 338, n. 42; Giblin, *Revelation*, 143.
[67] Bauckham, 'Worship', 338, n. 42.   [68] Ibid.

seems to require direction through an angel. It is possible, therefore, that the distinction between Christ and the angels is less than
'sharp' at this point. That is, the human-like figure in 14.14–20 is
more closely aligned with the angels than with God. We suggest
that in 14.14–20 we see Jesus taking up angelic form and serving
alongside angels because this is how John envisages Jesus Christ
manifesting himself. It is not that Jesus is understood as an angel in
the sense of a heavenly creature distinct from its Creator (and thus
we might speak of a 'full-blown' angel christology) but that Jesus
temporarily adopts angelic form for the purposes of action towards
humanity and takes his place alongside angels rather than over and
above them. Instead of bearing 'traces' of an angel christology
Apocalypse 14.14–15 in fact correlates well with the angelomorphic
christology of the *Ascension of Isaiah* where Jesus temporarily takes
up the form of an angel.

Karrer develops the remark of Bauckham cited above. He sees
Jesus Christ portrayed 'in angelophaner Tradition' but more
pithily than in Apocalypse 1.13–16. He sees a further difference
between 1.13–16 and 14.14: in the latter the appearance of Jesus is
integrated into a series of angels. Both 1.13–16 and 14.14 have
been formulated 'under the influence of an emerging angel christology'. This emerging angel christology at a later point is
witnessed to, for example, by Justin, *Apology* i.63 and *Dialogue
with Trypho* 127.4. There is some evidence that it remained an
influence in Asia Minor for some time.[69] Karrer further points out
that John does not shun '*Archontenterminologie*' (cf. Apc. 1.5a),
which was later rejected by the church because of its angelological
tradition. Also, in Apocalypse 1.1 there is 'a subordinationist
component' in the christology because God gives the revelation to
Jesus Christ. Yet the tendency of the christology of the Apocalypse is not towards subordination but to the identification of
Jesus the Son of God with God. In the Apocalypse, according to
Karrer, we run into an early stage in christological development
when the tension between the status of Jesus and the maintenance
of monotheism is not yet resolved.[70] With some of this analysis we
are in agreement. But we question whether it is most accurate to
speak of the influence of an emerging angel christology behind
1.13–16 and 14.14. Our study of 1.13–16 has suggested that John
applies familiar elements from descriptions of glorious angels to

[69] So Karrer, *Johannesoffenbarung*, 148, n. 45.   [70] Ibid., 147–9.

the risen Jesus. Our study of 14.14 has suggested that John may have drawn on both Danielic material and imagery already woven into the fabric of his visions to create a picture of Jesus which is characteristically John's own. In other words, the influence on these two passages is most likely to have been the developing angelology of Jewish apocalyptic traditions rather than an emerging angel christology in Christian circles. Rather than representing a stage in the development of an already existing angel christology, the Apocalypse may represent at best an anticipation of developments in angel christology – for example, the later dispensational angel christology of Origen.

Another response to Apocalypse 14.14 worth noting has been made by Giblin who suggests that although the son of man figure is Jesus Christ, he appears 'as an "angel"'. One reason for regarding Jesus as an angel is that 'he is God's special emissary in judging mankind'. But Giblin then suggests that a more likely explanation lies in the idea of 'distancing'. That is, apocalyptic language distinguishes between the reality of a person and the representation of a person. John 'sees' Jesus Christ, a real person, yet does not, in 14.14, see him as he really is: what he sees is Jesus present *in a vision*, a representation of Jesus. Giblin does not say much more than this but we presume he means that Jesus appearing to be an angel in a vision is not to be taken as evidence that Jesus *is* actually an angel.[71] This explanation accords with ours in as much as it is compatible with the idea that Jesus temporarily appears like an angel.

Conclusions

We have argued that 'one like a son of man' in Apocalypse 14.14 is an appearance of Jesus Christ. The identification is not without difficulties, but the difficulties can be resolved if we understand that this appearance of Jesus involves a *temporary* separation from the divine throne and the *temporary* assumption of angelic form and function. In other words, the portrayal of Jesus Christ in 14.14 is considerably influenced by angelology. In form and function Jesus is like the angels. He appears as a seventh angelic figure in a series of seven such figures. Thus in our view it is preferable to understand Apocalypse 14.14 as a portrayal of Jesus Christ influenced by

[71] Giblin, *Revelation*, 143.

angelology which anticipates later developments in angel christology rather than as a portrayal which reflects existing developments in angel christology. In essence, the angelologically influenced christology of Apocalypse 14.14 is the same as that of Apocalypse 1.13–16.

10

APOCALYPSE 19.11–16

In Apocalypse 19.11–16 we have a vision of a heavenly rider whose appearance suggests that he is identical to the figure in the christophany in Apocalypse 1.13–16. Many details in this vision are quite different from those in the christophany. Consequently, we have some reason for thinking that reflection on this vision might extend our discussion of the influence of angelology on the christology of the Apocalypse. In the first section of this chapter we cite Apocalypse 19.11–16 and then discuss a number of preliminary issues before examining four features which show definite signs of angelological influence.

Preliminary issues

Καὶ εἶδον τὸν οὐρανὸν ἠνεῳγμένον, καὶ ἰδοὺ ἵππος λευκὸς καὶ ὁ καθήμενος ἐπ᾽ αὐτὸν [καλούμενος] πιστὸς καὶ ἀληθινός, καὶ ἐν δικαιοσύνῃ κρίνει καὶ πολεμεῖ. ¹²οἱ δὲ ὀφθαλμοὶ αὐτοῦ [ὡς] φλὸξ πυρός, καὶ ἐπὶ τὴν κεφαλὴν αὐτοῦ διαδήματα πολλά, ἔχων ὄνομα γεγραμμένον ὃ οὐδεὶς οἶδεν εἰ μὴ αὐτός, ¹³καὶ περιβεβλημένος ἱμάτιον βεβαμμένον αἵματι, καὶ κέκληται τὸ ὄνομα αὐτοῦ ὁ λόγος τοῦ θεοῦ. ¹⁴Καὶ τὰ στρατεύματα [τὰ] ἐν τῷ οὐρανῷ ἠκολούθει αὐτῷ ἐφ᾽ ἵπποις λευκοῖς, ἐνδεδυμένοι βύσσινον λευκὸν καθαρόν. ¹⁵καὶ ἐκ τοῦ στόματος αὐτοῦ ἐκπορεύεται ῥομφαία ὀξεῖα, ἵνα ἐν αὐτῇ πατάξῃ τὰ ἔθνη, καὶ αὐτὸς ποιμανεῖ αὐτοὺς ἐν ῥάβδῳ σιδηρᾷ καὶ αὐτὸς πατεῖ τὴν ληνὸν τοῦ οἴου τοῦ θυμοῦ τῆς ὀργῆς τοῦ θεοῦ τοῦ παντοκράτορος, ¹⁶καὶ ἔχει ἐπὶ τὸ ἱμάτιον καὶ ἐπὶ τὸν μηρὸν αὐτοῦ ὄνομα γεγραμμένον· Βασιλεὺς βασιλέων καὶ κύριος κυρίων. (Apc. 19.11–16)

A number of observations demonstrate that the rider of the white horse (hence, the Rider) is certainly Jesus Christ. First, we find the Rider 'called Faithful and True' (καλούμενος πιστὸς καὶ ἀληθινός, 19.11), which recalls the description of Jesus Christ as 'the faithful witness' (ὁ μάρτυς, ὁ πιστός, 1.5), and 'the faithful and true witness' (ὁ μάρτυς ὁ πιστὸς καὶ ἀληθινός, 3.14). Secondly, his eyes resemble those of the exalted Jesus who appears to John in the earlier christophany (οἱ δὲ ὀφθαλμοὶ αὐτοῦ ὡς φλὸξ πυρός, 19.12; οἱ ὀφθαλμοὶ αὐτοῦ ὡς φλὸξ πυρός, 1.14; cf. 2.18). Thirdly, the sword in the mouth of the Rider also draws on the earlier appearance of the risen Jesus (καὶ ἐκ στόματος αὐτοῦ ἐκπορεύεται ῥομφαία ὀξεῖα, 19.15; καὶ ἐκ τοῦ στόματος αὐτοῦ ῥομφαία δίστομος ὀξεῖα ἐκπορευομένη, 1.16; cf. 2.12). Fourthly, the allusion to Psalm 2.9 in Apocalypse 19.15 (ποιμανεῖ αὐτοὺς ἐν ῥάβδῳ σιδηρᾷ) corresponds to a similar allusion made (i) by Jesus about himself (ποιμανεῖ αὐτοὺς ἐν ῥάβδῳ σιδηρᾷ ὡς τὰ σκεύη τὰ κεραμικὰ συντρίβεται, 2.26–8) and (ii) in the vision of the woman who bears a son (ὃς μέλλει ποιμαίνειν πάντα τὰ ἔθνη ἐν ῥάβδῳ σιδηρᾷ, 12.5). Finally, the Rider bears the name, 'King of kings and Lord of lords' (ἐπὶ τὸν μηρὸν αὐτοῦ ὄνομα γεγραμμένον· Βασιλεὺς βασιλέων καὶ κύριος κυρίων, 19.16), which mirrors the description of Jesus the Lamb (τὸ ἀρνίον νικήσει αὐτούς, ὅτι κύριος κυρίων ἐστὶν καὶ βασιλεὺς βασιλέων, 17.14).).[1]

A number of text-critical issues arise from Apocalypse 19.11–16, but for our purposes only one is significant and that is the question of whether or not βεβαμμένον is the correct reading in Apocalypse 19.13: καὶ περιβεβλημένος ἱμάτιον βεβαμμένον αἵματι. Both NA[26] and *UBSGNT*[3] read βεβαμμένον in the main body of the text.[2] That is, the Rider wears a robe 'dipped' or 'washed' or even 'dyed'[3] in or with blood. In the apparati to these editions variants to βεβαμμένον stemming from the verbs ῥαίνω and ῥαντίζω (both meaning 'I sprinkle') are listed. Thus, NA[26]/*UBSGNT*[3] list: ῥεράντισμένον, P (1006.1841).2329 *al*; περιρεραμμένον, א[(2)]; ἐρ-ραμμένον, (1611).2053.2062. Additionally, *UBSGNT*[3] cites: ῥεραμ-μένον, 1611, Origen; περιρεραντισμένον, א[c] syr[ph?] Cyprian; ἐρραντισμένον, 172.256.792.911. Some scholars have argued that βεβαμμένον is not a convincing choice.[4] On the one hand, βεβαμ-μένον could be a copyist's error from ῥεραμμένον which itself might be original (all other variants could plausibly stem from

---

[1] So Lohse, 93; Allo, 279; Prigent, 291.   [2] NA[26] cites as witnesses A 051 𝔐.
[3] BAG, 132–3.   [4] E.g. Kraft, 249; Swete, 248.

this)[5] or a variant of one of the forms of ῥαίνω and ῥαντίζω. On the other hand, the undoubted influence of Isaiah 63.3 on Apocalypse 19.13 suggests that βεβαμμένον is unlikely to be original since the underlying verb *nzh* is normally rendered in the LXX by ῥαίνω or ῥαντίζω, but never by βάπτω. Curiously, Isaiah 63.3 LXX itself does not use either ῥαίνω or ῥαντίζω and in fact is a rather free translation of *wyz nṣḥm ʻl bgdy wkl mlbšy ʼgʼlty*, thus: καὶ κατέθλασα αὐτοὺς ὡς γῆν καὶ κατήγαγον τὸ αἷμα αὐτῶν εἰς γῆν. In some MSS associated with the (so-called) Lucianic recension, however, we find ἐρραντίσθη is used.

A number of counter-arguments, however, may be brought forward. For example, even if John were familiar with the idea that βάπτω was an inappropriate verb with which to translate *nzh*, it does not follow that he felt constrained not to use βάπτω. John in a number of places exercises freedom in his use of sources. He does not merely adopt his sources; he also adapts them.[6] Βεβαμμένον is a word which carries definite Christian connotations. It is conjugated from βάπτω which is a cognate of βαπτίζω. The noun associated with the latter verb, βάπτισμα, is employed in the gospels as an allusion to the cross (Mark 10.38; Luke 12.50). Thus it is possible, as some scholars have observed, that John, by virtue of his choice of vocabulary,[7] deliberately alludes to the death of Jesus on the cross.[8] Alternatively, Prigent has pointed out that βεβαμμένον may reflect the influence of the Palestinian *Targum* of Genesis 49.11,[9] a passage which in turn has been influenced by Isaiah 63.3.[10] In *Targum Jerusalmi II* and *Targum Neofiti* Genesis 49.11 a warrior figure is described whose clothes are 'soaked in the blood' (*lbwšwy mʻgʻgyn bʼdmh*).[11] We need not go into the complex question of whether the Palestinian *Targum*s witness to a reading of

[5] Ibid., cf. Westcott and Hort (*New Testament*, ii, 139 (= Appendix)) who argue that 'all variations are easily accounted for if the form used was ῥεραμμένον'.
[6] Charles, ii, 133–4. Rissi (*Future* 24), argues for a minimal influence of Isa. 63.1–3 on Apc. 19.13–15.
[7] Cf. Ford, 321.
[8] A. T. Hanson, *Wrath*, 176; Sweet, 232, 249, 282; Boring, 196; Rissi, *Future*, 24.
[9] Note that Gen. 49.9 is in the background to Apc. 5.5, and Gen. 49.11 lies behind Apc. 7.14, so that John's familiarity with Gen. 49 is not in doubt even if his familiarity with the *Targum*(s) to Gen. 49 is a matter of continuing discussion.
[10] Prigent, 294–5; cf. McNamara, *New Testament*, 232; Grelot, 'L'exégèse', 374–81.
[11] According to Jastrow (*Dictionary*, 1042): 'rolled in blood'; and according to Sokoloff (*Dictionary*, 395): 'soiled with blood'. The author is grateful to Dr Robert Hayward (University of Durham) for his clarification of various matters concerning this phrase.

the text which dates from the first century CE or earlier.[12] The relevant point is that the Palestinian *Targum* reminds us that someone like John, who was undoubtedly familiar with synagogue practice (cf. Apc. 2.9, 3.9), could well have been influenced not only by the Hebrew text of the OT, but also by the kinds of interpretations which eventually became encapsulated in the *Targums*.

Thus we need not suppose that the only *Vorlage* for Apocalypse 19.13 was provided by Isaiah 63.3. It is quite possible that an interpretative reading of Genesis 49.11 was also in the background and that as a consequence the (unexpected) use of βεβαμμένον is to be explained by this.[13] As far as the suggestion that βεβαμμένον is an error for ρεραμμένον is concerned, we can only note that ρεραμμένον is scarcely upheld by as strong support from the textual witnesses as βεβαμμένον enjoys. Moreover, from an original verb stemming from ῥαίνω or ῥαντίζω there are no texts which suggest reasons for changing it to βεβαμμένον. Conversely, it is quite plausible to explain the variants cited in the apparati as natural attempts to correct βεβαμμένον in the light of Isaiah 63.3.[14] Consequently, there seems to be no substantive argument for overturning the judgement of the editors of NA[26] and *UBSGNT*[3] that βεβαμμένον was found in the original text of Apocalypse 19.13. Later in this chapter we shall explore a possible christological significance for the use of this word.

A related issue to the textual question just explored is the question of the meaning of the phrase βεβαμμένον αἵματι. It has been argued that the blood stems from the enemies of God and the Rider,[15] from the martyr deaths of the Rider's followers,[16] from

---

[12] McNamara argues for the Palestinian *Targum* reflecting, for the most part, traditions which date from the early Christian and pre-Christian eras. One reason adduced for this is the apparent witness of the NT to the antiquity of these traditions and within the NT a major witness is the Apocalypse (e.g. *New Testament*, 189–237.) Syrén (*Blessings*, 105, n. 116) has questioned McNamara's thesis, particularly in relation to the latter's work on Apc. 19.

[13] I.e., perhaps as a translation of 'g'g, to roll.

[14] Charles, ii, 133–4; cf. Metzger, *Textual*, 761–2; Bousset (p. 431, n. 2) who argues that βεβαμμένον became ρεραμμένον by a scribal error, and the other variants are then corrections of ρεραμμένον.

[15] E.g. Charles, ii, 133; Beckwith, 733; Kraft, 249; Bousset, 431; Holtz, *Christologie*, 172; Prigent, 295. Note that 'Edom' (Isa. 63.1) was a code word for Rome in some first-century CE circles: see, e.g., 4 Ezra 6.8–10; cf. Hunzinger ('Babylon', 69–71) and Grelot ('L'exégèse') 373. Charles', ii, 133 explanation that the blood belongs to the Parthian kings and their armies (cf. Apc. 17.14) is not sustainable (so Caird, 243; cf. Hanson (*Wrath*, 175):'This is a desperate expedient!').

[16] E.g. Caird, 242–4.

the Rider himself,[17] from the enemies and from the Rider,[18] and from both the followers and the Rider.[19] Finally, there is the view of Lohmeyer that the blood simply acts as a sign of victory, so that it is not necessary to ask whence it came.[20] We cannot enter here into a detailed attempt to resolve this issue which is relevant but not vital to our subsequent discussion in this chapter. We would suggest, however, that in view of the wide range of solutions offered, and in view of the fact that no consensus seems about to be reached, that consideration be given to the possibility that βεβαμμένον αἵματι is a multivalent image that incorporates all the above suggestions. That is, βεβαμμένον αἵματι alludes to the blood of the slain Lamb,[21] to the blood of the enemies of the Rider (either looking backwards to Apc. 14.20,[22] or forwards to the slaughter envisaged in 19.17–20, or both),[23] to the blood of the martyrs,[24] and symbolizes the victory of the Rider. These suggestions are by no means the limit of what the bloodied robe alludes to. It is conceivable, for example, that the robe, which must have been reminiscent of the purple robes of imperial office,[25] also symbolized the Rider's kingly status, along with the diadems (19.12) and the name 'King of kings and Lord of lords' (19.16).

[17] E.g. Sweet, 283; Brütsch, ii, 302; Farrar, 197; Rissi, 'Erscheinung', 89; cf. Swete, 248–9.

[18] E.g. Allo, 280.

[19] Boring (p. 196) emphasizes the blood as the Rider's own, but allows that it is 'his own martyr blood in union with the martyr blood of his followers'.

[20] Lohmeyer, 155.

[21] Charles, ii, 133 argues that the Rider is the Slayer not the Slain (i.e. the Lamb), but overlooks the explicit link between the Rider and the Lamb (19.16; cf. 17.14), and the fact that the Lamb is a wrathful figure (6.16–17; cf. 19.15).

[22] Space does not permit a full discussion of the identity of the treader of the vintage in Apc. 14.20. That it is Jesus is argued by, e.g., Bauckham, *Theology*, 97. Caird (pp. 242–4) interprets Apc. 14.18–20 as 'a profound disclosure about the great martyrdom', and hence suggests that the blood stains are 'the indelible traces of the death of [the horseman's] followers'. But Apc. 14.18–20 is most naturally read as an account of the slaying of God's enemies (cf. Yarbro Collins, *Combat*, 37). The enigmatic phrase 'outside the city' (14.20) recalls the crucifixion of Jesus (cf. Heb. 13.12–13) and hence is suggestive of martyrdom, but it does not require the interpretation Caird proposes since it could, e.g., be meant ironically: God's enemies are killed in the same location as God's Son.

[23] Cf. Rissi (*Future*, 24) who draws attention to the difficulty that the bloodied garment is seen *before* the Rider slaughters the enemies. Note, however, a suggested solution in Beckwith, 733.

[24] Cf. Boring, 196–7. Note also the references to the blood of the martyrs in passages preceding Apc. 19.11–16: 16.6, 17.6, 18.24, 19.2. It is reasonable to suppose that the Rider who comes in judgement (19.11) comes to avenge this blood (cf. 19.2).

[25] Caird, 213.

Another issue we need to discuss briefly concerns the 'names' of the Rider. Later in this chapter we will reflect on the angelological associations of the 'secret name' (19.12) and the '*Logos*-name' (19.13). At this point we briefly consider the suggestions that (i) the *Logos*-name is an addition to the text by an unknown hand in an attempt to solve the mystery of the secret name,[26] and that (ii) on stylistic and exegetical grounds the secret name is an interpolation.[27] We will address these two matters in turn.

There is, in fact, good cause to presume that the *Logos*-name clause, καὶ κέκληται τὸ ὄνομα αὐτοῦ ὁ λόγος τοῦ θεοῦ (Apc. 19.13), is germane to the whole passage. First, there is no text-critical reason to presume that the clause containing the *Logos*-name has been interpolated. Secondly, it is possible to think of reasons other than explanation of the unknown name to account for the employment of the *Logos*-name. We will elaborate on this below, but it suffices for now simply to draw attention to the appropriateness of the *Logos*-name for Jesus Christ as the one who reveals the truth of God.

R. H. Charles has put forward three observations to support the notion that the clause which contains the secret name, ἔχων ὄνομα γεγραμμένον ὃ οὐδεὶς οἶδεν εἰ μὴ αὐτός (Apc. 19.12), is an interpolation: (i) the clause represents an unnatural intrusion in the description of the Rider; (ii) the parallelism of the verse is restored when the clause is omitted; (iii) it contradicts the statement in 19.13 about a known name (i.e. the *Logos*-name). The first two of these are fair observations. First, the reference to the secret name interrupts a descriptive series which, *without* this name, runs through the items 'eyes', 'head', 'clothing', 'name' (i.e. the *Logos*-name). Secondly, the clause in which this name occurs begins with ἔχων and not καὶ, unlike each of the other clauses; and when this clause is omitted the remaining clauses exhibit a certain parallelism as Charles demonstrates. Yet neither of these observations proves that the clause in which the secret name occurs is an interpolation. They simply highlight the awkwardness of the composition of the Rider's description.

Furthermore, there is no text-critical reason to suppose that this clause did not belong to the original text of the Apocalypse.

[26] E.g. Bousset, 431; cf. Charles, ii, 134.
[27] E.g. Charles, ii, 132–3.

Although there is a textual variant involved within the clause itself this does not imply that the clause as a whole is an interpolation. In fact this variant offers supporting evidence for the originality of the clause. Thus instead of the majority reading, ἔχων ὄνομα γεγραμμένον ὃ οὐδεὶς οἶδεν εἰ μὴ αὐτός καὶ, some witnesses have ἔχων ὀνόματα γεγραμμένα καὶ.[28] The latter reading then links the 'name' motif to the description of the head so that the Rider's head 'has many crowns having names written (on them)'. The intrusive element introduced by the secret name is removed by submerging reference to 'names' into the description of the 'head', and its mystery is dissolved by omission of ὃ οὐδεὶς οἶδεν εἰ μὴ αὐτός. The textual variant, then, has every appearance of being precisely the kind of correction which later scribes, uncomfortable with the awkwardness of the original clause, would make in order to render the text both more intelligible and stylistically coherent.

Charles' third objection, that the secret name is contradicted by the disclosure in the next verse of the *Logos*-name, is most unsatisfactory. This objection implies that the Rider can have only one name. Yet even without the unknown name or the *Logos*-name the Rider has more than one name (cf. 19.11,16). There is no good reason why the Rider should not have one secret name in addition to having three disclosed names.[29] On the positive side of the argument for the clause's originality is the fact that the idea of a secret name for Jesus Christ is not unknown in contemporary apocalypses.[30] Thus, there seems to be no reason to overturn the judgement of modern editions of the Greek NT which retains the clauses in which the secret name and the *Logos*-name feature in Apocalypse 19.12–13.

Finally, in this introductory part of the chapter we must remark on some of the angelic and non-angelic characteristics of the Rider. In our investigations into the appearance of Jesus Christ in Apocalypse 1.13–16 and 14.14 we found that most of the descriptive elements given corresponded to descriptions of angels or angelomorphic figures either in the Apocalypse itself or in other

[28] Witnesses to this variant reading include 1006.1841.1854.2030 𝔐ᴷ syʰ.

[29] Cf. Philo, *Conf.*, 146: '[The Word] has many names, "The Beginning," and the Name of God, and the Word and the Man according to his image, and "the one who sees," that is, Israel.'

[30] E.g. *Asc. Isa.* 9.5: 'the Lord Christ, who is to be called in the world Jesus; but you cannot hear his name until you have come up from this body' (Knibb, *OTP*, ii, 169–70).

apocalyptic literature and related writings. In Apocalypse 19.11–16 the situation is different since a number of elements in the description of the Rider admit of no particular angelological influence. These elements include: being called Faithful and True, and coming to judge and make war in righteousness (19.11), the blood-stained robe (19.13), trampling the winepress of the fury of the wrath of God, striking down the nations, having a sharp sword in the mouth, and ruling the nations with an iron rod (19.15). Most, if not all, of these details reflect the influence of texts, often characterized as 'messianic', which look forward to the coming of a human agent appointed by God for a special role in the fulfilment of God's plan for Israel (e.g. Ps. 2.9; Isa. 11.4, 49.2, 63.1–3).

Our present concern, however, has to do with angelological influence on the portrayal of Jesus Christ in Apocalypse 19.11–16. We have already observed that a number of features of the portrayal serve to identify the Rider with portrayals of Jesus Christ elsewhere in the Apocalypse. In particular, two aspects of the description link the Rider to 'one like a son of man' in Apocalypse 1.13–16: (i) οἱ δὲ ὀφθαλμοὶ αὐτοῦ [ὡς] φλὸξ πυρός, 19.12; cf. καὶ οἱ ὀφθαλμοὶ αὐτοῦ ὡς φλὸξ πυρός, 1.14; and (ii) καὶ ἐκ τοῦ στόματος αὐτοῦ ἐκπορεύεται ῥομφαία ὀξεῖα, 19.15; cf. καὶ ἐκ τοῦ στόματος αὐτοῦ ῥομφαία δίστομος ὀξεῖα ἐκπορευομένη, 1.16. The first detail stands firmly, as we have seen, in the tradition of the glorious principal angel, while the second detail underlines the messianic character of Jesus. Unlike the vision of the exalted Jesus in Apocalypse 1.13–16 we are told little about the physical form of the Rider. It is possible of course that the two details which recall the earlier vision are meant to imply that all the other features described there are also present here. There is nothing in 19.11–16 to rule out this possibility. There is simply nothing said, for example, about the wearing of a belt, the colour of the hair, and the appearance of the face. Admittedly, there is a difference with respect to the wearing of a robe: 1.13 has ἐνδεδυμένον ποδήρη, while 19.12 has περιβεβλημένος ἱμάτιον. But these two descriptions are not necessarily contradictory. They could be, for instance, complementary descriptions, with ἐνδεδυμένον ποδήρη referring to an inner garment and περιβεβλημένος ἱμάτιον referring to an outer cloak. Although there is little resemblance in appearance between Jesus as 'one like a son of man' (14.14–16) and Jesus as the Rider (19.11–16) it is interesting to compare the opening to each vision:

Καὶ εἶδον, καὶ ἰδοὺ νεφέλη λευκή, καὶ ἐπὶ τὴν νεφέλην καθήμενον ὅμοιον υἱὸν ἀνθρώπου.   (Apc 14.14)

Καὶ εἶδον τὸν οὐρανὸν ἠνεῳγμένον, καὶ ἰδοὺ ἵππος λευκὸς καὶ καθήμενος ἐπ᾽ αὐτὸν [καλούμενος].   (Apc 19.11)

Essentially, the introduction to each vision is the same (καὶ εἶδον . . . καὶ ἰδοὺ), the initial object seen has the same colour (λευκὸς), and in each case the figure seated on a white object is Jesus Christ. Thus the Rider is essentially the same angelomorphic figure who appears in Apocalypse 1.13–16 and 14.14. What is then of interest are at least four features of the Rider which are not found in either of the previous visions but which, as we shall demonstrate, suggest that yet more angelological material has influenced the portrayal of Jesus Christ in the Apocalypse. The four features which we will consider are: (i) Jesus Christ as a rider on a horse; (ii) leadership of the heavenly armies; (iii) the secret name; and (iv) the *Logos*-name.

Jesus Christ as a rider on a horse

It is noticeable that none of the 'messianic' texts influential on this vision such as Genesis 49.11, Psalm 2.9, and Isa. 11.4, 49.2, 63.1–3 depicts a figure riding a horse into battle. Indeed, Isaiah 63.1–3 specifically envisages a figure '*marching* in his great might'. Genesis 49.11 mentions the foal and the donkey's colt of Judah, but there is no reference to their employment in battle. In the synoptic gospels Jesus is shown entering Jerusalem on horseback (Matt. 21.1–11, *par.*), but not as a warrior.[31] In the first instance the appearance of the Rider on a white horse directly recalls the appearance of the rider on a white horse in Apocalypse 6.2: ἰδυὸ ἵππος λευκὸς καὶ ὁ καθήμενος ἐπ᾽ αὐτὸν [καλούμενος]. Whether we recognize the first rider as an appearance of Jesus Christ, or the anti-Christ, or an angelic figure matters little for our present purpose.[32] The resemblance between the two riders suggests that the background to Apocalypse 6.2 is also the background to Apocalypse 19.11, even if this background material has been applied in different ways. In particular, the coloured horses of Zechariah 1.8 and 6.1–8 appear to have contributed to the vision in Apocalypse 6.1–8, and there is

---

[31] Michel, 'ἵππος', 337.
[32] Contrast, e.g., Rissi, 'Rider', 416 (anti-Christ), with Sweet, 137–8 (Christ).

no reason to suppose that they are not also in the background to
19.11–16.[33] It is striking, however, to note that with one exception
no riders are mentioned in Zechariah 1.8 and 6.1–8, so that the
horses are not explicitly viewed as the conveyances of angels.[34] The
exception is, of course, the reference in Zechariah 1.8 to 'a man
riding on a red horse'. We have already raised the possibility that
the 'man', also described as the 'angel of the LORD' lies in the
background to the opening of the vision of 'one like a son of man'
in Apocalypse 1.12–13. The description of this angel could, at best,
have been only slightly influential in the vision recorded in Apocalypse 19.11–16 since (i) the colour of the horse is changed: 'red' to
'white', and (ii) in Zechariah the angel does not lead an army into
battle. Given that Zechariah was a book which made an important
contribution to the development of the visions of the Apocalypse, it
seems reasonable to presume that Jesus as a rider on a white horse
reflects at least the partial influence of the visions of coloured
horses in Zechariah 1.8 and 6.1–8. We must also reckon, however,
with the possible influence of a 'messianic' text from Zechariah in
which God's ruler is envisaged 'riding on a donkey, on a colt, the
foal of a donkey' (9.9). This ruler will disarm the enemies of God's
people, establish peace, and rule over the earth (9.10).

Attention can be drawn to other passages which refer to heavenly
figures mounted on horseback who come to earth with militant
intentions. In 2 Maccabees 3.1–40 we find that heavenly interven-
tion saves the day in the story of the attempt by Heliodorus, the
agent of king Seleucus of Asia, to plunder the treasury of the
temple in Jerusalem. First appears 'a magnificently caparisoned
horse, with a rider of frightening mien' (3.25). After the horse has
struck Heliodorus with its hooves, two young men who appeared
with the rider flog him severely (3.26). The two young men are
described in 3.26 in such a way that their appearance must have
been akin to that of the various exalted figures we have looked at in
the course of the previous chapters: they are 'remarkably strong,
gloriously beautiful and splendidly dressed'. The 'rider of frightening mien' has little specifically in common with the Rider in the
Apocalypse. The former has no names, has 'armour and weapons
of gold' rather than 'a sword coming out of his mouth', and does

---

[33] Cf. Charles, ii, 131.
[34] Swete (p. 84) says that John has borrowed 'only the symbol of the horses and their colours'.

not lead heavenly armies. Nevertheless, the Maccabean rider is an example of a figure on horseback who comes from God in order to carry out the judgement of God. While there is no explicit reference to this figure as an angel, it is difficult to think of the figure as being anything other than an angel. In another Maccabean passage, 2 Maccabees 10.29–31, five angelic horsemen also feature in saving the Jews from a difficult situation. Although there is no specific recall of either of these passages in Apocalypse 19.11–16, they illustrate the fact that angels on horseback intervening from heaven in human affairs were a feature of Jewish angelology. It is, of course, quite unnecessary to suppose that any sort of angelological influence lies behind the portrayal of Jesus as the Rider on horseback. Military commanders riding on horseback were a familiar feature of the world in which John lived. None the less it is striking that within writings such as the Book of Zechariah and 2, 3 Maccabees angelic horsemen were to be found, and this raises the possibility that this aspect of angelology was influential on the vision in 19.11–16.[35]

Leadership of the heavenly armies

The composition of the armies which accompany the Rider has been the subject of some debate. Noting the reminiscence in Apocalypse 19.14 to 17.14 where the Lamb is accompanied by 'called and chosen and faithful', and in particular, noting the parallel between ἠκολούθει αὐτῷ (19.14) and οὗτοι οἱ ἀκολουθοῦντες τῷ ἀρνίῳ ὅπου ἂν ὑπάγῃ (14.4), some scholars have argued that the armies are composed of the martyrs.[36] Others have argued that the martyrs are beyond such battles and consequently the armies consist of angels.[37] In favour of this identification is the fact that heavenly armies of angels have already made an appearance in Apocalypse 12.7,[38] and the fact that an army consisting of angels on horseback is not unknown in the background literature: for example, 'angels on horseback' (ἔφιπποι . . . ἄγγελοι, 4 Macc.

---

[35] Cf. Prigent, 291; Michel, 'ἵππος', 337.
[36] E.g. Beckwith, 731; Sweet, 283; Caird, 244; Farrar, 199; cf. Prigent, 296; Charles, ii, 135.
[37] E.g. Kraft, 250. Cf. Bousset, 432; Lohse, 94; Rissi, *Future*, 25; Satake, *Gemeindeordnung*, 142.
[38] Swete, 250; cf. Allo, 281.

4.10–11).[39] We may also note 2 Thessalonians 1.7–8 which has certain resonances with Apocalypse 19.11–16: 'when the Lord Jesus is revealed from heaven with his mighty angels in flaming fire, inflicting vengeance'. Alternatively, it has been suggested that the armies in fact consist of both angels and martyrs.[40] This suggestion is not without parallel in contemporary apocalyptic literature. *Ascension of Isaiah* 4.14, for example,[41] envisages the coming of the LORD 'with his angels and with the hosts of the saints'.[42] It is difficult to find sufficient evidence to decide firmly in favour of one identification or the other.

For our present purposes it does not, in fact, seem crucial to attempt to decide the composition of the armies one way or the other. What is important is that they are *heavenly* armies. The Rider as *leader* of these takes up a role with both angelic and divine roots. The idea that an angel leads the heavenly army stems from the entitlement of an angel as 'the commander of the army of the LORD' (*śr ṣb' yhwh*; ἀρχιστράτηγος δυνάμεως κυρίου, Josh. 5.13 MT/LXX). The title ἀρχιστράτηγος subsequently came to be applied in a wide range of apocalyptic writings to the angel who commanded the angelic hosts of God. In some texts this angel is Michael (e.g. 2 *Enoch* 2.28, 33.10; *Test. Abr.* Rec. A, 7 and 19; *Apoc. Esdras* 4.24). In other texts the ἀρχιστράτηγος is unnamed (e.g. *Jos. and Asen.* 14.7).[43] On other occasions the leadership of the heavenly forces was in the hands of the LORD, who is a warrior (e.g. Exod. 15.3) and leads Israel into battle (e.g. Deut. 7 and 10). Psalm 68, for example, seems to have the LORD in view as leader of the heavenly army. The LORD 'rides upon the clouds' (v. 4), 'scatters kings' (v. 14), and is accompanied by 'mighty chariotry, twice ten thousand' (v. 17). Thus Longman argues that in Apocalypse

---

[39] In Hab. 3.8 'horses' form part of God's army, but there is no mention of angelic riders. In 1QM 12.7–12 the angelic army is not specifically described as riding on horseback; but there is reference to 'the host of His spirits is with our foot-soldiers and horsemen' (12.9).

[40] Lohmeyer, 155.

[41] Noted by Bauckham ('Note', 138) who argues that 1 *Enoch* 1.9 in Codex 42. Panopolitanus is to be similarly understood; cf. 1QM 12.4. Space does not permit an account of other parallels between *Asc. Isa.* 4.14–18 and Apc. 19.11–20.3.

[42] Knibb, *OTP*, ii, 162.

[43] Greek text from Philonenko, *Joseph*, 178. Philonenko, idem, argues that the angel is, in fact, Michael. Daniel 8.11 LXX also mentions the *archistrategos*, but it is not clear whether this is a reference to an angelic figure (so, Bampfylde, 'Prince', 130) , or to God (so, Driver, *Daniel*, 116; Charles, *Daniel*, 207; Montgomery, *Daniel*, 335).

19.11–16 we find 'a description of Christ the Divine Warrior which
. . . connects him with Yahweh the Divine Warrior in the OT'.[44]
Further, our supposition that the Book of Zechariah was well
known to the seer means that we must reckon with the possibility
that John had in mind a text such as Zechariah 14.5 ('then the LORD
my God will come, and all the holy ones with him') and thus saw
Jesus the Rider as one who acted in the place of God.[45]

Nevertheless, we know from Apocalypse 12.7 that John was
familiar with the idea of Michael as the leader of the heavenly
army. In that verse Michael and the angels fight the dragon and his
angels and drive them out of heaven. In 19.19 the Rider and his
army fight against the beast and the kings of the earth and their
armies. The location of the second battle is undoubtedly the earth,
and the opponents are different from those in the first battle,
although not unrelated since the beast is the chief agent of the
dragon (13.2). However, a similar battle is being waged, between
the forces of God and the forces of the anti-God power and thus it
does not seem unreasonable to suppose that Jesus the Rider is
presumed to have taken over from Michael as the commander of
the heavenly army. The notion that John may have thought of
Jesus as one who superseded Michael is already raised in the
Apocalypse in 12.7–10. There we are informed that Michael and his
angels have been responsible for the defeat of the dragon and his
angels. The heavenly response to this is notable for its reference to
Christ, even though there has been no mention of any role for him
in the war against the dragon. Thus John hears a voice proclaiming,
'Now have come the salvation and the power and the kingdom of
our God and the authority of his Christ' (Apc. 12.10).[46]

Collins argues that this is an example of 'angelic christology'.
The role allotted to Michael is transferred to Jesus Christ.[47]
Certainly, the thought that Jesus is leader of the heavenly armies in
19.14 instead of Michael is consistent with this understanding of
12.7–10. We have seen in our survey of angel christology in
chapter 5 that close links between Jesus and Michael were a

---

[44] Longman, 'Divine', 298; cf. Schmitt, 'Christologische', 287.
[45] Bauckham ('Note', 137) notes the following examples of the interpretation of οἱ
ἅγιοι in Zech. 14.5 as the angelic army of the 'divine Warrior': Matt. 16.27, 25.31;
Mark 8.38; Luke 9.26; 2 Thess. 1.7; (Ethiopic) *Apoc. Peter* 1; *Sib. Or.* 2.242; and
(probably) 1 Thess. 3.13.
[46] Further on Christ in Apc. 12, see Satake, 'Sieg' (1975).
[47] Collins, *Vision*, 146.

relatively common feature of ancient Christian writings and inscriptions. In *Hermas Similitudes* 8.3.3, Michael and Jesus even appear to be identified.[48] Yet careful consideration of this passage above led to the conclusion that Jesus is not necessarily being understood as an angel or being identified with Michael. In Apocalypse 19.14 there seems to be no particular reason to think that Jesus leading the heavenly armies means that he is either an angel per se, or that he is identified with Michael. Rather, the role of Michael seems to have been transferred to him. The view that Jesus and Michael are not to be identified is supported by the possibility that the 'heavenly armies' which the Rider leads is not the army in 12.7 but one which has expanded to include the martyrs: the larger army is led by one who is greater than Michael.

Why might John have depicted Jesus Christ as one who superseded Michael? We venture to suggest that John must have been struck by the relevance of the prophecy in Daniel 12.1–2 to Jesus Christ.[49] The nexus of themes in Daniel 12.1–2 – resurrection, judgement, deliverance, book – is mirrored in the Apocalypse, but with the crucial difference that it is not Michael who has arisen to effect salvation for the people of God and to be the key figure in connection with judgement, resurrection, and the book of life, but Jesus the Lamb. In the Apocalypse it is those written *in the Lamb's* book of life who will be saved (13.8, 17.8). The painful struggle of the church would cease when Jesus *came in glory* (cf. 1.7, 22.20). *Salvation* was through Jesus Christ and his death on a cross (cf. 1.5–6, 5.9) and not through Michael. Consequently, it is reasonable to presume that John believed that Daniel understood God's intentions in a limited way. Michael had a role to play in the salvation of God's people – hence John includes the reference to Michael and his angels defeating the dragon and his angels (12.7) – but the most important role belonged to Jesus Christ. Thus in 12.10 it is not Michael who is glorified but Christ. In 19.14 it is not Michael who leads the heavenly armies but Jesus the Rider. In other words, the role prophesied for Michael in Daniel 12.1–2 may have led to the conclusion that some attributes and actions associated with Michael should be transferred to Jesus Christ. As a result, consideration of John's portrayal of Jesus as the Rider who

---

[48] Cf. *Herm. Vis.* 3; *Herm. Sim.* 9.12.7–8. See discussion above (pp. 106–8); also Longenecker, *Christology*, 26, n. 5.
[49] See above, p. 135, on John's familiarity with Daniel 12.

leads the heavenly armies opens up the possibility that in this role Jesus stands in for God 'the Divine Warrior' and takes up a role formerly associated with Michael. Once again, the portrayal of Jesus in the Apocalypse shows signs of angelological influence.

The secret name

The Rider has several names: πιστός καὶ ἀληθινός (Apc. 19.11);[50] ὄνομα γεγραμμένον ὃ οὐδεὶς οἶδεν εἰ μὴ αὐτός (19.12); ὁ λόγος τοῦ θεοῦ (19.13); and βασιλεὺς βασιλέων καὶ κύριος κυρίων (19.16).[51] This feature is different from the visions in Apocalypse 1.13–16 and 14.14 where 'one like a son of man' is neither named nor 'called' anything. In view of the influence of 'messianic' texts on Apocalypse 19.11–16 it is interesting that none of these names is drawn from Isaiah 9.6 which gives several names for God's chosen one: 'Wonderful Counsellor, Mighty God, Everlasting Father, Prince of Peace'. We have already noted in our review of Origen that the expression Μεγάλης βουλῆς ἄγγελος, which is found in the LXX version of this verse, has had no influence on the Apocalypse. Two of the four names in Apocalypse 19.11–16 have particular angelic connections and we must explore their significance for the portrayal of Jesus Christ in that text. In this section we consider the 'secret name': ἔχων ὄνομα γεγραμμένον ὃ οὐδεὶς οἶδεν εἰ μὴ αὐτός (19.12).

This 'secret name' may be linked to Jesus' own words about 'names' in the letters to the seven churches. To the conquering Christians at Pergamum Jesus promises hidden manna and a white stone. On the stone will be written a name ὃ οὐδεὶς οἶδεν εἰ μὴ ὁ λαμβάνων (2.17). To the conquering Christians at Philadelphia Jesus promises that he will write on them 'the name of my God, and the name of the city of my God . . . and my own new name (καὶ τὸ ὄνομά μου τὸ καινόν)' (3.12). The close parallel between 19.12 and 2.17 suggests something of a conundrum. On the one hand, Jesus' secret name is described in 19.12 in the same way as the 'new name' of the conquering Christians. Since Jesus also receives a 'new name' (3.12) it would be reasonable to conclude

---

[50] Note 3 Macc. 2.11 as the only occasion in the LXX when πιστὸς and ἀληθινός are found together (where they refer to God).

[51] On 'king of kings and lord of lords' see Beale ('Origin'), who argues that in Apc. 17.14 this title draws on Daniel 4.37 LXX, with approval from Slater ('Revisited'), using Apc. 19.11–21 as a parallel.

that the name in 19.12 is Jesus' 'new name'. On the other hand, the name in 19.12 is one which no one knows except Jesus, whereas the 'new name' of Jesus is one which will be written on the foreheads (presumably, cf. 14.1) of the conquering Christians. That is, Jesus' 'new name' appears to be a public name in contrast to his 'secret name'. We conclude, therefore, that although the form of words used to introduce the secret name of Jesus suggests that the 'new name' of Jesus is in view, in fact another name is meant.

Presumably, the common factor between Apocalypse 2.17 and 19.12, then, is not anything to do with newness but something to do with the private character of the names. In this case it is noticeable that the names in 2.17 are inscribed on 'white stones'. A number of explanations for these stones have been advanced,[52] and one which accounts for the combination of 'stone', 'inscribed name', and 'secrecy' by supposing a kind of amulet in which the name has power to secure protection against evil powers cannot be ruled out.[53] This explanation would then imply that the point of Jesus having a secret name in 19.12 is that it is a sign of his power to conquer evil. Few commentators, however, have drawn attention to the angelic roots of the concept of a heavenly being with a mysterious or secret name. One exception is Swete who points out that the question of an unknown angelic name arises in the story of Jacob's struggle at Jabbok (Gen. 32.22–32) and in the story of the appearance of the angel of the LORD to Manoah (Judg. 13.2–25).[54] In the first story Jacob wrestles with 'a man' through the night prior to his meeting with Esau (Gen. 32.22–32). At daybreak their struggle ends with the man blessing Jacob and telling him that he will henceforth be called 'Israel'. Jacob then asks the man to tell him his name. The man responds with the question, 'Why is it that you ask my name?' (Gen. 32.30). He then blesses Jacob and recognition dawns on Jacob who names the place Peniel, saying, 'For I have seen God face to face and yet my life has been preserved' (Gen. 32.30). In the second story the angel of the LORD replies to Manoah's inquiry as to his name in similar vein: 'Why do you ask my name? It is too wonderful' (Judg. 13.18).

There is no direct link between these stories and the secret name in Apocalypse 19.12. We are not told in the OT stories, for instance,

---

[52] See, e.g., Beckwith, 462–3; Swete, 39–40; Hemer, *Letters*, 96–105.
[53] Beckwith (p. 463) favours this explanation. Hemer (*Letters*, 103), however, concludes that 'the popular amulet theory is more problematical'.
[54] Swete, 248.

that the name is only known to the angel, just that the humans concerned may not know. Conversely, in Apocalypse 19.12 we are not told that the secret name is 'wonderful'. The three passages are only related in the sense that when we are told that the Rider has a name which 'no one may know' there is engendered a sense of mystery which resonates with the refusal of the angels who appear to Jacob and to Manoah to divulge their names.[55] Thus, the secret name of the Rider may indirectly reflect the influence of at least two ancient angelophanies.

The secret name of the Rider has led to various explanations concerning its significance. Some scholars have stressed the connection between 'name' and the 'being' of a person. Holtz, for example, suggests that just as a name expresses the being of a person so the secret name expresses the innermost being of Christ.[56] Other scholars have suggested that the secret name is the *Tetragrammaton*, the name of God itself.[57] Some scholars, however, in line with what we have just mentioned concerning the connection between 'name' and 'white stone', have pointed to the ancient belief that there is a link between the name and the power of a being. Bousset, for example, suggests that the name is kept secret from the Rider's adversaries according to the ancient view that power resides in a person's name.[58] Beckwith argues that mention of the name 'is based on the current belief in the marvellous power of a secret name'.[59] He cites 1 *Enoch* 69.14 as evidence for this: 'His name was (then) Beqa; and he spoke to Michael to disclose to him his secret name[60] so that he would memorize this secret name of his, so that he would call it up in an oath in order that they shall tremble before it and the oath.'[61] If the secret name of the Rider is indicative of the Rider's power to conquer then it is interesting to see that the text quoted by Beckwith in support of his interpretation of the secret name also mentions Michael! In 1 *Enoch* 69.14 Michael has a secret name which is sought in connection with a powerful 'oath'. Although the connection between the name and the oath is not

---

[55] Contrast with *Jos. and Asen.* 15.12 where the influence of Judg. 13.17–18 is clear.

[56] Holtz, *Christologie*, 174; see also Caird, 242; Swete, 248; Schillebeeckx, *Christ*, 442–3; cf. Kraft, 248–9.

[57] Allo (p. 280) following Cullmann (*Christology*, 314); cf. Prigent, 293–4; Farrar, 198. Note *Odes Sol.* 4.8 where the angels are clothed with the Divine Name.

[58] Bousset, 431; cf. Lohmeyer, 155.

[59] Beckwith, 732.   [60] Some MSS. 'the secret name'.

[61] Isaac, *OTP*, i, 48. Note also *Asc. Isa.* 9.5; Sir. 47.18; Pr Man 3; *Ps. Clem. Homilies* 16.18.

clearly explained the impression given is that the oath involves swearing by a name on the basis that the greater the name the more powerful the oath which invokes it. The oath is described in a manner which invites comparison with 'wisdom' in respect of its role as God's agent in the inauguration and maintenance of creation (cf. Prov. 8.22–30; Wis. 7.22–8.1). Thus the writer of the *Similitudes of Enoch* speaks, for example, of how 'By that oath, the sea was created' (69.18) and 'By the same oath the sun and moon complete their courses of travel, and do not deviate from the laws (made) for them, from the beginning (of creation)' (69.20).[62] Michael's role in this work of creation is significant for the oath is placed in his hand (1 *Enoch* 69.15).[63] Moreover, 1 *Enoch* 69.27 describes reoicing in heaven because 'the name of that (Son of) Man was revealed to them'.[64] Obviously, there is much more that can be said about this enigmatic episode in the *Similitudes* but our concern is simply to demonstrate that in this document, which is probably contemporaneous with the Apocalypse, the motif of a *secret name* is associated with an angel.

That the secret name according to 1 *Enoch* 69 has a certain kind of power and is able to enhance the oath which appears to be analogous to *Sophia* in its function in creation suggests that the name may be some form of the name of God itself.[65] Such a name in association with an angel is not unknown in Jewish angelology when we recall the name 'Yahoel', a name applied to the chief angel (and to God) in the *Apocalypse of Abraham*. Whether or not the secret name of the Rider might be something similar we can only speculate. But if it is, then it is consistent with the similar duality concerning the Rider as leader of the heavenly armies, whereby the background to this role lies both in angelology and theology. In sum: the possession of a secret name by the Rider may well represent a further sign of angelological influence on the portrayal of Jesus Christ in the Apocalypse.[66]

[62] Isaac, *OTP*, i, 48.
[63] Just who gives this oath to Michael is unclear. Cf. 'The Evil One (*'ekuy*) placed this oath in Michael's hand' (Isaac, *OTP*, i, 48); '[Kesbeel, the chief of the oath] placed this oath Akae in the charge of the holy Michael' (Knibb, *AOT*, 253). Both translations recognize the difficulty engendered by the underlying Ethiopic. Knibb (*AOT*, 253, n. 19) suggests that it may be a corruption of the word 'other'.
[64] Isaac, *OTP*, i, 49.
[65] Black, *Enoch*, 248, suggests that the text which was copied included a version of the consonants, *'š*, that is, the Gematria for *yhwh 'dny*. Cf. Segal, *Powers*, 196–7.
[66] Cf. Smith, 'Prayer', 31, n. 13, who argues that the heavenly revealer possessing a

The *Logos*-name

The fact that the Rider is named ὁ λόγος τοῦ θεοῦ (Apc. 19.13) is noteworthy in the first instance because it is a name which 'stands alone' within the Apocalypse. Whereas the remaining three names for the Rider may be linked to other entitlements and references to names for Jesus Christ, the *Logos*-name is independent of any other such occurrences.[67] Of course, the expression ὁ λόγος τοῦ θεοῦ in itself is not unique within the Apocalypse but it is never used as a name on the four other occasions when it is found. These four instances are: (i) John describes himself as one who has 'testified to the word of God and to the testimony of Jesus Christ, (1.2); (ii) the reason for John being on Patmos is 'because of the word of God and the testimony of Jesus' (1.9); (iii) the souls under the heavenly altar are those 'who had been slaughtered for the word of God and for the testimony they had given' (6.9); and (iv) similarly, souls are seen by John 'who had been beheaded for their testimony to Jesus and for the word of God' (20.4).

The fact that the *logos* of God is linked in parallel to the *testimony* of Jesus probably means that Jesus' testimony is not considered to be additional to 'the word of God' but a reformulation of God's truth by Jesus.[68] If we assume that John was on Patmos because of a negative response to the *logos* of God, then on three out of four occasions, the phrase 'the *logos* of God' is directly associated with suffering (i.e. 1.9, 6.9, 20.4). Why should exile or death be the experience of the Christian on account of the *logos* of God and the testimony of Jesus? A strong hint is given in 12.17 and 14.12. In the former we are told that the anger of the dragon against the woman who has given birth to the child-messiah leads to his making war on her children. Her children are described as 'those who keep the commandments of God and hold the testimony of Jesus'. In the latter 'the saints' are described as 'those who keep the commandments of God and hold fast the faith of Jesus'. In

---

(secret) celestial name while having another (known) earthly name is a standard feature of Hellenistic revelatory literature (e.g. Homer, *Iliad* 20.74: further references, Smith, ibid.). See also the discussion in Gruenwald (*Apocalyptic*, 175) with reference to *Merkavah Rabbah*.

[67] 'Faithful and True' evokes the titles 'the faithful witness' (Apc. 1.5) and 'the faithful and true witness' (3.14); the 'secret name' recalls 'a new name that no one knows except the one who receives it' (2.17; cf. 3.12); and 'King of kings and Lord of lords' recalls a similar description of the Lamb (17.14).

[68] Charles, i, 7.

other words, the *logos* of God as the reason for suffering seems to mean that *the keeping of God's commandments has led to an oppressive reaction by the secular authorities*. (Presumably it is not those commandments which prohibit stealing and murder but those concerned with allegiance to the one God ahead of all other earthly and heavenly powers which have provoked this reaction.) Thus the expression 'the *logos* of God' in three out of four instances seems to focus on that truth which demands a commitment conflicting with the requirements of good citizenship in Asia Minor.

In the remaining instance we have a slightly different emphasis. In 1.2 'the *logos* of God and the testimony of Jesus' are interpreted as 'all that [John] saw'. In other words, the *logos* of God and the testimony of Jesus are understood as the *particular* revelation which John receives on Patmos. Yet to describe the particular revelation given on Patmos as 'the *logos* of God and the testimony of Jesus' presumably means that it is continuous with *that* to which martyrs such as Antipas and saints who remain alive have already borne faithful witness (cf. 2.13). At the heart of the revelation granted to the churches through John is not some completely new truth but a restatement of what has already been revealed in the history of Israel, the coming of Jesus Christ, and the life of the primitive church. In some respects, however, the revelation contains some new elements since what was formerly a mystery is now explained (cf. 10.7).

What, then, can we say *from the perspective of the Apocalypse itself* about the significance of the *Logos*-name? Important at this point is our investigation into the significance of the phrase βεβαμμένον αἵματι (Apc. 19.13; cf. pp. 199–200 above). We saw that this image could be understood multivalently and includes an allusion to the blood of the martyrs. In this case, the mission of the Rider can be interpreted as a mission of vengeance and the name 'the *Logos* of God' can be understood ironically. Jesus has the *Logos*-name because he comes to avenge those who have died on account of 'the *logos* of God'. The rejected testimony of the martyrs has (so to speak) become the legal testimony which secures the condemnation of their persecutors.[69] The faithful witnesses such as Antipas (2.13) have not died in vain. Their opponents may have thought that they had made a mockery of the *logos* of God and the testimony of Jesus by moving against the church. But by

---

[69] Bauckham, 'War scroll', 33.

bearing the name, 'The *Logos* of God', it is the Rider who 'has the last laugh' and taunts the opponents of the church. The *Logos*-name conveys the justification for the Rider's crusade against them.

Secondly, if the *logos* of God is that which has come to particular expression through the witness of Jesus, and if it is the revelation of Jesus Christ (Apc. 1.1), then it is entirely appropriate that the *Logos*-name should be applied to Jesus. The *Logos*-name encapsulates the function of Jesus as the revealer. But to say that the *Logos*-name is an *appropriate* name for Jesus the Rider in the light of what we understand about 'the *logos* of God' elsewhere in the Apocalypse is scarcely to exhaust the significance of this name for the Rider and for our study of the christology of the Apocalypse. One crucial observation may be noted at this point. When the Rider is called 'Faithful and True' (19.11) and is described as having the regal name, 'King of kings and Lord of lords' (19.11), we are told something about the Rider which is true concerning his character and function. These names are not given like so many – as ones which are incidental to the actual nature of the named person. Jesus is called 'Faithful and True' because he is faithful and he is true. He has the regal name because he is king over all kings and lord over all lords. Consequently, it is likely that Jesus has the *Logos*-name because he is in himself the personal expression of the *logos* of God. To the extent that we can speak of a personal being called the *Logos* who comes from God from the perspective of the Apocalypse, Jesus is that being.[70] It follows from this conclusion that it is worth exploring beyond the confines of the Apocalypse to material which may lie in its background in order to understand better the implications of the *Logos*-name for the Rider.

There is no particular link between the Rider with the *Logos*-name and 'the *Logos*' of the Fourth Gospel. There is a general connection in as much as both figures have a function in revealing the truth of God. But apart from this 'community of interest' there is no reason to think of mutual influence between John 1 and Apocalypse 19.13. Other texts speak of the *logos* (or *rhema*) in terms of similes involving (sharp, two-edged) swords (e.g. Heb. 4.12; Eph. 6.17). In Apocalypse 19.15 the Rider is shown to have 'a sharp sword with which to strike down the nations' which comes

---

[70] Against Schillebeeckx (*Christ*, 442–3) who does not sufficiently undergird his claim that ὁ λόγος τοῦ θεοῦ is a 'designation' rather than a 'name'; cf. Prigent, 295; Lohse, 94.

from his mouth. Immediately in the background here are Isaiah 11.4 and 49.2. But there are other texts focusing on the 'mouth' of the Messiah but making explicit the thought that it is the 'word' or 'words' coming out of it which effect the judgement. These include *Psalms of Solomon* 17.24,35; 1 *Enoch* 62.2; and Hosea 6.5. However, in none of these texts is the messiah called or named 'the *Logos* (of God)'. There is one source, however, which appears to lie behind the portrayal of Jesus as a heavenly figure who comes to judge and make war wielding a sword and is *called* 'the *Logos* of God'. This is Wisdom 18.15–16 which we have already examined in chapter 4:[71]

> your all-powerful word leaped from heaven (ὁ παντο-δύναμός σου λόγος ἀπ' οὐρανῶ), from the royal throne, into the midst of the land that was doomed, a stern warrior carrying the sharp sword of your authentic command, [16]and stood and filled all things with death, and touched heaven while standing on the earth'.

In two particular ways this passage differs from Apocalypse 19.11–16. First, Wisdom's concern at this point is with the Exodus story rather than the last judgement. Secondly, there is no mention of the *logos* riding on a horse. Differences such as these make it difficult to determine whether John had this passage specifically in mind when describing the Rider as bearing the *Logos*-name. Never-theless, Wisdom 18.15–16 is the closest passage in the OT to the portrayal in 19.11–16 of a heavenly figure with the *Logos*-name. It has motifs which resonate strongly with Apocalypse 19.11–16: descent from heaven, warrior figure called *logos*, sword, and royal connotations. If John was not familiar with Wisdom 18.15 itself then he was familiar with the set of motifs represented there. When we considered Wisdom 18.15–16 above we saw that it was an example, alongside the writings of Philo, of a tendency to interpret angelological material in the OT. For the writer of Wisdom the 'destroyer' or 'destroying angel' is an expression of the *logos* of

---

[71] See pp. 91–2 above; also Prigent, 295; Lohse, 94; Ford, 313, 321. It is interesting to speculate on the possible influence of another text, Hab. 3.5, where 'pestilence' goes before God and behind him follows 'plague' (cf. 'Death' and 'Hades' in Apc. 6.8). As a result, the nations and mountains are shaken (3.6–12, cf. Apc. 6.12–17). The Hebrew consonants for 'plague' are the same as for 'word' (*dbr*), and in fact the LXX offers λόγος instead of a Greek equivalent for 'plague'. Does John understand Jesus the Rider as 'the plague/*logos* of God'?

God. For Philo 'the angel of the LORD' is the form in which the *Logos* of God manifests itself. It is interesting, therefore, to note that in Apocalypse 19.11–16, where so much material illustrates the 'messianic' character of the Rider, John uses the *Logos*-name. It is true that the *Logos*-name in 19.13 may be simply explained in terms of the Apocalypse itself, as we outlined above: the *Logos*-name ironically illustrates the nature of the Rider's mission to avenge those who have suffered for the sake of the word of God. But when the portrayal of Jesus as the Rider shows signs of the influence of angelology it is conceivable that John uses the *Logos*-name because an angelic figure coming out of heaven on a mission of judgement recalls the kind of development represented in Wisdom 18.15–16. John does not just see Jesus-messiah in his vision wielding the sword-like *logos*, he sees the *Logos* of God in person. In other words, the application of the *Logos*-name to the Rider may well reflect traditions in which the *Logos* manifests itself in angelic form. Our discussion of the Philonic view of the *Logos*, its possible misinterpretation, and the possible influence of *Memra* theology on Apocalypse 19.13 (cf. pp. 95–6 above) left open the alternatives that Jesus the *Logos* of God could be an angelic figure quite separate and distinct from God or a figure who appears separate from God, yet ultimately is indistinguishable from God. Our exploration in this section indicates that the second alternative better captures the nature of the *Logos* in Apocalypse 19.13.

Conclusions

In the vision of Jesus as the heavenly, equine warrior we have found a number of signs of angelological influence. In this picture of eschatological war the 'messiah' sits on a horse, an image more readily associated with OT visions of angels than of prophecies about the messiah. As leader of the heavenly armies the Rider appears to have taken up the role of Michael as commander of the army of God. Two of the Rider's four names – 'secret' and *Logos* – have particular angelic associations. Further, the actual form of the Rider suggests that John may have seen a reappearance of the risen angelomorphic Jesus as described in Apocalypse 1.13–16. As the Rider, then, Jesus Christ is a messianic and angelic figure. Yet this is not the whole of the matter. Jesus does not simply bear the name 'the *Logos* of God'; rather, he is the *Logos* – appearing angelomorphically yet ultimately indistinguishable from God. It is also possible that the 'secret name' in 19.12 points to a (so to speak) dual identity in which Jesus is 'seen' as an angelic figure and yet in reality is distinguished from the angels by virtue of his sharing in the very being of God. Once again, therefore, we see Jesus in angelic form carrying out angelic function but bearing signs of being one who is coordinate with God rather than subordinate, and as one who comes from the throne of God itself.

11

CONCLUSION

Summary and results

Reviewing previous study of the christology of the Apocalypse and of the significance of angelology for the development of early christology, we determined that such an investigation of the influence of angelology on the christology of the Apocalypse would be a contribution to a little-researched area of study. We noted that a useful starting point would be a significant recent proposal by Rowland concerning the influence of angelology on the christophany in Apocalypse 1.13–16. This starting point led to a review of angelological and epiphanic material in the Books of Zechariah, Ezekiel, and Daniel with sideward glances to the angel of the LORD in the OT and to the human-like figure of Daniel 7.13 in other literature. We argued that aspects of the development behind the christophany proposed by Rowland are doubtful. We questioned whether (i) the figure in Ezekiel 8.2 represented a bifurcation in the deity; (ii) the figure in Daniel 10.5–6 represented a development through Ezekiel 1.26–8 and 8.2–4; and (iii) Daniel 7.13 LXX had influenced the combination of Danielic texts in Apocalypse 1.13–16. Positively, we suggested that the origin, from a literary perspective, of the 'glorious man' in Daniel 10.5–6 lies in the 'man clothed in linen' introduced in Ezekiel 9.2. While other aspects from Ezekiel 1 have undoubtedly contributed to the portrayal in Daniel 10.5–6, it is not in such a way that necessitates the conclusion that the 'man' is anything other than an angel. This point was confirmed by the observation that the 'man' is 'sent' and therefore is clearly distinct from God.

We then reviewed examples of principal angels, observing, among other matters, that (i) some angelophanies are reminiscent of theophanies; (ii) Yahoel has the divine name; (iii) Melchizedek is designated *'lwhym*; and (iv) the angel of the presence, according to

Jubilees 48, uses the first-person plural when speaking of his work
with God. We saw how some angels, such as Raphael and Jacob-
Israel, open out the possibility of a powerful angel coming to earth,
and either feigning human appearance or indwelling a known figure
in order to function in the service of God. It was noticeable,
however, that the power, majesty, and closeness to God of these
angels probably did not result in any of these angels being
worshipped or acclaimed as a second power in heaven before the
end of the first century CE. The possibility that angels were
worshipped by some Jews and Christians on a number of occasions
before 100 CE cannot be completely excluded. But we noted that
such practices seem to have had a minimal impact on the apocalypses and related writings which feature glorious angels of high
status.

We also observed that there is no consistent identity for the chief
angel. Thus there is no reason to think that one angelic figure was
the subject of widespread speculation about sharing in divine status
or standing alongside God as an equal. The variety of angels
observed in the position of chief angel and the fact that in some
cases four or seven angels form the leading group of angels suggest
that the significance of an apparent dualism between God and one
outstanding angel should not be exaggerated. Thus, although
glorious in form and exalted in status, the angels we have considered push at the boundaries of monotheism but in the end do not
break them before the second century CE (and even then with a
strong and vigorous response). In other words, the angelology
which influenced the christology of the Apocalypse was, in all
likelihood, one in which an angel was an angel and not more than
an angel (in the sense of being perceived to have divine status or
legitimately to receive worship).

Our discussion of the angelological context of the christology of
the Apocalypse was then extended to include angelomorphic figures
such as exalted humans and the *Logos*. We saw in our survey of
texts featuring exalted humans that such figures were gloriously
depicted in similar form to the glorious angels previously considered. The inclusion of theophanic imagery or the use of the term
θεός in the descriptions of exalted humans such as Abel, Noah, and
Moses, as with the glorious principal angels, did not correlate to
their enjoyment of divine status. At the most, humans such as Abel
and Moses represented God as a vizier-like figure, or, in the case of
Enoch, may have been identified with the greatest heavenly figure

apart from God. We also noted material which demonstrates the widespread belief in the possibility of human transformation in the milieu in which the Apocalypse was composed. A different kind of angelomorphic figure is the *Logos* who, as God in his self-revelation, sometimes appeared in the likeness of an angel. But we noted that the presentations of the *Logos* in Wisdom and in Philo's writings were ambiguous to such an extent that it would not be inconceivable that the *Logos* was held by some to be a separable and distinct figure alongside God. We also briefly noted that if the *Memra* lies behind Apocalypse 19.13 then we must consider that Jesus as 'the *Logos* of God' is ultimately indistinguishable from God although able to appear as a separate figure.

A number of ancient texts from the first Christian centuries which speak of Jesus Christ as an 'angel' were examined and we saw that there were a number of possible meanings for this kind of talk. Frequently, the title 'Angel (of Great Counsel)' was applied to Christ. In some cases, Christ becomes an angel *temporarily*, analogously to his becoming the human Jesus, while in others he *functions* as an angel. In *Ascension of Isaiah* 9.30, for example, 'the Beloved' appears to be transformed into an angel as a concession to Isaiah who otherwise could not look on him. Some ancient theologians such as Tertullian and Origen clearly denied the validity of a 'full-blown' angel christology, but others such as the Ebionites and Elkesaites appeared to have held the belief that Jesus Christ was created an (arch)angel. We also saw that in some writings the relationship between Michael and Christ is ambiguous. Thus we concluded that talk of Jesus as an angel in the first centuries CE, outside of the NT, mostly falls under the category of 'angelomorphic christology'.

Turning to the Apocalypse itself, we considered Jesus in relation to God and to the revealing angel. In the context of a strict adherence to monotheism we saw that no encouragement is given in the Apocalypse to a belief that Jesus is a second god. Rather, there is a monotheistic approach which allows for Jesus to be included with God as the object of worship and which envisages Jesus eternally sharing the divine throne with God. In other words, the exalted Jesus is bound with God in a unity. We also concluded that the exalted Jesus who, united with God, sends the revealing angel, is *functionally equivalent* to this angel since he closely shares in the process of unveiling the revelation to John and his fellow servants. An apparent doubling up between Jesus and the revealing angel was explained in terms of a pastoral motive (Jesus comes close to his church) and a christological motive (to prevent Jesus from being identified as an angel by making the angel a point of comparison). In the process of developing this part of our study we sketched out the involvement of the revealing angel in the Apocalypse, arguing that this angel is present at key points in the unfolding of the vision to John (Apc. 1, 4, 10, 17–19, 21–2).

The next stage in our investigation was to compare the risen Jesus of Apocalypse 1.13–16 to the glorious angels, the living creatures, and the elders in the Apocalypse. We found that in certain respects Jesus is similar to each, though also distinct. There is, for example, a degree of similarity between Jesus in Apocalypse 1.13–16 and the form of the mighty angel in 10.1–3 yet we have argued, contrary to some scholars, that Jesus is not to be identified with this angel. We concluded that in the context of the angelology of the Apocalypse the form of the exalted Jesus was consistent with the form of a glorious angel. We also concluded that the christophany in Apocalypse 1.13–16 is sharply distinguished from the theophany in 4.3. Yet we discovered no reason to question our supposition that Jesus Christ in the Apocalypse is divine and we were able to confirm this through comparison of Jesus and the living creatures. Great though the living creatures are, they do not occupy the centre of the divine throne and they themselves bow the knee to Jesus the Lamb. In our view, the divine Jesus Christ was perceived to have taken up angelic form temporarily, in line with some observations made in our study of angel(omorphic) christology, particularly in connection with the *Ascension of Isaiah*.

We then considered the christophany in Apocalypse 1.13–16 in the light of our earlier investigation of epiphanies outside of the Apocalypse and confirmed what is well known, namely that the language of 1.13–16 reflects the influence of texts from Daniel, Ezekiel, and other OT writings. We drew attention to the possible influence of Zechariah 1.8 on the setting of the christophany, noted that most elements of the christophany recall the appearance of other glorious angels and angelomorphic figures, and argued that the form of the risen Jesus was consistent with the form of an angel. We questioned whether the divinity of Jesus Christ is being illustrated in Apocalypse 1.14, notwithstanding the undoubted influence of Daniel 7.9 on it. We noted that the influence of Daniel 7.9 was a feature of other epiphanies which did not involve divine figures. We continued to question the explanation for the conflation of elements from Daniel 7.9,13 and 10.5–6 in terms of the influence of Daniel 7.13 LXX and proposed an alternative explanation based on the epiphany of Noah in 1 *Enoch* 106. 2–6. In other words, we again confirmed that the christophany is more akin to an angelophany than to a theophany. The christology of Apocalypse 1.13–16 is appropriately described as an 'angelomorphic christology'.

The identification of the human-like figure in Apocalypse 14.14 is not as straightforward as might at first appear. After careful consideration of this vision and the issues arising from it, we concluded that the figure is an appearance of Jesus Christ and suggested that the angelic features of his portrayal can be understood in terms of a *temporary* separation from the divine throne and the *temporary* assumption of angelic form and function. In other words, the portrayal of Jesus Christ in 14.14 is considerably influenced by angelology. We also suggested that it is preferable to understand 14.14 as a portrayal of Jesus Christ influenced by angelology anticipating later developments in angel christology, rather than as a portrayal reflecting existing developments in angel christology. In essence, the angelologically influenced christology of Apocalypse 14.14 is the same as that of Apocalypse 1.13–16.

Our final study concerned the vision in Apocalypse 19.11–16. In the vision of Jesus as the heavenly, equine warrior we found a number of signs of angelological influence. In this picture of eschatological war the 'messiah' sits on a horse, an image more readily associated with OT visions of angels than of prophecies about the messiah. As leader of the heavenly armies the Rider appears to have taken up the role of Michael as commander of the army of God. Two of the Rider's four names – 'secret' and *Logos* – have particular angelic associations. Further, the actual form of the Rider suggests that John may have seen a reappearance of the risen angelomorphic Jesus as described in Apocalypse 1.13–16. As the Rider, then, Jesus Christ is a messianic and angelic figure. But this is not the whole of the matter: Jesus does not simply bear the name 'the *Logos* of God'; rather, he is the *Logos* who appears angelomorphically yet is ultimately indistinguishable from God. It is also possible that the 'secret name' in 19.12 points to a (so to speak) dual identity in which Jesus is 'seen' as an angelic figure and yet in reality is distinguished from the angels by virtue of his sharing in the very being of God. Once again, therefore, we saw Jesus in angelic form carrying out angelic function yet bearing signs of being one who is coordinate with God rather than subordinate, and as one who comes from the throne of God itself.

A number of investigative threads may now be drawn together. In our discussion of the background to the possibility of angelological influence on the christology of the Apocalypse we have observed the high status of certain angels and angel-like figures in Jewish and Christian literature from the period of our concern, but we have not concluded that interest in these great figures signified a compromised or broken monotheism. In this we side with some scholars (e.g. Dunn, Hurtado, Bauckham) but not with others (e.g. Fossum, Barker, Hayward). With the majority of scholars we have accepted the divinity of Christ within the Apocalypse. We have been particularly interested in the proposals of Rowland concerning bifurcatory developments behind angelomorphic christology but have not been convinced by them. We have read the developmental relationship between angelic figures in Daniel and Ezekiel in a different way and have argued that Daniel 7.13 LXX is unlikely to have contributed to the conflation of epiphanic texts from Daniel 7 and 10 in Apocalypse 1.13–16. Just as likely, we suggest, is the possibility that 1 *Enoch* 106.2–6 has provided the necessary background key to this conflation.

At this point, we have started to break new ground and the significant theses of our study begin to come into view. First, we have argued that Apocalypse 1.14, which strongly reflects the language of the theophany in Daniel 7.9, is not necessarily illustrative of the divinity of the risen Jesus as has commonly been supposed. Against the background of similar epiphanic accounts featuring clearly non-divine figures, the use of Daniel 7.9 in Apocalypse 1.14 is unremarkable. Corroboration of this argument comes from the observation that in the context of the epiphanies of the Apocalypse itself the christophany is quite distinct from the theophany in Apocalypse 4. In sum: we have argued that the christophany is essentially an angelophany, although because Jesus Christ in the Apocalypse is not an angel, we more accurately speak in terms of an angelomorphism – the christophany is the appearance of an angelomorphic figure. Secondly, in order to understand *why* the divine Jesus appears equivalent to angels in form and function in the context of an extended vision featuring glorious principal angels we have argued that there were two motives for doing so: one *pastoral* and the other *christological*. The pastoral motive was to present Jesus as visibly close to his church. The christological motive was to demonstrate, through comparison with the glorious angels in the Apocalypse, that the risen Jesus should not be confused with an angel. Thirdly, we have argued that the angelomorphic appearance of the divine Jesus is a temporary phenomenon – with some similarity to the angelomorphism of the Beloved in the *Ascension of Isaiah*, and to a degree anticipating the dispensational angel christology of Origen. A corollary of this conclusion is that we can make sense of Apocalypse 14.14–16 where some descriptive elements point to an identification of the human-like figure with Jesus, but other elements seem to contradict this. By supposing Jesus to be *temporarily* separated from the divine throne the contradictory elements can be largely reconciled. Fourthly, we have demonstrated that three christophanic passages (Apc. 1.13–16, 14.14, 19.11–16) in the Apocalypse have been significantly influenced by angelology.

Can we, then, encapsulate our study in terms of one overarching thesis? The following statement offers an appropriate summing up. Angelology has influenced the christology of the Apocalypse in such a way that one of its important strands is an angelomorphic christology which upholds monotheism while providing a means for Jesus to be presented in visible, glorious form to his church.

Broader considerations

Our first remarks are directed to the christology of the Apocalypse. In our view, the fact that Jesus appears as the Lamb as well as in angelic form is significant: it offers confirmation that the angelomorphic appearances are temporary and do not constitute a guide to the ontological nature of Jesus. That is, Lamb christology is an effective counter to any attempt to argue that Jesus is an angel (meaning a created, non-divine, heavenly being). It is as the Lamb that Jesus is distinguished from the angels by being the joint object of worship and the one who is united with God on the divine throne (see especially Apc. 5.13, 7.17, 22.3–4). Conversely, in our study we have drawn on Lamb passages in the Apocalypse to enable us to understand better the relationship between Jesus and God. Thus it is not possible to separate completely angelomorphic christology from Lamb christology, a point which is reinforced by noting the shared title 'King of kings and Lord of lords' for the Lamb and the Rider (Apc. 17.14, 19.16). A similar point may be made about Son of God christology. Although the use of the title ὁ υἱὸς τοῦ θεοῦ (Apc. 2.18) reflects messianic influence from Psalm 2.7–9 (Apc. 2.26–8,) it is noticeable that this title is directly linked to a part of the christophany in Apocalypse 1.13–16 which has been influenced by angelology: 'the Son of God, who has eyes like a flame of fire, and whose feet are like burnished bronze' (2.18).

Our study has consistently presupposed the monotheistic outlook of the Apocalypse. In doing so, we have followed the arguments of other scholars such as Bauckham. But we have been able to add one new supporting argument, namely that the sharp distinction between the angelomorphic christophany of Apocalypse 1.13–16 and the theophany of Apocalypse 4 reinforce the singular character of God in the Apocalypse.

Our final broader consideration with respect to the christology of the Apocalypse concerns *Logos* christology. We have seen from the Wisdom of Solomon and Philo's writings that the *Logos* of God was envisaged moving towards God's people in angelic form. Consequently, if Jesus Christ shares in the being of God yet comes close to his church in angelomorphic form while participating in the process of disclosing the revelation of God's word, then, independently of Apocalypse 19.13, we could appropriately characterize the christology of the Apocalypse as a *Logos* christology. In fact, of course, in 19.13 Jesus is specifically named 'the *Logos* of God' so that *Logos* christology is not only implicit but explicit in the Apocalypse. Our study suggests, therefore, that a profound understanding of Jesus as the *Logos* of God lies behind the christology of the Apocalypse.

What, then, can we say, if anything, of the broader considerations of our study for the christology of the NT period? We begin with a recommendation for caution. There has been something of a tendency in recent scholarship to see in the christology of the Apocalypse the expression of a christology whose comparative age belies the lateness of the book itself. Thus Hurtado has argued that the christophany in Apocalypse 1.13–16 is 'probably representative' of visionary experiences in the first decades of the church's life,[1] and in a recent article Yarbro Collins argues that consideration of the 'son of man' tradition in the Apocalypse leads to the conclusion that, 'In the book of Revelation . . . we seem to have an independent development of a very early christological tradition.'[2] Since our study has said nothing about visionary experiences in the life of

---

[1] Hurtado, *God*, 120.   [2] Yarbro Collins, 'Tradition', 568.

the fledgling church nor about the 'son of man' tradition in the NT period prior to the composition of the Apocalypse, we do not deny these possibilities. But we do advocate some caution about supposing that angelomorphic christology as expressed in the Apocalypse reflects developments stretching back to the earliest history of the church. We have noticed, for instance, that the christophany in Apocalypse 1.13–16 compares favourably with angelophanies found in (probably) late first-century CE (or later) apocalypses and related writings such as the *Apocalypse of Abraham*, the *Apocalypse of Zephaniah* and *Joseph and Aseneth*. The use of the expression υἱὸς ἀνθρώπου (Apc. 1.13, 14.14) may be placed alongside the results of apparently comparable meditative reflection on Daniel 7.13 in (probably) late first-century CE works such as the *Similitudes of Enoch*, 4 Ezra, and the *Syriac Apocalypse of Baruch*. The temporary and transformational nature of the angelomorpic christology of the Apocalypse bears comparison with the angelomorphic christology of the late first-century (or later) apocalypse, the *Ascension of Isaiah*.

By contrast, presenting Jesus Christ as an explicitly angelomorphic figure is not well attested by the earliest Christian writings. For example, whatever we may make of Paul's visionary experiences, such as his encounter with the risen Christ (Acts 9.3), his 'visions and revelations of the Lord' (2 Cor. 12.1), his ascent to the third heaven (2 Cor. 12.2), his claim to have received the gospel 'through a revelation of Jesus Christ' (Gal. 1.12), and however we understand his emphasis on 'the glory of God in the face of Jesus Christ' (2 Cor. 4.6), it is not at all clear that Paul encountered an angelomorphic Christ in a similar manner to John. On the one hand, we are simply not given any descriptive detail which correlates to that given in the Apocalypse. On the other hand, Paul has clearly grasped what is almost completely absent from the angelomorphic christology of the Apocalypse, namely an image of the crucified Christ (cf. 1 Cor. 1.23; 2 Cor. 4.10; Gal. 2.19, 3.1, 6.17). In sum: one broader consideration of our study for NT christology is that it may have very little to contribute to the continuing investigation into the origins of christology in the earliest period of Christianity.

If anything, the significance of the angelomorphic christology of the Apocalypse is likely to be in terms of christological developments taking place contemporaneously with, and following after, the Apocalypse. The links between christology in the Apocalypse (and contemporary apocalypses) and the angel(omorphic) christology of the fathers such as Justin and Origen remain under researched. Likewise, much work remains to be done on comparative study of angelomorphic christology in the Apocalypse and contemporary apocalypses (especially the *Ascension of Isaiah*).

Nevertheless, we can note a number of illuminating possibilities for study of NT christology offered by angelomorphic christology in the Apocalypse. First, an illumination of Hebrews 1 (and Col 2.18): the Apocalypse witnesses to a rich angelology pervading the imaginative world of at least some first-century Christians; one that apparently led to sharp warnings for some (e.g. Col. 2.18) and to heavy corrective arguments for others (e.g. Heb. 1). In Hebrews there is a positive appreciation of the role of angels (as servants of God sent to serve Christians, Heb. 1.14) and an acknowledgement that angels were part of the Christian community (Heb. 13.1). Our study suggests that such appreciation could be genuinely felt since, in the case of the Apocalypse, it was able to be extended to a positive presentation of Jesus as an angel-like figure. Also, the presentation of an angelomorphic Jesus in the context of a rich angelology in the Apocalypse suggests that Hebrews may have been written to a group of Christians who were similarly familiar to the audience of the Apocalypse with such a mixture yet failed to properly distinguish between the angelic Jesus and the angels.

Secondly, in the course of our study we have observed a degree of familiarity with the ideas that the *Logos* could appear in angelic form and that angels could appear in human form (e.g. Jacob in the *Prayer of Joseph*; Raphael in the Book of Tobit). In particular, our study of christophanic passages in the Apocalypse suggests that John may be an example of a Christian who recognized at least the former transformation. In broad terms both John 1.1–14 and Philippians 2.5–11 embrace the concept of the divine becoming human (the divine *Logos* in the former, the divine *morphe* in the latter). This incarnational transformation is unique in the period we are concerned with, particularly in the explicit terms of John 1.14, 'the Word became flesh'. The question of how this christological conception was able to be absorbed into the theology of the early Christians can be answered (for example) in terms of familiarity on their part with talk of *Sophia* in Jewish Wisdom literature and Philonic and Hellenistic discussion of the *Logos*. But the answer may also include familiarity with the two transformations, *Logos/morphe* to angel, angel to human, combined in John 1 and

Philippians 2 into one (two-stage) transformation. Our study of angelomorphic christology in the Apocalypse, which has emphasized the temporary transformation of the divine Christ into an angelomorphic figure, freshly suggests that Christians in the first century CE were not averse to thinking along such transformational lines.

Finally, in a certain paradoxical sense, our study throws fresh light on the portrayal of the humanity of Jesus Christ in the NT gospels. We have been made aware of the interest of Jews and Christians in angelology in the first century CE. We have also noticed examples of important men and women of God being portrayed in angelomorphic form (e.g. Jacob and Aseneth in *Joseph and Aseneth*, Noah in 1 *Enoch*). The NT gospels themselves witness to familiarity with angels and their involvement in the affairs of humanity and to the possibility of angelomorphic transformation. To give just four examples in keeping with our investigations in this study: (i) at the tomb of Jesus a glorious angel appears (Matt. 28.3); (ii) the son of man will come with 'great power and glory' and with his angels (Mark 2.26–7 *par*.); (iii) the angels of God will be seen 'ascending and descending upon the Son of Man' (John 1.51); and (iv) those who are resurrected will be 'like angels' (Luke 20.36 *par*.). Consequently, it is striking that the gospels generally portray Jesus in human rather than angelic terms. We find, in fact, surprisingly little attempt made to portray Jesus in glorious form – the obvious exception being the transfiguration story (Matt. 17.1–8 *par*.). If angelomorphic christology in the Apocalypse reinforces the divinity of Jesus Christ then in the NT gospels it reinforces his humanity.

These broader considerations suggest possibilities for further study. The angelologically influenced christology of the Apocalypse is not without profound applications in fresh appraisal of familiar territory in the NT period and beyond.

BIBLIOGRAPHY

Primary sources

The Holy Bible: Old and New Testaments with the Apocryphal/Deutero-canonical Books (New Revised Standard Version), Nashville, Tennessee: Nelson, 1989.

Aberbach, M. and Grossfeld, B. *Targum Onkelos to Genesis: A Critical Analysis Together with an English Translation of the Text (Based on A. Sperber's Edition)*, Denver: Ktav Publ., 1982.

Babbit, F. C. (ed.) *Plutarch's Moralia*, Loeb Classical Library, 14 vols., London: Heinemann, 1927.

Black, Matthew (ed.) *Apocalypsis Henochi Graece: Fragmenta Pseudepigraphorum Quae Superunt Graeca* (PVTG 3), Leiden: Brill, 1970.

The Book of Enoch or 1 Enoch: With Commentary and Textual Notes, Leiden: Brill, 1985.

Box, G. H. (ed.) *The Apocalypse of Abraham: Edited, with a Translation from the Slavonic Text and Notes*, London: SPCK, 1919.

Braunde, William G. (trans.) *Pesikta Rabbati*, 2 vols., New Haven, CT/London: Yale University Press, 1968.

Bright, W. (ed.) *Eusebius' Ecclesiastical History*, 2nd edn, Oxford: Clarendon Press, 1881.

Charles, R. H. (ed.) *The Ascension of Isaiah*, London: Black, 1900.

The Apocrypha and Pseudepigrapha of the Old Testament in English, 2 vols., Oxford: Clarendon Press, 1913.

Charlesworth, James H. (ed.) *Old Testament Pseudepigrapha*, 2 vols., London: Darton, Longman & Todd, 1983, 1985.

Cohen, Martin Samuel *The Shi'ur Qomah: Texts and Recensions*, Tübingen: Mohr (Paul Siebeck), 1985.

Colson, F. H., Whitaker, G. H., and Marcus, R. (eds.) *Philo*, Loeb Classical Library, 12 vols., London: Heinemann, 1929–53.

Denis, A.-M. *Concordance Grecque des Pseudépigraphes d'Ancien Testament: Concordance, Corpus des Textes, Indices*, Louvain: Université Catholique de Louvain, 1987.

Díez Macho, A. *Neophyti 1*, vols.1–6, Madrid: Conjejo Superiro de Investigaciones Cientificas, 1970.

Dods, M., Reith, G., and Pratten, B. P. *The Writings of Justin Martyr and Athenagoras* (ANCL 2), Edinburgh: T. & T. Clark, 1867.

Elliger, K. and Rudolph, W. (eds.) *Biblia Hebraica Stuttgartensia*, Stuttgart: Deutsche Bibelstiftung, 1977.

Epstein, I. (ed.) *The Babylonian Talmud*, London: Soncino Press, 1935–52.

Fairclough, H. Rushton (trans.), *Virgil: Eclogues Georgics, Aeneid I–VI*, 2nd edn, Loeb Classical Library, London: Heinemann, 1935.
   Virgil: Aeneid VII–XII, The Minor Poems, 2nd edn, Loeb Classical Library, London: Heinemann, 1934.

Field, F. *Origenis Hexaplorum: Veterum Interpretum Graecorum Fragmenta*, 2 vols., Oxford: Clarendon Press, 1875.

Fitzmyer, Joseph A. *The Genesis Apocryphon of Qumran, Cave 1: A Commentary*, Rome: Pontifical Biblical Institute, 1966.

Friedlander, G. *Pirkê de Rabbi Eliezer*, London: Kegan Paul, Trench, Trubner, 1916.

Funk, F. X. (ed.) *Die Apostolischen Väter*, Tübingen: Mohr (Paul Siebeck), 1906.

Geissen, A. *Der Septuaginta-Text des Buches Daniel Kap. 5–12, zusammen mit Susanna, Bel et Draco sowie Esther Kap. 1, 1a–2, 15* (PTA 5), Bonn: Rudolf Habelt Verlag, 1968.

Goodwin, W. W. (ed.) *Plutarch's Morals IV*, Boston: Little, Brown & Co, 1874.

Heine, R. E. (ed.) *Origen: Commentary on the Gospel of John Books 1–10* (The Fathers of the Church, 80), Washington, DC: Catholic University of America, 1989.

Hennecke, E. and Schneelmelcher, W. (ed.) *New Testament Apocrypha*, 2 vols., 1959, 1964 (ET: R. McL. Wilson, (ed.) Philadelphia: Westminster, 1963, 1964).

Homer, *The Iliad* (trans. R. Fagles), London: Penguin, 1991.

James, M. R. (ed.) *The Apocryphal New Testament*, Oxford: Clarendon Press, 1924.

Jongeling, B., Labuschagne, C. J., van der Woude, A. S. (eds.) *Aramaic Texts from Qumran: With Translations and Annotations* (SSS iv, vol. i), Leiden: Brill, 1976.

Kenyon, F. G. *The Chester Beatty Biblical Papyri: Descriptions and Texts of Twelve Manuscripts on Papyrus of the Greek Bible, Fasciculus vii: Ezekiel, Daniel, Esther: Text*, London: Emery Walker, 1937.

Klijn, A. F. J. and Reinink, G. J. *Patristic Evidence for Jewish–Christian Sects* (NovTSup 36), Leiden: Brill, 1973.

Knibb, M. A. (ed.) *The Ethiopic Book of Enoch: A New Edition in the Light of the Aramaic Dead Sea Fragments* (vol. i: Text and Apparatus; vol. ii: Introduction, Translation, and Commentary), Oxford: Clarendon Press, 1978.

Lake, K. (ed.) *The Apostolic Fathers*, Loeb Classical Library, 2 vols., London: Heinemann, 1912–13.

Levey, S. H. (trans.) *The Targum of Ezekiel* (The Aramaic Bible 13), Edinburgh: T. & T. Clark, 1987.

Lohse, Eduard (ed.) *Die Texte aus Qumran: Hebräisch und Deutsch*, 2nd edn, Munich: Kösel-Verlag, 1971.

Mangan, C., Healey, J. F., and Knobel, P. S. (trans.) *The Targums of Job,*

Proverbs, and Qohelet (The Aramaic Bible 15), Edinburgh: T. & T. Clark, 1991.

Metzger, Bruce M. *et al.* (eds.) *The Greek New Testament,* 3rd edn, Stuttgart: United Bible Societies, 1983.

Migne, J.-P. (ed.) *Patrologia Graeca,* 161 vols., Paris, 1857–66. *Patrologia Latina,* 221 vols., Paris, 1844–90.

Milik, J. T. (ed.) *The Books of Enoch: Aramaic Fragments of Qumran Cave 4,* Oxford: Clarendon Press, 1976.

Milik, J. T. and Barthélemy, D. (eds.) *Discoveries in the Judean Desert 1,* Oxford: Clarendon Press, 1955.

Morgan, Michael A. (trans.) *Sepher ha-Razim: The Book of Mysteries* (SBLTT 25), Chico, CA: Scholars Press, 1983.

Naveh, J. and Shaked, S. *Amulets and Magic Bowls: Aramaic Incantations of Late Antiquity,* Leiden: Brill, 1985.

Nestle, E., Aland, K., and Aland, B. (eds.) *Novum Testamentum Graece,* 26th edn, Stuttgart: Deutsche Bibelgesellschaft, 1979.

Newsom, Carol *Songs of the Sabbath Sacrifice: A Critical Edition* (HSS 27), Atlanta, GA: Scholars Press, 1985.

Odeberg, Hugo *3 Enoch or the Hebrew Book of Enoch: Edited and Translated for the First Time with Introduction, Commentary, and Critical Notes,* Cambridge: Cambridge University Press, 1928 (repr. New York: Ktav Publishing House, 1973).

Philonenko, Marc *Joseph et Aséneth: Introduction, Texte Critique, Traduction et Notes* (*SPB* 13), Leiden: Brill, 1968.

Pratten, B. P., Dods, M., and Smith, T. *The Writings of Theophilus and the Clementine Recognitions* (ANCL 3), Edinburgh: T. & T. Clark, 1867.

Preuschen, E. (ed.) *Origenes Werke Vol. 4: Der Johanneskommentar* (GCS), Leipzig: J. C. Hinrichs, 1903.

Rahlfs, A. (ed.) *Septuaginta,* 2 vols. in 1, Stuttgart: Deutsche Bibelgesellschaft, 1979.

Roberts, A. and Donaldson, J. *The Clementine Homilies, The Apostolical Constitutions* (ANCL 17), Edinburgh: T. & T. Clark, 1870.

Rolfe, J. C. (ed.) *Suetonius: Lives of the Caesars,* Loeb Classical Library, 2 vols., London: Heinemann, 1913–14.

Schäfer, Peter (ed.) *Synopse zur Hekhalot-Literatur* (TSAJ 2), Tübingen: Mohr (Paul Siebeck), 1987.

Sparks, H. E. D. (ed.) *The Apocryphal Old Testament,* Oxford: Clarendon Press, 1984.

Sperber, A. *The Bible in Aramaic,* vols. i–ivb, Leiden: Brill, 1959–73.

Stone, Michael E. *The Testament of Abraham: the Greek Recensions* (SBLTT 2: PS 2), Missoula: Society of Biblical Literature, 1972.

Thackeray, H. St. J. and Marcus, R. (eds.) *Josephus,* Loeb Classical Library, 9 vols., London: Heinemann, 1926–65.

Trollope, W. (ed.) *S. Justini: Philosophie et Martyris: Apologia Prima,* Cambridge: Macmillan, 1845.

VanderKam, J. C. (ed.) *The Book of Jubilees: A Critical Text* (CSCO 510; ScripAeth 87), Louvain: Peeters, 1989.

(trans.) *The Book of Jubilees* (CSCO 511; ScripAeth 88), Louvain: Peeters, 1989.

Vermes, Geza *The Dead Sea Scrolls in English*, 3rd edn, London: Penguin, 1987.
Yadin, Yigael *The Scroll of the War of the Sons of the Light against the Sons of Darkness: Edited with Commentary and Introduction*, Oxford: Oxford University Press, 1962.
Ziegler, J. (ed.) *Susanna, Daniel, Bel et Draco* (Septuaginta: Vetus Testamentum Graecum Auctoritate Academiae Scientiarum Gottingensis editum 16/2), Göttingen: Vandenhoeck & Ruprecht, 1954.

Commentaries on the Apocalypse of John

Allo, E.-B. *L'Apokalypse*, 2nd edn, Paris: Librairée Victor Lecoffre, 1921.
Andreas *Comment. in Apocalypsim* in Migne, *PG* 106, 1863, pp. 207–485.
Arethas *Comment. in Apocalypsim* in Migne, *PG* 106, 1863, pp. 486–786.
Augustine *Expositio in Apocalypsim b. Joannis* in Migne, *PL* 35, 1864, pp. 2417–52.
Beasley-Murray, G. R. *The Book of Revelation* (NCB), 2nd edn, London: Oliphants, 1978.
Beckwith, I. T. *The Apocalypse of John: Studies in Introduction with a Critical and Exegetical Commentary*, London: Macmillan, 1919 (repr. Grand Rapids: Baker Book House, 1967).
Boring, M. Eugene *Revelation* (Int.), Louisville: John Knox Press, 1989.
Bousset, Wilhelm *Die Offenbarung Johannis*, 6th edn, Göttingen: Vandenhoeck & Ruprecht, 1906.
Brütsch, Charles *Die Offenbarung Jesu Christi: Johannes-Apokalypse*, 3 vols., Zurich: Zwingli Verlag, 1970.
Caird, G. B. *The Revelation of St. John the Divine*, 2nd edn, London: Black, 1984.
Charles, R. H. *A Critical and Exegetical Commentary on the Revelation of St. John* (ICC), 2 vols., Edinburgh: T. & T. Clark, 1920.
Farrar, Austin *The Revelation of St. John the Divine*, Oxford: Clarendon Press, 1964.
Ford, J. Massyngberde *Revelation: Introduction, Translation, and Commentary* (Anchor), Garden City, NY: Doubleday, 1975.
Kiddle, M. *The Revelation of St. John*, London: Hodder & Stoughton, 1940.
Kraft, Heinrich *Die Offenbarung des Johannes* (HNT 16a), Tübingen: Mohr (Paul Siebeck), 1974.
Lohmeyer, Ernst *Die Offenbarung des Johannes* (HNT 16), Tübingen: Mohr (Paul Siebeck), 1926.
Lohse, Eduard *Die Offenbarung des Johannes* (NTD 11), Göttingen: Vandenhoeck & Ruprecht, 1960.
Loisy, Alfred *L'Apocalypse de Jean*, Paris: Emile Noury, 1923.
Morris, Leon L. *The Revelation of St. John: An Introduction and Commentary* (Tyndale), Eerdmans: Grand Rapids, 1969.
Mounce, Robert, H. *The Book of Revelation* (NLC), London: Marshall, Morgan & Scott, 1977.
Prigent, Pierre, *L'Apocalypse de Saint Jean* (CNT 2.14), 2nd edn, Geneva: Labor et Fides, 1988.

Primasius *Comment. in Apocalypsim* in Migne, *PL* 68, 1866, pp. 793–936.

Ritt, H. *Offenbarung des Johannes* (NEBNT 21), Würzburg: Echter Verlag, 1986.

Roloff, Jürgen *Die Offenbarung des Johannes* (ZBKNT 18), Zurich: Theologischer Verlag, 1984.

Ruperti Tuitensis *Comment. in Apocalypsim* in Migne, *PL* 169, 1854, pp. 827–1214.

Schüssler Fiorenza, E. *Revelation: Vision of a Just World* (Proclamation Commentaries), Fortress: Minneapolis, 1991.

Scott, Walter *Exposition of the Revelation of Jesus Christ*, London: Pickering & Inglis, 4th edn, no date.

Sweet, John *Revelation*, London: SCM, 1990.

Swete, H. B. *The Apocalypse of St. John: The Greek Text with Introduction, Notes, and Indices*, London: Macmillan, 1906.

Victorinus *Comment. in Apocalypsim* in I. Haussleiter (ed.), *Victorini Episcopi Petavironensis Opera*, CSEL 49, Vindobonae: F. Tempsky, 1916, pp. 12–154.

Secondary works

Alexander, P. '3 (Hebrew Apocalypse of) Enoch' in James H. Charlesworth (ed.), *Old Testament Pseudepigrapha*, vol. i, London: Darton, Longman & Todd, 1983, pp. 223–316.

Andersen, F. I. '2 (Slavonic Apocalypse of) Enoch' in James H. Charlesworth (ed.), *Old Testament Pseudepigrapha*, vol. ii, London: Darton, Longman & Todd, 1983, pp. 91–222.

Aune, David E. 'The social matrix of the Apocalypse of John', *BR* 26 (1981), 16–32.

'The influence of Roman court ceremonial in the Apocalypse of John', *BR* 28 (1983), 5–26.

The New Testament in its Literary Environment, Philadelphia: Westminster, 1987.

'The Apocalypse of John and Graeco-Roman revelatory magic', *NTS* 33 (1987), 481–501.

'The prophetic circle of John of Patmos and the exegesis of Revelation 22.16', *JSNT* 37 (1989), 103–16.

'The form and function of the proclamations to the seven churches', *NTS* 36 (1990), 182–204.

'Intertextuality and the genre of the Apocalypse', SBLSP (1991), 142–60.

'Christian prophecy and the messianic status of Jesus' in J. H. Charlesworth (ed.), *The Messiah: Developments in Earliest Judaism and Christianity*, Minneapolis: Fortress, 1992, pp. 404–22.

Bakker, Adolphine 'Christ an angel? A study of early Christian docetism', *ZNW* 32 (1933), 255–65.

Balz, H. R. *Methodische Probleme der Neutestamentlichen Christologie* (WMANT 25), Neukirchen-Vluyn, Neukirchener Verlag, 1967.

Bampfylde, Gillian 'The prince of the host in the Book of Daniel and the Dead Sea Scrolls', *JSJ* 14 (1983), 129–34.

Barbel, Joseph *Christos Angelos: Die Anschauung von Christus als Bote und*

Engel in der gelehrten und volkstümlichen Literatur des christlichen Altertums, Bonn: Peter Hanstein, 1941 (repr. w. *Anhang*: 'Christos Angelos: Die frühchristliche und patristische Engelchristologie im Lichte der neueren Forschung', 1964).

Barker, Margaret *The Lost Prophet: The Book of Enoch and its Influence on Christianity*, London: SPCK, 1988

'Temple imagery in Philo: an indication of the origin of the Logos?' in W. Horbury (ed.), *Templum Amicitiae: Essays on the Second Temple Presented to Ernst Bammel* (JSNTSup. 48), Sheffield: JSOT Press, 1991, pp. 70–102.

The Great Angel: A Study of Israel's Second God, London: SPCK, 1992.

Barr, James 'Theophany and anthropomorphism in the Old Testament', VTSup 7 (1960), 3.1–8.

'The image of God in the Book of Genesis: A study of terminology', *BJRL* 51 (1968), 11–26.

Barton, J. M. T. 'The Ascension of Isaiah' in H. F. D. Sparks (ed.), *The Apocryphal Old Testament*, Oxford: Clarendon Press, 1984, pp. 775–812.

Bauckham, Richard J. 'Synoptic parousia parables and the Apocalypse', *NTS* 23 (1977), 162–76.

'Synoptic parousia parables again', *NTS* 29 (1983), 129–34.

'The rise of apocalyptic', *Themelios* 3 (1978), 10–23.

'The figurae of John of Patmos' in A. Williams (ed.), *Prophecy and Millenarianism: Essays in Honour of Marjorie Reeves*, London: Longman, 1980, pp. 109–25.

'The role of the Spirit in the Apocalypse', *EvQ* 52 (1980), 66–83.

'The worship of Jesus in apocalyptic Christianity', *NTS* 27 (1981), 322–41.

'A note on a problem in the Greek version of 1 *Enoch* 1.9', *JTS* 32 (1981), 136–8.

'The apocalypses in the new pseudepigrapha', *JSNT* 26 (1986), 97–117.

'The Book of Revelation as a Christian war scroll', *Neot* 22 (1988), 17–40.

Jude and the Relatives of Jesus in the Early Church, Edinburgh: T. & T. Clark, 1990.

The Theology of the Book of Revelation, Cambridge: Cambridge University Press, 1993.

'The Apocalypse of Peter: an account of research', *ANRW* 2.25.6, pp. 4712– 50.

Bauer, W., Arndt, W. F., and Gingrich, F. W. *A Greek–English Lexicon of the New Testament and Other Early Christian Literature*, 4th edn, Cambridge: Cambridge University Press, 1952.

Beagley, A. J. *The 'Sitz im Leben' of the Apocalypse with Particular Reference to the Role of the Church's Enemies*, Berlin: Walter de Gruyter, 1987.

Beale, Gregory K. 'The problem of the man from the sea in IV Ezra 13 and its relation to the messianic concept in John's Apocalypse', *NovT* 25 (1983), 182–8.

The Use of Daniel in Jewish Apocalyptic Literature and in the Revelation of St. John, Lanham, MD: University Press of America, 1984.

'The origin of the title "King of Kings and Lord of Lords" in Revelation 17.14', *NTS* 31 (1985), 618–20.

'A reconsideration of the text of Daniel in the Apocalypse', *Bib* 67 (1986), 539–43.

'Revelation' in D. A. Carson and H. G. M. Williamson (eds.), *It Is Written: Scripture Citing Scripture* (*FS*: B. Lindars), Cambridge: Cambridge University Press,1988, pp. 318–36.

'The interpretative problem of Rev 1.19', *NovT* 34 (1992), 360–87.

Beck, Dwight M. 'The christology of the Apocalypse of John' in Edwin P. Booth (ed.), *New Testament Studies: Critical Essays in New Testament Interpretation with Special Reference to the Meaning and Worth of Jesus*, New York: Abingdon-Cokesbury Press, 1942, pp. 253–77.

Bell, Albert A. 'The date of John's Apocalypse: the evidence of some Roman historians reconsidered', *NTS* 25 (1979), 93–105.

Bergmeier, Roland 'Die Buchrolle und das Lamm (Apk 5 und 10)', *ZNW* 76 (1985), 225–42.

Betz, Hans Dieter 'On the problem of the religio-historical understanding of apocalypticism' in R. W. Funk (ed.), *Apocalypticism* (JTC 6), New York: Herder & Herder, 1969, pp. 134–56.

Betz, Hans Dieter and Smith, E. W. 'De Iside et Osiride' in Hans Dieter Betz (ed.), *Plutarch's Theological Writings and Early Christian Literature*, Leiden: Brill, 1975, pp. 36–84.

Bietenhard, Hans *Die himmlische welt im Urchristentum und Spätjudentum* (WUNT 2),Tübingen: Mohr (Paul Siebeck), 1951.

Black, Matthew 'The throne-theophany prophetic commission and the "Son of Man": a study in tradition-history' in R. G. Hamerton-Kelly and R. Scroggs (eds.), *Jews, Greeks, and Christians: Religious Culture in Late Antiquity* (*FS*: W. D. Davies), Leiden: Brill,1976, 57–73.

'The "Parables of Enoch" (1 Enoch 37–71) and the "Son of Man"', *ExpTim* 88 (1976), 5–8.

'The messianism of the Parables of Enoch: their date and contributions to christological origins' in J. H. Charlesworth (ed.), *The Messiah: Developments in Earliest Judaism and Christianity*, Minneapolis: Fortress, 1992, pp. 145–68.

Böcher, Otto 'Die Johannes-Apokalypse in der neueren Forschung', *ANRW* 2.25.2, pp. 3850–93.

'Die Johannes-Apokalypse und die Texte von Qumran', *ANRW* 2.25.2, pp. 3894–8.

Boring, M. Eugene 'Narrative christology in the Apocalypse', *CBQ* 54 (1992), 702–3.

'The voice of Jesus in the Apocalypse of John', *NovT* 34 (1992), 334–59.

Bousset, W. *Die Religion des Judentums*, 2nd edn, Berlin: Reuther & Reichard, 1906.

Bovon, François 'Le Christ de l'Apocalypse', *RTP* 21 (1972), 65–80.

Boyd, W. J. P. 'I am Alpha and Omega (Rev 1.8; 21.6; 22.13)', *Studia Evangelica* 2 (1964), 526–31 = F. L. Cross (ed.), TU 87, Berlin: Akademie, 1964, pp. 526–31.

Braun, F. M. 'Les Testaments des XII Patriarchs et leur problème de leur origine', *RB* 67 (1960), 516–49.

Brighton, L. A. 'The Angel of Revelation: an Angel of God and an icon of Jesus Christ' (PhD Diss., St Louis University, 1991).

Bruce, F. F. 'The Spirit in the Apocalypse' in B. Lindars and S. Smalley (eds.), *Christ and Spirit in the New Testament* (*FS*: C. F. D. Moule), Cambridge: Cambridge University Press, 1973, pp. 333–44.

'The oldest Greek version of Daniel', *OTS* 20 (1977), 22–40.

A Mind for What Matters: Collected Essays, Grand Rapids: Eerdmans, 1990.

Büchsel, Friedrich *Die Christologie der Offenbarung Johannis*, Halle: Druck von C. A. Kämmerer, 1907.

Bühner, Jan-A. *Der gesandte und Sein Weg im 4 Evangelium: Die kultur-und religionsgeschichtlichen Grundlagen der johanneischen Sendungs-christologie sowie ihre traditionsgeschichtliche Entwicklung* (WUNT 2.2), Tübingen: Mohr (Paul Siebeck), 1977.

Burchard, C. *Untersuchungen zu Joseph und Aseneth* (WUNT 8), Tübingen: Mohr (Paul Siebeck), 1965.

'Zum Text von "Joseph und Aseneth"', *JSJ* 1 (1970), 3–34.

'Joseph et Aséneth: questions actuelles' in W. C. van Unnik (ed.), *La littérature Juive entre Tenach et Mischna*, Leiden: Brill, 1974, pp. 77–100.

Joseph and Aseneth (JSHRZ 2), Gütersloh: Gerd Mohn, 1983.

'Joseph and Aseneth' in James H. Charlesworth (ed.), *Old Testament Pseudepigrapha*, vol ii, London: Darton, Longman & Todd, 1985, pp. 177–248.

'The importance of Joseph and Aseneth for the study of the New Testament', *NTS* 33 (1987), 102–34.

Caird, G. B., 'Review: *Die Christologie der Apokalypse des Johannes* [T. Holtz]', *JTS* 15 (1964), 141–3.

Caragounis, Chrys C. *The Son of Man* (WUNT 38), Tübingen: Mohr (Paul Siebeck), 1986.

Carmignac, J. 'Le document de Qumran sur Melchisedeq', *RevQ* 7 (1970), 343–78.

Carnegie, David R. 'Worthy is the Lamb: the hymns in Revelation' in H. H. Rowden (ed.), *Christ the Lord: Studies in Christology Presented to Donald Guthrie*, Leicester: Intervarsity Press, 1982, pp. 243–56.

Carr, Wesley *Angels and Principalities: The Background, Meaning and Development of the Pauline Phrase 'hai archoi kai hai exousiai'* (SNTSMS 42), Cambridge: Cambridge University Press, 1981.

Carrell, Peter '"Lamb" christology in the Apocalypse of John' (BD Diss., University of Otago, 1986).

Casey, Maurice 'The use of the term "son of man" in the Similitudes of Enoch', *JSJ* 7 (1976), 11–29.

Son of Man: The Interpretation and Influence of Daniel 7, London: SPCK, 1979.

From Jewish Prophet to Gentile God: The Origins and Development of New Testament Christology, Cambridge: James Clarke, 1991.

Casey, R. P. 'The earliest christologies', *JTS* 9 (1958), 253–77.

Charles, R. H. *A Critical and Exegetical Commentary on the Book of Daniel: With Introduction, Indexes, and a New English Translation*, Oxford: Clarendon Press, 1929.

Charlesworth, James H. 'The portrayal of the righteous as an angel' in J. J. Collins and G. W. E. Nickelsburg (eds.), *Ideal Figures in Ancient Judaism: Profiles and Paradigms* (SBLSCS 12), Chico, CA: Scholars Press, 1980, pp. 135–51.

'The Jewish roots of christology: the discovery of the hypostatic voice', *SJT* 39 (1986), 19–41.

(ed.) *The Old Testament Pseudepigrapha and the New Testament: Prolegomena for the Study of Christian Origins* (SNTSMS 54), Cambridge: Cambridge University Press,1985.

Chernus, Ira 'Visions of God in merkabah mysticism', *JSJ* 13 (1982), 123–46.

Chesnutt, R. D. 'Joseph and Aseneth', *ABD*, iii, p. 971.

Collins, John J. 'The son of man and the saints of the Most High in the Book of Daniel' *JBL* 93 (1974), 50–66.

'Pseudonymity, historical reviews and the genre of the Revelation of John', *CBQ* 39 (1977), 329–43.

The Apocalyptic Vision of the Book of Daniel (HSM 16), Missoula: Scholars Press, 1977.

'Introduction: towards the morphology of a genre', *Semeia* 14 (1979), 1–20.

'The Jewish apocalypses', *Semeia* 14 (1979), 21–60.

'The heavenly representative: "the son of man" in the Similitudes of Enoch' in J. J. Collins and G. W. E. Nickelsburg (eds.), *Ideal Figures in Ancient Judaism: Profiles and Paradigms* (SBLSCS 12), Chico, CA: Scholars Press, 1980, pp. 111–33.

The Apocalyptic Imagination; An Introduction to the Jewish Matrix of Christianity, New York: Crossroad, 1984.

'The son of man in first-century Judaism', *NTS* 38 (1992), 448–66.

Colpe, C. 'ὁ υἱός τοῦ ἀνθρώπου', *TDNT*, viii, 400–77.

Comblin, J. *Le Christ dans l'Apocalypse* (Bibliothèque de Théologie: Théologie biblique 3/6),Paris: Desclée, 1965.

Cook, D. E. 'The christology of the Apocalypse' (PhD Diss., Duke University, NC, 1962).

Cooke, G. A. *A Critical and Exegetical Commentary on the Book of Ezekiel* (ICC), Edinburgh: T. & T. Clark, 1936.

Coppens, J. 'La mention d'un Fils d'homme angélique en Ap 14,14' in J. Lambrecht (ed.), *L'Apocalypse johannique et l'Apocalyptique dans le Nouveau Testament* (BETL 53), Louvain: Leuven University Press, 1980, 229.

Court, John M. *Myth and History in the Book of Revelation*, Atlanta, GA: John Knox Press, 1979

Cullmann, Oscar *The Christology of the New Testament*, 2nd edn, London: SCM, 1963.

Cuss, Dominique *Imperial Cult and Honorary Terms in the New Testament*, Fribourg: the University Press, 1974.

Daniélou, Jean *The Theology of Jewish Christianity*, London: Darton, Longman and Todd, 1964.

240   *Bibliography*

Davidson, Maxwell, J. *Angels at Qumran: A Comparative Study of 1 Enoch 1–36, 72–108 and Sectarian Writings from Qumran* (JSPSup 11), Sheffield: JSOT Press, 1992.

Day, John *God's Conflict with the Dragon and the Sea*, Cambridge: Cambridge University Press, 1985.

De Jonge, Marinus 'Once more: Christian influence in the Testaments of the Twelve Patriarchs', *NovT* 5 (1962), 311–19.

'Christian influence in the Testaments of the Twelve Patriarchs' in M. De Jonge (ed.), *Studies in the Testament of the Twelve Patriarchs: Text and Interpretation* (SVTP 3), Leiden: Brill, 1975, pp. 193–246.

'The use of the expression ὁ χριστός in the Apocalypse of John' in J. Lambrecht (ed.), *L'Apocalypse johannique et l'Apocalyptique dans le Nouveau Testament* (BETL 53), Louvain: Leuven University Press, 1980, pp. 267–81.

'The Testaments of the Twelve Patriarchs' in H. F. D. Sparks (ed.) *The Apocryphal Old Testament*, Oxford: Clarendon Press, 1984, pp. 505–600.

Christology in Context: The Earliest Christian Response to Jesus, Philadelphia: Westminster Press, 1988.

De Jonge, Marinus and van der Woude, A. S. '11Q Melchizedek and the New Testament', *NTS* 12 (1966), 301–26.

Delcor, M. 'Les sources du chapitre VII de Daniel', *VT* 18 (1968), 290–312.

'Melchizedek from Genesis to the Qumran texts and the Epistle to the Hebrews', *JSJ* 2 (1971), 115–35.

De Moor, J. C. *The Rise of Yahwism: The Roots of Israelite Monotheism* (BETL 41), Louvain: Leuven University Press, 1990.

Dillon, John *The Middle Platonists: A Study of Platonism, 80 B.C. to A.D. 220*, Duckworth: London, 1977.

Dix, G. 'The seven archangels and the seven spirits', *JTS* 28 (1927), 233–85.

Downing, F. G. 'Pliny's prosecution of Christians: Revelation and 1 Peter', *JSNT* 34 (1988), 105–23.

Driver, S. R. *The Book of Daniel*, Cambridge: Cambridge University Press, 1936.

D'Sousa, J. D. *The Lamb in the Johannine Writings*, Allohabad: St Paul Publications, 1968.

Duensing, H. 'Epistula Apostolorum' in E. Hennecke, W. Schneelmelcher, and R. Wilson (eds.), *New Testament Apocrypha*, vol. i, Philadelphia: Westminster, 1963, pp. 126–55.

'Apocalypse of Paul' in E. Hennecke, W. Schneelmelcher, and R. Wilson (eds.), *New Testament Apocrypha*, vol. ii, Philadelphia: Westminster, 1964, pp. 755–98.

Duensing, H. and Maurer, C. 'Apocalypse of Peter' in E. Hennecke, W. Schneelmelcher, and R. Wilson (eds.), *New Testament Apocrypha*, vol. ii, Philadelphia: Westminster, 1964, pp. 663–83.

Duling, D. C. 'Testament of Solomon' in James H. Charlesworth (ed.), *Old Testament Pseudepigrapha*, vol i, London: Darton, Longman & Todd, 1983, pp. 935–88.

Dunn, James D. G. *Jesus and the Spirit: A Study of the Religious and*

Charismatic Experience of Jesus and the First Christians as Reflected in the New Testament, London: SCM, 1975.

'Was Christianity a monotheistic faith from the beginning?', *SJT* 35 (1982), 303–36.

Christology in the Making: A New Testament Inquiry into the Origins of the Incarnation, 2nd edn, London: SCM, 1989.

Unity and Diversity in the New Testament: An Enquiry into the Character of Earliest Christianity, 2nd edn, London: SCM, 1990.

The Partings of the Ways: Between Christianity and Judaism and their Significance for the Character of Christianity, London: SCM, 1991.

Edelstein, E. J. and Edelstein, L. *Asclepius: A Collection and Interpretation of the Testimonies*, 2 vols., Baltimore: Johns Hopkins, 1945.

Edwards, Sarah A. 'Christological perspectives in the Book of Revelation' in R. F. Berkey and S. A. Edwards (eds.), *Christological Perspectives* (*FS*: H. K. McArthur), New York: The Pilgrim Press, 1982, pp. 139–54.

Ehrhardt, A. A. T. 'Judaeo-Christians in Egypt, the Epistula Apostolorum and the Gospel to the Hebrews', *Studia Evangelica* 3 (1964), 360–82 = F. L. Cross (ed.), TU 88, Berlin: Akademie-Verlag, 1964, pp. 360–82.

Eichrodt, W. *Theology of the Old Testament*, 2 vols., London: SCM, 1961, 1967.

Eissfeldt, O. 'El and Yahweh', *JSS* 1 (1956), 25–37.

Ellwanger, Walter H. 'The christology of the Apocalypse', *CTM* 1 (1930), 512–28.

Emerton, J. A. 'The origin of the son of man imagery', *JTS* 9 (1958), 225–42.

Farnell, L. R. *Greek Hero Cults and Ideas of Immortality* (Gifford Lectures), Oxford: Clarendon Press, 1921.

Ferch, A. J. 'Daniel 7 and Ugarit: a reconsideration', *JBL* 99 (1980), 75–86.

Feuillet, André 'Le fils de l'homme de Daniel et la tradition biblique', *RB* 60 (1953), 170–202, 321–46.

L'Apocalypse: Etat de la question (SN 3), Paris: Desclée, 1963.

'Le premier cavalier de l'Apocalypse', *ZNW* 57 (1966), 229–59.

Fischer, Karl M. 'Die Christlichkeit der Offenbarung Johannes', *TLZ* 106 (1981), 165–72.

Fitzmyer, Joseph A. 'The Aramaic 'Elect of God' text from Qumran Cave IV', *CBQ* 27 (1965), 348–72.

'Further light on Melchizedek from Qumran Cave 11', *JBL* 86 (1967), 25–41.

Fossum, Jarl 'Jewish–Christian christology and Jewish mysticism', *VC* 37 (1983), 260–87.

The Name of God and the Angel of the Lord: Samaritan and Jewish Concepts of Intermediation and the Origin of Gnosticism (WUNT 36) Mohr (Paul Siebeck): Tübingen, 1985.

'Kyrios Jesus as the angel of the Lord in Jude 5–7', *NTS* 33 (1987) 226–43.

'The new Religionsgeschichtliche Schule: the quest for Jewish christology', *SBLSP* (1991), 638–46.

Francis, Fred O. 'Humility and angelic worship in Col 2.18', *ST* 16 (1962), 109–34.

Friedman, D. N. (ed.), *Anchor Bible Dictionary*, 6 vols., New York: Doubleday, 1992.

Fuhs, H. F. *Ezechiel 1–24*, Würzburg: Echter-Verlag, 1984.

Gaechter, Paul 'The original sequence of Apocalypse 20–22', *TS* 10 (1949), 485–521.

Gammie, John 'Spatial and ethical dualism in Jewish wisdom and apocalyptic Literature', *JBL* 93 (1974), 356–85.

Gentry, Kenneth L. *Before Jerusalem Fell: Dating the Book of Revelation, An Exegetical and Historical Argument for a Pre-A.D. 70 Composition*, Tyler, TX: Institute for Christian Economics, 1989.

Gerhardsson, Birger 'Die christologischen Aussagen in den Sendschrieben der Offenbarung (Kap. 2–3)' in A. Fuchs (ed.), *Theologie aus dem Norden: Studien zum Neuen Testament und Seiner Umwelt* (Serie A, Band 2), Linz: privately published, 1977, pp. 142–66.

Giblin, C. H. 'Structural and thematic correlations in the theology of Revelation 16–22', *Bib* 55 (1974), pp. 487–504.

The Book of Revelation: The Open Book of Prophecy (GNS 34), Collegeville, MN: Liturgical Press , 1991.

Glasson, T. F. 'The son of man imagery: Enoch 14 and Daniel 7', *NTS* 23 (1977), 82–90.

Goldingay, John *Daniel* (WBC 30), Dallas, TX: Word Books, 1989.

Goodenough, E. R. *By Light, By Light: The Mystic Gospel of Hellenistic Judaism*, New Haven, CT: Yale University Press, 1935.

The Theology of Justin Martyr: An Investigation into the Conceptions of Early Christian Literature and its Hellenistic and Judaistic Influences, Jena: Frommannsche Buchhandlung, 1923 (repr. Amsterdam: Philo Press, 1968).

An Introduction to Philo Judaeus, 2nd edn, Oxford: Blackwell, 1962.

Goodrick, A. T. S. *The Book of Wisdom: With Introduction and Notes*, London: Rivingtons, 1913.

Goulder, Michael D. 'The Apocalypse as an annual cycle of prophecies', *NTS* 27 (1981), 342–67.

Gregg, J. A. E. *The Wisdom of Solomon: In the Revised Version with Introduction and Notes*, Cambridge: Cambridge University Press, 1909.

Grelot, Pierre 'Les versions grecques de Daniel', *Bib* 47 (1966), 381–402.

'L'exégèse messianique d'Isaie, LXIII, 1–6', *RB* 70 (1963), 371–80.

Gressmann, Hugo *Der Ursprung der Israelitisch-jüdischen Eschatologie*, Göttingen: Vandenhoeck & Ruprecht, 1905.

Gruenwald, I. *Apocalyptic and Merkabah Mysticism* (AGJU 24), Brill: Leiden, 1980.

Gundry, Robert H. 'Angelomorphic christology in the Book of Revelation', SBLSP 1994 (ed. E. H. Lovering, Atlanta, GA: Scholars Press, 1994), pp. 662–78.

Guthrie, Donald 'The Lamb in the structure of the Book of Revelation', *VE* 12 (1981), 64–71.

The Relevance of John's Apocalypse, Exeter: Paternoster Press, 1987.

Hahn, Ferdinand *Christologische Hoheitstitel* (FRLANT 83), Göttingen: Vandenhoeck & Ruprecht, 1963.

Hall, R. G. 'Living creatures in the midst of the throne: another look at Revelation 4.6', *NTS* 36 (1990), 609–13.

Halperin, D. J. *The Merkabah in Rabbinic Literature* (AOS 62), New Haven, CT: American Oriental Society, 1980.

The Faces of the Chariot: Early Jewish Responses to Ezekiel's Vision, Tübingen: Mohr (Paul Siebeck), 1988.

Hammond, N. G. L. and Scullard, H. H. (ed.), *The Oxford Classical Dictionary*, 2nd edn, Oxford: Clarendon Press, 1970.

Hanson, Anthony Tyrell *The Wrath of the Lamb*, London: Dartons Longman & Todd, 1957.

Hanson, P. D. *The Dawn of Apocalyptic: The Historical and Sociological Roots of Jewish Apocalyptic Eschatology*, Philadelphia: Fortress, 1979.

Hare, D. R. A. *The Son of Man Tradition*, Minneapolis: Fortress, 1990.

Harlé, P.-A. 'L'Agneau de l'Apocalypse et le Nouveau Testament', *ETR* 31 (1956), 26–35.

Harrington, D. J. 'Pseudo-Philo' in James H. Charlesworth (ed.), *Old Testament Pseudepigrapha*, vol. ii, London: Darton, Longman & Todd, 1985, pp. 297–378.

Hartman, Lars *Prophecy Interpreted: The Formation of Some Jewish Apocalyptic Texts and of the Eschatological Discourse Mark 13 Par*, Lund: Gleerup, 1966.

'Form and message. A preliminary discussion of < partial texts > in Rev 1–3 and 22,6ff' in J. Lambrecht (ed.), *L'Apocalypse johannique et l'Apocalyptique dans le Nouveau Testament* (BETL 53), Louvain: Leuven University Press, 1980, pp. 129–49.

Hartman, Louis F. and Di Lella, Alexander, A. *The Book of Daniel: A New Translation With Introduction and Commentary* (Anchor), Garden City, NY: Doubleday, 1978.

Hayman, Peter 'Monotheism – a misused word in Jewish studies?', *JJS* 42 (1991), 1–15.

Hayward, Robert 'The Holy Name of the God of Moses and the prologue of St John's Gospel', *NTS* 25 (1978), 16–32.

Divine Name and Presence: The Memra, Totowa, NJ: Allenheld, Osmun & Co., 1981.

Heidt, W. G. *The Angelology of the Old Testament*, Washington, DC: Catholic University of America, 1949 (repr. Ann Arbour: 1980).

Hellholm, David 'The problem of apocalyptic genre and the Apocalypse of John', *Semeia* 36 (1986), 13–64.

Hemer, Colin J. *The Letters to the Seven Churches of Asia in their Local Setting* (JSNTSup 11), Sheffield: JSOT Press, 1986.

Hengel, Martin *The Son of God: The Origin of Christology and the History of Jewish–Hellenistic Religion*, London: SCM, 1976.

The Johannine Question, London: SCM, 1989.

'Christological titles in early Christianity' in J. H. Charlesworth (ed.), *The Messiah: Developments in Earliest Judaism and Christianity*, Minneapolis: Fortress, 1992, pp. 425–48.

Hillyer, Norman ' "The Lamb" in the Apocalypse', *EvQ* 39 (1967), 228–36.

Himmelfarb, Martha *Tours of Hell: An Apocalyptic Form in Jewish and Christian Literature*, Philadelphia: Fortress, 1983.

Hirth, V. *Gottes Boten im Alten Testament: Die alttestamentliche Malʿak-Vorstellung unter besonderer Berücksichtigung des Malʿak-Jahwe-Problems* (TA 32), Berlin: Evangelisches Verlagsanstalt, 1975.

Hohnjec, N. *Das Lamm – τὸ ἀρνίον in der Offenbarung des Johannes: Eine exegetisch-theologische Untersuchung*, Rome: Pontificia Universitas Gregoriana, 1980.

Holladay, Carl R. 'The portrait of Moses in Ezekiel the Tragedian', *SBLSP* (1976), 447–52.

Theios Aner in Hellenistic Judaism (SBLDS 40), Missoula: Scholars Press, 1977.

Hollander, H. W. and De Jonge, M. *The Testaments of the Twelve Patriarchs: A Commentary* (SVTP 8), Leiden: Brill, 1985.

Holtz, Traugott 'Christliche Interpolationen in > Joseph and Aseneth < ', *NTS* 14 (1968), 484–97.

Die Christologie der Apokalypse des Johannes (*TU* 85) 2nd edn, Berlin: Akademie Verlag, 1971.

'Gott in der Apokalypse' in J. Lambrecht (ed.), *L'Apocalypse johannique et l'Apocalyptique dans le Nouveau Testament* (BETL 53), Louvain: Leuven University Press, 1980, pp. 242–65.

Horbury, William 'The messianic associations of "the Son of Man"', *JTS* 36 (1985), 34–55.

Horton, Fred L. *The Melchizedek Tradition: A Critical Examination of the Sources to the Fifth Century A.D. and in the Epistle of the Hebrews* (SNTSMS 30), Cambridge: Cambridge University Press, 1976.

Hultgard, A. 'Das Judentum in der hellenistisch-römischen Zeit und die iranische Religion – ein religionsgeschichtliches Problem', *ANRW*: 2.19.1, pp. 512–90.

Hunzinger, Claus-Hunno 'Babylon als Deckname für Rom und die Datierung des 1 Petrusbriefes' in H. G. Reventlow (ed.), *Gottes Wort und Gottes Land* (*FS*: H. W. Hertzberg), Göttingen: Vandenhoeck & Ruprecht, 1965, pp. 67–77.

Hurtado, Larry W. 'Revelation 4–5 in the light of Jewish apocalyptic analogies', *JSNT* 25 (1985), 105–24.

One God, One Lord: Early Christian Devotion and Ancient Jewish Monotheism, London: SCM, 1988.

Isaac, E. '1 (Ethiopic Apocalypse of) Enoch' in James H. Charlesworth (ed.), *Old Testament Pseudepigrapha*, vol. i, London: Darton, Longman & Todd, 1983, pp. 5–90.

Jacobsen, H. 'Mysticism and apocalyptic in Ezekiel's Exagoge', *ICS* 6 (1981), 272–95.

The Exagoge of Ezekiel, Cambridge: Cambridge University Press, 1983.

Jankowski, A. 'Chrystus Apkalipsy Janowy a con obecny (De Christo Apocalypseos Johanneae hoc in aevo agente)', *Analecta Cracoviensia* 14 (1982), 243–94.

Jastrow, M. *A Dictionary of the Targumim, Talmud Babli, Yerushalmi, and Midrashic Literature*, New York: Judaica Press, 1992.

Jeffery, A. *The Book of Daniel* (IB), Nashville: Abingdon, 1956.

Jeremias, Joachim 'Μωυσῆς', *TDNT*, iv, 848–73.

Jeske, Richard L. 'Spirit and community in the Johannine Apocalypse', *NTS* 31 (1985), 452–66.

Johnson, M. D. 'Life of Adam and Eve' in James H. Charlesworth (ed.), *Old Testament Pseudepigrapha*, vol. ii, London: Darton, Longman & Todd, 1985, pp. 249–98.

Johnson, S. E. 'Asia Minor and early Christianity' in J. Neusner (ed.), *Christianity, Judaism, and Other Greco-Roman Cults* (*FS*: Morton Smith), part 2, Leiden: Brill, 1975, pp. 77–145.

Jones, Benny Joseph 'A study of the son of man in Revelation with special reference to the suffering servant motif' (PhD Diss., New Orleans Baptist Theological Seminary, 1990).

Jones, D. L. 'Christianity and the Roman imperial cult', *ANRW* 2.23.2 , pp. 1023–54.

Kalenkow, H. B. 'The angelology of the Testament of Abraham' in G. W. E. Nickelsburg (ed.), *Studies in the Testament of Abraham* (SBLSCS 6), Missoula: Scholars Press, 1976, pp. 153–62.

Kaplan, C. 'The angelology of the non-canonical Jewish Apocalypses', *JBL* 67 (1948), 217–32.

Karrer, Martin *Die Johannesoffenbarung als Brief: Studien zu ihrem literarischen, historischen und theologischen Ort* (FRLANT 140) Göttingen: Vandenhoeck & Ruprecht, 1986.

Kee, Howard C. 'Self-definition in the Asclepius cult' in Ben F. Meyer and E. P. Sanders (eds.), *Jewish and Christian Self-Definition, Volume Three: Self-Definition in the Graeco-Roman World*, London: SCM, 1982, pp. 118–36.

Miracle in the Early Christian World: A Study in Socio-Historical Method, New Haven, CT/London: Yale University Press, 1983.

'Testaments of the Twelve Patriarchs' in James H. Charlesworth (ed.), *Old Testament Pseudepigrapha*, vol. i, London: Darton, Longman & Todd, 1983, pp. 775–828.

'The socio-cultural setting of *Joseph and Aseneth*', *NIS* 29 (1983), 394–413.

Kim, Seyoon *The Origin of Paul's Gospel*, Grand Rapids: Eerdmans, 1982.

Kirby, J. T. 'The rhetorical situations of Revelation 1–3', *NTS* 34 (1988), 197–207.

Kittel, G. and Friedrich, G. (eds.) *Theological Dictionary of the New Testament*, 10 vols., Grand Rapids: Eerdmans, 1964–76.

Klauck, H.-J. 'Der Sendschreiben nach Pergamon und der Kaiserkult in der Johannesoffenbarung', *Bib* 73 (1992), 153–82.

Klijn, A. F. J. '2 (Syriac Apocalypse of) Baruch' in James H. Charlesworth (ed.), *Old Testament Pseudepigrapha*, vol. i, London: Darton, Longman & Todd, 1983, pp. 615–52.

Knibb, M. A., 'The date of the Parables of Enoch: a critical review', *NTS* 25 (1979), 345–59.

'1 Enoch' in H. F. D. Sparks (ed.), *The Apocryphal Old Testament*, Oxford: Clarendon Press, 1984, pp. 169–320.

'Martyrdom and Ascension of Isaiah' in James H. Charlesworth (ed.),

Old Testament Pseudepigrapha, vol. ii, London: Darton, Longman & Todd, 1985, pp. 143–76.

Knight, Jonathan M. 'Disciples of the Beloved One: a study in the Ascension of Isaiah with respect to its christology, social setting, and relevance for New Testament interpretation' (PhD Diss., University of Cambridge, 1990).

Knox, W. L. 'The "Divine Hero" christology in the New Testament', *HTR* 41 (1948), 229–49.

Kobelski, P. J. *Melchizedek and Melchiresa* (CBQMS 10), Washington, DC: Catholic Biblical Association of America, 1981.

Kraft, Heinrich 'Zur Offenbarung Johannes', *TRu* 38 (1973), 81–98.

Kramer, Werner *Christ, Lord, Son of God* (SBT 50), London: SCM, 1966.

Kreitzer, L. 'Apotheosis of the Roman emperor', *BA* 53 (1990), 211–17.

Kretschmar, G. *Studien zur frühchristlichen Trinitätstheologie* (BHT 21), Tübingen: Mohr (Paul Siebeck), 1956.

Kselman, John S. and Barré, Michael L. 'Psalms' in R. E. Brown, J. A. Fitzmyer, and R. E. Murphy (eds.), *The New Jerome Biblical Commentary*, Englewood Cliffs, NJ: Prentice Hall, pp. 523–52.

Kuhn, K. H. 'The Apocalypse of Zephaniah and an Anonymous Apocalypse' in H. F. D. Sparks (ed.), *The Apocryphal Old Testament*, Oxford: Clarendon Press, 1984, pp. 915–26.

Kuhn, Peter *Offenbarungsstimmen im Antiken Judentum: Untersuchungen zur Bat Qol und verwandten Phänomenen* (TSAJ 20), Tübingen: Mohr (Paul Siebeck), 1989.

Kvanvig, Helge S. *Roots of Apocalyptic: The Mesopotamian Background of the Enoch Figure and of the Son of Man* (WMANT 61), Neukirchen: Neukirchener Verlag, 1988.

Läpple, Alfred 'Das Geheimnis des Lammes: Das Christusbild der Offenbarung des Johannes', *BiKi* 39 (1984), 53–8.

Laubscher, F. du T. 'God's Angel of Truth and Melchizedek: a note on 11QMelch 136', *JSJ* 3 (1972), 46–51.

Le Grys, A. 'Conflict and vengeance in the Book of Revelation', *ExpTim* 104 (1992), 76–80.

Levison, John R. *Portraits of Adam in Early Judaism: From Sirach to 2 Baruch* (JSPSup. 1), Sheffield: JSOT Press, 1988.

Lieberman, Saul 'Metatron, the meaning of his name and his functions' Appendix in I. Gruenwald, *Apocalyptic and Merkabah Mysticism* (AGJU 24), Leiden: Brill, 1980, pp. 235–41.

Linton, G. 'Reading the Apocalypse as an apocalypse', *SBLSP* (1991), 161–86.

Lohse, Eduard 'Apokalyptik und Christologie', *ZNW* 62 (1971), 48–67.

   'Die alttestamentliche Sprache des Sehers Johannes', *ZNW* 52 (1961) 122–6.

   'Der Menschensohn in der Johannesapokalypse' in E. Lohse, *Die Vielfalt des Neuen Testaments* (ESTNT ii), Göttingen: Vandenhoeck & Ruprecht, 1982, 82–7.

   'Wie christlich ist die Offenbarung des Johannes', *NTS* 34 (1988), 321–38.

Longenecker, Richard N., *The Christology of Early Jewish Christianity* (SBT ii.17), London: SCM, 1970.

Longman, T. 'The Divine Warrior: the New Testament use of an Old Testament motif', *WTJ* 4 (1982), 290–307.

Lueken, W. *Michael: eine Darstellung und Vergleichung der jüdischen und der morgenländisch-christlichen Tradition vom Erzengel Michael*, Göttingen: Vandenhoeck & Ruprecht, 1898.

Lunt, H. G. 'Ladder of Jacob' in James H. Charlesworth (ed.), *Old Testament Pseudepigrapha*, vol. ii, London: Darton, Longman & Todd, 1985, pp. 401–12.

Lust, J. 'Daniel 7,13 and the Septuagint', *ETL* 54 (1978), 62–9.

MacDonald, William Graham 'Christology and "The Angel of the Lord"' in G. F. Hawthorne (ed.), *Current Issues in Biblical and Patristic Interpretation* (*FS*: M. C. Tenney), Grand Rapids: Eerdmans, 1975, pp. 324–35.

Mach, Michael *Entwicklungsstadien des jüdischen Engelsglaubens in vorrabbinischer Zeit* (TSAJ 34), Tübingen: Mohr (Paul Siebeck), 1992.

McNamara, Martin *The New Testament and the Palestinian Targum to the Pentateuch*, Rome: Pontifical Biblical Institute, 1966.

'*Logos* in the Fourth Gospel and the *Memra* of the Palestinian Targum (Ex 12.42)', *ExpTim* 79 (1968), 115–17.

Targum and Testament: Aramaic Paraphrases of the Hebrew Bible, A Light on the New Testament, Shannon: Irish University Press, 1972.

Manson, T. W. 'The Son of Man in Daniel, Enoch and the Gospels', *BJRL* 32 (1949–50), 171–93.

Mazzaferri, F. D. *The Genre of the Book of Revelation from a Source-Critical Perspective* (*BZNW* 54), Berlin/New York: Walter de Gruyter, 1989.

Mearns, C. L. 'Dating the Similitudes of Enoch', *NTS* 25 (1979), 360–9.

Meeks, Wayne A. *The Prophet-King: Moses Traditions and the Johannine Christology* (NovTSup 14), Leiden: Brill, 1967.

'Moses as God and king' in J. Neusner (ed.), *Religions in Antiquity* (*FS*: E. R. Goodenough), Leiden: Brill, 1968, pp. 354–71.

Metzger, Bruce *A Textual Commentary on the Greek New Testament*, 2nd edn, London: United Bible Society, 1975.

'The Fourth Book of Ezra' in James H. Charlesworth (ed.), *Old Testament Pseudepigrapha*, vol. i, London: Darton, Longman & Todd, 1983, pp. 561–80.

Meyers, C. L. and Meyers, E. M. *Haggai, Zechariah 1–8* (Anchor) New York: Doubleday, 1987.

Michaelis, W. *Zur Engelchristologie im Urchristentum: Abbau der Konstruction Martin Werners*, Basel: Maier, 1942.

Michaels, J. Ramsey 'Revelation 1.19 and the narrative voices of the Apocalypse', *NTS* 37 (1991), 604–20.

Michel, Otto 'ἵππος', *TDNT*, iii, pp. 336–9.

Michl, J. *Die Engelvorstellungen in der Apokalypse des Hl. Johannes*, Munich: Max Huebert, 1937.

'Engel I-IX' in T. Klauser (ed.), *Reallexikon für Antike und Christentum*, vol. 5, Stuttgart: A. Hiersemann, 1962, pp. 54–258.

Milik, J.T. '*Milkî-sedeq et Milkî-resaʿ* dans les anciens ecrits juifs et chretiens', *JJS* 23 (1972), 95–144.

Minear, Paul S. 'The cosmology of the Apocalypse' in W. Klassen and G. F. Snyder (eds.), *Current Issues in New Testament and Interpretation: Essays in Honour of Otto A. Piper*, London: SCM, 1962, pp. 23–37.

Mitchell, H. G., Smith, J. M. P., and Bewer, J. A. *A Critical and Exegetical Commentary on Haggai, Zechariah, Malachi, and Jonah* (ICC), Edinburgh: T. & T. Clark, 1912.

Moberly, R. B. 'When was Revelation conceived?', *Bib* 73 (1992), 376–93.

Molina, F. Contreras *El Espiritu en el libro del Apoclipsis* (Koinonia 28), Salamanca: Secretariado Trinitario, 1987.

Montgomery, J. A. 'The education of the seer of the Apocalypse', *JBL* 45 (1926), 70–80.

   A Critical and Exegetical Commentary on the Book of Daniel (ICC), Edinburgh: T. & T. Clark, 1927.

Moore, M. S. 'Jesus Christ: "Superstar" (Revelation xxii 16b)', *NovT* 24 (1982), 82–91.

Morray-Jones, C. R. A. 'Merkabah Mysticism and Talmudic Tradition: A Study of the Traditions Concerning Ham-merkabah and Ma'aseh Merkabah in Tannaitic and Amoraic Sources' (PhD Diss., University of Cambridge, 1989).

   'Transformational mysticism in the apocalyptic-merkabah tradition', *JJS* 43 (1992), 1–31.

Moule, C. F. D. *The Origin of Christology*, Cambridge: Cambridge University Press, 1977.

Mounce, R. H. 'The christology of the Apocalypse', *Foundations* (Rochester, USA) 11 (1969), 42–51.

Moxnes, Halvor 'God and his angel in the Shepherd of Hermas', *ST* 28 (1974), 49–56.

Muilenberg, J. 'The Son of Man in Daniel and the Ethiopic Apocalypse of Enoch', *JBL* 79 (1960), 197–209.

Mullen, E. Theodore, Jr. *The Divine Council in Canaanite and Early Hebrew Literature* (HSM 24), Chico, CA: Scholars Press, 1980.

Müller, Ulrich B. *Messias und Menschensohn in jüdischen Apokalypsen und in der Offenbarung des Johannes* (SNT 6), Gütersloh: Gerd Mohn, 1972.

   Zur frühchristlichen Theologiegeschichte: Judenchristentum und Paulismus in Kleinasien an der Wende vom ersten zum zweiten Jahrhundert n. Chr., Gütersloh: Gerd Mohn, 1976.

Mussies, G. *The Morphology of Koine Greek as Used in the Apocalypse of St. John: A Study in Bilingualism* (NovTSup 27), Leiden: Brill, 1971.

Newsom, Carol A. 'Angels: Old Testament', *ABD*, i, pp. 248–53.

Nickelsburg, G. W. E. 'Enoch, First Book of', *ABD*, ii, pp. 508–16.

   Studies in the Testament of Abraham (SBLSCS 6), Missoula: Scholars Press, 1976.

Ozanne, C. G. 'The language of the Apocalypse', *TynBul* 16 (1965), 3–9.

Pace Jeansonne, Sharon *The Old Greek Translation of Daniel 7–12* (CBQMS 19), Washington, DC: The Catholic Biblical Association of America, 1988.

Parker, H. M. 'The scripture of the author of the Revelation of John', *Iliff Review* 37 (1980), 35–51.

Pennington, A. 'The Apocalypse of Abraham' in H. F. D. Sparks (ed.), *The Apocryphal Old Testament*, Oxford: Clarendon Press, 1984, pp. 363–92.

Pernveden, Lage *The Concept of the Church in the Shepherd of Hermas*, Lund: Gleerup, 1966.

Pesce, M. (ed.) *Isaia, il Diletto e la Chiesa: Visione ad esegese profetica cristiano-primitiva nell' Ascensione de Isaia*, Brescia: Poideia Editrice, 1983.

Pesch, Rudolph 'Offenbarung Jesu Christi: eine Auslegung von Apk 1.1–3', *BibLeb* 11 (1970), 15–29.

Porteous, Norman W. *Daniel: A Commentary*, London: SCM, 1965.

Prigent, Pierre 'Pour une théologie de l'Image: les visions de l' Apocalypse', *RHPR* 59 (1979), 373–8.

Procksch, O. 'Die Berufungsvision Hesekiels', BZAW 34 (1920), 141–9.

Quispel, G. 'Ezekiel 1.26 in Jewish mysticism and gnosis', *VC* 34 (1980), 1–13.

Rainbow, Paul 'Jewish monotheism as the matrix for New Testament christology: a review article', *NovT* 33 (1991), 78–91.

Rebell, W. *Neutestamentliche Apokryphen und Apostolische Väter*, München: Kaiser, 1992.

Reddish, Mitchell G. 'Martyr christology in the Apocalypse', *JSNT* 33 (1988), 85–95.

Rengstorf, Karl Heinrich 'ἀποστέλλω', *TDNT*, i, pp. 398–406.

Rissi, Mathias 'The rider on the white horse: a study of Revelation 6.1–8', *Int* 18 (1964), 407–18.

'Die Erscheinung Christi nach Off. 19,11–16', *TZ* 21 (1965), 81–95.

Was ist und was geschehen soll danach: Die Zeit- und Geschichtsauffassung der Offenbarung des Johannes (ATANT 46), Zurich: Zwingli Verlag, 1965.

'The kerygma of the Revelation to John', *Int.* 22 (1968), 3–17.

The Future of the World: An Exegetical Study of Revelation 19.11–22.15 (SBT 23), London: SCM, 1972.

Roberts, J. H. 'The Lamb of God', *Neot* 2 (1968), 41–56.

Robertson, R. G. 'Ezekiel the Tragedian' in James H. Charlesworth (ed.), *Old Testament Pseudepigrapha*, vol. ii, London: Darton, Longman & Todd, 1985, pp. 803–20.

Robinson, John A. T. *Redating the New Testament*, London: SCM, 1976.

Robinson, S. E. *The Testament of Adam: An Examination of the Syriac and Greek Traditions* (SBLDS 52), Chico, CA: Scholars Press, 1982.

Rohland, Johannes Peter *Der Erzengel Michael: Arzt und Feldherr, Zwei Aspekte des vor- und frühbyzantinischen Michaelskultes* (BZRGG 19), Leiden: Brill, 1977.

Rowe, Robert D. 'Is Daniel's "Son of Man" messianic?' in H. H. Rowden (ed.), *Christ the Lord: Studies in Christology Presented to Donald Guthrie*, Leicester: Intervarsity Press, 1982, pp. 71–96.

Rowland, Christopher C. 'The visions of God in apocalyptic literature', *JSJ* 10 (1979), 137–54.

'The vision of the risen Christ in Rev. i.13ff: the debt of an early christology to an aspect of Jewish angelology', *JTS* (1980), 1–11.

The Open Heaven, London: SPCK, 1982.
'A man clothed in linen: Daniel 10.6ff and Jewish angelology', *JSNT* 24 (1985), 99–110.
'Apocalyptic literature' in D. A. Carson and H. G. M. Williamson (eds.), *It is Written: Scripture Citing Scripture* (*FS*: B. Lindars), Cambridge: Cambridge University Press, 1988, pp. 170–89.
Rubinkiewicz, R. 'Apocalypse of Abraham' in James H. Charlesworth (ed.), *Old Testament Pseudepigrapha*, vol. i, London: Darton, Longman & Todd, 1983, pp. 681–706.
Ruiz, Jean-Pierre *Ezekiel in the Apocalypse: The Transformation of Prophetic Language in Revelation 16,17–19,10* (EUS 23: Theology: 376), Frankfurt am Main: Peter Lang, 1989.
Russell, D. S. *The Method and Message of Jewish Apocalyptic: 200 BC–AD 100*, London: SCM, 1964.
Sabugal, S. 'El titulo Χριστός en el Apocalipsis', *Aug* 12 (1972), 319–40.
Salmon, G. *An Historical Introduction to the Study of the Books of the New Testament*, 7th edn, London, 1885.
Sanders, E. P. 'Testament of Abraham' in James H. Charlesworth (ed.), *Old Testament Pseudepigrapha*, vol. i, London: Darton, Longman & Todd, 1983, pp. 871–902.
Sanders, J. A. 'Dissenting deities and Philippians 2.1–11', *JBL* 88 (1969), 279–90.
Sandmel, S. 'Philo Judaeus: an introduction to the man, his writings, and his significance', *ANRW* 2.21.1, pp. 3–46.
Satake, Akira *Die Gemeindeordnung in der Johannesapokalypse*, Neukirchen-Vluyn: Neukirchener Verlag, 1966.
'Sieg Christi–Heil der Christen: eine Betrachtung von Apc XII', *AJBI* 1 (1975), 105–25.
'Christologie in der Johannesapokalypse im Zusammenhang mit dem Problem des Leidens der Christen' in C. Breytenbach and P. Henning (eds.), *Anfänge der Christologie* (*FS*: F. Hahn), Göttingen: Vandenhoeck & Ruprecht, 1991, pp. 307–22.
Schäfer, Peter *Rivalität zwischen Engeln und Menschen: Untersuchungen zur rabbinischen Engelvorstellung* (SJ 8), Berlin/New York: Walter de Gruyter, 1975.
'New Testament and hekhalot literature: the journey into heaven in Paul and in merkavah mysticism', *JJS* 35 (1984), 19–35.
Scherman, N. and Goldwurm, H. *Daniel: A New Translation with a Commentary Anthologized from Talmudic, Midrashic, and Rabbinic Sources*, 2nd edn, Brooklyn, NY: Mesorah, 1980.
Schillebeeckx, Edward *Christ: The Christian Experience in the Modern World*, London: SCM, 1980.
Schmidt, C. *Gespräche Jesu mit seinen Jüngern nach der Auferstehung*, Leipzig: J. C. Hinrichs, 1919 (repr. Hildesheim: Georg Olms, 1967).
Schmidt, Daryl D. 'Semitisms and septuagintalisms in the Book of Revelation', *NTS* 37 (1991), 592–603.
Schmitt, Eugen 'Die Christologische Interpretation als das Grundlegende der Apokalypse', *TQ* 140 (1960), 257–90.
Schneelmelcher, W. 'Kerygma Petrou' in E. Hennecke, W. Schneelmelcher,

R. Wilson (eds.), *New Testament Apocrypha*, vol. ii, Philadelphia: Westminster, 1964, pp. 94–102.

Schoeps, H. J. *Theologie und Geschichte des Judenchristentums*, Tübingen: Mohr (Paul Siebeck), 1949.

Scholem, Gershom G. *Major Trends in Jewish Mysticism*, 3rd edn, New York: Schocken, 1954.

Jewish Gnosticism, Merkabah Mysticism, and Talmudic Tradition, New York: The Jewish Theological Seminary, 1960.

Schüssler Fiorenza, Elisabeth *Priester für Gott: Studien zum Herrschafts- und Priestermotiv in der Apokalypse* (NTAbh 7), Münster: Verlag Aschendorff, 1972.

The Book of Revelation: Justice and Judgement, Philadephia: Fortress, 1985.

Schweizer, Eduard 'Die sieben Geister in der Apokalypse' in E. Schweizer *Neotestamentica: Deutsche und englische Aufsätze 1951–1963*, Zürich and Stuttgart: Zwingli Verlag, 1963, pp. 190–202.

Scott, E. F. *The Book of Revelation*, London: SCM, 1939.

Scott, R. B. Y. ' "Behold, he cometh with clouds" ', *NTS* 5 (1958–9), 127–32.

Segal, Alan F. *Two Powers in Heaven: Early Rabbinic Reports About Christianity and Gnosticism* (SJLA 25), Leiden: Brill, 1977.

'Ruler of this world: attitudes about mediator figures and the importance of sociology for self-definition' in E. P. Sanders, A. I. Baumgarten, and A. Mendelson (eds.), *Jewish and Christian Self-Definition Vol II: Aspects of Judaism in the Greco-Roman Period*, Philadelphia: Fortress, 1981, pp. 245–68.

'The risen Christ and the angelic mediator figures in the light of Qumran' in J. H. Charlesworth (ed.), *Jesus and the Dead Sea Scrolls*, New York: Doubleday, 1992, pp. 302–28.

'Heavenly ascent in hellenistic Judaism, early Christianity, and their environment', *ANRW* 2.23.2, pp. 1333–94.

Silberman, L. H. 'Farewell to ὁ ἀμήν. A note on Rev 3.14', *JBL* 82 (1963), 213–15.

Simonetti, M. 'Note sulla cristologia dell' *Ascensione de Isaia*' in M. Pesce (ed.), *Isaia, il Diletto e la Chiesa: Visione ad esegese profetica cristiano-primitiva nell' Ascensione de Isaia*, Brescia: Poideia Editrice, 1977, pp. 185–210.

Sjöberg, E. *Der Menschensohn im äthiopischen HenochbuchT*, Lund: Gleerup, 1946.

Skehan, Patrick W. 'A fragment of the "Song of Moses" (Deut. 32) from Qumran', *BASOR* 136 (1954), 12–15.

Skrinjar, A. 'Les sept esprits (Apoc 1,4; 3,1; 4,5; 5,6)', *Bib* 16 (1935), 1–24, 113–40.

Slater, T. B. ' "King of kings and lord of lords" Revisited', *NTS* 39 (1993), 159–60.

Smith, Jonathan Z. 'The Prayer of Joseph' in J. Z. Smith, *Map Is Not Territory: Studies in the History of Religion* (SJLA 23), Leiden: Brill, 1978, pp. 24–66 = J. Neusner (ed.), *Religions in Antiquity*, Leiden: Brill, 1968, pp. 253–94.

'Prayer of Joseph' in James H. Charlesworth (ed.), *Old Testament Pseudepigrapha*, vol. ii, London: Darton, Longman & Todd, 1985, pp. 699–714.

Smith, Morton 'The account of Simon Magus in Acts 8' in *Harry Austyn Wolfson Jubilee Volumes*, Jerusalem: American Academy for Jewish Research, 1965, vol. ii, pp. 735–50.

'Ascent to the heavens and deification in 4QM^a' in L. H. Schiffman (ed.), *Archaeology and History in the Dead Sea Scrolls* (JSPSup. 8) (*FS*: Y. Yadin), Sheffield: JSOT Press, 1990, pp. 181–8.

Smith, Ralph C. *Micah–Malachi* (WBC 32), Waco, TX: Word, 1984.

Sokoloff, M. *A Dictionary of Jewish Palestinian Aramaic*, Ramat-Gan: Bar Ilan University, 1990.

Steenburg, D. 'The case against the synonymity of *Morphe* and *Eikon*', *JSNT* 34 (1988), 77–86.

'The worship of Adam and Christ as the image of God', *JSNT* 39 (1990), 95–109.

Stevenson, J. and Frend, W. H. C. (eds.) *A New Eusebius: Documents Illustrating the History of the Church to AD 337*, 2nd edn, London: SPCK, 1987.

Stier, F. *Gott und Sein Engel im Alten Testament*, Münster: Aschendorffschen, 1934.

Stone, Michael E. *Fourth Ezra* (Hermeneia), Minneapolis: Fortress, 1990.

'Apocalyptic – vision or hallucination' in M. E. Stone, *Selected Studies in Pseudepigraphal Apocrypha: With Special Reference to the Armenian Tradition*, Leiden: Brill, 1991.

Stone, Michael E. and Greenfield, J. C. 'The Enochic pentateuch and the date of the *Similitudes*', *HTR* 70 (1977), 51–65.

Strack, H. L. and Billerbeck, P. *Kommentar zum Neuen Testament: Aus Talmud und Midrasch*, 4th edn, 6 vols., Munich: C. H. Beck'sche, 1965.

Strugnell, John 'The angelic liturgy at Qumran – 4Q Serek Sîrôt Olat Hassabbat', VT Sup. 7 (1959), 318–45.

Stuckenbruck, Loren T., 'An angelic refusal of worship: the tradition and its function in the Apocalypse of John', SBLSP 1994 (ed. E. H. Lovering, Atlanta, GA: Scholars Press, 1994), pp. 679–96.

Syrén, Roger *The Blessings in the Targums: A Study on the Targumic Interpretations of Genesis 49 and Deuteronomy 33*, Åbo: Åbo Akademe, 1986.

Tabor, J. D. *Things Unutterable: Paul's Ascent to Paradise in its Greco-Roman, Judaic, and early Christian Contexts*, Lanham, MD: University Press of America,1986.

Takahashi, M. 'An oriental's approach to the problems of angelology', *ZAW* 78 (1966), 346–8, 343–50.

Talbert, C. H. 'The myth of the descending-ascending redeemer in Mediterranean antiquity', *NTS* 22 (1976), 418–40.

Temporini, H. and Haase, W. (eds.) *Aufstieg und Niedergang der römischen Welt*, Berlin/New York: Walter de Gruyter, 1972.

Thompson, L. L. 'A sociological analysis of tribulation in the Apocalypse of John', *Semeia* 36 (1986), 147–74.

The Book of Revelation: Apocalypse and Empire, Oxford: Oxford University Press, 1990.

Thompson, Steven *The Apocalypse and Semitic Syntax* (SNTSMS 52), Cambridge: Cambridge University Press, 1985.

Tobin, Thomas H. 'Logos', *ABD*, iv, pp. 348–56.

Trakatellis, Demetrius C. *The Pre-Existence of Christ in Justin Martyr: An Exegetical Study with Reference to the Humiliation and Exaltation Christology* (HDR 6), Missoula: Scholars Press, 1976.

Trebilco, Paul R. *Jewish Communities in Asia Minor* (SNTSMS 69), Cambridge: Cambridge University Press, 1991.

Trigg, J. W. 'The Angel of Great Counsel: Christ and the angelic hierarchy in Origen's theology', *JTS* 42 (1991), 35–51.

Trites, Alison A. 'Μάρτυς and martyrdom in the Apocalypse: a semantic study', *NovT* 15 (1973), 77–80.

Trudinger, L. Paul 'Some observations concerning the text of the Old Testament in the Book of Revelation', *JTS* 17 (1966), 82–8.

Turdeanu, E. 'L'Apocalypse d'Abraham en slave', *JSJ* 3 (1972), 153–80.

Turner, N. 'The Testament of Abraham' in H. F. D. Sparks (ed.), *The Apocryphal Old Testament*, Oxford: Clarendon Press, 1984, pp. 393–422.

Van der Horst, P. W. 'Moses' throne vision in Ezekiel the Dramatist', *JJS* 34 (1983), 21–9.

VanderKam, J. C. *Textual and Historical Studies in the Book of Jubilees*, Missoula: Scholars, 1977.

Enoch and the Growth of an Apocalyptic Tradition (CBQMS 16), Washington, DC: Catholic Biblical Association of America, 1984.

'Righteous One, Messiah, Chosen One, and Son of Man in 1 Enoch 37–71' in J. H. Charlesworth (ed.), *The Messiah: Developments in Earliest Judaism and Christianity*, Minneapolis: Fortress, 1992, pp. 169–91.

Vanhoye, Albert 'L'utilisation du livre d'Ezéchiel dans l'Apocalypse', *Bib* 43 (1962), 436–72.

Vanni, Ugo 'L'Apocalypse johannique. Etat de la question' in J. Lambrecht (ed.), *L'Apocalypse johannique et l'Apocalyptique dans le Nouveau Testament* (BETL 53), Louvain: Leuven University Press, 1980, pp. 21–46.

'Liturgical dialogue as a literary form in the Book of Revelation', *NTS* 37 (1991), 348–72.

Van Schaik, A. P. '"Αλλος ἄγγελος in Apk 14' in J. Lambrecht (ed.), *L'Apocalypse johannique et l'Apocalyptique dans le Nouveau Testament* (BETL 53), Louvain: Leuven University Press, 1980, pp. 217–28.

Van Unnik, W. C. ' "Worthy is the Lamb": the background of Apoc. 5' in A. Descamps and A. de Halleux (eds.), *Mélanges bibliques* (*FS*: B. Rigaux), Gembloux, 1970, pp. 445–61.

Völter, D. 'Der Menschensohn in Dan 7.13', *ZNW* 3 (1902), 173–4.

Von Rad, Gerhard *Old Testament Theology*, 2 vols., Edinburgh: Oliver & Boyd, 1962, 1965.

Vos, Louis A. *The Synoptic Traditions in the Apocalypse*, Kampen: Kok, 1965.

Wernberg-Møller, P. *The Manual of Discipline: Translation and Annotated with Introduction* (STDJ 1), Leiden: Brill, 1957.

Werner, M. *The Formation of Christian Dogma: An Historical Study of its Problem* (trans. S. G. F. Brandon), London: Black, 1957.

Westcott, B. F. and Hort, F. J. A. *The New Testament in the Original Greek*, 2nd edn, 2 vols., London, 1896.

Whittaker, M. 'The Testament of Solomon' in H. F. D. Sparks (ed.), *The Apocryphal Old Testament*, Oxford: Clarendon Press, 1984, pp. 733–52.

Wicker, K. O'Br. 'De defectu oraculorum' in H. D. Betz (ed.), *Plutarch's Theological Writings and Early Christian Literature*, Leiden: Brill, 1975, pp. 131–235.

Winston, D. *Logos and Mystical Theology in Philo of Alexandria*, Cincinnati NJ: Hebrew Union College, 1985.

Wintermute, O. S. 'Apocalypse of Zephaniah' in James H. Charlesworth (ed.), *Old Testament Pseudepigrapha*, vol. i, London: Darton, Longman & Todd, 1983, pp. 497–516.

'Jubilees' in James H. Charlesworth (ed.), *Old Testament Pseudepigrapha*, vol. ii, London: Darton, Longman & Todd, 1985, pp. 35–142.

Wolfson, H. A. 'The pre-existent angel of the Magherians and Al-Nahawandi', *JQR* 51 (1960–1), 89–106.

Yarbro Collins, Adela *The Combat Myth in the Book of Revelation* (HDR 9), Missoula: Scholars Press, 1976.

'The history-of-religions approach to apocalypticism and the 'Angel of the Waters' (Rev 16:4–6)', *CBQ* 39 (1977), 367–81.

'The early Christian apocalypses', *Semeia* 14 (1979), 61–122.

Crisis and Catharsis: The Power of the Apocalypse, Philadelphia: Westminster Press, 1984.

'Review: *The Use of Daniel in Jewish Apocalyptic Literature and in the Revelation of St. John* [G. K. Beale]', *JBL* 105 (1986), 734–5.

'Eschatology in the Book of Revelation', *Ex Auditu* 6 (1990), 63–72.

'Appreciating the Apocalypse as a whole', *Int.* 45 (1991), 187–9.

'The "Son of Man" tradition and the Book of Revelation' in J. H. Charlesworth (ed.), *The Messiah: Developments in Earliest Judaism and Christianity*, Minneapolis: Fortress, 1992, pp. 536–68.

Young, R. *Christology of the Targums, or the Doctrine of the Messiah as it is Unfolded in the Ancient Jewish Targums*, Edinburgh (self publication), 1853.

Zevit, Z. 'The structure and individual elements of Daniel 7', *ZAW* 80 (1968), 394–6.

'The exegetical implications of Daniel viii 1, ix 21', *VT* 28 (1978) 488–92.

Zimmerli, W. *Ezekiel 1: A Commentary on the Book of the Prophet Ezekiel, Chapters 1–24* (Hermeneia), Philadelphia: Fortress, 1979.

Ezekiel 2: A Commentary on the Book of the Prophet Ezekiel, Chapters 25–48 (Hermeneia), Philadelphia: Fortress, 1983.

Zimmermann, F. *The Book of Tobit: An English Translation with Introduction and Commentary*, New York: Harper, 1958.

INDEX OF BIBLICAL AND ANCIENT WRITINGS

Early Christian, Gnostic, and other ancient writings

INDEX OF SUBJECTS